5080

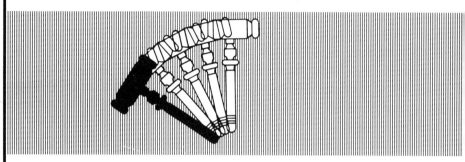

CONSTITUTIONAL LAW

Gary Goodpaster
Professor of Law
University of California, Davis

CASENOTES PUBLISHING CO., INC.
1640 Fifth Street, Suite 208
Santa Monica, CA 90401
(310) 395-6500

Fourth Edition, 2000

ISBN 0-87457-180-4

With the introduction of *Casenote Law Outlines,* Casenotes Publishing Company brings a new approach to the legal study outline. Of course, we have sought out only nationally recognized authorities in their respective fields to author the outlines. Most of the authors are editors of widely used casebooks. All have published extensively in respected legal journals, and some have written treatises cited by courts across the nation in opinions deciding important legal issues on which the authors have recommended what the "last word" on those issues should be.

What is truly novel about the *Casenote Law Outlines* concept is that each outline does not fit into a cookie-cutter mold. While each author has been given a carefully developed format as a framework for the outline, the format is purposefully flexible. The student will therefore find that all outlines are not alike. Instead, each professor has used an approach appropriate to the subject matter. An outline on Evidence cannot be written in the same manner as one on Constitutional Law or Contracts or Torts, etc. Accordingly, the student will find similar features in each *Casenote Law Outline,* but they may be handled in radically different ways by each author. We believe that in this way the law student will be rewarded with the most effective study aid possible. And because we are strongly committed to keeping our publications up to date, *Casenote Law Outlines* are the most current study aids on the market.

For added studying convenience, the *Casenote Law Outlines* series and the *Casenote Legal Briefs* are being coordinated. Many titles in the *Casenote Legal Briefs* series have already been cross-referenced to the appropriate title in the *Casenote Law Outlines* series, and more cross-referenced titles are being released on a regular basis. A tag at the end of most briefs will quickly direct the student to the section in the appropriate *Casenote Law Outline* where further discussion of the rule of law in question can be found.

We continually seek law student and law professor feedback regarding the effectiveness of our publications. As you use *Casenote Law Outlines,* please do not hesitate to write or call us if you have constructive criticism or simply would like to tell us you are pleased with the approach and design of the publication.

Best of luck in your studies.

CASENOTES PUBLISHING CO., INC.

CASENOTE LAW OUTLINES — SUPPLEMENT REQUEST FORM

Casenotes Publishing Co., Inc. prides itself on producing the most current legal study outlines available. Sometimes between major revisions, the authors of the outline series will issue supplements to update their respective outlines to reflect any recent changes in the law. Certain areas of the law change more quickly than others, and thus some outlines may be supplemented, while others may not be supplemented at all.

In order to determine whether or not you should send this supplement request form to us, first check the printing date that appears by the subject name below. If this outline is less than one year old, it is highly unlikely that there will be a supplement for it. If it is older, you may wish to write, telephone, or fax us for current information. You might also check to see whether a supplement has been included with your *Casenote Law Outline* or has been provided to your bookstore. If it is necessary to order the supplement directly from us, it will be supplied without charge, but we do insist that you <u>send a stamped, self-addressed return envelope.</u> If you request a supplement for an outline that does not have one, you will receive the latest *Casenotes* catalogue.

If you wish to request a supplement for this outline:

#5080, CONSTITUTIONAL LAW by Goodpaster ▸ 2000

please follow the instructions below.

TO OBTAIN YOUR COMPLIMENTARY SUPPLEMENT(S), *YOU MUST FOLLOW THESE INSTRUCTIONS PRECISELY* **IN ORDER FOR YOUR REQUEST TO BE ACKNOWLEDGED.**

1. **REMOVE AND SEND THIS ENTIRE REQUEST FORM:** You *must* send this *original* page, which acts as your proof of purchase and provides the information regarding which supplements, if any, you need. The request form is only valid for any supplement for the outline in which it appears. *No photocopied or written requests will be honored.*

2. **SEND A STAMPED, SELF-ADDRESSED, FULL-SIZE (9" x 12") ENVELOPE:** *Affix enough postage to cover at least 3 oz.* We regret that we absolutely cannot fill and/or acknowledge requests unaccompanied by a stamped, self-addressed envelope.

3. **MULTIPLE SUPPLEMENT REQUESTS:** If you are sending supplement requests for two or more different *Casenote Law Outlines,* we suggest you send a return envelope for each subject requested. If you send only one envelope, your order may not be filled immediately should any supplement you requested still be in production. In that case, your order will not be filled until it can be filled completely, *i.e.,* until all supplements you have requested are published.

4. **PLEASE GIVE US THE FOLLOWING INFORMATION:**

    Name: _____ Telephone: (____)_____-_____

    Address: _____ Apt.: _____

    City: _____ State: _____ Zip: _____

    Name of law school you attend: _____

    Name and location of bookstore where you purchased this *Casenote Law Outline:*_____

    _____

    Any comments regarding *Casenote Law Outlines?*_____

    _____

CASENOTES PUBLISHING CO., INC., 1640 Fifth Street, Suite 208, Santa Monica, CA 90401
TELEPHONE (310) 395-6500

LAW

OUTLINES

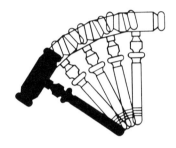

CONSTITUTIONAL
LAW

To the just and compassionate

INTRODUCTION

Those who drafted, debated, and adopted the United States Constitution designed a fundamental charter outlining the basic purposes, arrangements, and limits of governmental power. While the Constitution is short and succinct, Americans accept it as the authoritative basic source and guide for use in determining important questions about the uses of governmental power and the scope and range of human freedoms. But the Constitution does not often speak either directly or clearly on the countless and myriad issues that representative government and liberty claims raise, and therefore, needs interpretation. The United States Supreme Court has taken on the role of principal, and final, interpreter of the Constitution. Consequently, the study of American constitutional law is, almost entirely, the study of United States Supreme Court decisions about the meaning of the Constitution, its various provisions, and the practical, institutional arrangements which makes the Constitution an operative, effective charter.

Approximately 200 years of Supreme Court decisions applying the Constitution, first to the problems of nation-building and then to the ever and increasingly changing circumstances and conditions of American society, economy, and government, constitute an immense, complicated, and sometimes confusing gloss on that brief document. Students quickly learn that text, history, tradition, practice, politics, major public debates, intellectual currents, contested conceptions of liberty and the role of various governmental institutions, as well as the felt necessities of the times, all contribute to shape constitutional law rulings and doctrines. This makes the study of constitutional law fascinating and exciting and opens it, in a qualitatively different way than other law courses, to important debates about social policy, the ends and aims of government, the role of the courts, the executive, and the legislature and the contemporary meaning of constitutional liberties.

The current body of constitutional law doctrine is something of a palimpsest — a writing on top of another writing — revealing different layers of constitutional growth and different paradigms of constitutional understanding. In particular, the Civil War, the New Deal, the Second World War and subsequent Cold War, and the civil rights revolution have all profoundly influenced constitutional thinking and shaped or re-shaped constitutional doctrine.

There is one other factor of considerable importance to anyone seeking to understand and reconcile Supreme Court constitutional law decisions, a task sometimes frustratingly difficult. The United States Supreme Court is essentially a committee, and its decisions are committee decisions. While one Justice usually authors a majority opinion, the opinion must be written in a way that commands the majority vote. There are disparate and shifting majorities on the Supreme Court, depending on the issue, however, and this tends to mean, as far as opinion-writing goes, that doctrinal coherence, clarity, or consistency is often sacrificed simply to command a majority vote for a particular result. In contrast to the relatively unified Court of the Warren era, subsequent courts have been deeply divided and often badly splintered, unable, in a number of important decisions, to find a majority voice. During the Reagan and Bush presidencies, there emerged a working conservative majority which effected transformations of dominating judicial philosophies and some constitutional doctrine. This was most evident in criminal, particularly death penalty, cases and in civil rights and habeas corpus cases. Recently, this same majority has begun to effect significant developments in the law relating to state and federal relations, affirmative action, and religious freedom.

What this all means for students of constitutional law decision-making and constitutional doctrine is that the track of the law zigs and zags. The student, just as the careful scholar, will sometimes find lines of cases hard to harmonize, intelligible rationale difficult to state, and jerry-built rules.

Constitutional law is a wonderful, and sometimes difficult, subject. I wrote this work to ease the student's burden in learning and understanding it: to provide students with a clear, well-organized, and concise survey statement of American constitutional law, related as coherently and comprehensively as possible in an expanded outline format. This work does not simply string together a series of seemingly disconnected rules. Instead, it seeks to digest the law and state rules coherently, giving them a context and fitting them into the larger body of constitutional doctrine. The book thus strikes a middle ground between outline and hornbook, providing a detailed statement of all the important rules and principles, together with sufficient background, explanatory material, and examples to make them intelligible, understandable, useful, and usable.

The student can best use this book in conjunction with a constitutional law casebook. It works as a principal aid: making cases and casebooks more intelligible and assisting the reader's understanding of them once read; organizing and synthesizing the teaching of lines of cases; and clarifying and stating rules and bodies of doctrine. In greatly easing the student's burden of mining and refining the ore of constitutional law, this book provides students with the information and knowledge base necessary to understanding contemporary issues and controversies and to "doing" constitutional law.

CAPSULE OUTLINE

CO

CHAPTER 1: JUDICIAL POWER, FUNCTIONS, AND JURISDICTION

I. FEDERAL COURTS

A. Article III Courts: The Constitution vests judicial power in one Supreme Court and lower federal courts that Congress creates.

B. Constitutionally Assigned Jurisdiction: Cases or controversies involving the following subjects fall within the jurisdiction of the federal judicial power:

1. The Constitution, federal laws, and treaties;

2. Ambassadors, public ministers, and consuls;

3. Admiralty;

4. The United States as a party;

5. Controversies between states, a state and a citizen of another state, and citizens of different states;

6. Controversies between a state or state citizens and foreign states or their citizens or subjects.

C. Original and Appellate Jurisdiction

1. *Original jurisdiction:* The Supreme Court has "original" jurisdiction in cases involving ambassadors, other public ministers and consuls, and states as parties.

2. *Appellate jurisdiction:* In all other cases, the Supreme Court has appellate jurisdiction, subject to such exceptions Congress establishes.

D. Supreme Court Review Jurisdiction

1. *Discretionary review:* Almost all appellate review is discretionary by writ of certiorari, rather than a matter of right.

2. *Review of state court decisions:* The Supreme Court may only review state court decisions regarding federal issues and will even deny review of some cases involving incorrect application of federal law, as long as the state court decision rests on independent state law grounds.

3. *Review of state court refusal to hear federal claims:* State courts are required to hear federal claims, as long as they are appropriately presented.

II. THE DOCTRINE OF JUDICIAL REVIEW AND ITS CONSEQUENCES

A. Supreme Court Authority to Review Governmental Actions and Declare Them Unconstitutional

1. *"Judicial review" defined:* "Judicial review" is the practice of court review of legislative and executive acts to determine their constitutionality.

2. *The doctrine:* The doctrine of judicial review holds that courts are the final arbiters of the meaning of the laws. In constitutional matters, it essentially means that the Supreme Court can test legislative, executive, and other judicial action against constitutional requirements and hold invalid those the Court deems violative of the Constitution.

3. Judicial review is countermajoritarian, and the Supreme Court has developed a number of doctrines, such as retroactivity and severability rules, and rules of construction in constitutional cases to limit the impact of judicial review.

B. Retroactivity: Once a statute is declared unconstitutional, the new interpretation applies retroactively to all cases pending on direct review.

C. Severability: When a court declares a portion of a statute unconstitutional, that portion may be held severable, leaving the remainder of the statute in force. Whether an unconstitutional part of a statute is merely severed or the entire statute is stricken depends on the structure of the statute and on legislative intent.

D. Supreme Court Review of State Statutes and State Court Judgments: The Supremacy Clause declares that the Constitution, federal laws, and treaties take precedence over state law and requires state courts to apply them where applicable. The clause endows the Supreme Court with the authority to hold state statutes unconstitutional and to review state court decisions regarding federal questions.

E. Congressional Power to Restrict Judicial Review by Limiting Federal Court Jurisdiction

1. *Article III and the Exceptions Clause:* The Exceptions Clause of Article III authorizes Congress to define and regulate the appellate jurisdiction of the Supreme Court. Although a matter of some concern, Congress has not used this power to strip the Court of its jurisdiction so as to imperil constitutional rights; in appropriate cases, it may "channel" jurisdiction in order to direct certain claims to other courts.

III. CONSTITUTIONAL LIMITS ON FEDERAL JUDICIAL REVIEW

A. The "Case or Controversy" Requirement: Article III, § 2 limits federal judicial power to "cases and controversies," that is, actual, concrete legal disputes between real adversary parties that are capable of judicial resolution and relief.

CO

1. ***Justiciability:*** A case is justiciable if there is standing to sue, the issue is judicially resolvable, and there are no reasons for judicial restraint. Hypothetical, moot, collusive, or premature cases are all examples of nonjusticiable cases.

2. ***Standing:*** This requirement ensures that there is a genuine issue that a court can and should resolve. In order to have standing to sue a plaintiff must: show injury in fact; suffer the injury personally; be able to trace the injury to the defendant's wrongful conduct; and demonstrate that relief from the court will eliminate or redress the injury.

B. Political Question Doctrine: Courts will refuse to hear a question when the issue is committed to another governmental branch, lacks judicial standards for resolution, requires a policy decision from the political branches, or necessitates deference to another branch.

1. ***Separation of powers:*** The political question doctrine is partially based on the idea that one branch of government — here, the judiciary — cannot constitutionally exercise powers belonging to another branch.

2. ***Unresolvable or unmanageable cases:*** A question is also "political" if the court concludes that the case is not judicially resolvable or its resolution would create serious institutional problems.

C. Eleventh Amendment Limits on Federal Judicial Power in Suits against States: The Eleventh Amendment creates a form of state sovereign immunity and effectively prohibits citizens of one state, or citizens or subjects of a foreign state, from suing a state in federal court without the sued state's consent.

1. ***Congressional legislation overriding state sovereign immunity:*** Congress, acting under Constitutional provisions or amendments that limit state power or sovereignty may use its conferred powers to authorize such suits. In general, Congress may not use its Article 1 powers to override state sovereign immunity, but it may do so under the Fourteenth and Fifteenth Amendments. Nor may Congress, with certain exceptions, authorize suits against states in their own courts.

2. ***Suits against state officials:*** The Eleventh Amendment also bars suits against state officials if damages are to be paid from the state treasury. When a state official has acted unconstitutionally, however, he may be sued in federal court.

IV. JUDICIALLY IMPOSED LIMITS ON FEDERAL CONSTITUTIONAL REVIEW

A. Abstention: Federal courts should postpone cases involving unsettled or unclear state law until a state court has had a chance to interpret the law. Abstention promotes federalism, preserves state court authority, and may obviate the need for a federal hearing if no federal constitutional issue remains after the state court ruling.

B. Equitable Restraint in Prosecutions and Civil Enforcement Proceedings: Federal courts may not intervene in pending state prosecutions unless the state action was brought in bad faith or prevented adequate litigation of federal claims.

C. Avoiding Constitutional Questions: The following rules are designed to help federal courts circumvent constitutional questions:

    1. ***Alternative nonconstitutional ground of decision:*** If there is some alternative nonconstitutional ground that will dispose of a case, the court will not decide a constitutional question.

    2. ***Construction:*** Courts must reasonably construe statutes in such a way as to avoid declaring them unconstitutional.

    3. ***Competing interpretations:*** If competing interpretations are possible, courts must adopt the one that renders the statute constitutional.

    4. ***Facial challenges:*** One who challenges an act or regulation on its face must show that there are no circumstances under which the act or regulation would be valid.

CHAPTER 2: THE FEDERAL STRUCTURE OF AMERICAN GOVERNMENT

I.   FEDERAL-STATE RELATIONS IN GENERAL

A. Federal system: Under our system of dual sovereign governments — state and federal — state governments possess independent governmental power.

    1. ***Delegation and limitation of powers:*** The Constitution delegated certain essential powers to the federal government while prohibiting the states from exercising certain powers.

    2. ***Values of federalism:*** Decentralized government facilitates governmental responsiveness, provides checks on the federal government, and encourages local diversity and experimentation.

B. Powers Delegated to Congress

    1. ***Necessary and Proper Clause:*** Congress has the power to make all laws "necessary and proper" for executing its other powers and to enable the executive and judicial branches to exercise their powers and carry out their functions.

    2. ***Doctrine of enumerated powers and congressional regulation of unenumerated matters:*** Congress has those powers the Constitution specifically confers and those powers necessarily implied or useful to carrying out its delegated powers. Congress may use its powers for any ends the Constitution does not forbid, and it may regulate unenumerated matters as a rational means of promoting some legitimate federal aim.

3. ***Exclusive federal power:*** The Constitution expressly prohibits the states from exercising some powers; other powers are exclusively federal by their very nature, *e.g.*, the power to declare war.

4. ***Concurrent state and federal power:*** States may, however, exercise nonexclusive federal powers, as long as Congress has not expressly or implicitly enacted laws that supersede or preempt state laws.

II. **INTERGOVERNMENTAL IMMUNITIES**

A. **Federal Immunities — Limits on State Power to Regulate or Tax Federal Activities:** The federal government and its properties are presumed immune from state taxation or regulation.

1. ***Presumption:*** Federal immunity is a presumption only if Congress does not act. Congress may consent to state taxation and regulation.

2. ***Interference rule:*** Federal employees are only exempt from state laws that interfere with their official duties.

3. ***Federal enclaves:*** Unless Congress passes legislation to the contrary, existing state law continues to apply once the federal government obtains state property.

4. ***State income taxation:*** States may tax the salaries of federal employees.

5. ***Other state taxes — incidence rule:*** States may not impose a direct tax on the federal government, but the government may pay a tax whose incidence falls on other parties, *e.g.,* a state tax falling on a federal contractor operating under a cost-plus contract.

B. **State Immunities — Limits on Congressional Power to Legislate Regarding the States**

1. ***The Tenth Amendment and federalism-based limits on congressional power:*** The Tenth Amendment provides that those powers the Constitution neither delegates to the United State nor prohibits the states are reserved to the state or the People.

2. ***Plain statement rule:*** To avoid interference with state sovereignty, courts should enforce federal legislation infringing on essential state powers only when Congress plainly states that it desires that result.

3. ***Other constraints on congressional regulation of state activity:*** These include Congress's inability to eliminate states as independent political entities, the requirement that Congress justify its legislation as rational means to a legitimate end, and the ability of states to protect themselves through their representation in Congress.

C. **Federal Taxation of State Employees, Activities, and Property:** Absent discrimination or possibly undue interference with state functions, there is no state immunity from federal taxation.

III. **RELATIONS BETWEEN STATES**

A. **Required Cooperation between States:** The Full Faith and Credit Clause of the Constitution requires that the states recognize and give appropriate effect to legal acts and proceedings of other states.

B. **Interstate Compacts:** The Constitution requires that Congress consent to agreements or compacts between states, at which time the agreement becomes federal law. However, the Clause requires congressional consent only for those agreements that may increase the political power of the states and encroach on the supremacy of the federal government; all other agreements are exempt from congressional approval.

IV. **STATE RELATIONS TO CITIZENS OF OTHER STATES: INTERSTATE PRIVILEGES AND IMMUNITIES**

A. **Provision:** The Interstate Privilege and Immunities Clause of the Constitution provides that "[t]he Citizens of each State shall be entitled to all Privileges and Immunities of Citizens of the several states."

B. **Definition:** States must accord residents and nonresidents equal treatment with regard to certain interests "fundamental" to national economic union and interstate harmony, including the rights to own property, engage in gainful employment, travel, and receive medical care.

C. **Rule — Fundamental Interests:** However, a state may lawfully discriminate against a nonresident if the state has a substantial and legitimate reason justifying the different treatment.

D. **Rule — Nonfundamental Interests:** If a state treats a nonresident differently than a resident with respect to a nonfundamental interest, it need only show that it has not acted arbitrarily.

E. **Limited Application:** The Interstate Privileges and Immunities Clause applies only to citizens, not to corporations or to aliens.

CHAPTER 3: POWERS OF THE FEDERAL GOVERNMENT

I. **THE PRINCIPAL CONGRESSIONAL LEGISLATIVE POWERS**

A. **The Commerce Power:** In order to create an integrated national economy and to eradicate barriers to trade, the Constitution gave Congress the power to regulate

CO

commerce between the states; it may be the most important regulatory power Congress possesses.

1. ***Defining commerce:*** Earlier distinctions about whether various activities constituted commerce have given way to determinations whether an activity is in interstate commerce, uses its channels, or affects it.

2. ***Defining the reach of Congress' commerce power:*** Congress can clearly regulate all commerce that is interstate. The significant question, however, is whether Congress can regulate intrastate commerce because of its effect on, or relationship to, interstate commerce. Recently, the Court has limited some expansive interpretations of Congress' Commerce Clause power by requiring its exercise in conjunction with activities or problems that relate to commercial or economic activity.

B. **The Taxing Power:** Congress may tax in order to raise revenue and, as long as the tax produces revenue, may regulate activities by taxing them. Congress may even impose taxes so great as to effectively prohibit the taxed activity.

C. **The Spending Power:** Congress has the power to spend for the common defense and general welfare. Essentially, Congress may spend for any appropriate public purpose. It can use the Spending Power to regulate indirectly, through conditional grants, what it cannot regulate directly.

D. **War and Military Affairs Powers:** Congress has the power to declare war and to create and regulate military forces. During, and even after, a war, Congress has broad authority to enact economic and social legislation necessary for waging war or remedying its evils. Congress may establish a draft, as well as a system of military justice and courts-martial.

E. **Treaty Power:** The Constitution gives the president, with the advice and consent of the Senate, the power to make treaties. Treaties requiring no enabling legislation take precedence over inconsistent state law and federal law existing at the time of the treaty's enactment.

F. **The Immigration Power:** Congress has exclusive control over immigration. It may accord resident aliens different treatment than citizens but may not deny them certain procedural due process rights guaranteed by the Fifth Amendment. Congress may not treat naturalized citizens differently than native-born citizens.

G. **Congressional Investigatory Power:** Congress has the implied power to conduct investigations into any matters subject to its legislative powers. In investigating, Congress may compel persons to testify and may punish refusals to testify by contempt, but witnesses may lawfully assert the Fifth Amendment privilege against self-incrimination and any other protections provided by the Bill of Rights.

H. **Constitutional Qualifications for Membership in Congress:** The Constitution establishes qualifications for membership in each house of Congress, but each house of Congress has the power to *judge* the qualifications of its own members. The states have no power to alter or add to these qualifications.

CO

II.   **POWERS OF THE PRESIDENT (Summary Introduction)**

    A.   **Powers in General:** Article II of the Constitution vests the executive power of the United States in the president and gives him the power to make treaties, appoint officers, receive ambassadors, administer laws, grant pardons, and approve or veto laws, the last power being subject to a two-thirds congressional override.

    B.   **General Relationship between Congressional and Presidential Powers:** Given its constitutional authority to legislate regarding many matters within the president's domain, Congress can shape and, to some degree, control the exercise of presidential powers.

CHAPTER 4:   PRESIDENTIAL POWERS, IMMUNITIES, AND PRIVILEGES

I.   **PRESIDENTIAL POWERS**

    A.   **Executive Power:** Despite the relatively few powers expressly conferred on the president by the Constitution, he exercises vast powers derived from his executive and political role in federal government, from statutory authority conferred by Congress, and from the resources he has at his command.

    B.   **The Foreign Affairs Power:** Both the president and Congress have some foreign affairs powers. For example, the president appoints and receives ambassadors and makes treaties with Senate advice and consent, while Congress regulates foreign commerce, lays duties, and declares war. Other than such specific power allocations, the limits of the two branches' constitutional authority over foreign affairs is uncertain and the Constitution seems to contemplate some collaboration. As a practical matter, Congress must abdicate management of foreign affairs on a day-to-day basis to the executive branch.

    C.   **Exclusive Presidential Foreign Affairs Powers**

        1.   *Recognition of foreign governments:* The president has the sole authority to recognize foreign governments or to withdraw recognition.

        2.   *Making treaties:* The president negotiates treaties and, upon Senate consent, ratifies them.

        3.   *Executive agreements:* Pursuant to presidential power, a prior treaty, or authorization by Congress, the president may enter into international agreements without seeking Senate consent. If not entered into pursuant to one of those three authorities, the agreement should not supersede prior inconsistent federal law.

        4.   *The president's military powers and foreign affairs:* As commander-in-chief, the president may suppress insurrections, repel invasions, and use military force to

CO

protect American citizens and property abroad without prior Congressional authority.

5. ***Presidential wars and the War Powers Resolution:*** After the Vietnam War, Congress enacted the War Powers Resolution in an attempt to define and enlarge the Congressional role in the use of military power. Its major provision requires the president to terminate the use of armed forces within sixty days unless Congress declares war or authorizes their continued use.

D. **Delegated Legislative Power:** The president approves legislation and, under Congressional authorization and guidelines, may make policy choices and draft rules and regulations.

E. **The "Take Care" Power and Duty:** The Constitution provides that the president "shall take Care that the Laws are faithfully executed." Congress usually gives the president discretion in enforcing laws. In addition, limited resources and the necessity to choose between various trade-offs also entail executive discretion in law enforcement.

F. **The Appointments Power:** The president has the power to nominate and appoint, with the advice and consent of the Senate, ambassadors, other public ministers, consuls, Supreme Court judges, and all other officers of the United States, i.e., those appointees who exercise significant authority under the laws of the United States.

1. ***Inferior officers:*** Under the Appointments Clause, Congress may vest the appointment of inferior officers in the heads of departments.

2. ***Removal power:*** The president has the power to terminate at will those officials whose exercise of discretion is essential to the functioning of the executive branch; Congress has the power to provide for the removal of other officials only "for cause."

G. **The Veto Power:** The Constitution grants the president the power to disapprove legislation passed by Congress. A vote of two-thirds of each house of Congress is needed to override a presidential veto.

H. **The Pardon Power:** The president has the power to grant reprieves and pardons for federal offenses, free from congressional limits of any kind.

II. **PRESIDENTIAL IMMUNITIES AND PRIVILEGES**

A. **Executive Immunity:** Absent contrary congressional legislation, the president is absolutely immune from civil damages liability for official acts. However, the president has no immunity, not even temporary immunity while in office, from civil litigation arising out of events that occurred before he took office. Presidents may also be immune from criminal liability unless convicted in an impeachment proceeding. Yet they are not completely immune from judicial process and may be required to comply with subpoenas.

B. Executive Privilege: In order to facilitate presidential candor, the Supreme Court has inferred that presidents have a presumptive executive privilege to refuse to reveal confidential communications. The privilege may be overridden if essential to ensuring justice in a pending criminal trial. The president may also refuse to disclose information that would endanger national security.

CHAPTER 5: SEPARATION OF POWERS

I. THE DOCTRINE OF SEPARATION OF POWERS: Although not mentioned in the Constitution, this doctrine divides the major powers of government among three branches — the legislative, the executive, and the judicial — and holds that only that branch of the government vested with a particular power may exercise it.

    A. Purpose and Theory of the Doctrine: Since each branch may exercise only those powers conferred on it by the Constitution, the separation of powers creates countervailing governmental power centers which check and balance each other and insure against abuses.

II. MAJOR ISSUES UNDER THE DOCTRINE OF SEPARATION OF POWERS

    A. Exclusive Congressional Authority to Legislate Domestically

        1. *Delegation of powers:* As long as Congress sets policy and lays down guidelines and standards, it may broadly delegate authority to make law.

        2. *Bicamerality and presentment:* In order for a bill to become law, it must pass both houses of Congress (bicamerality) and be presented to the president for his approval (presentment). The Constitution provides but four instances in which one house's action has the force of law: The House alone has the power to initiate impeachments, while the Senate alone conducts impeachment trials, approves presidential appointments, and ratifies treaties.

    B. Separation of Powers and the Power to Remove Officials

        1. *Congressional exercise of a power to remove officials:* Congress may reserve the power to remove its own employees but not officials of the executive branch.

        2. *Congressional restriction of executive power to remove officials:* Congress may not override the president's power to remove officials central to the function of the presidency at will; Congress may, however, provide for-cause removal of other executive branch officials.

    C. Separation of Powers and the Judiciary: The Constitution confers the judicial power of the United States on Article III courts.

        1. *The constitutional role of Article III federal judges:* Federal judges are limited to deciding "cases and controversies" and may not take on executive or administrative

duties of a "nonjudicial" nature. However, Congress may assign some nonadjudicatory tasks to the judiciary, as long as the tasks do not interfere with the judicial function, are not more appropriately undertaken by other branches, and do not threaten judicial integrity. Furthermore, Congress can establish Article I "legislative" courts in specialized areas, such as customs and taxes.

2. *Independence, impartiality, and tenure of the federal judiciary:* In order that they may be free from outside influence, Article III judges enjoy life tenure, subject to removal only by impeachment.

3. *Legislative reopening or setting aside of final court judgments:* The judicial power of Article III courts is the power to decide cases dispositively, subject to review only by superior Article III courts. Congress therefore violates the doctrine of separation of powers when it orders courts to reopen final judgments.

D. **Separation of Powers, Legislative and Executive Immunities, and Protection from Criminal and Civil Processes:** To prevent misuse of power as between branches, the Constitution provides the following protections:

1. *Congressional privilege against arrest:* Except in cases of treason, felony, and breach of the peace, the Constitution provides members of Congress with a privilege against civil arrest.

2. *Congressional protection from executive or judicial inquiry:* Members of Congress are absolutely protected by the Speech and Debate Clause from executive or judicial inquiry into what they say or do during the legislative process.

3. *Executive immunities and privileges:* See Chapter 4, II., *supra.*

E. **Separation of Powers and the Political Question Doctrine:** Where the Constitution clearly assigns decisions regarding some particular issue to a specific branch of the government, the judiciary cannot review that branch's decision and must decline to hear the matter under the "political question" doctrine.

CHAPTER 6: STATE REGULATION AFFECTING COMMERCE, CONTRACTS, AND PRIVATE PROPERTY

I. **THE DORMANT OR "NEGATIVE" COMMERCE CLAUSE: The Commerce Clause, Article I, § 8 of the Constitution gives Congress broad authority to regulate commerce between the states. Although the Commerce Clause is couched in terms of an affirmative grant to Congress, the Supreme Court has also interpreted it to imply a limit on the capacity of states to inhibit or prevent interstate trade. Using a two-tiered analysis, the Court has struck down many state attempts to regulate commerce and economic activity on the basis of this so-called dormant or "negative" Commerce Clause.**

A. Modern Commerce Clause Cases and the Two-Tier Approach

1. ***Discriminatory regulation of, or unjustifiable state burdens on, interstate commerce:*** With few exceptions, state legislation that discriminates against interstate commerce is unconstitutional.

2. ***The two-tier approach:*** The second tier applies to nondiscriminatory restrictions that affect interstate commerce. Using a balancing test, the Court will invalidate state regulations that are not justified by interests outweighing the burdens imposed on interstate commerce. Such restrictions will be struck down if they impose a substantial burden on commerce.

B. Trade Cases: Where state regulations affecting interstate commerce have a discriminatory purpose, use discriminatory means, or impose an unjustifiable burden on interstate commerce, they are unconstitutional. Laws which, on their face, expressly single out interstate commerce for disparate treatment are per se unconstitutional. State statutes which are not facially discriminatory, but which have discriminatory effects, will be upheld only if legitimate, nonprotectionist state interests justify the regulation and there are no other nondiscriminatory alternatives available.

C. Market Participant Doctrine – State Actions Not Subject to Dormant Commerce Clause Invalidation: When the state acts as a proprietor or entrepreneur, the dormant Commerce Clause does not apply to its activities. A state acting as a market participant may favor its own citizens over non-residents in its subsidies, purchases, or employment opportunities. However, in drawing distinctions between residents and nonresidents, a state may neither impose conditions that have substantial regulatory effects outside of the market in which it is participating nor violate the Privileges and Immunities Clause of the Constitution.

D. The Twenty-First Amendment as a Limitation on the Dormant Commerce Clause: The Twenty-First Amendment authorizes states to regulate the importation and use of intoxicating liquors. States may thus constitutionally prohibit the importation of intoxicating liquors or otherwise regulate their importation and use within state borders. They may not, however, favor local liquor interests over outside interests by imposing competitive disadvantages on them.

II. STATE TAXATION OF INTERSTATE COMMERCE

A. Practical Effect Test: In order for state taxation of interstate commerce to pass Commerce Clause scrutiny, the tax must be on activity having a substantial nexus with the state, be fairly apportioned, not discriminate against interstate commerce, and be fairly related to services that the state provides.

B. Property Taxes: States may impose property taxes on commercial entities that have sufficient presence or contacts in the state to justify the tax but may not tax goods merely in transit. Taxing the gross receipts for the sale of services having an interstate component, and only a partial in-state component, does not violate the Commerce Clause when the service is purchased within the taxing state.

III. **STATE TAXATION OF FOREIGN COMMERCE**

A. **Instrumentalities of Commerce:** Because of the enhanced risk of multiple taxation and of multiple, rather than uniform, regulation, judicial review of taxation on foreign commerce is more rigorous than the four-part practical effect test applied to taxation on interstate commerce.

B. **State Taxation of a Domestic Entity's Foreign Income:** States may tax foreign-derived income of unitary business enterprises.

C. **The Import-Export Clause:** This Clause prohibits state taxation of foreign commerce while it is in transit, although the income of importers or exporters may be taxed.

IV. **THE CONTRACT CLAUSE: Although the Contract Clause prohibits a state from passing any "law impairing the Obligation of Contracts," enactments having effects on existing contracts are rarely considered impairments under the Clause.**

A. **Reserved Power Doctrine:** States may not contract away essential state powers, but they may enter into, and subsequently impair, financial or debt contracts when the impairment is reasonable and necessary to serve an important public purpose. When private individuals, not the state, are parties to a contract, the state may act in the public interest regardless of any effect or impairment its legislation may have on that private contract.

V. **TAKINGS AND THE JUST COMPENSATION CLAUSE: The Fifth Amendment prohibits the governmental taking of private property for public use, without just compensation.**

A. **Takings and Eminent Domain Distinguished:** When the government exercises the power of eminent domain and condemns private property for public use, it pays compensation, thus satisfying the Just Compensation Clause. However, when it attempts to take property without payment, restricts property use, or reduces or destroys the value of private property, a takings case may arise. On the other hand, when government regulates private property for police power purposes — *i.e.,* health, welfare, or safety — diminution of property values due to regulation will not give rise to a compensable taking.

B. **Public Use Clause:** Governments may take private property only for public purposes, not merely in order to give it to another private party.

C. **Property:** Protected property is defined broadly and includes intellectual property.

D. **Compensable Takings**

1. *Physical invasion or occupation:* When not justified by nuisance or preexisting property law, governmental appropriation, invasion, or destruction of private property amounts to a compensable taking.

2. ***Regulation denying all economically beneficial or productive use:*** Unless justified by nuisance or property law, when government deprives a property owner of all viable use of the property, there is a regulatory taking.

3. ***Appropriation for public functions:*** When the government takes private resources to facilitate uniquely public functions, its actions may amount to a taking.

E. **Noncompensable Regulation:** The government need not compensate when it takes property to end a public harm or when the owner retains economically viable use of the land.

F. **Nexus between Public Purpose and Regulation:** The regulatory means that a government chooses must reasonably further its stated public purpose.

G. **Remedy for "Temporary" Regulatory Takings:** When governmental action constitutes a taking, the remedy is not merely invalidation of the action. The government must also pay damages for the temporary taking effected during the period before the ordinance was invalidated.

CHAPTER 7: FOURTEENTH AMENDMENT LIBERTY AND DUE PROCESS

I. **THE BILL OF RIGHTS AND THE FOURTEENTH AMENDMENT:** As originally interpreted, the Bill of Rights, or first ten amendments to the Constitution, applied only to the federal government, not to the states. Over time, however, the Fourteenth Amendment Due Process Clause, which prohibits states from depriving "any person of life, liberty, or property, without due process of law," became the vehicle for requiring the states to accord individuals the protections found in virtually all of the important specific provisions of the Bill of Rights.

II. **THE MEANING OF FOURTEENTH AMENDMENT "LIBERTY" AND "DUE PROCESS"**

A. **"Incorporation" of the Bill of Rights:** Interpretation of the Fourteenth Amendment term "due process" has evolved over time to mean "fundamental fairness," reflected by, but not limited to, most of the protections found in the Bill of Rights. The Fourteenth Amendment is thus said to "incorporate" — make applicable to the states — most of the freedoms and rights of the Bill of Rights, as well as additional rights.

B. **Substantive Due Process:** Due process has both a procedural and a substantive aspect. The procedural view of due process permits governments to do anything not forbidden as long as they act in accordance with fair procedures. The substantive view, on the other hand, recognizes that there are some things the state cannot do, even if not forbidden, no matter how fair its procedures.

1. ***Substantive due process and "liberty of contract":*** Starting with the infamous case *Lochner v. New York*, 198 U.S. 45 (1905), the Court invalidated numerous laws regulating prices, labor, and business entry on grounds of interference with liberty of

CO

contract. The Court later abandoned this emphasis on economic substantive due process analysis and instead substituted the now pervasive and highly deferential "rational basis" test to evaluate socioeconomic legislation.

2. *Noneconomic substantive due process:* However, substantive due process analysis lives on in cases involving noneconomic fundamental rights. To justify infringing such a right, states must show a compelling state interest and no alternative way to achieve it than through the infringement. Substantive due process recognizes the following rights of personal liberty: the right to refuse unwanted medical treatment; the right to die (physician assisted suicide); certain liberty rights while in state custody; and a fundamental right of privacy, which includes within it rights to create, maintain, or change a family relationship, to procreate, to educate children, and the right to abortion without undue state interference.

C. **Procedural Due Process**

1. *Procedural due process in criminal cases:* States must accord suspected or accused persons virtually all the criminal procedural protections of the Bill of Rights, excepting certain requirements, such as a twelve-person jury, deemed not "fundamental."

2. *Procedural due process in civil governmental matters:* Both the Fifth and the Fourteenth Amendment proscribe the governmental taking of life, liberty, or property without due process of law. The "life" interest protected by procedural due process is ill-defined but obviously protected by procedural requirements in death penalty cases. The Court has, however, acknowledged the following liberty interests: those contained in the Bill of Rights and acknowledged in case law, including the rights of privacy and autonomy; those granted by state law; "federal" freedom from governmental restraint; and it has also recognized various property interests and expectations.

3. *Figuring out what procedures procedural due process requires in any given case:* Three factors determine what procedural protections are appropriate in any given case: (1) the private interest affected; (2) the risk of error inherent in the given procedure; and (3) the interest the government is seeking to protect, along with the fiscal and administrative burdens of alternative procedures.

D. **The Conclusive Presumption Doctrine:** Looked at a certain way, overinclusion and underinclusion legislation classifications create a presumption that anyone covered has the characteristics that comprised the reason for the legislation. This may not be true; thus, such statutes appear to create irrebutable presumptions. When a court strikes such a statute down because of the irrebutable presumption, a court is really just substituting its judgment about the appropriateness of the classification for that of the legislation — in effect, exercising a form of rigorous scrutiny review. After employing the doctrine in a number of cases, the Supreme Court, realizing the doctrine would inappropriately invalidate much social and economic legislation, arrested its further development by limiting it to a requirement for individualized hearings when an important liberty interest is affected.

CHAPTER 8: EQUAL PROTECTION (I)

I.   **OVERVIEW: The Fourteenth Amendment guarantees that no state shall deny any person the equal protection of the law, while the Fifth Amendment Due Process Clause, as interpreted by the Court, requires the federal government to accord equal protection as well. In order to determine whether the government has an appropriate justification when its legislation differentiates between people, the Supreme Court scrutinizes the action with one of three levels of intensity.**

A.   **Levels of Judicial Review under the Equal Protection Clause:**

1.   ***Rational basis review:*** The most deferential form of review, rational basis review, requires merely that the state have a legitimate legislative purpose and permits the state to use any rational means to reach its goal.

2.   ***Intermediate review:*** This standard requires that the state have some "substantial and important" goal and that the means it uses to reach its goal serve it reasonably well.

3.   ***Strict scrutiny:*** The most stringent form of review requires the state to justify its actions by showing that it has a compelling state interest and that its choice of means entails the least amount of infringement on the exercise of individual rights.

B.   **Classifications and Equal Protection:** Most statutes and regulations classify persons or situations in order to regulate. Equal protection analysis evaluates the ways that laws classify individuals and the justifications for those classifications. Defending on the level of judicial scrutiny involved, classifications must be rational, *i.e.,* tend to serve the purposes for which they were designed, or have a good means-end fit and be perfectly tailored to the problem they are designed to alleviate. Classifications based on race, religion, national origin, alienage, or ethnicity are "suspect" classifications and will be accorded strict scrutiny. Strict scrutiny will also be applied to classifications affecting fundamental rights. Classifications based on gender, mental, social, or birth status receive intermediate review. All other classifications are subject to rational basis review.

II.   **RATIONAL BASIS REVIEW**

A.   **Basic Principles:** Rational basis review is applied in cases involving social and economic regulation that contain no suspect classifications and that implicate no fundamental rights. Over- and underinclusiveness, without more, will not invalidate a classification undergoing rational basis review. Furthermore, the classification will be upheld if any conceivable grounds justify it.

B.   **Inconsistency in Rationality Review:** Although the standard is extremely deferential, the Court has occasionally applied rational basis review more rigorously than usual to overturn statutory classifications on the ground that they were irrational, especially when they reflect unreasoned fears, hatred, or prejudice.

III. STRICT SCRUTINY REVIEW: SUSPECT CLASSIFICATIONS

A. Classifications Based on Race, Ethnicity, or National Origin: The Equal Protection Clause bans discrimination on the basis of race, color, ethnicity, and national origin; any classifications based on these attributes will be subject to strict scrutiny.

B. Racial Segregation: In the ground-breaking case of *Brown v. Board of Education,* 347 U.S. 483, the Court held racial segregation in public education unconstitutional. Ultimately, the Court applied the Brown desegregation rule to all state-sanctioned segregation. Ending segregation produced tremendous resistance and involved practical, social, and financial problems which continue to this day.

C. Proving Purposeful Discrimination

1. *Disproportionate or disparate impact:* When an action affects one distinctive group more heavily than another, it is said to have a disproportionate impact, or to have discriminatory effects. Such an impact may be intentional or inadvertent.

2. *General rule:* In order to establish a violation of the Equal Protection Clause, one must prove there was a discriminatory intent or purpose behind the action in question.

3. *Mixed-motivation cases:* Where a decision-maker manifests mixed motives, the plaintiff need only prove that a discriminatory motive played a substantial role in the decision taken.

4. *Neutral criteria maintained for a discriminatory purpose:* In these cases, an intent to maintain innocently adopted, neutral criteria because of their discriminatory impact is sufficient to establish an Equal Protection violation.

5. *Foreseeability:* That one can foresee that a certain discriminatory effect will follow is merely evidence, not proof, of discriminatory intent.

IV. HEIGHTENED SCRUTINY FOR CERTAIN OTHER CLASSIFICATIONS

A. Gender Classifications: Unlike racial classifications, classifications based on gender do have valid purposes and may be useful or essential for regulation. The Court therefore requires that a gender classification fairly and substantially relate to the achievement of important and articulated (not hypothetical) governmental objectives — an intermediate rather than strict scrutiny standard of review.

B. Alienage Classifications: The Constitution expressly gives Congress plenary authority to regulate immigration and nationalization. States, on the other hand, have no constitutional role to play in immigration and may not act to discourage or burden lawful immigration. Therefore, when Congress regulates on the basis of alienage, the Court applies rational basis review, whereas state classifications based on alienage are inherently suspect and are thus subject to strict scrutiny. States may, however, require citizenship as a condition of employment for employees who participate in the formulation and execution of governmental policy, the so-called political function exception.

C. **Illegitimacy As a Classification:** Although it may be morally wrong to punish or disadvantage a child because its parents were not married, filiation remains important: The provision of support and inheritance rights are often tied to biological or legally recognized relationships to parents. In addition, benefits or compensatory awards, such as Social Security and insurance, are predicated on a child's establishing dependency on a covered individual, and legitimacy has some evidentiary value in proving dependency. Since illegitimacy as a classification may have some rational and relevant purposes, it does not qualify as a suspect classification. While its standard of review has shifted from time to time, the Court now applies intermediate scrutiny to classifications that distinguish between legitimate and illegitimate children.

D. **Other Classifications as Possible Suspect or Quasi-suspect Classifications:** The Court has rejected attempts to add new classifications, such as age and mental retardation, to the list of suspect or quasi-suspect classifications. Instead, the Court reviews state use of such classifications under the rational basis standard, although it may scrutinize classifications based on mental disability with special care.

CHAPTER 9: EQUAL PROTECTION (II)

I. "BENIGN" SUSPECT OR QUASI-SUSPECT CLASSIFICATIONS

A. **"Benign" Racial Classifications:** Strict scrutiny review of racial classifications is a barrier that governments or state agencies must overcome when they seek to use such classifications in order to provide educational and employment opportunities to disadvantaged racial minorities.

   1. *Constitutional limits on the use of race-conscious remedies:* Race-conscious classifications may only be used to remedy prior or current discrimination against an identifiable group of victims. All racial classifications, whether harmful or benign, receive strict scrutiny review. A strong minority of the Court has argued otherwise, albeit unsuccessfully; it would apply an intermediate level of scrutiny to beneficial racial classifications, which do not entail the sort of victimization of a minority that suspect classifications traditionally imply.

   2. *Diversity in education as a compelling state interest:* Racial admission quotas that make race solely determinative are unconstitutional, although public universities may use race as one factor to help ensure a diverse student body.

   3. *Congressional use of race-based classifications — strict scrutiny:* Congress may employ race-conscious classifications not merely to remedy past discrimination but also to further important governmental objectives. Such classifications will receive strict scrutiny.

CO

4. *State and local race-based policy decisions:* Except to redress prior or current discrimination, state and local governments may not use racial classifications to further affirmative action programs.

B. **"Benign" Use of Gender Classifications**

1. *Affirmative governmental use of quasi-suspect classifications:* Unlike racial classifications, cases involving gender classifications receive only intermediate scrutiny, requiring only an important, rather than a compelling, governmental purpose. Consequently, government can use gender-based classifications to correct a significant sex-based discrimination or in situations where the sexes are differently situated and the classification is well tailored to reflect that difference.

C. **Affirmative Action Under Title VII:** Title VII of the Civil Rights Act of 1964 bans employment discrimination based on race, color, religion, sex, or national origin. Title VII authorizes the use of race- and gender-based classifications to correct traditionally segregated job situations. Under Title VII, Congress has even banned the use of neutral employment criteria and discretionary hiring and promotional practices that have discriminatory or disproportionate effects.

II. **FUNDAMENTAL RIGHTS AND EQUAL PROTECTION**

A. **The List of Fundamental Rights:** When evaluating classifications impinging on fundamental rights, the Court balances the important interests of the state against the impact of the regulation on the exercise of the rights. Where a regulation severely restricts the exercise of a fundamental right, it must be narrowly tailored to meet a compelling state interest. The following fundamental rights are protected by this branch of equal protection law:

B. **The Right to Vote**

1. *Voting qualifications or restrictions:* Where a state electoral regulation severely restricts voting rights, it must be narrowly drawn to advance a compelling state interest. On the other hand, if rights are reasonably, but not severely, restricted, an important state interest will suffice.

2. *Vote dilution:* The government must treat each person's vote equally; consequently, electoral schemes that accord greater weight to some votes than to others are unconstitutional unless justified by an important state interest.

3. *Ballot access restrictions:* Restricting the access of candidates to a place on the election ballot impairs voters' rights to cast their votes for candidates of their choice. However, as long as access requirements afford minority parties and candidates "a real and substantially equal opportunity" to qualify for a ballot, and alternative requirements would not serve state interests in significantly less burdensome ways, the state may impose them.

CO

C. **The Indigent's Right of Fair Treatment in State Adjudication Processes**

1. *Criminal cases:* Where the state permits criminal appeals as of right, it must provide an attorney and trial transcripts without charge to indigent appellants. Where the state has already provided one appeal as of right, it need not provide counsel for subsequent discretionary appeals.

2. *Imprisonment for inability to pay fines:* States may not discriminate against indigent criminals by imprisoning them for nonpayment of fines unless there are no adequate, alternative forms of punishment.

3. *Civil cases:* Although technically a due process, rather than equal protection issue, when access claims involve some fundamental interest, such as divorce proceedings, the state must waive filing fees for indigents.

D. **The Right to Migrate Interstate:** States cannot bar persons from immigrating into, and taking up residence in, the state or penalize them for doing so. Without a compelling interest, states also may not impose a substantial residency requirement as a condition for receiving welfare or necessary medical care but may do so as a condition for obtaining a divorce.

E. **Other Fundamental Rights:** Since individuals have no fundamental constitutional right to the basic necessities of life, states need not meet strict scrutiny review when providing, or reducing, welfare benefits. Nor, at least where the state provides education, is there a fundamental right to education, which would require the state to equalize per-pupil expenditures.

CHAPTER 10: STATE ACTION AND CONGRESSIONAL AUTHORITY TO REACH PRIVATE ACTION TO PROTECT CIVIL RIGHTS

I. **STATE ACTION: To support an action against private parties for infringement of Fourteenth and Fifteenth Amendment-based civil rights, it is usually necessary to show some kind of state involvement or responsibility; otherwise, the action is merely a private wrong pursuable only through ordinary remedies. This is because only states, not private parties, are prohibited from denying those civil rights.**

A. **State Action through the Undertaking of Public Functions:** When private parties exercise powers traditionally reserved exclusively to the state, there is state action. Action by a company town, for example, which has the facilities and functions of an ordinary town, will be construed as state action.

B. **State Action through State Involvement:** One can infer state action when there is "significant state involvement" in the conduct in question. A private party's use of state courts to enforce a racially restrictive covenant, for example, constitutes state action. On the other hand, mere state licensing or funding of private parties does not constitute state action.

CO

C. **State Authorization or Encouragement:** Where the state can be said to be responsible for the action the private actor took, there is state action: Affirmative state acts designed to authorize or encourage private violations of civil rights constitute sufficient state action to make the state liable for the actions of private parties.

D. **Private Actors Operating under State Statutes:** Private actors will be deemed state actors depending on the extent of reliance on state assistance, whether the actor is performing a traditional government function, and whether apparent state authority aggravates the injury.

E. **State Inaction:** State inaction, in the absence of state responsibility and of a constitutional duty to act, cannot constitute state action.

II. **CONGRESSIONAL AUTHORITY TO REACH PRIVATE ACTION INFRINGING CIVIL RIGHTS**

A. **The Civil Rights Statutes:** These statutes provide for criminal and civil remedies for private interference with the exercise of federally protected civil rights.

1. *Criminal civil rights legislation:* 18 U.S.C. § 241 prohibits conspiracies against the rights of citizens; 18 U.S.C. § 242 criminalizes the deprivation of federally protected rights "under color of law." These two statutes provide federal criminal sanctions and a federal forum for the prosecution of racially motivated crimes. The "color of law" requirement is met when the wrongdoer was "clothed" with the authority of the state, had an "actual semblance" of state authority, or participated in an activity jointly with the state.

2. *Civil rights statutes with civil sanctions:* 42 U.S.C. § 1985(c) provides civil remedies for conspiracies to deny "equal protection of the laws, or of equal privileges and immunities under the laws." 42 U.S.C. § 1983 provides civil remedies for deprivations of rights "under color of law."

B. **Congressional Power under the Thirteenth Amendment:** The Thirteenth Amendment bans all slavery and involuntary servitude, whether public or private, and has no state action requirement. By empowering Congress to abolish all incidents of slavery, the Thirteenth Amendment sanctions statutes banning racial discrimination in housing and in the making and enforcement of contracts.

C. **Congressional Power under the Enabling Clauses of the Fourteenth and Fifteenth Amendments:** Congress has greater powers to prevent or remedy violations of the Fourteenth and Fifteenth Amendments than courts have. As long as Congress uses a rational means to effect the constitutional prohibitions against discrimination, the Court will uphold its action. Congress thus has the power to prohibit state action that, while itself not violative of those amendments, nonetheless perpetuates the effects of past intentional discrimination. Further, where there has been a history of intentional racial discrimination, Congress may forbid neutral state actions that have a discriminatory impact and create risks of purposeful discrimination. Congress does not actually have the power to define constitutional violations, but it has a greater fact-finding competence than courts and may determine that certain state actions or practices which a court would find neutral or justified so create risks of screening actual discrimination that they should be outlawed. Congress must use these powers in ways that are congruent and proportional to the identified harms it seeks to prevent or remedy.

CHAPTER 11: FREEDOM OF SPEECH (I)

I. **THEORIES OF THE FIRST AMENDMENT: The First Amendment provides that Congress shall make no law abridging the freedom of speech or of the press. Several theories attempt to define the kinds of speech protected by the First Amendment.**

    A. **Instrumental Theories:** These theories view free speech as a means to ensure that government remains open, responsive, and democratic, or to facilitate a robust exchange of ideas, or to symbolize and make workable a tolerant society.

    B. **Free Speech and Self-expression:** This theory holds that self-expression is an ultimate value, that is, an end in itself.

    C. **Freedom of Speech as a Default Principle:** This theory is based on the notion that since the government cannot be entrusted with the delicate task of regulating speech, it should not be attempted at all.

II. **THE FIRST AMENDMENT AND "DANGEROUS" SPEECH HAVING SOCIAL OR POLITICAL AIMS**

    A. **Historical Background:** In the first half of this century, the fear of radical ideas encouraged various legislation aimed at prohibiting acts or effects thought to endanger the war effort or the fragile public order. Ironically, modern free speech consciousness was born out of these efforts.

    B. **Unlawful or Subversive Advocacy Directed at the State or Major State Goals:** States may seek to prohibit or punish speech that advocates unlawful action in order to reach speech that actually causes such action and to prevent speech thought to be inherently dangerous. In early formulations, the Court held that a state could proscribe or punish only that speech that poses a "clear and present danger" of some harm. Over time, the clear and present danger principle has been refined in ways making it more speech protective. With respect to the Communist Party, for example, the Court has held that Congress could not punish abstract advocacy of ideas, even if those ideas postulated violent overthrow of the government, but could punish such advocacy coupled with action directed at, or creating a danger of, immediate overthrow. Similarly, Congress could proscribe the advocacy involved in creating a disciplined group prepared to take action when the time was ripe.

    C. **Incitement:** Following *Brandenburg v. Ohio*, 395 U.S. 444 (1969), the government can

CO

forbid or proscribe advocacy of force or illegal action in incitement situations only when the speaker intends to incite or produce imminent lawless action and is likely to do so.

D. Fighting Words: Direct personal insults likely to cause the hearer to react violently were traditionally considered unprotected speech. Subsequent developments call into question the continuing vitality of the fighting words doctrine.

E. Group Libel: False and derogatory statements about a group, tending to produce hate or prejudice, have been held unprotected, but the *Brandenburg* rule and current defamation law have rendered group libel's status uncertain.

F. Defamation of Government Officials, Public Figures, and Private Parties

1. *Actual malice required:* In order for a public official to recover for libelous false statements regarding her official conduct, the official has to prove by clear and convincing evidence that the statements were made with "actual malice," *i.e.,* with knowledge of falsity of in reckless disregard of the truth. *New York Times v. Sullivan,* 376 U.S. 254 (1964).

2. *Public figures:* In addition to public officials, the *New York Times* rule also applies to public figures, that is, famous individuals or those who have thrust themselves into the public spotlight.

3. *Fact and opinion:* Opinions not reasonably interpretable as stating or implying actual facts about an individual are not actionable.

4. *Inaccurate, distorted, or fabricated quotations:* If paraphrasing does not change the speaker's meaning, there is no actual malice.

5. *Private persons:* Individuals who place themselves in a particular public controversy may become public figures for purposes of the *New York Times* rule.

G. Invasion of Privacy

1. *Privacy cases:* The *New York Times* rule appears to apply to disclosures of true information which may be embarrassing or damaging. Disclosure of information already in the public record is not actionable.

2. *"False light" privacy cases:* Publication of true, but misleading, facts may give rise to liability if published with actual malice.

III. EROTIC, OBSCENE, AND PORNOGRAPHIC EXPRESSION

A. Definitions

1. *Obscenity:* That aspect or character of expression about sex which is disgusting, offensive, filthy, foul, loathsome, or repulsive.

2. *Pornography:* The graphic depiction of ultimate sexual acts or sexual organs intended to cause sexual excitement.

B. **Attempts to Restrict Censorship:** The Supreme Court has held that works of serious literary, artistic, political, or scientific value may not be suppressed regardless of their sexual content. However, legitimate state interests in order, safety, and morality may justify obscenity laws.

C. **Three-Part Test:** For First Amendment purposes, an expression is obscene if (1) to the average person, applying contemporary community standards, the dominant theme of the material taken as a whole appeals to the prurient interest, and (2) the work depicts or describes, in a patently offensive way, sexual conduct specifically defined by statute as unlawful to portray, and (3) the work taken as a whole lacks serious literary, artistic, political, or scientific value.

D. **Obscenity and Privacy:** With the exception of child pornography, the state cannot make it a crime to possess obscene material in one's own home. However, the state can prohibit buying or transporting obscene material.

E. **Dealing in or Distributing Obscene Materials:** The state may punish those who create or trade in obscene materials.

F. **Child Pornography:** The trier of fact in child pornography cases need not find an appeal to an average person's prurient interest, establish patent offense, or consider the work as a whole.

G. **Juvenile Obscenity:** States may outlaw for sale or distribution to minors nonobscene but sexually stimulating material.

H. **Sexually Violent and Degrading Expression:** Since some evidence suggests that exposure to sexually violent pornographic material causes sexually violent behavior toward women, the Attorney General's Commission on Pornography has recommended increased enforcement against such expression. Recently, pornography opponents have gone further by attempting to redefine pornography as a systematic practice of sexual exploitation and subordination of women or their surrogates.

IV. **INDECENT AND OFFENSIVE SPEECH**

A. **Words Not Per Se Proscribable:** There are no words that can be forbidden per se.

B. **Offensive Displays:** The First Amendment strictly limits government's ability to ban merely offensive expression on the basis of its content.

C. **Zoning and Offensive Expression:** However, as long as content and access are not significantly restricted, government may use land use regulation to limit sexually explicit displays to certain areas of a community.

CO

D. Content Neutrality: That the state may not regulate expression on the basis of its content is a hallmark of First Amendment jurisprudence.

E. Content Neutrality and Secondary Effects of Speech: In some circumstances, possibly limited to sexually explicit speech, government may treat different kinds of speech differently, as long as the regulation is not based on the message of the expression but on its "secondary effects."

F. Regulation of Offensive Speech According to Content: Because broadcast media invade the privacy of the home, where children may be listening, the FCC may regulate obscene, indecent, and offensive exposure. A total ban on indecent phone recordings simply in order to protect children, however, would be unconstitutional, as the ban applies to adults as well.

G. Uncertainty over the Status of Offensive or Other Low-Value Speech: Members of the Supreme Court disagree as to whether certain "low-value" speech should be accorded less constitutional protection or whether all protected speech should be treated similarly.

V. COMMERCIAL SPEECH

A. Definitions

1. *Commercial Speech:* The core meaning of "commercial speech" is any speech that does no more than propose a commercial transaction, *e.g.,* an offer to sell.

2. *Promotion:* "Promotional advertising," a subset of commercial speech, promotes a product or service or provides economically useful information.

3. *Motivation:* "Commercially or economically motivated speech" is motivated by profit but does not necessarily propose any commercial transaction.

B. The First Amendment Protects Truthful Commercial Speech Concerning Lawful Activities: Because of its special characteristics, the government may regulate commercial speech on the basis of its content to insure its truthfulness. The government may ban forms of communication which are likely to deceive or which solicit or promote illegal activity.

C. Level of Scrutiny: Truthful commercial speech has less First Amendment value than other forms of protected speech and is less protected. Government may regulate it when seeking to serve some substantial state interest. Furthermore, government may reduce demand of lawful-but-harmful products, like cigarettes, by banning their advertisement.

D. Lawyers and Commercial Speech: The commercial speech doctrine protects truthful attorney advertising concerning routine legal services. But the state may regulate some promotional activities to protect legal services consumers from undue influence and deception.

VI. NONCOMMERCIAL SOLICITATION

A. Charitable and Interest Group Solicitation: These activities are protected First Amendment activity.

B. Narrow Tailoring: Regulations affecting non-commercial solicitations must be narrowly tailored.

C. Door-to-Door Canvassing: Government may not ban door-to-door canvassing or handbilling.

CHAPTER 12: FREEDOM OF SPEECH (II)

I. FIRST AMENDMENT VARIABLES

A. Prior Restraint: Because the First Amendment forbids censorship, there is a very strong presumption against any form of prior restraint.

1. *Prior restraint possible:* This presumption is not an absolute, however. For example, national security interests may be sufficiently compelling to warrant a restraint on publication.

2. *Procedural requirements for injunction:* Restraints against publications may issue only after an adversarial hearing, unless time is of the essence.

3. *Prior restraints and nonprotected speech:* Technically, the prior restraint prohibition does not apply to inciting or libelous speech, but the nature of these forms of speech affords little opportunity for prior restraint. The state may delay publication of allegedly obscene expression, however, in order to review it. Such reviews must be conducted promptly, place the burden of proof on the censor, and provide for prompt judicial review.

4. *Licensing and permit systems as prior restraints:* If aimed at, or adaptable to, forbidding speech, such systems are unconstitutional.

5. *Seizure as a prior restraint:* Large-scale confiscations of allegedly obscene materials constitute prior restraints. Seizure of a single copy of a book for evidence does not.

6. *Forfeitures as prior restraints:* Forfeitures of protected materials following racketeering convictions are considered subsequent punishments, not prior restraints.

B. Overbreadth and Vagueness: A statute is overbroad if it applies to both protected and unprotected speech. One who seeks to challenge the constitutionality of a facially overbroad statute need only show that the statute applies to a substantial amount of protected speech, even if the statute does not infringe on his rights personally. A statute

CO

may also be held unconstitutional due to vagueness. A statute is vague if "persons of common intelligence must necessarily guess at its meaning and differ as to its application."

C. **Content-based Restrictions on Speech and Content Neutrality:** The First Amendment generally prohibits governmental regulation of speech based on its content or the speaker's point of view, and the court subjects such speech discriminations to strict scrutiny.

D. **The Speech-Conduct Distinction:** While government may not regulate speech, it may regulate conduct, as long as its aim is not to regulate associated speech, the regulation is reasonably tailored to reach the conduct harms that concern it, and it does not unduly burden speech.

E. **Conduct and Symbolic Speech:** In order to avoid treating all actions as protected First Amendment expression, courts must be able to distinguish between expressive and nonexpressive conduct.

   1. *Expressive conduct:* Conduct is expressive when undertaken in order to convey a particularized message that its audience is highly likely to understand.

   2. *Regulation of expressive conduct:* In a draft-card burning case, *United States v. O'Brien,* 391 U.S. 367 (1968), the Court adopted a two-track test: (1) When the government seeks to regulate expression as expression, the Court applies strict scrutiny analysis; (2) if governmental regulation merely incidentally affects expression, then the Court balances the government's interest and mode of regulating against their impact on expression.

F. **Discriminatory Motivations for Conduct:** The First Amendment does not protect bias-motivated conduct, such as hate crimes.

G. **Time, Place, and Manner Regulations**

   1. *Regulation permitted:* The state may reasonably regulate the time, place, and manner of access to, or uses of, public fora opened for expressive purposes.

   2. *Requirements for time, place, and manner regulations:* Such regulations must be content neutral, must serve a significant governmental purpose, and be well tailored to serve those purposes, while leaving open alternative channels of communication.

H. **The Captive Audience Problem:** In circumstances where individuals cannot protect their own privacy, the government may have an interest in doing so. Streets, parks, public monuments, etc., are traditional public gathering places, and there the audience is not involuntarily subjected to inescapable unwanted expression. However, in other places, like a subway or at home, government may protect a captive audience by limiting expression.

I. **Public Forum Doctrine:** A "traditional public forum" is a publicly owned place or property open to First Amendment activities under long-standing public practice, *e.g.,* a street. The Court applies a strict scrutiny analysis to content-based regulation in the public forum. A "public forum by designation" is a place transformed into a forum by government action, and the standard of review depends on the character of the forum. In a "limited public forum" created for a special use, like a zoo, the government may restrict speech uses to those compatible with the forum. A "nonpublic forum," not open to the public except for specialized public business, may be subject to reasonable distinctions between speakers and subject matter, so long as they are viewpoint neutral.

II. **RIGHTS OF ACCESS IN PRIVATE FORA**

   A. **Shopping Malls:** Privately owned facilities are not public fora, even though open to the public for other purposes.

   B. **State Law Opening Private Property to Free Speech Access:** States may grant their residents broader free speech rights than those granted by the U.S. Constitution and may thus consider shopping malls to be public fora.

   C. **Access to the Media and Other Institutions:** Congress may regulate the broadcast media without showing a compelling need to do so, and the FCC may require broadcasters to give candidates and opposing viewpoints equal access to airtime. By contrast, government has no authority to require the press, or any private print media, to grant rights of access to its publications.

CHAPTER 13: FREEDOM OF SPEECH, ASSOCIATION, AND THE PRESS

I. **FREE SPEECH IN SPECIAL CONTEXTS**

   A. **Money and Political Speech:** Government may not limit the amount spent by individuals, candidates, or campaigns to advance a candidate or a cause since such limits would transgress on the right to political speech and skew the free market in ideas. Although not persons for purposes of constitutional law, corporations have a right of free speech, and states may not prohibit corporations from spending money to influence the outcome of referenda. Governments, however, may limit contributions to candidate campaigns.

   B. **Free Speech in Public Schools:** Students have free speech rights while on school grounds and may express themselves freely as long as they do not significantly interfere with school activities or the rights of others. Schools may, however, impose standards that effectively limit speech based on the activity involved and the maturity of the audience.

   C. **Speech Interfering with the Administration of Justice:** Courts may punish in-court conduct with contempt, but contempt punishment for out-of-court speech must be

CO

justified by serious and imminent danger to, or actual interference with, the administration of justice. States may also restrict extrajudicial statements of litigants and attorneys likely to materially prejudice pending litigation.

D. **Picketing and Boycotts As Free Speech:** Picketing is communicative and therefore involves First Amendment activity, but the state may nonetheless regulate conduct on the picket line to reduce the potential for violence or possible interference with other legitimate activities. The state, however, may ban picketing having illegal goals. While the state can regulate economic activity and ban economically motivated boycotts, even though they may involve the communication of ideas, the state cannot prohibit the free speech activities associated with a politically motivated boycott.

II. FREEDOM OF ASSOCIATION

A. **First Amendment Freedom of Association:** The First Amendment protects the right to associate with others for the advancement of beliefs, ideas, and opinions.

B. **Compelled Disclosure of Associations and Other Information:** State-compelled disclosure of associational ties, without a compelling state interest, which may subject members to sanctions or embarrassment, violates the freedom of association. Compelling state interests, however, do justify disclosures about political campaign contributions and inquiries into fitness and competence of potential employees and license applicants.

C. **Loyalty Oaths:** Government cannot condition employment by requiring job applicants or employees to take oaths denying having engaged in, or forswearing future engagement in, protected First Amendment activity.

D. **Litigation as Expression:** Litigation for political ends and association for the purpose of litigating constitutional rights are protected First Amendment activities. Therefore, states may not curb ideological interest group informational activities designed to stimulate litigation. Neither may they bar or impede association designed to obtain meaningful access to the courts.

E. **Freedom Not to Associate:** Governments may not require individuals to provide support for political views, candidates, or causes with which they disagree. Similarly, government may not force exclusive organizations formed for expressive purposes to broaden their memberships, although it may require groups organized merely for general social or commercial purposes not to limit membership discriminatorily.

F. **First Amendment Protection of Speech and Association Activities of Public Employees and Contractors:** In the interests of fair and effective government performance, the government may restrict public employees' exercise of their First Amendment rights to a certain degree.

1. *Proscribing public employee partisan political activity:* Public employee involvement in political campaigns may be proscribed in a content-neutral fashion.

2. ***Public employee speech:*** The First Amendment protects public employee speech related to "matters of public concern," which is not knowingly or recklessly false, does not involve the disclosure of confidential information, and does not undermine employer-employee relationships.

3. ***Public contractors:*** The First Amendment protects even at-will governmental contractors from governmental termination or refusal to renew contracts in retaliation for an exercise of free speech rights.

4. ***Patronage or political affiliation dismissals:*** Public employers cannot fire, dismiss, or otherwise sanction employees based on political affiliation, if such affiliation is irrelevant to their effectiveness.

5. ***Denial of benefits because of speech:*** Although government is not required to subsidize expression, it may not deny governmental benefits because of speech.

G. **Legislative Investigations and Free Speech:** Need for an investigation directed at beliefs or associations must be balanced against the burden imposed on First Amendment rights.

III. FREEDOM OF THE PRESS

A. **Background:** The Supreme Court has developed a small body of constitutional law, in addition to prior restraint and libel law, relating specifically to the press.

B. **No Special Press Immunity from Governmental Inquiries, Obligations, or Processes:** There is no constitutionally implied special news-gathering privilege, nor does the press have special privileges exempting it from ordinary criminal processes, *e.g.,* the press is not exempt from search warrants or grand jury inquiries.

C. **Public and Press Access to Information:** In general, the press has no greater right of access to public institutions and information than the public itself has. As criminal trials have historically been open to the public, government may not close criminal trials to the press or the public unless closure is essential to serve an overriding governmental interest.

D. **Laws Directed at the Press:** Government may not enact laws specially applicable to the press which create a risk of punishing or censoring the press or which discriminate between classes of publications.

CHAPTER 14: FREEDOM OF RELIGION

I. THE ESTABLISHMENT CLAUSE

A. **Aid to Sectarian or Religious Schools:** In order for a state statute or program that in some sense arguably aids or endorses religion to succeed under the Establishment Clause,

(1) it must have a secular, not religious, purpose; (2) its primary effect must neither advance nor inhibit religion; and (3) it must not foster excessive government entanglement with religion.

1. *Application:* This three-part formula (the so-called *Lemon* test) has been used to render the following forms of aid impermissible. In recent cases, Court has revisited its Establishment Clause decisions and has articulated modifidations of the *Lemon* test less restrictive of state aid to sectarian schools. Presently, direct tuition aid, teacher salary supplements, and primary and secondary school building funds are unconstitutional. Conversely, permissible aid includes bus transportation, secular book loans, instructional materials and equipment simple diagnostic services, and off-site auxiliary services provided by non-sectarian school personnel.

B. **State Sponsorship of Prayer, Religious Practice, or Doctrinal Teaching in Public Schools:** The Court also uses the *Lemon* test to analyze other issues regarding government involvement with religion and has concluded that the government may not require or sponsor prayer in public school or require the teaching of certain theories designed to protect or promote religion.

C. **Grant of Government Powers to Religious Bodies:** The government may not grant or cede the exercise of governmental powers to religions.

D. **State Conferral of Benefits or Exemptions.**

1. *Benefits or exemptions generally available:* The Establishment Clause is not violated when a general benefit or exemption program incidentally benefits a religion.

2. *Benefits or exemptions conferred solely on religion:* Even these benefits may not be unconstitutional since a government may permissibly accommodate the free exercise of religion. The Civil Rights Act of 1964, for example, permits religious organizations to discriminate on the basis of religion when hiring or discharging employees.

E. **State Funding of Religious Groups:** When the government has a secular purpose, it may provide aid to sectarian as well as secular groups to carry out that purpose.

F. **Government Association with Religion in Other Contexts:**

1. *Sunday closing laws:* These laws provide a uniform day of rest for all, apart from their traditional religious significance, and thus do not constititute an establishment of religion.

2. *Legislative prayer and chaplains:* The long-standing practice of opening legislative sessions with a prayer is more an acknowledgment of belief than an establishment of religion.

CO

3. *Religious gerrymandering:* Laws that create denominational preferences violate the Establishment Clause.

4. ***Governmental use of, or association with, religious symbols:*** When there is a secular purpose in celebrating the holiday, no endorsement of religion, and no primary effect of advancing religion, a governmental display of a creche along with other holiday accoutrements at Christmas does not amount to an establishment of religion.

II. FREE EXERCISE OF RELIGION

A. Generally Applicable Laws: Generally applicable laws, not specifically directed at religious practices, which happen to govern acts that a religious belief requires or forbids are constitutional. On the other hand, laws that are neither neutral nor of general applicability are subject to strict scrutiny review, *i.e.,* must be justified by a compelling state interest. In special "hybrid" cases, certain neutral, generally applicable laws may also be subject to strict scrutiny and invalidated if they burden both free exercise and some other fundamental right, such as the parental right to educate children.

B. Free Exercise in Special Contexts: In special circumstances involving the military and prisons, the Court applies a deferential "reasonableness" standard of review to free exercise claims.

III. ADJUDICATION OR OTHER STATE SETTLEMENT OF RELIGIOUS MATTERS

A. Intrachurch Matters: The state may not ally itself with any side in an intrachurch controversy over religious authority or dogma. Courts may, however, apply neutral criteria to resolve non-doctrinal matters such as church property disputes.

B. Determining What Constitutes a Religion: In determining whether an individual's claim has a religious basis, the state may decide whether a religious belief is sincerely held but not what constitutes a religion or whether particular beliefs qualify as religious.

C. The Religion Clauses and the Conscientious Objection Exemption: A person may obtain conscientious objection status if his objection to war stems from beliefs held with the strength of religious convictions, regardless of whether or not he believes in God.

JUDICIAL POWER, FUNCTIONS, AND JURISDICTION

▶ **CHAPTER SUMMARY**

CHAPTER 1: JUDICIAL POWER, FUNCTIONS, AND JURISDICTION

Introduction. Traditionally, constitutional law courses begin with a study of the role of the judiciary and courts in the constitutional system. The study is a bit abstract, focusing, as it does, on the institution of courts and on some of the important rules regarding how they undertake to do their business. Nonetheless, it is essential, for it is ultimately a study of the power to decide constitutional issues.

Understanding the role of the courts in the constitutional system is fundamental to understanding constitutional law. In the United States, courts have asserted the authority to declare the meaning, import, and legal consequences of constitutional provisions. Over the years since the founding of the country, the United States Supreme Court has decided thousands of constitutional cases and issues and has created the immense body of constitutional rules and doctrines that comprise constitutional law. It is therefore important to understand the nature and extent of the power to adjudicate constitutional issues, how parties raise them, and how courts in general go about deciding them. This requires a study of the U.S. constitutional provisions relating to the judicial power and courts, and a consideration of jurisdiction and the relationship between state and federal courts and state and federal law. It also entails a study of what matters or issues courts will decide, what parties can raise constitutional issues, and various doctrines regarding limits on judicial review of constitutional questions.

FEDERAL COURTS

I. FEDERAL COURTS

A. Article III Courts: In Article III, § 1, the Constitution vests the judicial power of the United States in one Supreme Court and in such lower federal courts as Congress creates. The Constitution does not require Congress to create lower federal courts but rather authorizes it to do so. As an incident of its power to create lower federal courts, Congress also has the power to define their jurisdiction (or the cases they have authority to hear). *Sheldon v. Sill,* 49 U.S. 441 (1850). If Congress failed to create federal courts which could hear cases falling within the federal judicial power, or some portion of it (*see* II., *infra*), only state courts could hear them.

B. Constitutionally Assigned Jurisdiction: Article III, § 2 outlines the classes of cases or controversies coming within the jurisdiction of the federal judicial power. Principally, these are cases involving:

1. *The Constitution, federal laws, and treaties;*

2. *Ambassadors, public ministers and consuls;*

3. *Admiralty;*

4. *The United States as a party;*

5. *Controversies between states, a state and a citizen of another state, and citizens of different states;*

6. *Controversies between a state or state citizens and foreign states or their citizens or subjects.*

C. Original and Appellate Jurisdiction

1. *Original jurisdiction:* Article III, § 2 also provides that the Supreme Court shall have "original" jurisdiction – meaning the authority to first hear or try – in cases involving ambassadors, other public ministers and consuls, and cases in which a state is a party. Congress may not enlarge the original jurisdiction of the Supreme Court, *Marbury v. Madison,* 5 U.S. 137 (1803), but may give concurrent original jurisdiction to lower courts, *Bors v. Preston,* 111 U.S. 252 (1884), with the result that the Supreme Court would hear such cases on review.

2. *Appellate jurisdiction:* In all other (nonoriginal jurisdiction) cases coming within the federal judicial power, the Supreme Court has appellate jurisdiction. Article III, § 2 has a further provision, sometimes called the Exceptions Clause, which gives Congress the power to define and regulate the Supreme Court's appellate jurisdiction. (For further discussion, *see* II.3., *infra.*)

D. Supreme Court Review Jurisdiction

1. *Discretionary review:* Originally, Congress provided for appellate review in the Supreme Court as a matter of right. It later introduced discretionary Supreme Court review in certain kinds of cases through a system of petition for a writ of certiorari. In 1988, Congress revised the basic statute providing for Supreme Court review by making almost all its appellate review discretionary by writ of certiorari. 28 U.S.C. § 1257 (as amended, 1988).

2. *Review of state court decisions:* A federal jurisdictional statute, 28 U.S.C. § 1257, limits Supreme Court review of state court decisions to final judgments, regarding federal issues, made by the highest state court in which a decision could be had. As the Supreme Court has no authority to pass on state law questions unrelated to federal issues, it will not review state court decisions that rest on substantive "adequate and independent state grounds." *Herb v. Pitcairn,* 324 U.S. 117 (1945). In other words, even though a state court may rule incorrectly on federal law, if it adequately justifies its decision on state law grounds independently of its ruling on federal law, there is little point in federal review. Correction of the federal error would not change the result in the case.

Example: Suppose in a criminal case that a state court finds that some police interrogation practice violates both the U.S. Constitution's Fifth Amendment privilege against self-incrimination and a similar privilege in the state constitution. Assume further that the Supreme Court would find the state court ruling on the Fifth Amendment wrong as a matter of federal constitutional law. As long as the state court's decision is properly grounded in state constitutional law, the Supreme Court will not review it, notwithstanding the federal constitutional error.

a. *Uncertain cases – plain statement rule:* State courts sometimes fail to distinguish clearly between the federal and the state grounds for their decisions. Furthermore, state courts may believe that federal law requires a certain construction of state law. In either case, it is difficult to determine whether federal law effectively controlled the decision. Consequently, adequate and independent state grounds operate to avert federal review only when the state court clearly and expressly indicates that its decision is "alternatively based on bona fide separate, adequate, and independent grounds." *Michigan v. Long,* 463 U.S. 1032 (1983).

3. ***Review of state court refusal to hear federal claims:*** State courts are required to hear appropriately presented federal claims. Sometimes state courts refuse to hear such claims because of a litigant's failure to comply with some state procedural requirement. That failure may constitute an adequate and independent state ground where the procedural requirement serves some legitimate state interest, rather than being a convenient tool to evade federal claims or deprive litigants of federal rights. *Henry v. Mississippi,* 379 U.S. 443 (1965).

II. THE DOCTRINE OF JUDICIAL REVIEW AND ITS CONSEQUENCES

A. Supreme Court Authority to Review Governmental Actions and Declare Them Unconstitutional

1. ***"Judicial review" defined:*** "Judicial review," as used in this outline, means the practice of court review of legislative and executive acts to determine their constitutionality.

2. ***The doctrine:*** The doctrine of judicial review holds that courts, where relevant in cases coming before them, have the duty to interpret and apply the Constitution and have the power and authority to declare acts contrary to the Constitution invalid and unenforceable. *Marbury v. Madison,* 5 U.S. 137 (1803).

   a. *Theory:* The theory of the doctrine of judicial review is that the Constitution, which is supreme law, established a federal government of limited powers, that the branches of government may exercise only those powers the Constitution grants them, and that governmental acts inconsistent with such powers are unconstitutional and unenforceable. Where relevant to issues in cases before them, courts must apply the Constitution as fundamental law and therefore must refuse to enforce acts contrary to the Constitution.

   b. *Controversy regarding the doctrine of judicial review*

      (1) The meaning of *Marbury v. Madison*: As the Constitution itself is silent as to which of the three branches of government, the executive, the legislative, or the judiciary, shall be the authoritative interpreter of the meaning of the Constitution, there are at least three major possibilities to consider. These are as follows. Each branch, in matters falling within its sphere of authorized power, is to interpret the Constitution authoritatively. Alternatively, in cases coming before the Supreme Court, the Supreme Court is the formal, authoritative interpreter for all parties to the cases, including other branches of the government if parties, but not otherwise. Finally, the Supreme Court is the final, authoritative interpreter of the Constitution, and holdings in constitutional cases are binding on all, even those not parties to the litigation. *Marbury v. Madison* stands for the first proposition, is often read for the second, and commonly taken for the third.

      (2) The countermajoritarian character of judicial review: Supreme Court judges are appointed for life, not elected. When the Court declares legislative or executive acts unconstitutional, it strikes down acts thought to have broad majority support. The Court is thus antidemocratic and countermajoritarian in character, and Supreme Court judges have often been accused of substituting their personal moral, and social predilections

for the choices the people's popularly elected representatives have made. Given the breadth, generality, and indeterminateness of many constitutional provisions, this is a telling criticism. On the other hand, various constitutional provisions are countermajoritarian in character, *e.g.,* two senators for each state regardless of population, and it is clear that the framers of the Constitution intended in various ways to limit the power of transient political majorities to effect their will.

(3) Consequences: For all practical purposes, Supreme Court rulings regarding the Constitution are taken to state the law of the land. Over the years, however, controversy regarding the propriety of judicial review has caused the Court to develop a number of corollary constitutional law doctrines designed in part to limit or mitigate constitutional conflict with the popularly elected branches of government. These doctrines, such as judicial restraint, the presumption of the constitutionality of statutes, standing, the political question doctrine, and deferential judicial review, are discussed below.

B. **Retroactivity:** Statutes generally remain in effect until amended or declared unconstitutional. If a statute is declared unconstitutional or interpreted in a new way, however, what is the status of the actions taken under it prior to the declaration of unconstitutionality or the new interpretation?

1. *Old approach:* Because a newly declared rule can have greatly disruptive effects where parties relied on an earlier, different understanding of the law, the Court followed a policy of deciding the issue of the retroactive application of newly declared rules on a case-by-case basis. *Chicot Co. Drainage Dist. v. Baxter State Bank,* 309 U.S. 695 (1940). In doing so, the Court took into account such factors as reliance, the interests affected, and the foreseeability of the ruling.

2. *Problems of old approach:* Some justices, however, perceived unfairness in the practice, for it did not treat similarly situated parties equally. For example, if the Court declared that a new rule was to be applied prospectively only, the party in whose favor the Court had ruled would nonetheless obtain relief in her case, as would all subsequent parties raising the same issue. Other litigants, however, including all those whose cases were on direct appeal, would not receive the benefit of the new rule. In addition, deciding to give prospective, rather than retroactive, relief seems much more a legislative than a judicial act.

3. *Current approach:* For the reasons stated immediately above, the Court has recently held that all newly declared rules, whether civil or criminal, must be applied retroactively to all cases pending on direct review. *Harper v. Virginia Dept. of Taxation,* 61 U.S.L.W. 4664 (1993); *Griffith v. Kentucky,* 479 U.S. 314 (1987).

Severability: Some portions of a statute may be unconstitutional while others are not. Whether the entire statute stands or falls depends on the legislative intent in enacting the statute. Where the legislature has not made its intent clear, such intent is inferred from statutory structure. If the valid parts of the statute are self-sufficient and can be enforced without major difficulty, the unconstitutional part is in effect excised – declared severable – while the remainder of the statute remains in force. If, however, the statute or parts of it make an integral whole, the integral whole or section falls together.

D. **Supreme Court Review of State Statutes and State Court Judgments**

1. *The Supremacy Clause:* The Supremacy Clause of the Constitution, Article VI, provides that the U.S. Constitution, all federal laws, and treaties are supreme law which takes precedence over state law, and requires state court judges to apply them where applicable. In effect, the Supremacy Clause, by requiring state courts to hear and enforce federal claims, makes state courts a part of the federal legal system.

2. *Authority to invalidate state statutes:* The Supremacy Clause entails Supreme Court authority to hold state statutes unconstitutional. *Fletcher v. Peck,* 10 U.S. (6 Cranch) 87 (1810).

3. *Federal authority to review state court decisions:* Similarly, because of the Supremacy Clause and the need for uniformity in the interpretation of national law, federal statutes providing for Supreme Court appellate jurisdiction over state court decisions regarding federal law, U.S. treaties, and the U.S. Constitution are constitutional. *Martin v. Hunter's Lessee,* 14 U.S. 304 (1816); *Cohens v. Virginia,* 19 U.S. 264 (1821).

E. **Congressional Power to Restrict Judicial Review by Limiting Federal Court Jurisdiction**

1. *Article III and the Exceptions Clause:* Article III of the Constitution describes the original and appellate jurisdiction of the Supreme Court. The Exceptions Clause of Article III, however, authorizes Congress to define and regulate the appellate jurisdiction of the Supreme Court.

   a. *Jurisdiction-stripping statutes:* In *Ex parte McCardle,* 74 U.S. 506 (1869), the Supreme Court appeared to read the Exceptions Clause to confer virtual absolute power on Congress to withdraw or otherwise limit the Supreme Court's appellate jurisdiction.

      (1) The only recognized exceptions to Congress's "jurisdiction-stripping" authority appear to be situations in which Congress uses a jurisdictional statute as a means to force a court to apply an unconstitutional rule or the statute itself violates some other constitutional limitation. *United States v. Klein,* 80 U.S. (13 Wall.) 128 (1872).

      (2) Some commentators find this reading of the Exceptions Clause problematic, however, for it means that Congress, opposed to some Supreme Court constitutional ruling, *e.g.,* busing as an appropriate school desegregation remedy, could withdraw Supreme Court appellate jurisdiction from cases involving that issue. Congress could thus facilitate lower-court deviation from Supreme Court-established constitutional norms. They argue that Congress cannot exercise its Exceptions Clause power in ways which would destroy the essence of Article III judicial power – in other words, that there are inviolate essential or core judicial functions.

      (3) Congress's jurisdiction-stripping authority may not be quite the problem it appears to be. Congress, notwithstanding widespread opposition to a number of Supreme Court decisions, has not enacted any major

jurisdiction-stripping statutes arguably detrimental to the enforcement of established constitutional rights. Furthermore, most jurisdiction-stripping statutes are in fact "jurisdiction-channeling"; that is, such statutes, by withdrawing certain courts' jurisdiction over some claims in effect direct that the claims be finally heard in other courts. For example, withdrawing Supreme Court jurisdiction in school desegregation cases does not mean that they will not be heard, but rather that they will be heard in lower federal courts and in state courts. This might lead to disparate and even inconsistent interpretations of federal law, but could not be said to deny constitutional rights.

III. CONSTITUTIONAL LIMITS ON FEDERAL JUDICIAL REVIEW

A. The "Case or Controversy" Requirement: Article III, § 2 limits federal judicial power to "cases and controversies." A case or controversy is an actual, concrete legal dispute between real adversary parties which is capable of judicial resolution and relief. *Aetna Life Ins. Co. v. Haworth,* 300 U.S. 227 (1937).

CONSTITU-TIONAL LIMITS ON FEDERAL JUDICIAL REVIEW

1. ***Justiciability:*** Justiciability concerns the fitness of a case for adjudication. A case is said to be justiciable if it constitutes a case or controversy, and if, in deciding it, the Court would not exceed the discretionary self-restraint limits it sets for itself. In other words, a case is justiciable if there is "standing to sue" (*see* III.A.2., *infra*), the issue is judicially resolvable, and there are no reasons for judicial restraint. If the Court states that a case is nonjusticiable, it may mean either that there is no case or controversy (no standing), that the Constitution does not permit the judiciary to decide the issue, or that the Court *refuses* to decide the case.

a. *Types of nonjusticiable cases:* The following cases are nonjusticiable because there is no case or controversy:

(1) Cases requesting advisory opinions: Hypothetical cases, not involving concrete disputes between genuine adversaries, are not fit for federal adjudication because they do not meet the case or controversy requirement. A court decision in such a case would have no real world effect and in that sense would simply constitute an advisory opinion. *Cf. Muskrat v. United States,* 219 U.S. 346 (1911). Advisory opinions are objectionable because they may not bind the parties, might prompt collusive suits without full adversariness, and might force a court to render an opinion on a constitutional matter that it might otherwise avoid.

(2) Moot cases: Cases are moot when the underlying controversies are not real or when, for some reason, the underlying issue which generated the lawsuit has been resolved or dissolved in some fashion prior to adjudication.

Thus a case may be mooted when the law underlying it has changed, when it is settled, when the plaintiff no longer has a complaint, *Arizonans for Official English and Park v. Arizona,* 520 U.S. 43 (1997), dies, receives the relief requested without judicial intervention, and so on. Moot cases present no live dispute affecting the rights of parties and thus are not fit for adjudication.

(b) The following cases, which may have the appearance of mootness, are not moot.

i) Cases involving continuing harm: Even though circumstances may have changed and a plaintiff's major complaint no longer remains a live issue, the plaintiff may suffer continuing injury. For instance, a convict who has served his sentence may seek to have his conviction reviewed by way of a petition for a writ of habeas corpus. Although his major injury, imprisonment, has ended, he continues to suffer the civil disabilities that are the collateral consequences of a criminal conviction. His case is therefore not moot.

ii) Cases involving harms which, although ended, may recur: In periodic nuisance cases, the nuisance may cease, only to begin again at a later time. Although there is no present nuisance, if it is likely to recur, the case is not moot.

iii) Cases capable of repetition but evading review: Some cases are mooted when the plaintiff obtains the relief requested before a court decision. Nonetheless, it is clear that defendant's action will be repeated and cause new injury either to the plaintiff or to another not before the court. Although the plaintiff has obtained relief, the case is not moot. If it is probable that the same controversy, involving the same complainant, will recur, the case is not moot. *Murphy v. Hunt*, 455 U.S. 478 (1982).

Example: In *Roe v. Wade,* 410 U.S. 113 (1973), the famous abortion case in which plaintiff sought to terminate a pregnancy, the plaintiff was no longer pregnant when the Court heard and decided the case. As the appellate process generally takes more than nine months to complete, under normal mootness rules such a case would be mooted before there was a decision. Notwithstanding that, it was clear that the situation could have arisen again, either for the plaintiff or for another in her situation. Consequently, the Court refused to treat the issue as moot.

iv) Voluntary cessation of conduct: A defendant cannot moot a case merely by voluntarily ending a challenged injurious practice. A defendant asserting mootness must show that the allegedly wrongful behavior cannot reasonably be expected to recur. *Friends of the Earth, Inc. v. Laidlaw Environmental Services (TOC), Inc.*, 120 S. Ct. 693 (2000). Suppose that, after the filing of a suit, the defendant city states to the court hearing the case that it will not enforce the ordinance that is the basis of the plaintiff's complaint. If it is possible that the city will reinstate or enforce the ordinance after the suit is dismissed, the case is not moot. Were the case treated as moot, the defendant could always avoid litigation – but gain the benefits of challenged practices – through temporary cessation followed by reinstatement. *City of Mesquite v. Aladdin's Castle, Inc.*, 455 U.S. 283 (1982).

(3) Collusive cases: Where parties collude to bring a case, the situation is like that involving cases seeking advisory opinions.

(4) "Premature" cases and the ripeness requirement: Cases harboring a potential real controversy may be brought before the controversy ripens

into a genuine, concrete dispute with the possibility of real adverse consequences for the parties. Such cases are said not to be ripe for adjudication, and a federal court will not decide them because it is not yet necessary to do so.

Example: Suppose a state adopts a new criminal statute giving prosecutors the authority to charge misdemeanor drunk driving as felony drunk driving. Suppose further that the authority has never been used. Assuming there is a possible alleged constitutional defect in the statute, may a driver sue to enjoin the local prosecutor from using the statute against him should he be found drinking and driving, which he alleges, because of habit, is sure to happen? In the foregoing case, a federal court would refuse jurisdiction on the ground that the case was not ripe and tell the plaintiff to come back, or interpose a constitutional defense, when he was actually charged.

b. *Political question cases:* Even though there may be an actual case or controversy, political question cases (*see* III.B., *infra*) are also nonjusticiable.

2. *Standing:* "Standing" is a judicial review jurisdictional requirement inferred from the "case or controversy" requirement and from the institutional role of the judiciary. Essentially, standing comprises that set of attributes, fairly determinable from a plaintiff's complaint, which assures there is a genuine issue the judiciary can and should resolve and remedy. The standing requirement ensures that there is a genuine issue of practical, rather than merely theoretical, import, and that there is a real adversary contest that can illuminate all of the important contours of an issue.

a. *Injury in fact:* In order to have standing to sue and obtain judicial relief, a plaintiff must allege facts, which, if true, demonstrate her injury in fact. Injury in fact is any real, concrete injury, whether economic, property, aesthetic, environmental, or other injury, which the plaintiff suffers as a consequence of defendant's actions. *Sierra Club v. Morton*, 405 U.S. 727 (1972).

Injury in fact – quantum: The injury can be a small or trifling injury, but must be real, and the plaintiff must actually suffer it. "Ideological" and "stigmatic" injuries do not constitute injuries in fact.

Equal protection – competitive benefits cases: In equal protection cases involving access to competitive government benefits programs, the complainant need not show that, but for the challenged government action, she would actually have received the benefit. To establish "injury in fact," she need only show denial of an *equal opportunity to compete* for the benefit. *Northeastern Florida Chapter of the Associated General Contractors of America v. City of Jacksonville, Fla.,* 61 U.S.L.W. 4626 (1993).

Example: A cooperative of potato growers formed to negotiate for the purchase of a processing facility that would have been eligible for benefits under a new capital gains tax provision. After passage of the tax break in a comprehensive spending bill, the president line-item vetoed the tax break. The Court held that the growers had standing to challenge the constitutionality of the line-item veto because they suffered a concrete injury when they lost the tax advantage. *Clinton v. New York*, 66 U.S.L.W. 4543 (1998).

The antiprivate attorneys general rule: The plaintiff must suffer the injury personally. Others, whether co-plaintiffs or not, may suffer it as well, but the Court has held that, as a matter of judicial restraint, it will not recognize generalized injuries or grievances the plaintiff suffers in common with all other citizens as conferring standing. Consequently, the harm *every* citizen suffers from improper application of the Constitution and laws does not confer standing. *Lujan v. Defenders of Wildlife*, 112 S. Ct. 2130 (1992).

(1) Federal taxpayer suits, where the injury alleged is governmental misuse of tax funds, do not meet the standing requirement. *Frothingham v. Mellon*, 262 U.S. 447 (1923). The taxpayer's interest in any particular federal program is minute, and permitting such suits would mean that any federal taxpayer could challenge federal expenditures. Similarly, citizenship alone does not confer standing.

(a) Hypothetical: Suppose the president, without authority, shifts funds from a welfare program to a defense conversion program. Arguably, every taxpayer has a complaint for misallocation of tax funds. The complaint or "injury" which each taxpayer shares with every other is insufficient to confer standing. On the other hand, identified welfare recipients whose funds or services were actually cut would have standing to sue.

(b) Exception – double-nexus test: The Constitution itself does not require the rules against taxpayer standing, and the Court has recognized exceptions to it. A taxpayer plaintiff can establish standing by alleging that Congress has unconstitutionally exercised its taxing and spending power *and* that it has violated some *specific* constitutional limitation on the exercise of that power.

Example: A taxpayer sued, alleging that the government was unconstitutionally using tax monies to support or establish a religion in violation of the First Amendment, which forbids the government establishment of religion. Because in such cases the members of the supported religion would not be expected to sue, unless an ordinary taxpayer has standing, it is unlikely that there would be anyone who could challenge the unconstitutional action. While members of other churches might sue, they might also have difficulty showing a specific injury distinct from that suffered by all other citizens. In such circumstances, the taxpayer was held to have standing. *Flast v. Cohen*, 392. U.S. 83 (1968).

(c) Narrow rule: The *Flast* rule is apparently quite narrow. Since *Flast*, the Court has not found any other constitutional provision to be a specific limitation on the taxing and spending power. The *Flast* rule therefore may well be limited to First Amendment establishment cases.

c. *Causation and redressability:* The defendant must cause plaintiff's injury, legally speaking. In other words, the injury must be fairly traceable to the defendant's alleged wrongful conduct. The plaintiff must also show redressability – that if she wins, the relief to which she is entitled will substantially eliminate or redress the injury. A plaintiff must show standing for each form of relief sought, but relief need not always flow directly to the plaintiff. *Friends of the Earth, Inc., v. Laidlaw, supra.* For example, civil penalties awarded to the government, but not to private plaintiffs, nonetheless have a deterrent effect that may redress private plaintiffs. *Id.*

Examples: The mother of an illegitimate child sued to compel the local prosecutor to enforce against the alleged father a state criminal law penalizing parents for nonsupport of children. If convicted, the father would be jailed. There was no standing because the prosecutor's failure to enforce the law could not be said to have caused the injury of nonsupport. Furthermore, if the prosecutor were forced to prosecute and the alleged father were convicted, there was no showing that the relief desired, child support, would have been forthcoming. *Linda R.S. v. Richard D.,* 410 U.S. 614 (1972). The injury is not fairly traceable to the prosecutor nor can her action redress it.

A group of nonresident low-income persons sued a town because of its exclusionary zoning ordinance, claiming the ordinance effectively precluded low- and moderate-income persons from living there. In their complaint, however, they failed to make factual allegations tending to show that but for the zoning ordinance, developers and builders would have built housing affordable to plaintiffs. There was no standing because plaintiffs had not alleged facts showing that defendants caused their plight, nor facts showing a substantial likelihood that grant of the relief requested would result in affordable housing. The availability of housing depended on the actions of third parties not before the court. *Warth v. Seldin,* 422 U.S. 490 (1975).

d. *Standing in cases where the plaintiff is not directly affected:* Where third parties, rather than the plaintiff, are the object of the challenged action or inaction, the plaintiff has a heavier burden of adducing facts showing that it has been, or will be, injured and that the requested relief will redress the injury. *Lujan v. Defenders of Wildlife, supra.*

e. *Standing to assert the rights of others:* As the standing rules require that the plaintiff suffer personally, parties generally may not assert the rights of others to establish standing. Note, however, that the party suing may actually suffer injury because of a violation of rights of third parties not before the court. For instance, a law which prohibits sale of 3.2% beer to males under the age of twenty-one, while permitting sale to females over age eighteen, injures beer sellers as well as young males. Because of the substantial derivative injury, which would be relieved if the law were invalidated, the sellers may assert the rights of the young males. *Craig v. Boren,* 429 U.S. 190 (1976). The following are exceptions to the general rule against asserting the rights of others:

(1) Vicarious assertion of rights: There are cases in which, if a party not directly injured by the defendant is not allowed to sue, the rights of the third party actually injured could not be vindicated. A third party may assert the rights of an injured nonparty if (1) the injury causes an injury in fact to the third party; (2) the third party is an effective advocate of the nonparty's rights; and, (3) the nonparty is unlikely or unable to pursue an action in his or her own behalf. *Powers v. Ohio,* 499 U.S. 400 (1991).

Examples: A child is injured in an automobile accident. The child's parents may sue as next friends.

A statute makes it a crime to distribute, but not to use, contraceptives. In such a case, individuals have a right to use contraceptives, but a distributor may not sell them. If the distributor is unable to assert the rights of users to get into court or to defend against a prosecution, the statutory scheme will affect the absent parties' right to use in a virtually unchallengeable way. The distributor may assert the absent parties' rights. *Eisenstadt v. Baird,* 405 U.S. 438 (1972).

A prosecutor's discriminatory use of peremptory challenges to exclude black jurors from a criminal trial harms those excluded. Because those excluded are unlikely to challenge the exclusion, a white defendant, who is motivated to be an effective advocate against their exclusion, has standing to raise their claim. *Powers, supra.*

Judges in a particular county never appointed a black person as foreperson of the county's grand jury, although twenty percent of the county's residents are black. A defendant indicted by the grand jury has standing to assert a claim on behalf of the black county residents. Defendant's injury, a violation of due process rights, derived from the discriminatory actions against black county residents in grand jury selection.

(2) First Amendment overbreadth cases: Parties to whom a substantially overbroad law, potentially violative of First Amendment rights, may *constitutionally* be applied, have standing to assert the rights of third parties, not before the Court, to whom the law *cannot* constitutionally be applied. *See* Chapter 12, I.B., *infra.*

(3) Associational standing: Associations, *e.g.,* unions, interest groups, clubs, and other organizations, have standing to assert their own rights. They may also assert the rights of their members in the following cases. (1) The members themselves would have standing. (2) The controversy in the lawsuit is relevant to the association's purpose. (3) The members themselves are not indispensable parties – the nature of the suit does not require the members' participation to establish either the claim or the relief requested. *Hunt v. Washington State Apple Advertising Comm'n,* 432 U.S. 333 (1977); *Friends of the Earth, Inc. v. Laidlaw Environmental Services (TOC), Inc.* 120 S. Ct. 693 (2000). Note, however, that associations may also have standing in their own right, independent of any role in representing the interests of members.

f. *Standing and "prudential considerations":* The only basic standing rule truly inferable from the Case and Controversy Clause requirement is the necessity that the plaintiff suffer some threatened or actual injury. The Supreme Court, however, has created additional standing rules under the rubric of "prudential considerations." Prudential considerations go beyond constitutional requirements but are discretionarily imposed as a matter of judicial restraint or wisdom. The basic idea is that, even if there is standing under the Constitution, the Court should not decide "abstract questions of wide public significance" where other governmental institutions may be more competent to address the questions and where judicial intervention may be unnecessary to protect individual rights. Prudential considerations are one of the Court's responses to the countermajoritarian problem and evidence a policy of judicial deference and restraint.

(1) "Prudential considerations": The idea of prudential considerations is an open-ended concept, created by the Court to describe self-imposed discretionary limits on jurisdiction. The concept is vague and ill defined, and while there is no definitive list of so-called prudential considerations, the following is suggestive:

(a) Judicial resolution of the issue would cause separation-of-powers difficulties, *e.g.,* restructuring the operations of the executive branch of government.

(b) In a noncivil rights case, judicial resolution of the issue would in some serious way short-circuit the normal operation of elective political processes.

(c) Conferring standing in the instant case would open the "floodgates" of litigation and use up scarce judicial resources because similar cases would likely be filed in great numbers.

(2) Prudential considerations and justiciability: Prudential considerations fall within the class of discretionary reasons the Court might invoke to refuse to hear a case in which there was standing. Prudential considerations, however, do not exhaust that class of cases. Political question cases (*see* III.B., *infra*) fall into that class, and some ripeness cases, where it is a question of a judgment call about just how mature a dispute has become, may fall into it as well. Technically speaking, cases involving a refusal of jurisdiction for prudential reasons are justiciable cases – meaning, unlike political question or insufficiently ripe cases, they are judicially decidable: it's just that a majority of the justices conclude that they shouldn't decide such cases.

g. *Statutory standing:* Congress can confer standing statutorily. In such cases, the questions to be answered are how far can Congress go to create standing and on whom did Congress confer standing.

Congressional authority to confer standing: Congress can create legal interests and can confer standing even in some cases where the Court has held there is no judicially cognizable injury and thus no standing. This is because the Court, in its standing decisions, has not always distinguished between the Article III "case or controversy" requirements for standing and those it itself has prudentially imposed. As the Constitution requires only that Article III be met, Congress can confer standing in those cases where there is the requisite Article III injury, but the Court has, for prudential reasons, declined to find standing. For instance, as long as a plaintiff suffers the minimal injury required to establish an Article III case or controversy, Congress can confer standing on taxpayers or on third parties. *Association of Data Processing Service Organizations v. Camp*, 397 U.S. 150 (1970).

"Zone of interests": When a plaintiff bases some or all of her claim for relief on a statute, the standing question is whether the plaintiff's claim falls within the "zone of interests" protected by the statute. This is essentially a question of statutory interpretation aimed at determining whether Congress meant to preclude judicial review.

h. *Legislators' standing:* Members of legislatures, whose votes that could have blocked legislative action were allegedly improperly nullified, have standing to sue if that action goes into effect. *Coleman v. Miller*, 307 U.S. 433 (1939). They have a particularized interest in maintaining the effectiveness of their vote. However, where legislators allege an injury to their institution, where the injury is abstract and suffered in common by all present and future legislators, there is no immediate particularized injury and therefore no standing. *Raines, Dir., Office of Management and Budget v. Byrd*, 65 U.S.L.W. 3813 (1997). Thus, members of Congress who object that the mere passage of the line item veto, a law that gives the president the power to cancel appropriations, deprives them of the opportunity to vote for or against the surviving appropriations measures, or for the repeal of legislation, do not have standing to challenge the legislation. *Id.* (A subsequent challenge to the President's line-item veto authority by individuals who incurred a direct loss because of a line-item veto resulted in invalidating the line-item veto. *See* Chapter IV, Section I. (G) (3).)

i. *Procedural rulings:* If a procedural ruling injures a party procedurally, that party has standing to challenge it. *International Primate Protection League v. Administrators of Tulane Educ. Fund,* 500 U.S. 72 (1991).

j. *State standing and federal review:* Some states permit their courts to give advisory opinions, and states may recognize standing to sue in cases, such as taxpayers' "good government" suits, derivative standing cases, or tenuous causation cases, where a federal court would not find standing. If, in such cases, the state court opines or rules on a federal matter, the question arises whether a federal court has jurisdiction to review.

  (1) State advisory opinions: Even when a state court issues an advisory opinion on a federal question, there is no case or controversy in the federal sense, and consequently, there is no federal jurisdiction to review the advisory opinion.

  (2) State standing cases: States are not bound by the federal case or controversy requirement and may grant standing in cases which a federal court could not hear for lack of standing.

   (a) As a case or controversy is a prerequisite for federal jurisdiction, where a state confers standing in a case not amounting to a "case or controversy," there should ordinarily be no federal jurisdiction to review;

   (b) On the other hand, if there is a "case or controversy," but a federal court would decline to find standing for prudential reasons, it would appear there is federal jurisdiction to review;

     Finally, if a state court hears a case involving federal issues and involving parties who do not have federal standing, it is possible that its judgment concerning federal law itself will cause the kind of concrete injury that establishes a federal case or controversy. In that case, there is federal jurisdiction to review. *Asarco Inc. v. Kadish,* 109 S. Ct. 2037 (1989).

State standing to protect state interests or to represent state citizens: A state has standing to sue to protect its own sovereign or proprietary interests, but may not generally sue as a representative of its citizens to challenge federal statutes. *Massachusetts v. Mellon,* 262 U.S. 447 (1923). States do, however, have standing to sue to protect the physical and economic health and well-being of their citizens and to ensure that their populations properly benefit from participation in the federal system. *Alfred L. Snapp & Son, Inc. v. Puerto Rico,* 458 U.S. 592 (1982). For example, states may sue other states to abate public nuisances such as pollution, and states may sue to ensure that other states do not discriminate against them in interstate commerce.

Standing and mootness: Standing and mootness, while related concepts, are not identical. It may be easiest to distinguish them by the relative burdens they impose on parties. A plaintiff must establish standing, while a defendant must establish mootness. There may be cases where the prospect that a defendant will engage in harmful conduct is too speculative to support standing, but not so speculative as to defeat mootness – because of the defendant's heavy burden in establishing mootness. *Friends of the Earth, Inc., v. Laidlaw, supra.*

B. **Political Question Doctrine:** In rare cases, the Court will invoke the political question doctrine and refuse to decide a question, even where a plaintiff could be said to have standing, on the grounds that the case involves a "political question." A question is political when there is (1) a "textually demonstrable constitutional commitment of the issue" to another branch; (2) "a lack of judicially discoverable and manageable standards for resolving it"; (3) a need for an antecedent policy decision by another branch; or (4) an imperative need for deference to other branches. *Baker v. Carr,* 369 U.S. 186 (1962). The political question doctrine is a composite doctrine generated from both constitutional and institutional considerations.

1. *Separation of powers:* A major strand of the political question doctrine derives from the concept of separation of powers, the idea that the Constitution distributes different governmental powers to different branches of government and that one branch cannot exercise powers belonging to another. Political question cases therefore are those involving issues the Constitution in terms assigns for resolution to a branch of government other than the judiciary.

   Example: Under the terms of the Constitution, the Senate ratifies treaties. No one could bring a case asserting that although the Senate had refused to ratify a treaty, it should be required to ratify it. The constitutional provision regarding Senate ratification commits the decision to the Senate and clearly does not generate enforceable rights in anyone.

   a. *Scope of assignment:* Note that even where the Constitution in some provisions appears to assign responsibility for resolution of an issue to another branch of government, the Court will still have to determine the exact meaning of the provision, that is, just exactly what is committed to other branch resolution.

Examples: Article I, § 5 of the Constitution provides that "[e]ach House shall be the Judge of the Qualifications of its own Members." Does this provision mean that each House may exclude those it thinks unfit or that it can exclude only if the member does not meet one of the membership qualifications of age, citizenship, and residence prescribed in the Constitution itself? In *Powell v. McCormack,* 395 U.S. 486 (1969), the Court held the provision referred to the constitutionally prescribed qualifications alone. Consequently, notwithstanding Article I, § 5, the Court heard the suit of Representative Powell, duly elected but excluded by Congress on grounds of having wrongfully diverted funds and having filed false reports.

Article I, § 2, which requires apportionment of congressional representatives among the states "according to their respective numbers," is not a constitutional provision involving a nonjusticiable political question. The provision is judicially interpretable and creates a judicially enforceable obligation on Congress to select an apportionment plan related to population. *Department of Commerce v. Montana,* 60 U.S.L.W. 4279 (1992).

2. ***Unresolvable or controversial cases:*** Other strands of the political question doctrine advise that questions are also "political" when the issue is not resolvable through judicially manageable standards or when judicial prudence concludes the case is too controversial or would create institutional problems if judicially resolved.

Example: The Impeachment Trial Clause, Art. I, § 3, cl. 6 provides that the "Senate shall have the sole Power to try all impeachments." In *Nixon v. United States,* 61 U.S.L.W. 4069 (1993), Nixon, a federal district court judge, was criminally prosecuted for and convicted of making false statements before a federal grand jury. He was sentenced to prison, but he refused to resign his judicial position. The U.S. House of Representatives voted articles of impeachment to remove him from office. A Senate committee conducted hearings on the impeachment, and the committee presented a transcript of the hearings, a report, and a summary of the evidence to the full Senate. The parties provided the full Senate with briefs and delivered oral arguments, and Senators questioned the parties. The Senate then convicted Nixon on two of the impeachment articles. Nixon sued to overturn his impeachment on the ground that the Constitution requires the Senate to "try" impeachments, and the full Senate did not participate in evidentiary hearings. The Court held that the Constitution textually committed the issue of trying impeachments to the Senate, and that the question was therefore nonjusticiable. Major reasons for the holding were that there were no judicially manageable standards for resolving it, and that a contrary holding would put the judiciary in the position of reviewing judicial impeachments, thus removing a check on the judiciary. Furthermore, judicial review of impeachments would prevent them from becoming final and could lead to political chaos.

C. **Eleventh Amendment Limits on Federal Judicial Power in Suits Against States:** The Eleventh Amendment provides that "The Judicial power of the United States shall not be construed to extend to any suit in law or equity, commenced or prosecuted against one of the United States by Citizens of another State, or by Citizens or Subjects of any Foreign State." This Amendment derives from ideas about state sovereignty and effectively prohibits citizens of one state, or citizens or subjects of a foreign state, from suing a state in federal court *without the sued state's consent.* (In many cases, states do consent.) As state immunity from suit is a fundamental aspect of sovereignty, the Supreme Court has interpreted this provision to prohibit citizens from suing their own state in federal court. *Hans v. Louisiana,* 134 U.S. 1 (1890). Congress must treat the states as sovereigns, and neither the Supremacy Clause nor Congress' enumerated powers give Congress authority to abrogate states' immunity from federal court suit, *Alden v. Maine,* — U.S — (1999), except in special circumstances. The Amendment also applies to Indian tribes seeking to sue states. Indian tribes have the status of foreign sovereigns. Under the Eleventh Amendment, states are immune from suit by them in federal court. *Blatchford v. Native Village of Noatak,* 501 U.S. 775 (1991).

The Court has also interpreted the Amendment to mean that Congress cannot, except under certain clear authorities, authorize suits against states in their own courts. *Alden, supra.* Were the rule to be otherwise, Congress could do in state courts what it could not do in federal courts. *Id.*

1. ***Congressional legislation overriding state sovereign immunity:*** Where the Constitution takes away state powers or limits state authority and empowers Congress to act, Congress may use its conferred powers in ways that override state sovereignty. *Fitzpatrick v. Bitzer,* 427 U.S. 445 (1976). In these cases, Congress may authorize citizens to sue their own state, even for money damages, in federal court. In order to abrogate state sovereign immunity, Congress' unmistakable intent to do so must be obvious. *Kimel v. Florida Board of Regents,* 120 S. Ct. 631 (2000).

   a. *Fourteenth Amendment overrides:* The Fourteenth Amendment limits state power and in Section 5 confers on Congress plenary authority to enact legislation enforcing the Amendment. Using this power, Congress may subject states to suits in federal court for money damages for violations of Fourteenth Amendment-protected civil rights. *Fitzpatrick, supra.*

   Congress, however, may not use its Section 5 power to define substantive constitutional rights. An attempt by Congress to override state sovereign immunity from suits for age discrimination in employment failed because the Age Discrimination in Employment Act was not appropriate legislation under Section 5 of the Fourteenth Amendment. This is because the Act extended protection beyond the requirements of the Equal Protection Clause, without a showing of any necessity for doing so. Under Court holdings, age classifications for employment do not generally violate the Clause. Given that states can make rational use of age classifications, and that there was no showing of any pattern of state age discriminations, the ADEA could not constitute remedial or preventive legislation in support of Fourteenth Amendment rights. *Kimel, supra.*

   Example: Congress amended a patent act expressly to abrogate state sovereign immunity. Arguably this was done to enforce the Fourteenth Amendment's Due Process Clause. The theory would be that patents confer property rights, and without redress, states could violate patents with impunity. Under *City of Boerne v. Flores,* 521 U.S. 507 (1997), legislation under Section 5 of the Fourteenth Amendment must be "appropriate". It is appropriate when remedial or preventive of rights violations. In the Patent Remedy Act, however, Congress identified no pattern of state patent infringement. Nor was there any significant showing that states did not respect patent rights, nor that they failed to provide remedies for their violation. Of course, there is no constitutional violation if the state does provide a remedy. As the Act doesn't respond to any "widespread and persisting deprivation of constitutional rights," it is unconstitutional as being greatly disproportionate to the identified harm. For these reasons, Congress could not override state sovereign immunity. *Florida Prepaid Postsecondary Education Expense Board v. College Savings Bank,* 527 U.S. 666 (1999).

    b. *Commerce Clause overrides:* The Commerce Clause gives Congress the authority to regulate commerce and withholds the same power from the states. Nonetheless, the Commerce Clause does not give Congress the authority to abrogate State's Eleventh Amendment immunity from suit. *College Savings Bank v. Florida Prepaid Post-secondary Ed. Expense Bd.,* 527 U.S. 666 (1999); *Seminole Tribe of Florida v. Florida,* 517 U.S. 44 (1996) (overruling *Pennsylvania v. Union Gas Co.,* 491 U.S. 1 (1989), which had held that Congress may use the Commerce Clause to enact legislation authorizing citizens to sue their states for environmental harms.)

    2. *Suits against state officials:* The Amendment does not bar suits against state officials alleged to have acted unconstitutionally, even if they were carrying out state law, for the state has no authority to authorize unconstitutional acts. *Ex parte Young,* 209 U.S. 123 (1908).

    3. *Money damages – suits against state officials:* The Amendment also bars federal court private suits against state officials which require an award of money damages as compensation to be paid from the state treasury. *Great Northern Life Ins. Co. v. Read,* 322 U.S. 47 (1944). It does not, however, bar federal court decrees against state officials which, in requiring them to shape their future conduct to a court mandate, have the effect of requiring payment of state funds as a necessary consequence of compliance. *Edelman v. Jordan,* 415 U.S. 651 (1974).

    4. *Indemnification:* Eleventh Amendment immunity from suit applies even when the federal government has agreed to indemnify a state or its instrumentalities for the costs of litigation. What triggers the Eleventh Amendment immunity is a state's potential *legal* liability, not its *financial* liability, and indemnification is therefore irrelevant. *Regents of the Univ. of California v. Doe,* 519 U.S. 357 (1997).

JUDICIALLY IMPOSED LIMITS ON FEDERAL CONSTITUTIONAL REVIEW

IV. JUDICIALLY IMPOSED LIMITS ON FEDERAL CONSTITUTIONAL REVIEW: The Court has developed a number of doctrines having the effect of limiting federal judicial review. Considerations of comity, efficiency, federalism, and the need to avoid conflict with the political branches of government, rather than the Constitution, prompted these doctrines. The principal doctrines, in addition to the idea of prudential considerations (*see* III.A.2.f., *supra*) are as follows:

    A. Abstention: In some cases, both state and federal claims are raised, and both federal and state courts have jurisdiction to hear the same case or the same issues. The abstention doctrine holds that federal courts should abstain from, or postpone, hearing a case involving an unsettled or unclear state statute, on whose construction a federal constitutional question turns, until a state court construes it. *Railroad Comm'n of Texas v. Pullman Co.,* 312 U.S. 496 (1941).

    1. *Typical abstention situation:* The typical abstention situation involves a federal constitutional claim arising out of the attempted application of a state statute which has yet to be authoritatively construed by a state court.

2. *Significance of abstention:* By abstaining from intervention in a state proceeding, federal courts promote federalism and pursue a policy of avoiding decisions on constitutional questions if at all possible.

   a. *Preserves state court authority:* Allowing state courts to adjudicate in the first instance preserves state authority, and the state court may construe the statute in such a way that no federal constitutional issue remains.

   b. *Postpones federal hearings:* The abstention doctrine forces a federal plaintiff into state court and postpones a federal hearing until state courts resolve state law issues.

3. *Exceptions:* A federal court need not abstain when:

   a. *No statutory ambiguity:* There is no ambiguity in the state statute, and therefore, no necessity for authoritative state interpretation;

   b. *Settled interpretation:* Where the statute has a settled, authoritative interpretation; or

   c. *Unconstitutionality:* Where, under any interpretation, the statute would be unconstitutional.

B. **Equitable Restraint in Prosecutions and Civil Enforcement Proceedings:** Where necessary to protect constitutional rights, federal courts have authority to enjoin state criminal actions. *Ex parte Young, supra.* Nonetheless, as a matter of equitable restraint, federal courts may not intervene, either by way of injunction or declaratory judgment, in *pending* state prosecutions or civil enforcement proceedings unless there is a showing the state action is brought in bad faith to harass, or the state procedures do not permit adequate litigation of federal claims. *Younger v. Harris,* 401 U.S. 37 (1971); *Samuels v. Mackell,* 401 U.S. 66 (1971); *Huffman v. Pursue, Ltd.,* 420 U.S. 592 (1975).

   1. *"Threatened" and "pending" distinguished:* There is, however, no equitable bar to federal relief in cases of threatened, as opposed to pending, state proceedings. *Steffel v. Thompson,* 416 U.S. 452 (1974); *Doran v. Salem Inn, Inc.,* 422 U.S. 922 (1975). In such a case, the federal action does not interfere with any state proceedings.

   2. *Effect of* Younger *doctrine:* Unlike abstention, which postpones federal court action, the *Younger* doctrine forces a defendant to litigate her federal claims in state court, subject only to federal review thereafter by way of discretionary review in the Supreme Court or through federal habeas corpus.

C. **Avoiding Constitutional Questions:** The Court has formulated rules of decision and construction designed to help it avoid passing on constitutional questions unless absolutely necessary. Principal instances of this are as follows:

   1. *Alternative nonconstitutional ground of decision:* The Court will not decide a properly presented constitutional question if there is some other present ground which will dispose of the case. *Ashwander v. TVA,* 297 U.S. 288 (1936).

2. ***Construction:*** In order to save statutes from declarations of unconstitutionality, courts must give them every reasonable construction. *Edward J. DeBartolo Corp. v. Florida Gulf Coast Bldg. and Constr. Trades Council,* 485 U.S. 568 (1988). When an otherwise reasonable construction of a statute "would raise serious constitutional problems, the Court will construe the statute to avoid such problems unless such construction is plainly contrary to the intent of Congress," *Id.* at 575, *Concrete Pipe and Products of California v. Construction Laborers Pension Fund,* 61 U.S.L.W. 4611 (1993).

3. ***Competing interpretations:*** Of two possible interpretations, one which makes a statute unconstitutional and one which makes a statute constitutional, courts must adopt the latter. *Blodgett v. Holden,* 275 U.S. 142 (1927).

4. ***Facial challenges:*** In order to succeed in a facial challenge to legislative acts or administrative regulations, the challenger must show that there are no circumstances under which the act or regulation would be valid. *United States v. Salerno,* 481 U.S. 739 (1987).

THE FEDERAL STRUCTURE OF
AMERICAN GOVERNMENT

▶ **CHAPTER SUMMARY**

CHAPTER 2: THE FEDERAL STRUCTURE OF AMERICAN GOVERNMENT

Introduction. Once cut away from England, the thirteen original states looked upon themselves as independent governments. They cooperated in fighting the Revolutionary War and created a loose federation of governments under the Articles of Confederation. The central government under the Confederation was, however, quite weak. For example, it lacked powers to tax or regulate commerce, and there was neither a national chief executive nor a judiciary. There were also serious economic and commercial rivalries and conflicts between the states, and individual states sometimes ignored treaties and other obligations.

While there were problems of Confederation that only a stronger central government could solve, many in the original states wished to retain as much state sovereignty and power as possible. They believed in governments responsive to local control and were concerned about the dangers to liberty and state authority posed by a powerful central government. They feared that various interests might ally to capture the control of the central government and use it to further their own ends. While democratically inclined, they were also concerned about the threat of mob rule – or the rule of transient political majorities – that direct democracy might entail. To solve these linked problems, the Constitution incorporated a number of structural features, the net effects of which it was hoped would limit central governmental power, create competing power centers that would check each other, and retain a large measure of state authority. Some of the principal features are: (1) representative government, that is, government by officials elected for terms; (2) a division of governmental powers between three branches, an executive, a legislature (Congress), and a judiciary; (3) state representation in Congress; (4) a federal system under which the central government exercised only delegated powers while state governments or the people retained existing powers not delegated. Later, the Bill of Rights, or the first ten amendments to the Constitution, was added to the Constitution to disable the federal government from invading listed rights.

FEDERAL-STATE RELATIONS IN GENERAL

I. FEDERAL-STATE RELATIONS IN GENERAL

A. **Federal System:** The Constitution created a federal system of government by retaining – indeed, presuming – independent state governments while creating a central government. Each citizen and resident of the United States is therefore a subject of two separate governments, a state government and the federal government. Under this system of dual sovereign governments, state governments are not simply administrative units of the federal government, but instead possess independent governmental power.

1. *Delegation and limitation of powers:* The Constitution created this system by giving, or delegating, certain essential central powers – such as the powers to control commerce between the states, to declare war, or to enter treaties – to the federal government. It prohibited the states from exercising certain powers. Finally, in the Tenth Amendment, the Constitution reserved to the states, or the People, powers neither delegated nor prohibited.

2. *Values of federalism:* The existence of states decentralizes government. This facilitates greater governmental responsiveness in matters of local concern. Similarly, the existence of states multiplies the number of political actors and political power centers in the country. These create institutional and political checks on the actions of the federal government and on factions that seek to control it. Their existence also permits and encourages diversity in local culture, experimentation in governmental programs, and the development of statewide political communities.

B. Powers Delegated to Congress: In Article I, § 1, the Constitution gives Congress the legislative power of the federal government. Section 8 lists specific legislative powers – or subject matters of the legislative power conferred on Congress. The major ones are to tax, spend for common defense and general welfare, borrow money, and regulate commerce; establish immigration, naturalization, bankruptcy, copyright, and patent laws; and coin money, create lower federal courts, create and provide for the regulation of armies and navies, and to declare war. In addition to these specific subjects, many of the amendments to the Constitution, such as the Thirteenth, Fourteenth, Fifteenth, and Nineteenth Amendments, both limit state power and give Congress the specific authority to enforce them by appropriate legislation.

1. ***Necessary and Proper Clause:*** Congress also has the power to make all laws "necessary and proper" for executing its other powers and all the other powers the Constitution placed in the federal government. Thus, Congress has the power to enact laws to enable the president and the judiciary to carry out their powers.

2. ***Doctrine of enumerated powers and congressional regulation of unenumerated matters:*** The federal government is a government of enumerated powers. That is, in domestic affairs, it has no inherent authority to deal with any subject matters but those which the Constitution assigns it. There are, however, constitutionally legitimate ways for Congress to legislate regarding matters not listed in the Constitution.

   a. *Scope of the Necessary and Proper Clause:* Article I, § 8, gives Congress the power to enact all laws "necessary and proper for carrying into [e]xecution" all the powers of the federal government. This clause gives Congress broad authority to choose the means for reaching some legitimate aim of government. It need not choose only indispensable means, but also those which are simply useful. *McCulloch v. Maryland,* 17 U.S. 316, 4 Wheat. 314 (1819).

      Example: Although the Constitution does not expressly give Congress the power to create a Bank of the United States, it may do so. *Id.* Such a bank might be a useful way of regulating currency, facilitating the borrowing of money or the regulation of commerce through credit creation – all proper ends of the federal government.

      (1) Under the Necessary and Proper Clause, Congress may regulate matters not listed in the Constitution as long as such regulation is a rational means of effecting or promoting some legitimate federal aim. *Heart of Atlanta Motel, Inc. v. United States,* 379 U.S. 241 (1964).

   b. *Use of enumerated powers as a means:* Congress's enumerated powers are plenary, and Congress may exercise these powers to achieve ends neither authorized nor forbidden by the Constitution. For example, Congress cannot legislate directly to outlaw or regulate gambling or prostitution within a state. Congress may, however, prohibit shipment of lottery tickets or gambling paraphernalia in interstate commerce, and it may prohibit the movement of women in interstate commerce for purposes of prostitution. Such prohibitions obviously may affect gambling or prostitution within a state, and Congress may intend that they do so. Nonetheless, as long as Congress uses a means within its power – here the power over interstate commerce – it may do so for any end not forbidden by the Constitution.

3. ***Exclusive federal power:*** Some of the powers of the federal government are exclusive; that is, they are powers that the states cannot exercise. Of these, some are either stated to be exclusive or are exclusive because the Constitution prohibits the states from exercising them, *e.g.,* the powers to enter treaties or coin money, or pass bills of attainder or *ex post facto* laws, Article I, § 10. Other powers, *e.g.,* the powers to create lower federal courts, declare war, provide for a common defense, or regulate the armed forces, are exclusive by their very nature.

4. ***Concurrent state and federal power:*** In the absence of conflicting federal legislation or state action interfering with the federal structure (*see, e.g.,* dormant Commerce Clause, Chapter 6, I, *infra*), states may exercise nonexclusive federal powers.

   a. *Supremacy Clause and preemption:* Under the Supremacy Clause, when Congress acts within its powers, it may expressly or implicitly enact laws that supersede, or preempt, state laws. Congress may preempt implicitly when it regulates a subject matter pervasively or when it enacts laws conflicting with state laws.

   b. *Statutory interpretation in preemption cases:* Almost all preemption questions are questions of statutory interpretation, that is, questions of determining congressional intent.

      (1) Occupying the field: Where Congress makes it clear that it intends its regulation to be the sole regulation of the subject matter, Congress is said to have "occupied the field." When Congress has occupied the field, the states may not regulate.

      (2) Express preemption: Even where Congress expressly preempts state laws, it does not necessarily follow that Congress has occupied the field. A court must determine just what it was that was preempted. If Congress has not occupied the field, state laws not inconsistent with the congressional regulatory scheme may be valid.

      (3) Implicit preemption: Where Congress preempts implicitly, the same questions as to the scope of preemption arise.

      (4) Preemption factors: In determining whether, and to what degree, Congress has preempted state law, courts consider the following, in addition to the usual factors of congressional expression of purpose, legislative history, plain meaning, and construction to avoid constitutional issues:

         (a) the nature of the subject matter regulated, including the need for uniform national regulation and the substantiality of the states' interest in regulating the same subject matter; the thoroughness or comprehensiveness of the federal regulation.

         Example: In 1996, Congress adopted a law imposing sanctions on Burma. The law conferred broad authority on the president to act in matters of national interest in relation to Burma. It also authorized the president to impose additional sanctions on Burma, authority that the president later exercised. Independently, Massachusetts had earlier adopted a law barring state entities from buying goods and services from any person identified as doing business with Burma. The state law was broader than the federal law and conflicted with it. The Court held that the federal scheme necessarily preempted the state law. *Crosby v. National Foreign Trade Council,* 68 U.S.L.W. 4545 (2000). The Congressional action, together with the conferral of broad authority on the president implied that there was no room for the states to act on their own.

c. *Federal regulation by inducement – grants-in-aid:* Through offering grants-in-aid to states, conditioned on state adoption of regulatory programs meeting congressional standards, Congress often achieves indirectly, through state cooperation, what it could not achieve directly. Such programs, even when involving offers states could hardly refuse, are constitutional as long as the states have, at least in theory, the option of choosing not to participate. *Steward Machine Co. v. Davis,* 301 U.S. 548 (1937); *Helvering v. Davis,* 301 U.S. 619 (1937).

II. INTERGOVERNMENTAL IMMUNITIES

A. Federal Immunities – Limits on State Power to Regulate or Tax Federal Activities: The Supremacy Clause entails that the federal government and its properties and activities are immune from state taxation or regulation. *McCulloch v. Maryland, supra.*

1. ***Presumption:*** The constitutional immunity is a presumption applied in the absence of congressional action. But Congress can consent to state taxation and regulation, and, contrarily, it can also confer immunity from it in cases where the constitutional immunity does not apply. *Cleveland v. United States,* 323 U.S. 329 (1945).

2. ***Interference rule:*** The constitutional immunity applies to those state regulations which "interfere" with the performance of federal operations or functions. *Hancock v. Train,* 426 U.S. 167 (1976). Consequently, federal employees carrying out their duties need not obtain state licenses to do so. *Johnson v. Maryland,* 254 U.S. 51 (1920). On the other hand, federal employees and agents are not exempt from ordinary state law, such as criminal or divorce law, which cannot be said to interfere with their duties.

3. ***Federal enclaves:*** Federal enclaves are federal properties, such as military bases or federal compounds, located within states.

   a. *Application of state law generally:* Absent federal legislation, state law existing at the time the federal government obtained the property and not inconsistent with federal policy continues to apply. *Pacific Coast Dairy, Inc. v. Department of Agric.,* 318 U.S. 285 (1943); *James Stewart & Co. v. Sadrakula,* 309 U.S. 94 (1940).

   b. *Application of state criminal law:* Since 1825, in a series of statutes known as the Assimilative Crimes Acts, Congress has provided that state criminal law, with some exceptions, is to apply to federal enclaves within the state. The effect is to assimilate state criminal law into federal law and permit federal enclave crime prosecutions based on state criminal law. *Cf. United States v. Sharpnack,* 355 U.S. 286 (1958).

4. ***State income taxation:*** States may tax the salaries of federal employees. *Graves v. New York ex rel. O'Keefe,* 306 U.S. 466 (1939).

5. ***Other state taxes – incidence rule:*** States may not impose a direct tax on either the United States or its instrumentalities, *i.e.,* departments or other effective "arms" of government. Whether federal tax immunity operates to bar state taxes, such as receipts, use, sales, or property taxes, on activity or property associated with the federal government depends upon the "legal incidence" of the tax, that is, who has the legal obligation to pay it under state law. If neither the United States nor instrumentalities integral to it have that obligation, the tax does not fall on the United States, and there is no implied constitutional immunity from it. This is so even if the United States actually ends up paying the tax, as, for example, it would under a contract with a private contractor wherein it agreed to pay for services or all costs associated with a project. *James v. Dravo Contracting Co.,* 302 U.S. 134 (1937); *Alabama v. King & Boozer,* 314 U.S. 1 (1941).

B. **State Immunities – Limits on Congressional Power to Legislate Regarding the States:** The Supreme Court's expansive reading of congressional legislative authority recognizes Congress's power to reach almost any activity within states and to influence and shape state legislation and programs.

1. ***The Tenth Amendment and federalism-based limits on congressional power:*** The Tenth Amendment provides that those powers the Constitution neither delegates to the United States nor prohibits the states are reserved to the states or the People. Until recently, the Court viewed this amendment as stating a truism, not in any way limiting the federal government's powers. *United States v. Darby,* 312 U.S. 100 (1941). Consequently, the Court consistently upheld federal laws which, in regulating state or local activities, arguably trenched on state sovereignty. *See, e.g., Case v. Bowles,* 327 U.S. 92 (1946); *Maryland v. Wirtz,* 392 U.S. 183 (1968). However, in *National League of Cities v. Usery,* 426 U.S. 833 (1976), the Supreme Court found the Tenth Amendment an effective limitation of federal power. There it held that Congress did not have the power, under the Commerce Clause, to override state laws concerning integral, traditional governmental "functions essential to the separate and independent existence" of the states. Specifically, it ruled unconstitutional a congressional attempt to require states and cities to follow federal minimum wage and maximum hour requirements for their employees. Subsequently, in *Garcia v. San Antonio Metropolitan Transit Authority,* 469 U.S. 528 (1985), the Court reversed *Usery,* finding its standard unworkable and sufficient protection of state sovereign interests through state participation in the federal political process. As the decisions in *Usery* and *Garcia* were close, there is some possibility the Court may again consider this issue.

   a. *Federal coercion of state lawmaking:* Under principles of federalism and separation of powers between the federal and state governments, Congress may not *compel* states to enact and enforce a federal regulatory program, nor require state officers to execute federal laws. *Printz v. United States,* 65 U.S.L.W. 3425 (1997); *New York v. United States,* 112 S. Ct. 2408 (1992).

      Examples: In *Printz, supra,* Congress's attempt, through the Brady Handgun Violence Prevention Act, to require state and local law enforcement officers to conduct background checks on prospective handgun purchasers was held unconstitutional.

In order to address the national problem of disposal of low-level radioactive waste, Congress enacted legislation. The legislation required, among other things, that states without appropriate disposal facilities either to take title to low-level radioactive waste produced in-state and become liable for all damages occasioned by it for failure to do so, or to regulate the waste according to federal law. In effect, by legislation operating directly on the states, Congress was forcing states into service for a federal regulatory purpose, and this violated state sovereignty. *New York v. United States, supra.*

   b. *Federal inducement of state lawmaking:* While Congress cannot order states to enact and enforce a federal regulatory program, Congress can prompt states to do so by encouragement and inducements in the form of grants-in-aid conditioned on adoption of a federal program. Congress may also offer states difficult choices, *e.g.,* regulate according to federal standards or suffer preemption. *New York v. United States, supra; Hodel v. Virginia Surface Mining and Reclamation Ass'n,* 452 U.S. 264 (1981).

2. ***Plain statement rule:*** While Congress, acting pursuant to constitutional powers, may legislate in areas traditionally controlled by the states, out of federalism concerns, courts should not readily assume Congress has done so. To avoid interference with state sovereignty, courts should enforce federal legislation infringing on essential state political functions and historic powers only when Congress plainly states it desires that result. *Gregory v. Ashcroft,* 111 S. Ct. 2395 (1991). When it is unclear that Congress intended to intrude on state functions, a court should assume that it did not. *Id.*

3. ***Other constraints on congressional regulation of state activity***

   a. *Structural constraint:* Although the Tenth Amendment does not limit the exercise of congressional power, the constitutional structure assumes the existence of states. This suggests that Congress cannot go so far as to eliminate the essential features of states as independent political entities. Thus, for example, absent extraordinary circumstances, such as a civil war or rebellion, Congress should not be able to designate a state governor, displace all state law, replace a state legislature, or dictate state governmental structure.

   b. *Further congressional constraint:* There is, of course, some further constraint in the requirement that Congress demonstrate that its regulation is either an exercise of an enumerated power or a rational means to achieve some legitimate aim.

   c. *Political and practical constraints:* As senators and representatives are elected by and responsible to state and local constituencies, state concerns and interests are amply represented in the Congress. Notwithstanding the immense scope of federal legislative authority, states are therefore capable of protecting themselves as entities.

C. **Federal Taxation of State Employees, Activities, and Property:** Unless a federal tax discriminates against a state or unduly interferes with essential state functions, there is no state immunity from federal taxation. *Massachusetts v. United States,* 435

U.S. 444 (1978); *Helvering v. Gerhardt,* 304 U.S. 405 (1938). Consequently, the federal government may tax state employees' salaries and a state's proprietary activities and, where relevant to a federal program, impose registration taxes on state vehicles such as aircraft.

2

III. RELATIONS BETWEEN STATES

A. Required Cooperation between States

1. ***Full faith and credit:*** The Full Faith and Credit Clause of the Constitution requires that the states recognize and give appropriate effect to legal acts and proceedings of other states. Article IV, § 1.

   Examples: Nongranting states should recognize a proper divorce decree of the granting state. However, a judgment of a state court is conclusive on the court of another state only if the first state had jurisdiction to pass on the merits. *Durfee v. Duke,* 375 U.S. 106 (1963).

   Even where the rendering court makes an error of law, as long as it fully and fairly considered its jurisdiction to adjudicate the issue, other courts must accord its judgment full faith and credit. *Underwriters Nat'l Assurance Co. v. North Carolina Life,* 455 U.S. 691 (1982).

2. ***Extradition:*** The Constitution calls upon a state to deliver, to a properly demanding state, persons found there who are fugitives from justice in the demanding state. Article IV, § 2. The Supreme Court, however, has held that this provision imports a moral, not a legal, duty, which a court cannot enforce against a noncomplying state. *Kentucky v. Dennison,* 65 U.S. 66 (1861).

B. Interstate Compacts: The Constitution requires that Congress consent to interstate agreements or compacts. Article I, § 10.

1. ***Interstate agreements requiring consent:*** The Compact Clause is not taken literally to reach all agreements between states. Instead, it applies only to agreements that would tend to increase the political power of member states in a way that would encroach on the supremacy of the federal government. *New Hampshire v. Maine,* 426 U.S. 363 (1976); *Virginia v. Tennessee,* 148 U.S. 503 (1893). Consequently, states can enter into many agreements with other states, even those involving reciprocal legislation and the creation of multistate commissions, without first obtaining congressional approval. *U.S. Steel Corp. v. Multistate Tax Comm'n,* 434 U.S. 452 (1978).

2. ***Law-of-the-union doctrine:*** If Congress consents to an interstate agreement, the agreement becomes federal law, *Pennsylvania v. Wheeling & Belmont Bridge Co.,* 54 U.S. 518 (1852), subject to federal rather than state construction, *Cuyler v. Adams,* 449 U.S. 433 (1981).

3. ***Congressional consent regarding other interstate agreements:*** Sometimes Congress consents to interstate agreements prior to their adoption. If Congress does so, and the subject matter of the agreement is one appropriate for congressional legislation, then, whether or not the agreement is one requiring congressional approval, it is transformed into federal law under the Compact Clause. *Cuyler, supra.*

Example: Congress consented in advance to interstate agreements to help prevent crime. Subsequently, states entered into an interstate agreement on detainers, an agreement that could hardly be said to enhance the political power of states and erode federal supremacy. Nevertheless, because of prior congressional approval, the agreement created federal law under the Compact Clause. *Id.*

IV. **STATE RELATIONS TO CITIZENS OF OTHER STATES – INTERSTATE PRIVILEGES AND IMMUNITIES**

    A. **Provision:** Article IV, § 2 of the Constitution provides that "[t]he Citizens of each State shall be entitled to all Privileges and Immunities of Citizens of the several States."

    B. **Definition:** The Interstate Privileges and Immunities Clause, which should be distinguished from the Fourteenth Amendment Privileges and Immunities Clause (*see* Chapter 7, I.A., *infra*) was one of a number of provisions intended to contribute to making the United States a single entity. It is therefore read as requiring states to accord residents and nonresidents equal treatment with regard to certain interests essential or "fundamental" to national economic union and interstate harmony. This definition of "privileges and immunities" appears open-ended, but includes the following protected personal privileges or rights of:

        1. *owning, possessing, and disposing of property;*

        2. *engaging in gainful employment;*

        3. *doing business on terms of substantial equality with state citizens;*

        4. *traveling through and within a state, including changing residence from one state to another;*

        5. *equal treatment by justice institutions;*

        6. *seeking medical care.*

    C. **Rule – Fundamental Interests:** A state cannot treat a nonresident differently from a resident in the exercise of a protected privilege – cannot discriminate against the nonresident – unless:

        1. *the state has a substantial reason for the different treatment; and*

        2. *that reason is a good justification for the difference in treatment* – in effect, the state must show that nonresidents cause the problem or are part of the problem that the state is attempting to solve and that there are no ways the state could solve it which would be less injurious to the exercise of the privilege or right. *Supreme Court of New Hampshire v. Piper,* 470 U.S. 274 (1985).

    D. **Rule – Nonfundamental Interests:** If a state treats a nonresident differently from a resident with respect to a nonfundamental interest, it need only show that it has not acted arbitrarily to justify its action.

        1. *Unconstitutional discrimination:* A state may not impose a residency requirement on nonresident women seeking abortions. *Doe v. Bolton,* 410 U.S. 179

INTERSTATE PRIVILEGES AND IMMUNITIES

(1973). Nor may a state require private employers to give state residents a hiring preference, *Hicklin v. Orbeck,* 437 U.S. 518 (1978); nor condition bar admission on residency, *Piper, supra; Supreme Court of Virginia v. Friedman,* 487 U.S. 56 (1988).

2. ***Constitutional discrimination:*** A state may charge nonresident hunters higher fees for hunting licenses than residents. *Baldwin v. Montana Fish and Game Comm'n,* 436 U.S. 371 (1978).

2

E. **Limited Application:** The Interstate Privileges and Immunities Clause in terms applies only to "Citizens." Only natural persons can be citizens, and only natural persons born in or naturalized in the United States are citizens. The Clause therefore does not apply to corporations or aliens.

1. ***Sources of protection for corporations and aliens:*** Note, however, that other interstate equality principles, that is, those found in the dormant Commerce Clause (*see* Chapter 6, *infra*) or Fourteenth Amendment equal protection (*see* Chapter 8, *infra*) would come into play to protect corporations and aliens from discriminatory state actions.

POWERS OF THE FEDERAL GOVERNMENT

▶ **CHAPTER SUMMARY**

3

CHAPTER 3: POWERS OF THE FEDERAL GOVERNMENT

Introduction. In theory, the Constitution established a federal government of limited powers. Congress, of course, has the legislative power of the federal government, but the Constitution limits that by expressly stating the specific legislative powers that Congress has, for example, the power to regulate foreign commerce and commerce between the states or the power to raise and support armies. The Constitution, however, did not define the meaning or scope of important legislative powers. Particularly in the early years of the Republic, and in the period culminating in the New Deal, there were many contests over Congress's authority to enact specific legislation. Challengers claimed that Congress was exceeding its constitutionally granted powers, and the Supreme Court had to define the powers to settle the issues raised. While there are cases involving every legislative power Congress has, constitutional law courses usually focus on the major juris-generative powers, such as the commerce power, and on the doctrines that effectively enhance congressional legislative power. The overall lesson is that while Congress has only those legislative powers the Constitution confers, those powers – particularly given the Supreme Court's expansive construction of the Necessary and Proper Clause (*cf.* Chapter 2, II.C., *supra*) – are very broad indeed. When Congress wants to legislate – on virtually anything except curtailing constitutional rights or the constitutional powers of the president or the judiciary – it can usually find a constitutional way to do so.

PRINCIPAL CON- GRESSIONAL LEGISLATIVE POWERS

I. THE PRINCIPAL CONGRESSIONAL LEGISLATIVE POWERS

A. The Commerce Power: Article I, § 8. One of the purposes of the Constitution was to create an integrated national economy, a common market, by ending trade restrictions, protective tariffs, and other barriers to trade. To help achieve this, the Constitution gave Congress the power to regulate commerce between the states. Over time, the changing and increasingly interdependent character of the national economy and the Supreme Court's ultimately expansive reading of the Commerce Power have made it perhaps the most important of Congress's regulatory powers. Historically, there were several major problems in determining the reach of Congress's power under the Commerce Clause, and the Court reached confused and often inconsistent results. The major problems were defining commerce; deciding whether and how far Congress could reach activities wholly within a state; and deciding whether Congress could use the Commerce Power not only to regulate the national economy, but also as a means to achieve health, safety, and welfare aims.

    1. *Defining commerce:* Early cases identified commerce with commercial activities, narrowly defined, or the movement of persons or goods between the states. Consequently, manufacturing, mining, and agricultural production were thought not to constitute commerce and were held to be activities Congress could not reach under the Commerce Clause. *United States v. E.C. Knight Co.,* 156 U.S. 1 (1895); *Hammer v. Dagenhart,* 247 U.S. 251 (1918); *Carter v. Carter Coal Co.,* 298 U.S. 238 (1936); *A.L.A. Schecter Poultry Corp. v. United States,* 295 U.S. 495 (1935). Such distinctions are no longer made, for the issue is not whether some activity is commerce, but whether it is in interstate commerce, uses its channels, or affects it. *Perez v. United States,* 402 U.S. 146 (1971).

    2. *Defining the reach of Congress' commerce power:* Congress can clearly regulate all commerce that is interstate. The significant question, however, is whether Congress can regulate intrastate commerce because of its effect on, or relationship to, interstate commerce.

a. *Substantial economic relation to interstate commerce, the national market, or the economy:* In *Gibbons v. Ogden,* 22 U.S. 1 (1824), Chief Justice Marshall stated that the Commerce Power does not reach the completely internal commerce of a state but that state lines do not define what is completely internal. As commerce within a state is often part of commerce outside a state, or "concerns" or affects it, Congress has the power to regulate it. This is now the accepted view, and as long as the activity Congress seeks to regulate has, or would have, a *substantial* effect on commerce, Congress can reach it. *United States v. Lopez,* 63 U.S.L.W. 4343 (1995); *Wickard v. Filburn,* 317 U.S. 111 (1942); *NLRB v. Jones & Laughlin Steel Corp.,* 301 U.S. 1 (1937). For example, Congress can apply a federal labor law to large-scale in-state industries, for work stoppages in them could have a serious effect on the national economy.

(1) Aggregate effects: Congress may regulate even small, individual activities which by themselves have no discernible effect on commerce as long as all such activities, in the aggregate, can have an effect on commerce. *Wickard, supra.* For example, the federal government can regulate wheat production for private consumption because the cumulative effect of all such production on the national wheat market may be substantial. *Id.* Similarly, Congress can prohibit racial discrimination in food service in private restaurants that buy food that has moved in interstate commerce. Such discrimination may deter interstate travel, and this would have an effect on the demand for businesses serving interstate travelers and for the interstate goods they sell. *Katzenbach v. McClung,* 379 U.S. 294 (1964).

(2) Enterprise regulation: If some part of the activity of an enterprise affects commerce, Congress may regulate the entire enterprise. Otherwise, the nonregulated part might adversely impact the part affecting commerce. For example, if a factory has two divisions, one producing goods for interstate commerce and one producing goods for intrastate commerce, Congress can require both divisions to conform to federal wage and hour standards for employees. *Maryland v. Wirtz,* 392 U.S. 183 (1968). Labor unrest in the intrastate division might well cause labor unrest in the interstate division, or goods produced by the intrastate division might compete unfairly with out-of-state goods produced by companies complying with federal standards.

b. *Limits of substantial effects doctrine; relation to commercial or economic activity:* There is a potential problem in the substantial effects doctrine depending on how one reads the words "substantial effects on commerce." If they are read broadly, as reaching anything that affects interstate commerce or the national economy in any way, Congress would have what amounted to a general police power to regulate virtually all activities within the states. This is because, in our integrated economy, arguably anything can affect the national commerce or economy. For example, average mathematics achievement scores for U.S. grade- and high-school children are lower than those of children of some other countries with which we compete. This may have an effect on national scientific, engineering, and technological competitiveness with other countries. May Congress therefore regulate all precollege mathematics courses taught in the country? Arguably, crime, particularly violent crime, affects economic productivity, insurance rates, costs of doing business, and so on. May Congress therefore federalize all crimes,

3

thereby replacing all state criminal codes? Such an expansive reading of the Commerce Clause would allow Congress to displace the states in areas such as education, law enforcement, and even divorce and family law, areas where historically states have been viewed as sovereign. To avoid such a result, it is possible to give the words "substantial effects on commerce" a narrower reading. The Supreme Court has recently done this by requiring that the matter Congress seeks to regulate itself be commercial or economic activity or significantly linked to such activity. *United States v. Lopez, supra.* In *Lopez,* Congress made it a federal offense for any individual knowingly to possess a firearm in a school zone. Lopez, a high-school student, carried a loaded .38-caliber handgun to school. He was arrested, prosecuted federally, and convicted. In adopting the legislation, Congress made no findings regarding the effects on interstate commerce of gun possession in a school zone. The Court rejected the government's arguments that violent crime and negative effects of gun possession on the educational process justified this law under the Commerce Clause. In the Court's view, gun possession in a school zone was not an economic activity that, even with repetition in other places, substantially affected interstate commerce.

(1) Recent developments. The Federal Violence Against Women Act of 1994 provides for a federal civil rights remedy for crimes of violence motivated, at least in part, by gender animus. In *United States v. Morrison,* 68 U.S.L.W. 4351 (2000), the Court held that, insofar as the Act was adopted under Congress' Commerce Clause power, it was unconstitutional. This was because the Act sought to regulate noneconomic, violent crimes based solely on their aggregate effects on interstate commerce. Apparently, noneconomic causes of economic effects, or some of them, are not regulable under the Commerce Clause. Undoubtedly, although the exact rationale is difficult to articulate, the fact that Congress seeks to federalize, through the Commerce Clause, areas traditionally regulated by the states, is important.

c. *Prohibiting or attaching conditions to the interstate movement of goods or persons:* Congress's control over interstate commerce is plenary. As long as Congress does not violate any other constitutional provision, it may prohibit or condition the movement of goods or persons in interstate commerce regardless of its motive for doing so. *United States v. Darby,* 312 U.S. 100 (1941). In other words, Congress need not have a commerce purpose but may exercise its prohibition power for any reason it deems proper. In addition, Congress may regulate intrastate activities in order to make such prohibitions effective. *Id.*

Example: Congress can prohibit the shipment in interstate commerce of goods produced by employees whose wages and hours do not meet the standards established in the federal Fair Labor Standards Act. To ensure that such products are not shipped in interstate commerce, it can require employers who produce goods for interstate commerce to conform to the wages and hours provisions of that Act. *Id.*

(1) Regulation after interstate movement: Congress may, to some degree at least, regulate what happens to articles after interstate movement. In *United States v. Sullivan,* 332 U.S. 689 (1948), the Supreme Court applied a federal statute which prohibited misbranding of drugs held for sale "after shipment in interstate commerce." It upheld a federal drug-misbranding

conviction against a retail druggist who, in refilling some pills for resale, failed to include warnings on use. The druggist had purchased the pills, properly labeled, in-state from a wholesaler who had purchased them interstate. This decision is understandable on a theory of prohibition to make a federal program effective or, perhaps, on an aggregate effect theory and should not be read as an independent theory on which to base federal regulation. Allowing Congress to continue to regulate articles or persons forever in any way deemed fit simply because of movement in interstate commerce would further extend already extremely extensive Congressional power and dissolve distinctions between interstate and intrastate commerce.

    d. *Instrumentalities of interstate commerce*: Congress has the power to regulate and protect the instrumentalities of interstate commerce, such as vehicles or aircraft, railways, and transportation terminals, as well as persons or things in interstate commerce, even where the threat comes from intrastate activities. *Shreveport Rate Cases*, 234 U.S. 342 (1914); *Southern R. Co. v. United States*, 222 U.S. 20 (1911).

    e. *Congressional findings:* As long as Congress's express or implied conclusion that an activity affects commerce is rational, courts will defer to it and not itself reexamine the question. *Hodel v. Virginia Surface Mining and Reclamation Ass'n,* 452 U.S. 264 (1981). Further, when Congress finds that a class or aggregate of activities affects commerce, it may regulate particular instances of the activity without a showing that they affect commerce. *Perez v. United States, supra.* Consequently, where Congress has outlawed loan sharking — using violence or other criminal means to collect loans — because it is often carried on in interstate commerce and affects it, federal prosecutors need not show that a particular loan-sharking operation took place in or had an effect on commerce. *Id.*

B. **The Taxing Power:** The Constitution grants Congress the power "[t]o lay and collect Taxes, Duties, Imposts, and Excises." Article I, § 8.

    1. ***Taxing to raise revenue or to regulate:*** There is no question that Congress may tax in order to raise revenue. Taxes, of course, have a regulatory effect, and there can be no objection to a tax that regulates activity as well as raising revenue. Congress may, however, enact taxes that either have purposes in addition to raising money or have no genuine money-raising purpose, but a purely regulatory one instead. The Supreme Court precedents in this area are difficult to reconcile, but the basic rule is that if the tax produces revenue, it will be upheld regardless of its regulatory effect. *United States v. Kahriger,* 345 U.S. 22 (1953).

    2. ***Collateral regulatory purposes and effects within congressional power:*** Congress may impose taxes so great as to effectively prohibit the taxed activity. As long as Congress could otherwise regulate the activity, its use of the taxing power as a means is constitutional.

    Example: In *Veazie Bank v. Fenno,* 75 U.S. 533 (1869), the Court upheld a congressional tax of ten percent on state bank notes, the effect of which was to make state bank note issuance prohibitively expensive. As Congress has the power to control currency, however, it may certainly use the taxing power to that end.

3. *Collateral regulatory purposes and effects – raising revenue and regulating:* The Supreme Court generally refuses to examine congressional motives for using the taxing power. Congress has the authority to set the objects to be taxed and the level of a tax, and the fact that Congress may have a motive of inhibiting an activity as well as raising revenue does not invalidate a tax.

   Example: In *McCray v. United States,* 195 U.S. 27 (1904), the Court upheld a tax structure which imposed a ten-cent-per-pound tax on oleomargarine when it was colored like butter, but one-quarter of a cent otherwise.

4. *Collateral regulatory purposes and effects – amount of revenue raised:* Regulations reasonably designed to make a tax effective are valid, even when the revenue raised is minuscule or nonexistent and the regulations have purposes other than raising revenue.

   Example: In *United States v. Doremus,* 249 U.S. 86 (1919), the Court upheld a registration and regulatory scheme which required persons dealing in opium and coca products to register with the federal government. The statute also made criminal the sale of such products to persons not presenting a written order for them on a form prescribed by the Commissioner of Internal Revenue. The tax on persons who sought to deal in such drugs was $1 a year. Obviously the regulatory scheme was designed to criminalize sales involving opium and coca products, most properly a subject for state regulation, yet it was upheld on a taxing fiction.

5. *Contrary precedents:* In a few cases, the Court found limits to Congress's use of the taxing power, holding that Congress could not use that power punitively in order to regulate matters of state concern it could not otherwise regulate. *Bailey v. Drexel Furniture Co.,* 259 U.S. 20 (1922) (Child Labor Tax Case); *United States v. Constantine,* 296 U.S. 287 (1935). This is, of course, a truism, and specific cases must turn on the scope of Congress's regulatory power. Given the broad reach of congressional power under the Commerce Clause, its use of the taxing power is equally large. Whatever Congress could reach under the commerce power, it could use the taxing power as a means to regulate.

C. **The Spending Power:** The Constitution gives Congress the power to spend for the common defense and general welfare. Article I, § 8. This is an independent grant of power, and Congress may spend not only in aid or the exercise of its other legislative powers, but also for any appropriate public purpose. *United States v. Butler,* 297 U.S. 1 (1936). While Congress could not, of course, spend in violation of some constitutional limitation, it may use its spending power, in effect, as an indirect form of regulation by conditioning receipt of funds on compliance with federal rules and standards. *Steward Machine Co. v. Davis,* 301 U.S. 548 (1937). In other words, through use of the spending power, Congress can regulate indirectly what it cannot regulate directly.

D. **War and Military Affairs Powers:** The Constitution gives Congress the powers to declare war, to raise and support armies and navies, to regulate the armed forces, to define offenses against the law of nations, and to organize, arm, and regulate the militia. Article I, § 8. These powers are treated generally below. As Congress's war and military affairs powers are intimately and intricately involved with the president's commander-in-chief and foreign affairs powers, these particular powers are treated together in detail in Chapter 4, I., *infra*.

1. ***Domestic war power:*** In time of war, Congress has broad authority to enact economic and other regulations, such as price, rent, wage, industry, or work force controls thought necessary or useful to wage war or remedy its evils. It may also control activities within states that it could not regulate absent war. *Yakus v. United States,* 321 U.S. 414 (1944); *Hamilton v. Kentucky Distilleries and Warehouse Co.,* 251 U.S. 146 (1919). This power does not necessarily end when war ends, but Congress may use it to restore the economy after the war, for example, by continuing rent controls until the severe housing shortage occasioned by war is alleviated. *Woods v. Cloyd W. Miller,* 333 U.S. 138 (1948).

2. ***Draft:*** Congress can establish a draft and conscript men for war, and it may use state militias to fight against foreign enemies. *Selective Draft Law Cases,* 245 U.S. 366 (1918).

3. ***Military justice and courts-martial:*** Pursuant to its authority to regulate and govern the armed forces, Congress may establish a military justice system for military discipline and may create courts-martial, or military courts, to try crimes. *Kinsella v. United States,* 361 U.S. 234 (1960); *Dynes v. Hoover,* 61 U.S. 65 (1858).

   a. *Bill of Rights inapplicable:* Courts-martial are legislatively created courts located in the executive branch, not Article III courts, and need not follow the Bill of Rights procedures, such as trial by jury, which the Constitution requires in Article III courts.

   b. *Courts-martial jurisdiction*

      (1) Generally speaking, with the exception of civilians of nations with whom the United States is at war, courts-martial jurisdiction extends only to those actually members of the armed forces, not to civilians, civilian dependents, or ex-service personnel. *Ex parte Milligan,* 71 U.S. 2 (1866); *Reid v. Covert,* 354 U.S. 1 (1957). *U.S. ex rel. Toth v. Quarles,* 350 U.S. 11 (1955).

      (2) Courts-martial jurisdiction extends to all offenses committed by service personnel while in the service. *Solorio v. United States,* 483 U.S. 435 (1987) (overruling *O'Callahan v. Parker,* 395 U.S. 258 (1969)).

E. **Treaty Power:** The treaty power is not one completely within congressional control, for the Constitution gives the president, with the advice and consent of the Senate, with a two-thirds majority, the power to make treaties. Article I, § 10. The Constitution expressly forbids the states to make treaties, Article I, § 10, and provides that treaties, like the Constitution itself and other federal laws, are the supreme law of the land. Article VI. (For a further discussion of treaties and international agreements of the United States, and the president's role in them, *cf.* Chapter 4, *infra.*)

   1. ***Self-executing and nonself-executing treaties:*** Treaties requiring no enabling legislation to put them into effect are called self-executing and become law on ratification. Treaties which require further acts of Congress to become effective are not self-executing and do not become law of the land until the requisite legislation is passed.

   2. ***Priority of treaties:*** Self-executing treaties take precedence over conflicting state law and federal law existing at the time the treaty was enacted. Federal law

enacted afterward, if inconsistent with a treaty, will take precedence. *The Chinese Exclusion Case,* 130 U.S. 581 (1889); *Whitney v. Robertson,* 124 U.S. 190 (1888).

3. **Conflict between treaty and Constitution:** While treaties are federal law, they are not equal in authority to the Constitution. In other words, the constitutional limitations that apply to exercises of federal power apply to treaties as well, *Reid v. Covert, supra,* and the federal government cannot do internally via a treaty what it could not otherwise do, for example, suppress free speech in violation of the First Amendment.

4. **Federalism and the treaty power:** Valid treaties regarding matters of international concern are binding on the states even if they regulate something normally the subject of state control which the federal government could not regulate absent the treaty. *Missouri v. Holland,* 252 U.S. 416 (1920).

F. **The Immigration Power:** The Constitution gives Congress the power to establish "a uniform rule of Naturalization." Article I, § 8.

1. **Control over immigration:** Congress has exclusive control over immigration. *Holmgren v. United States,* 217 U.S. 509 (1910). States may not enact laws affecting aliens which conflict with federal law or policy. *Truax v. Raich,* 239 U.S. 33 (1915); *Takahashi v. Fish and Game Comm'n,* 334 U.S. 410 (1948); *Graham v. Richardson,* 403 U.S. 365 (1971).

2. **Terms and conditions of alien entry:** Congress has virtual plenary power to regulate or condition immigration and naturalization, and it can admit noncitizens to the United States, or expel, deport, or exclude them. *Fiallo v. Bell,* 430 U.S. 787 (1977); *Kleindienst v. Mandel,* 408 U.S. 753 (1972); *Lapina v. Williams,* 232 U.S. 78 (1914). Congress may also accord resident aliens different treatment from citizens, but as they are persons within the meaning of the Fifth Amendment, they are entitled to some procedural due process rights. (*Cf.* Chapter 7, I.C. and Chapter 8, IV.B., *infra,* for a more extended discussion.)

3. **Citizenship:** The Fourteenth Amendment makes all persons born or naturalized in the United States citizens of the United States. Consequently, Congress may not treat naturalized citizens differently from native-born, for to do so would create two classes of citizenship. *Schneider v. Rusk,* 377 U.S. 163 (1964).

4. **Loss of citizenship:** Congress can impose loss of citizenship through denaturalization proceedings, applicable only to those who have become citizens through naturalization, or through expatriation, but there are constitutional limits on this power.

   a. *Denaturalization:* Congress may provide for the revocation of naturalization in cases where it was not validly granted, *e.g.,* when based on fraudulent misrepresentations. *Costello v. United States,* 365 U.S. 265 (1961).

   b. *Expatriation:* Because of the Fourteenth Amendment, absent a citizen's consent, Congress has no authority to expatriate or exile those who are citizens by virtue of birth or naturalization in the United States. *Afroyim v. Rusk,* 387 U.S. 253 (1967). In other words, Congress cannot impose loss of citizenship on such a citizen except in circumstances indicating the citizen has voluntarily renounced it. *Id.* The government must show, through the citizen's words or actions, that she intended to renounce. Congress may, however, establish the evidentiary standard used to determine whether there was an intention to renounce, and a statute requiring proof of intention by a preponderance of the evidence is constitutional. *Vance v. Terrazas,* 444 U.S. 252 (1980).

(1) Note that because of its great power over immigration and naturalization, Congress can confer citizenship on persons other than those born or naturalized in the United States. For instance, a federal statute confers citizenship on those born abroad to an American citizen who has resided in the United States. 8 U.S.C.A. § 1401(g). Because Congress, rather than the Fourteenth Amendment, confers this citizenship, Congress may revoke it. *Rogers v. Bellei,* 401 U.S. 815 (1971).

G. **Congressional Investigatory Power:** In order to obtain information necessary to legislate, examine problems facing the country, and assess the operation and effectiveness of federal laws and programs, Congress has the implied power to conduct investigations into any matters subject to its legislative powers.

1. *Scope of congressional investigatory power:* Congressional investigations must relate to topics concerning that which Congress has authority to legislate. Congressional investigative power is broad, however, and Congress may investigate to develop legislation, to determine how laws and government work, and to "inquire into and publicize corruption, maladministration or inefficiency" in governmental agencies. *Watkins v. United States,* 354 U.S. 178, n. 33 at 200 (1957).

   a. *Limits on committee authority:* Congressional resolutions creating investigating committees must state the authority of the investigating committee and show that it is related to a legitimate legislative purpose, and questions the committee asks witnesses must be pertinent to the investigation. *United States v. Rumely,* 345 U.S. 41 (1953); *United States v. Deutch,* 367 U.S. 456 (1961).

   b. *Committee guidelines:* These requirements ensure that committee questioners have guidelines for questioning witnesses, allow witnesses to determine whether to answer, and assist courts reviewing witness claims of rights violations.

   c. *No unlimited investigations:* Congress has no authority to conduct legislative trials nor investigate simply to pillory witnesses, bring them into public disrepute, or cause them shame.

2. *Subpoena and contempt powers:* In investigating, Congress may compel persons to testify, *McGrain v. Daugherty,* 273 U.S. 135 (1927), and it can punish by contempt refusals to provide relevant testimony, *Anderson v. Dunn,* 19 U.S. 204 (1821); *Jurney v. MacCrackern,* 294 U.S. 125 (1935). Witnesses appearing before Congress, however, have the protections of the Bill of Rights, and may sometimes assert the Fifth Amendment privilege against self-incrimination, First Amendment freedoms of association, or due process rights in refusing to answer questions. (*Cf.* Chapter 13, II.A., *infra.*)

H. **Constitutional Qualifications for Membership in Congress:** The Constitution establishes qualifications for membership in each house of Congress. For the U.S.

3 ▶

House of Representatives, it calls for an age of at least twenty-five, U.S. citizenship for at least seven years, and residency in the state the person is elected to represent. Article I, § 2, cl. 2. For the Senate, the requirements are an age of at least thirty, U.S. citizenship for at least nine years, and residency in the state from which the person is elected. Article I, § 3, cl. 3.

1. ***Congressional power to judge qualifications:*** Under the Constitution, each house of Congress has the power to judge the qualifications of its own members. Article 1, § 5, cl. 1. However, this does not include the power to alter or add to the qualifications stated in the Constitution. This is because the framers of the Constitution apparently intended the qualifications to be fixed. This precludes Congress from shaping its composition to its own liking and ensures that the people can choose whom they please to govern them. *Powell v. McCormack*, 395 U.S. 486 (1969).

2. ***Term limits — state power to set qualifications:*** The states have no power to alter or add to the qualifications for Congress that the Constitution sets out. While the Constitution does not, in terms, prohibit state-added qualifications, federal legislative offices are national offices, and the right to elect people to those offices is a right that arose from the Constitution and the existence of a national government, not from the states. The states therefore have no Tenth Amendment reserved powers to add qualifications. *U.S. Term Limits v. Thornton*, 63 U.S.L.W. 4413 (1995).

POWERS OF THE PRESIDENT

II. POWERS OF THE PRESIDENT (Summary Introduction)

A. **Powers in General:** In Article II, the Constitution, without defining it, vests the executive power of the United States in the president. It makes the president the commander-in-chief of the armed forces. With the advice and consent of the Senate, he has the power to make treaties and to appoint ambassadors and consuls, Supreme Court justices, and all other officers of the United States. He has the duties of receiving ambassadors and other public ministers, and of taking care that the laws are faithfully administered, each of which implies the requisite powers. The president also has the power to grant pardons and reprieves for offenses against the United States. Finally, in Article I, § 7, the Constitution gives the president a role in enacting laws. Congressional legislation becomes law only on presidential approval or, following a presidential veto, only on a two-thirds vote of Congress.

B. **General Relationship Between Congressional and Presidential Powers:** As one major power of the president is the executive power – the power to carry out and administer the laws – it is obvious that much presidential authority stems from acts of Congress. In addition, Congress has constitutional authority to legislate regarding many matters falling, in some sense, within the domain of presidential powers. For instance, while the president is commander-in-chief, Congress has the authority to create and regulate the armed forces, and to declare war. Furthermore, the Constitution gives Congress the appropriations power and the power to make all laws necessary and proper for executing laws it has passed under its enumerated powers, "and all other Powers vested . . . in the Government of the United States, or in any Department or Officer thereof." Article I, § 8. Congress, consequently, can shape and, at least to some degree, control the exercise of presidential powers. Because of the interrelated nature of the exercise of presidential and congressional powers, a full treatment of presidential powers requires a discussion of both. This follows in Chapter 4, *infra*.

PRESIDENTIAL POWERS, IMMUNITIES, AND PRIVILEGES

▶ **CHAPTER SUMMARY**

CHAPTER 4: PRESIDENTIAL POWERS, IMMUNITIES, AND PRIVILEGES

Introduction. The Constitution confers relatively few express powers on the president of the United States, yet the president exercises vast powers. Most of these powers derive from the executive and political roles the president plays in federal government, the statutory authority Congress has conferred on the president and the executive branch, and the resources the president has at his command. Basic constitutional law courses, however, do not much deal with the richness or breadth of practical presidential power, nor with the ways of power or political struggle, but instead with the boundaries of power and the frameworks for its exercise. That is not by any means a negligible study, for it defines the field in which political power may properly play and the ground rules by which it must play.

4 ▶

I. PRESIDENTIAL POWERS

PRESIDENTIAL POWERS

A. **Executive Power:** The Constitution, without defining it, confers the executive power on the president. While it is clear that the executive power includes the power to administer and carry out the laws, it is unclear how much more it includes.

1. *Executive power in emergencies:* During times of national emergency, particularly war, presidents have taken actions, such as the creation of agencies, the issuance of regulatory codes, or the seizing of goods, persons, and properties, without authorizing congressional legislation. Lincoln, Wilson, and Franklin Roosevelt are the primary examples. In many instances, the actions amounted to executive legislation but were justified as being within some constitutional power of the president, usually either "inherent" executive power to deal with emergencies, the commander-in-chief power, or the power to take care to see to it that the laws are faithfully executed. In many instances, Congress acquiesced after the fact. In other cases, Congress effectively delegated legislative authority to the president so great as to validate virtually any presidential action. In the latter situation, the president could rely on the authority conferred by Congress rather than on any independent presidential constitutional authority. Nonetheless, even then, presidents such as Roosevelt asserted their own constitutional authority, as well as congressional authority, as a basis for the action. The Supreme Court has never defined the full reach of presidential power, however, and the debate about it ranges over several views.

   a. *Stewardship theory:* In his autobiography, President Theodore Roosevelt advanced a theory expressive of the views and practices of a number of presidents regarding the nature of the executive power under the Constitution. His theory, known as the "stewardship theory," was that the president had the constitutional power to do anything not forbidden by the Constitution or by Congress in the proper exercise of its powers. In other words, in this view, presidential power is open-ended.

   b. *Enumerated powers theory:* The alternative view, espoused by President Taft and consistent with basic constitutional doctrine in other matters, is that the president can only exercise such powers as the Constitution confers and those powers which can reasonably be inferred from such specific grants of power.

   c. *Concurrent powers theory:* In *Youngstown Sheet & Tube Co. v. Sawyer* (The Steel Seizure Case), 343 U.S. 579 (1952), Justice Jackson, in concurrence, stated the constitutional power to deal with some emergencies may be concurrent so that either Congress or the executive might exercise it in the absence of action by the other branch. Jackson proposed a tripartite classification scheme, accepted as the proper starting point for analyzing presidential exercises of power.

(1) When the president acts with congressional authorization, he acts with maximum constitutional authority – that of his own office and that which Congress can properly delegate;

(2) When there is no congressional authorization for the president to act, he can rely only on his own constitutional powers, but where the Constitution does not indicate which branch has the power to act in a given situation, both Congress and the president may have the power concurrently;

(3) When the president acts against congressional will as expressed in legislation, he acts with least constitutional authority.

In *Crosby v. National Foreign Trade Council*, 68 U.S.L.W. 4545 (2000), Congress broadly authorized the president to take actions to develop a "multilateral strategy to bring democracy to and improve human rights practices and the quality of life in Burma." The Court held that a state law imposing sanctions on Burma interfered with the president's activities in circumstances where he was acting with maximum authority, as defined in *Youngstown, supra*.

2. ***Executive power in domestic emergencies:*** In the absence of congressional authorization, the president cannot take domestic action tantamount to legislation. *Youngstown Sheet & Tube, supra*. Consequently, President Truman's executive order directing seizure of steel mills to ensure continued production during the Korean war was unconstitutional.

B. **The Foreign Affairs Power:** While the Constitution mentions and allocates some specific foreign affairs powers, it is silent regarding the general external affairs power of the United States as a sovereign state among other sovereign states. This silence regarding the foreign affairs power has given rise to different theories regarding its origin and scope. While all theories agree that the power is plenary, some attempt, by broad and expansive construction, to derive the foreign affairs power from the Constitution itself. Others assert that the power does not derive from the Constitution, but arises independently. These latter theories of extraconstitutional origin, stated more fully below, deviate from the basic constitutional premise that the federal government is one of enumerated powers. While troubling for that reason, under any view, given modern, expansive interpretations of federal power, the federal government has virtual unlimited power to act in foreign affairs.

1. ***Theories of extraconstitutional origin***

    a. *Inherent power:* The United States is a sovereign entity under international law, and, as such, has whatever powers any nation could exercise regarding external affairs. In other words, the foreign affairs power flows from the fact of creation of a new nation, and the power is, unlike the enumerated powers the People conferred on the federal government through the Constitution, open-ended and unlimited.

b. *The* Sutherland *theory – inherited power:* In *United States v. Curtiss-Wright Export Corp.,* 299 U.S. 304 (1936), Justice Sutherland essayed that when the colonies collectively rebelled from England, "the powers of external sovereignty passed from the Crown not to the colonies severally, but to the colonies in their collective and corporate capacity as the United States of America."

2. *Allocation of foreign affairs powers:* The Constitution neither defines nor generally allocates the country's powers in foreign affairs. It does, however, give both the president and Congress powers which relate to foreign affairs. For instance, the president appoints and receives ambassadors, makes treaties with Senate advice and consent, while Congress has the powers of regulating foreign commerce, laying duties, and declaring war. Other than specific power allocations such as these, and whatever other foreign affairs powers they may reasonably imply, the limits of the respective constitutional authority of the president and Congress to control the nation's foreign affairs is uncertain. This is particularly problematic when foreign affairs powers are thought to derive from sovereignty alone, for then there is no guide at all as to which branch has authority to exercise a power.

   a. *The* Curtiss-Wright *theory of presidential power over foreign affairs:* In *United States v. Curtiss-Wright Export Corp., supra,* Justice Sutherland took the view that the locus of the external affairs power of the United States as sovereign was in the executive. The president, "as sole organ of the federal government in the field of international relations," had plenary and exclusive power over foreign affairs and could act without authorizing congressional legislation.

      (1) Critique: The *Curtiss-Wright* statements regarding an independent and plenary presidential power in foreign affairs were dicta. More importantly, the Constitution clearly gives Congress powers relating to foreign affairs. Furthermore, congressional authority to legislate and appropriate funds also implies congressional authority to shape foreign policy if it chooses to do so. In that sense, any general presidential foreign affairs power cannot be plenary and exclusive.

   b. *Concurrent or collaborative foreign affairs powers:* As a practical matter, even if it wished to do so, Congress could not "micromanage" foreign affairs on a day-to-day basis. Developing relations with foreign governments and dealing with the myriad and protean problems arising in a world of nation-states requires continuity, diplomacy, and secrecy and the abilities to respond rapidly, with one voice, and to make commitments. The constitutional arrangement effectively makes the president the agent of the United States in foreign affairs and similarly confers authority to formulate and initiate foreign policy, and the president should be able to act in the absence of legislation.

      (1) This is particularly true in those foreign affairs matters calling for immediate decision, action, and leadership.

      (2) This is not, however, to suggest that the Constitution gives the president a general and plenary foreign affairs power which could override congressional legislation or that Congress lacks authority to undo or revise presidential foreign affairs actions.

C. **Exclusive Presidential Foreign Affairs Powers:** The Constitution, by implication, assigns the executive some "exclusive" foreign affairs powers.

1. *Recognition of foreign governments:* The president has the sole authority to recognize foreign governments or to withdraw recognition from them, that is, to establish or break relations with other countries. *Banco Nacional de Cuba v. Sabbatino,* 376 U.S. 398 (1964); *United States v. Pink,* 315 U.S. 203 (1942). In recognizing foreign governments, the president can enter executive agreements or international compacts settling matters relating to recognition, for instance, the disposition of money claims against the foreign government. *United States v. Pink, supra; United States v. Belmont,* 301 U.S. 324 (1937). Such agreements may override state law to the contrary.

2. *Making treaties:* The president, with the advice and consent of the Senate, makes treaties. Article II, § 2. This essentially means that the president negotiates treaties, and, on Senate consent, ratifies them. It is unclear whether any general presidential foreign affairs power permits him to terminate treaties without Senate consent. *Cf. Goldwater v. Carter,* 444 U.S. 996 (1979). Presumably, however, the president could terminate a treaty as a necessary adjunct of the exercise of some other specific presidential power, *e.g.,* as an incident to recognition of a foreign government power.

3. *Executive agreements:* While the Constitution provides for treaty-making, it does not require that all international commitments derive from treaties. The executive has some constitutional authority to enter into international agreements, called "executive agreements," without seeking the consent of the Senate as required for treaties. *United States v. Belmont, supra.*

   a. *Kinds of executive agreements:* Executive agreements can be divided into four classes: (1) those based on the exercise of some presidential power, such as the commander-in-chief power or the power to recognize foreign governments; (2) those based on authorizing legislation; (3) those based on some prior treaty; and (4) those adopted by Congress (so-called congressional-executive agreements).

      (1) In a congressional-executive agreement, after negotiating the agreement, the president seeks approval of a majority of both houses of Congress. This circumvents the ability of one-third plus one of the members of the Senate to block an international agreement and also provides a way to obtain legislation implementing the international agreement domestically. The proposed North American Free Trade Agreement (NAFTA) is an example of a congressional-executive agreement.

      (2) While some also advance the position that the president derives the power to make executive agreements from his position as sole organ of the United States in international affairs, the reach of such independent authority is obscure. Any distinction between matters which call for a treaty and matters in which an executive agreement will suffice is also not clear. In fact, the United States enters most of its international agreements through congressional-executive agreements and there are comparatively few solely executive agreements.

      (3) In any case, presidential authority to enter nontreaty international agreements, without authorizing legislation, is clearest in cases involving

some exercise of a specifically granted executive power such as the power to recognize foreign governments or the commander-in-chief power.

    b.   *Analyzing the constitutionality of executive agreements:* In analyzing executive agreement issues, the categories of *Youngstown Sheet and Tube, supra,* are appropriate. Thus, an executive agreement entered pursuant to an exercise of presidential power or effectively authorized by Congress is constitutional. *Dames & Moore v. Regan,* 453 U.S. 654 (1981).

    c.   *Domestic legal effects of executive agreements:* Where properly entered, and absent conflicting federal legislation, executive agreements have the same effect as treaties under the Supremacy Clause and override state laws to the contrary. *Belmont, supra.* In other words, the president effectively can create domestic legislation through proper international agreements having domestic effects.

  4. **Executive agreements conflicting with federal law:** Where the president enters an executive agreement that conflicts with federal law, the executive agreement is constitutional and overrides conflicting law when:

    a.   the executive agreement was entered pursuant to a prior treaty or congressional authorization; or

    b.   the executive agreement was entered pursuant to an appropriate exercise of exclusive presidential power.

    c.   *Effect of no authority:* Where the executive agreement was not entered pursuant to a prior treaty, congressional authorization, or appropriate exercise of exclusive presidential power, it should not supersede prior inconsistent federal law.

  5. **The president's military powers and foreign affairs:** While Congress can authorize the president to take military action short of war, *cf. Bas v. Tingy,* 4 U.S. 37 (1800), the Constitution makes the president the commander-in-chief of the country's armed forces. His power, and its use as a means to carry out other substantive presidential powers, gives the president authority to take some military actions without congressional authorization.

    a.   *Suppressing rebellions and repelling attacks:* While the president has no authority to declare war, as commander-in-chief, he has the authority to suppress insurrections and repel invasions even in the absence of a congressional declaration of war. *The Prize Cases,* 67 U.S. 635 (1863). Note that the power to repel invasions could, under some circumstances and on a theory that a good offense is a good defense, support presidential authority to order invasion of a foreign country.

    b.   *Protecting citizens and property abroad:* The president has the power to use military force to protect American citizens and property abroad. *In re Neagle,* 135 U.S. 1 (1890); *Durand v. Hollins,* 8 Fed. Cases 111 (1860). The president also has authority to use force to suppress piracy or in "hot pursuit" of criminals fleeing the United States; although, historically, many such actions were not directed against sovereign nations and could not therefore be considered acts of war.

6. ***Presidential wars and the War Powers Resolution:*** Many recent presidents have asserted presidential power to commit the armed forces without congressional consent, either as an implication of the president's power in foreign affairs or as an emergency power related to national security. There was no congressional declaration of war in two of the major American twentieth century wars, the Korean War and the Vietnam War, nor have there been in most of the cases in which the United States has undertaken military action abroad. Although the executive has involved the country in undeclared wars, the cases are complicated by the fact that Congress, by raising troops, appropriating monies, or other displays of support, arguably implicitly authorized or ratified the presidential actions.

    a. *Purpose of the War Powers Resolution:* In response to presidential assertions of warmaking power, Congress adopted the War Powers Resolution, which regulates presidential use of armed forces in the absence of a declaration of war.

        (1) The major provision of the Resolution requires the president to terminate the use of the armed forces sixty days after commitment unless Congress declares war or specifically authorizes continued use of the armed forces.

        (2) It would also permit Congress, by concurrent resolution, to direct the president to remove American armed forces engaged in hostilities abroad.

    b. *Congress's view of the president's warmaking power:* As the War Powers Resolution does not purport to, and indeed could not, alter the constitutional authority of the president or Congress, it merely represents the congressional view that the president does not have the constitutional power to commit the country to long-term hostilities without express congressional agreement.

D. Delegated Legislative Power: Under the Constitution, while the president has no direct domestic legislative power, he does have a role in making law by approving legislation. Article I, § 7. Aside from this, Congress may, within limits, delegate some legislative powers to make policy choices or draft rules and regulations to executive branch administrative agencies.

1. ***Delegation requirements:*** As long as Congress establishes standards which guide and measure an administrator's actions under a statutory delegation, the delegation is constitutional. *Yakus v. United States,* 321 U.S. 414 (1944).

2. ***President's responsibilities:*** In such circumstances, as the president is responsible for the work of such agencies, the president may be said to have delegated legislative power.

E. The "Take Care" Power and Duty: The Constitution provides that the president "shall take Care that the Laws be faithfully executed," Article II, § 3,. This clause can be viewed as conferring the power to ensure that the laws are executed and the duty to see to it that they are. This imports some power to supervise subordinates, but does not otherwise suggest any authority to do more, or less, than enforce the laws. This raises the major question, however, whether the president must enforce all the laws.

1. ***The discretionary character of most laws:*** Many statutes give the executive branch considerable discretion as to enforcement. In addition, statutory language

often gives rise to varying interpretations regarding policy and application, and this, too, of necessity, creates both a need and an opportunity for discretionary enforcement. In such situations, it is obvious that the executive branch can exercise discretion in enforcing statutes.

2. ***Discretionary enforcement of criminal and civil statutes:*** There are never enough resources to enforce all criminal statutes, and legal questions relating to proof, the importance of particular cases, and the like properly affect prosecutorial judgment whether to proceed. For such reasons, the Supreme Court has recognized wide prosecutorial discretion not to enforce laws, holding such decisions presumptively nonreviewable. *Heckler v. Chaney,* 470 U.S. 821 (1985). As similar considerations exist in cases involving enforcement of civil regulatory programs, courts recognize executive discretion to engage in selective nondiscriminatory enforcement in civil matters as well.

3. ***Mandatory statutes – impoundment:*** Congress may, of course, expressly mandate that the executive do certain things. Assuming such a statute is clear and does not trench on any constitutional power of the president, the president would have an obligation to enforce it under the Take Care Clause.

   Example: Congress may direct that the executive expend money for certain purposes, and the president has no inherent executive power to ignore the mandate and impound funds. *Kendall v. United States,* 37 U.S. 524 (1838).

F. **The Appointments Power:** In Article II, § 2, the Constitution gives the president the power to nominate and appoint, with the advice and consent of the Senate, "Ambassadors, other public Ministers and Consuls, Judges of the Supreme Court, and all other Officers of the United States." Congress has the authority to vest the appointment of "inferior officers" in the president, the judiciary, or department heads. Congress also has the authority to appoint its own employees.

   1. ***"Officers of the United States":*** Appointees who exercise "significant authority under the laws of the United States" are officers of the United States. *Buckley v. Valeo,* 424 U.S. 1 (1976). This appears to include appointees who formulate governmental policy, exercise wide administrative powers such as rulemaking and adjudication, or who otherwise have broad governmental obligations. *Id.; cf. Morrison v. Olson,* 487 U.S. 654 (1988). While only the president may appoint such officials, Congress may set their qualifications.

      Examples: Members of the Federal Election Commission, whose duties included rulemaking, formulating policy for administration of the Federal Election Campaign Act, and the power to bring civil actions for violations of the Act, were "officers of the United States," and consequently had to be appointed by the president rather than by congressional officials. *Buckley, supra.*

      Special prosecutors, who have limited tenure and are removable by the attorney general for good cause, who have authority to investigate and prosecute for only certain federal crimes, and who do not formulate policy for the government, are "inferior officers" whose appointment Congress may vest in the judiciary. *Morrison, supra.*

   2. ***Inferior officers:*** Under the Appointments Clause, Congress may vest the appointment of inferior officers in the heads of departments. Inferior officers are

"officers whose work is directed and supervised at some level by others who were appointed by presidential nomination with the Senate's advice and consent." *Edmond v. United States*, 520 U.S. 651 (1997).

Example: Judges of the Coast Guard Court of Criminal Appeals, appointed by the secretary of transportation, were inferior officers for Appointments Clause purposes, and their appointment was constitutional. *Edmond, supra.*

3. ***Removal power:*** The power to remove officials is, in a way, the power to control their exercise of discretion. When an official is removable only for some reason stated in a statute (removal for cause) – usually malfeasance or misfeasance in office – that official has some independence. As long as she is doing her job, she will continue in office even if her superiors dislike her decisions or actions. When an official is removable at will, however, she may be discharged simply because her actions or decisions displease her superiors. In the latter case, the superior can command, on pain of discharge, that the job be carried out the way the superior wants it done. Aside from the impeachment and conviction provisions, the Constitution makes no mention of the power to remove presidential appointees. The Supreme Court, however, noting the differential impact of the two kinds of removal authorities, has inferred some constitutional restrictions on Congress's ability to control removal.

   a. *Officials removable at will:* The Supreme Court has effectively held that the Constitution requires that the president have the power to terminate at will those officials whose exercise of discretion is essential to the functioning of the executive branch. *Myers v. United States,* 272 U.S. 52 (1926); *Morrison, supra.*

   b. *Officials removable for cause:* Congress has the power to create "independent" executive branch agencies and officials relatively free of presidential control. Removal-for-cause provisions give the president enough control to see to it that the laws are faithfully executed. Consequently, as long as the "independent" agency which Congress creates is not one central to the functioning of the presidency, Congress may provide for the removal of its officials only "for cause." *Morrison, supra; Wiener v. United States,* 357 U.S. 349 (1958).

G. **The Veto Power:** The Constitution grants the president the power to disapprove legislation passed by Congress. Article I, § 7. This veto power is among the most important of presidential powers, for all congressional action, in order to become law, requires either the president's approval or a vote of two-thirds of each house of Congress following a presidential veto.

1. ***Difficulty in accomplishing overrides:*** The supermajority requirement for a veto override makes it difficult to accomplish. While the president is thus able to negate congressional legislative action, Congress is not equally able to overturn or undo presidential action, for to do so requires legislation that the president may veto.

   Political constraints on exercising vetoes: On the other hand, it is also important to note that political circumstances may prevent a president from vetoing legislation containing provisions which he disapproves. For example, it is common for Congress to include provisions in omnibus appropriations bills that the president would veto if presented separately.

Line-item veto authority: The Constitution's Presentment Clause prohibits Congress from granting the president line-item veto authority that the president can use to eliminate individual appropriations in omnibus spending measures. In *Clinton v. New York, supra,* the Court held that the Presentment Clause requires Congress to pass legislation and present it to the president for signature or veto. A line-item veto authority would permit the president to act legislatively by reshaping legislation presented for signature or veto.

H. **The Pardon Power:** The Constitution gives the president the power "to grant reprieves and pardons for offenses against the United States, except in Cases of Impeachment." Article II, § 2.

1. *Act of public welfare:* A pardon is an act for the public welfare and does not require consent or acceptance on the part of the person pardoned. *Biddle v. Perovich,* 274 U.S. 480 (1927).

2. *Scope of pardons:* The president can pardon individuals or whole classes of persons, *United States v. Klein,* 80 U.S. 128 (1872), any time after an offense is committed, *Ex parte Garland,* 71 U.S. 333 (1866). The effect of a pardon is either to preclude conviction or to remove or mitigate any penalties and disabilities flowing from conviction, *id.* The president may also impose conditions on pardons. *Ex parte Grossman,* 267 U.S. 87 (1925); *Shick v. Reed,* 419 U.S. 256 (1974).

3. *No congressional authority:* Congress has no power to undo or otherwise limit the effects of a presidential pardon. *Klein, supra.*

II. **PRESIDENTIAL IMMUNITIES AND PRIVILEGES**

A. **Executive Immunity**

PRESIDENTIAL IMMUNITIES AND PRIVILEGES

1. *Civil liability for official acts:* Given the unique nature of the office, the controversy often generated by presidential decisions, and the distraction from duties defending lawsuits would impose, absent congressional legislation to the contrary, the president is absolutely immune from civil damages liability for his official acts. *Nixon v. Fitzgerald,* 457 U.S. 731 (1982). Executive officials other than the president have only a qualified immunity from such liability. Such officials are treated differently, depending on their functions.

   a. *Derivative absolute immunity:* Where exercising sensitive functions delegated to them by the president, they may partake of derivative absolute immunity.

   b. *Qualified immunity:* Otherwise, executive officials have only a qualified immunity. They are immune only if they did not know or could not reasonably have been expected to know that their official actions would violate the "clearly established" rights of others. *Harlow v. Fitzgerald,* 457 U.S. 800 (1982); *Mitchell v. Forsyth,* 472 U.S. 511 (1985).

2. *Civil liability for unofficial acts:* The president has no immunity, not even temporary immunity while in office, from civil litigation arising out of events that occurred before he took office. *Clinton v. Jones,* 65 U.S.L.W. 4372 (1997). The burdens attending civil litigation defense are not so great as to impair the

president's ability to carry out his functions, and required submission to judicial process in such cases does not violate the doctrine of separation of powers. *Id.*

3. ***Criminal liability:*** The Constitution, in Article I, § 3, provides for impeachment as the only means to remove a sitting president and indicates that criminal proceedings may be brought following impeachment. As a criminal prosecution against a president might result in a conviction requiring removal from office, it appears that a president is immune from criminal liability until convicted in an impeachment proceeding.

4. ***Immunity from judicial process:*** The president is not completely immune from judicial process, and a court may order the president to comply with a subpoena. *United States v. Nixon,* 418 U.S. 683 (1974). The president could, of course, refuse to obey the court order, and it might therefore, as a practical matter, be unenforceable. *Cf. Nixon v. Sirica,* 487 F.2d 700 (D.C. Cir. 1973).

B. Executive Privilege

1. ***Presidential communications:*** The threat of revelation of confidential communications might inhibit presidential candor and affect his ability to deal with problems effectively. Consequently, although the Constitution makes no provision for an executive privilege regarding confidential communications, the Supreme Court has inferred that some such privilege is essential to the exercise of executive functions and has held that private presidential communications are presumed privileged.

    a. *Disclosure to ensure justice:* That privilege, however, may be overridden on a showing that disclosure of presidential communications, not involving military, diplomatic, or national security secrets, is essential to ensuring justice in a pending criminal trial. *United States v. Nixon, supra.*

    b. *Disclosure to ensure preservation of records:* Similarly, to ensure the preservation and appropriate use of presidential records, Congress may require that professional archivists, under guidelines taking due account of the need for executive confidentiality, review and catalog them. *Nixon v. Administrator of General Services,* 433 U.S. 425 (1977).

2. ***State secrets privilege:*** The executive may refuse to produce evidence or information the disclosure of which, *e.g.,* military secrets, would endanger national security. *United States v. Reynolds,* 345 U.S. 1 (1953).

SEPARATION OF POWERS

▶ **CHAPTER SUMMARY**

CHAPTER 5: SEPARATION OF POWERS

Introduction. The Constitution allocates certain authorities and responsibilities to the executive and certain authorities and responsibilities to Congress and to the Supreme Court. The government can't operate, however, unless the following occur: (1) each branch exercises its respective authorities and carries out its responsibilities, and (2) their work products mesh. The study of the separation of powers examines the constitutional allocation and coordination of governmental powers and concerns itself with improper exercise of power.

I. **THE DOCTRINE OF SEPARATION OF POWERS: While the Constitution does not mention separation of powers, it divides the major powers of government into three parts, the legislative, the executive, and the judicial, and confers them respectively on those branches of the government.**

DOCTRINE OF SEPARATION OF POWERS

A. **Purpose and Theory of the Doctrine:** The doctrine of separation of powers holds that only that branch of government in which the Constitution has vested a power can exercise it. The theory is that dividing the powers of government, and separately conferring them on different branches, creates countervailing governmental power centers which check and balance each other and thereby inhibit the abuse of power.

   1. *Ensuring accountability:* In addition, assigning certain types of governmental powers to specific branches helps ensure accountability and may create some governmental efficiencies not otherwise obtainable.

B. **Constitutionally Required Shared Exercise of Power:** In some cases, the Constitution requires a joint, or shared, exercise of powers to effect some result. For instance, legislation which passes both houses of Congress does not become law unless signed by the president. Similarly, certain presidential appointments require Senate approval.

MAJOR ISSUES UNDER THE DOCTRINE

II. **MAJOR ISSUES UNDER THE DOCTRINE OF SEPARATION OF POWERS: The major purpose of the doctrine of separation of powers is maintaining the constitutional allocation of powers. Consequently, its chief concerns are whether some branch is improperly exercising powers the Constitution has assigned to another branch; whether one branch is improperly inhibiting another branch's legitimate exercise of its powers; and whether one or another branch is improperly aggrandizing power at the expense of another branch.**

There are two major problems in this area of constitutional law. The first is that the Constitution does not define the powers that it confers on the branches of government. While perhaps everyone might agree on what is central to legislative or executive or judicial action, there are cases involving governmental activities difficult to characterize under these headings. The second problem arises out of the so-called fourth branch of government, the administrative agencies. Many administrative agencies exercise legislative, executive, and judicial powers, and there have been difficulties incorporating them into a rigorous scheme of separation of powers.

A. **Exclusive Congressional Authority to Legislate Domestically:** The Constitution confers exclusively on Congress the authority to make laws governing domestic affairs. *Youngstown Sheet & Tube Co. v. Sawyer*, 343 U.S. 579 (1952). While the president has a role in lawmaking, *i.e.*, by signing bills presented by Congress, the president has no independent domestic lawmaking authority, at least short of some extreme national emergency. *Id.*

1. ***Delegation of powers:*** As long as it sets policy and lays down some intelligible principles, guidelines, or standards to give guidance to an administrator, Congress may broadly delegate authority to make law. *Yakus v. United States,* 321 U.S. 414 (1944); *Mistretta v. United States,* 488 U.S. 361 (1989).

2. ***Bicamerality and presentment:*** To make valid law, Congress must follow the bicamerality and presentment procedures the Constitution requires. In order for a bill to become law, it must pass both houses of Congress, be presented to the president, and receive his approval by signature. Article I, § 7. If the president disapproves a bill and vetoes it, it may thereafter become law only on a two-thirds vote of each house of Congress. *Id.*

   a. *Legislative acts:* Congressional acts which have "the purpose and effect of altering the legal rights, duties and relations of persons . . . outside the legislative branch" are legislative acts requiring bicamerality and presentment. *INS v. Chadha,* 462 U.S. 919 (1983).

      Example: A statute authorizing one house of Congress to veto, by resolution, the attorney general's suspension of deportation pursuant to a statute conferring authority to suspend deportation in cases of extreme hardship was held unconstitutional. *Id.* This once oft-employed congressional technique of overriding executive functions is known as the "legislative veto." Such vetoes, by circumventing constitutional requirements regarding deliberative processes, erode the separation of powers and impermissibly allow Congress to intervene in executive activity.

   b. *Internal congressional affairs and unilateral House actions:* Because they do not affect the rights of parties outside the legislative branch, each house of Congress can adopt rules, regulations, and procedures regarding the organization of its own business. In addition, the Constitution provides four instances in which one house's actions have the force of law.

      (1) The House of Representatives alone has the power to initiate impeachments. Article I, § 2.

      (2) The Senate alone conducts impeachment trials. Article I, § 3.

      (3) The Senate alone has authority to approve or disapprove presidential appointments. Article II, § 2.

      (4) Finally, the Senate alone has the power to ratify treaties. Article II, § 2. Note, however, that the United States enters most of its international agreements through congressional-executive agreements.

B. **Separation of Powers and the Power to Remove Officials**

   1. ***Congressional exercise of a power to remove officials:*** While Congress may certainly reserve to itself the power to remove its own employees, it may not

similarly reserve the power to remove executive branch officials or other officials charged with execution of the laws. *Bowsher v. Synar,* 478 U.S. 714 (1986).

    a. *Power to remove – power to control:* The power to remove an official is, in a sense, the power to control the official: one beholden to another for his job is unlikely to take action that might displease the party who can remove him.

    b. *Congressional reservation of removal power:* Reservation of such a removal power, therefore, risks legislative control, other than by statute, of executive discretion and action. Consequently, Congress could not vest executive budget-reduction responsibilities in the comptroller general, an official answering to Congress and subject to its removal. *Id.*

2. ***Congressional restriction of executive power to remove officials:*** Some executive branch officials, such as the secretary of state, are so central to the functioning of the presidency that the president must, in order to control their exercise of discretion, be able to remove them at will.

    a. *Removal for cause:* On the other hand, there are statutes that permit the president to remove officials for cause, such as misfeasance or malfeasance in office. Such statutes, as long as they do not involve officials central to the presidency, give the president sufficient control over officials charged simply with executing the laws that the president can ensure the faithful execution of the laws.

    b. *Constitutionality of for-cause removal:* In such cases, for-cause removal provisions do not interfere with the proper exercise of presidential power and are constitutional. *Morrison v. Olson, supra.* Consequently, Congress may provide that an executive branch official, such as an independent prosecutor, is removable only for cause. *Id.* (For a further discussion of appointments and removal issues, *cf.* Chapter 3, I.F.2., *supra.*)

3. ***Separation of powers following*** **Bowsher** ***and*** **Chadha:** *Bowsher* makes clear that Congress cannot carry out executive functions. *Chadha's* bicamerality and presentment requirements clarify what constitutes valid congressional legislative action. In appropriate cases, where the nature of congressional action is unclear, both cases may be used to determine whether Congress has violated separation of powers principles.

    Example: Congress transferred Dulles and National Airports from the federal government to an airports authority conditioned on the authority's creation of a review board having veto power over the authority's decisions. The review board was to be composed of nine members of Congress. Viewed either as an exercise of executive or legislative power, the review board violated separation-of-powers principles. If the board's actions were executive, Congress was attempting to create an arm to carry out executive functions, contrary to *Bowsher.* If the board's actions were legislative, they would fail to meet the Constitution's bicamerality and presentment requirements, contrary to *Chadha. Metropolitan Washington Airport Auth. v. Citizens for the Abatement of Aircraft Noise,* 111 S. Ct. 2298 (1991).

C. **Separation of Powers and the Judiciary:** The Constitution confers the judicial power of the United States on Article III courts. Separation-of-powers problems can arise when Congress seeks to displace the judiciary from its constitutional role, or in some way threatens or inhibits its impartiality and independence.

1. ***The constitutional role of Article III federal judges:*** Federal judges are constitutionally limited to deciding "cases and controversies" and may also do whatever is reasonably related to that function. Essentially this means that federal judges may not take on executive or administrative duties of a "nonjudicial" nature. The reasons for this limitation are to ensure judicial integrity and independence, so that judges can decide cases without congressional or executive interference, and to prevent judicial encroachment into other branch functions.

   a. *Conferring rulemaking power on the judiciary:* Congress may confer rulemaking authority on the judiciary where the rulemaking is reasonably related to its functions.

      (1) Thus, Congress may authorize the federal judiciary to adopt rules of civil procedure. *Sibbach v. Wilson & Co.,* 312 U.S. 1 (1941).

      (2) Congress may also authorize courts to establish rules for the conduct of their own business or to revise the federal rules of evidence.

   b. *Vesting nonadjudicatory activities within the judicial branch:* Congress may vest some nonadjudicatory activities in federal judges or courts or in auxiliary bodies within the judicial branch. The judiciary may be assigned administrative or rulemaking duties as long as the tasks do not interfere with the judicial function, are not more appropriately undertaken by other branches, or are not threatening to the integrity of the judiciary. *Mistretta v. United States, supra.*

      Example: Congress can create within the judicial branch an independent sentencing commission whose duties include the formulation of sentencing guidelines. *Id.* Such a commission is not a court; sentencing has been a function of courts, and formulation of sentencing guidelines does not aggrandize the authority of the judicial branch. Further, the appointment of federal judges to serve on such a commission is also constitutional as long as such extrajudicial service does not threaten the independence and impartiality of the judiciary. *Id.*

2. ***Independence, impartiality, and tenure of the federal judiciary:*** To ensure that federal judges are free of legislative or executive influence in deciding cases, the Constitution provides that federal judges hold their offices "during good Behaviour" and that their compensation "shall not be diminished during their Continuance in Office." Article III, § 1. *Northern Pipeline Constr. Co. v. Marathon Pipe Line Co.,* 458 U.S. 50 (1982). The Good Behaviour Clause guarantees that Article III judges enjoy life tenure, subject to removal only by impeachment, *United States ex rel. Toth v. Quarles,* and the Compensation Clause guarantees a fixed and irreducible compensation, *United States v. Will,* 449 U.S. 200 (1980).

   a. *No Article III powers for Article I judges:* Congress may not confer Article III power on Article I judges. The Constitution requires that the authority to adjudicate private rights be vested in an Article III court, for only Article III courts, whose judges have life tenure, are free from possible domination or influence of the other branches of government. *Northern Pipeline, supra.*

b. *Article I – "legislative" – courts:* Under the Necessary and Proper Clause, however, Congress has the authority to establish Article I, or "legislative," courts. Such courts, such as the Tax Court and the Court of Customs Appeals, serve "specialized areas having particularized needs . . . warranting distinctive treatment." *Palmore v. United States,* 411 U.S. 389 (1973).

(1) Congress may create legislative courts of the following kinds:

(a) territorial courts: courts having jurisdiction in geographical areas where Congress exercises the general powers of government;

(b) courts-martial;

(c) courts trying cases denominated "public rights" cases: courts which try cases involving matters which, historically, Congress or the executive could have determined, *e.g.,* cases involving the administration of customs laws, which historically was committed to executive officers.

c. *Administrative courts or officials as "adjuncts" to Article III courts:* As long as an Article III court retains the final authority to deal with matters of law, Congress may, in cases involving congressionally created statutory rights, assign fact-finding functions to an administrative agency or official. *Crowell v. Benson,* 285 U.S. 22 (1932); *Northern Pipeline, supra.* Further, as long as an Article III court retains the *ultimate* decision-making authority regarding *all* matters, Congress may authorize preliminary adjunct adjudication even in cases involving constitutional rights. *United States v. Raddatz,* 447 U.S. 667 (1980); *Northern Pipeline, supra.* However, Congress may not vest non-Article III courts with the ordinary powers of federal district courts and authorize them to adjudicate private rights not created by Congress, if they are not made subject to the ultimate decision-making authority of an Article III court. *Northern Pipeline, supra.*

3. ***Legislative reopening or setting aside of final court judgments:*** The judicial power of Article III courts is the power to decide cases dispositively, subject to review only by superior Article III courts. Congress therefore violates the doctrine of separation of powers when it orders courts to reopen final judgments. *Plaut v. Spendthrift Farm, Inc.,* 63 U.S.L.W. 4243 (1995).

Example: In *Lampf, Pleva, Lipkind, Prupis & Petigrow v. Gilbertson,* 501 U.S. 350 (1991), the Supreme Court resolved a split among federal circuit courts regarding the statute of limitations applicable in implied Securities Exchange Act fraud suits by declaring a national, uniform statute of limitations for such actions. The Court held that such actions had to be commenced within one year after the discovery of the facts constituting the violation and within three years after the violation. *Lampf* also applied its new statute of limitations rule retroactively to all pending cases, thus requiring the dispositive dismissal of many actions. In response to the Court's decision, Congress passed legislation having the effect of undoing the Supreme Court's retroactive application of the statute of limitations rule and reviving the dismissed causes of action. This legislation would, in effect, have required courts to reopen final judgments and was therefore unconstitutional.

D. **Separation of Powers, Legislative and Executive Immunities, and Protection from Criminal and Civil Processes:** Legal actions, such as criminal prosecutions or civil actions, can intimidate, harass, and, certainly, distract a defendant. If governmental officials did not have some kind of immunity or protection from criminal or civil actions against them for their normal, official activities, those with power to institute legal proceedings against them could unduly influence, or otherwise interfere with them, in the performance of their duties. For instance, to ensure compliant attitudes on the part of Congress, a president might from time to time resort to grand jury investigations or even criminal prosecutions against members. To prevent such misuse of power as between branches, the Constitution provides some specific protections.

1. *Congressional privilege against arrest:* In Article I, § 6, the Constitution provides members of Congress with a privilege against arrest, except in cases of treason, felony, and breach of the peace, while attending or traveling to and from session business. This privilege applies only to arrest in civil cases, a kind of arrest common when the Constitution was adopted. *Long v. Ansell,* 293 U.S. 76 (1934). The privilege does not confer any immunity from service of civil process, *id.,* or from being forced to appear as a witness in a criminal case. *United States v. Cooper,* 4 U.S. 341 (1800).

2. *Congressional protection from executive or judicial inquiry:* The Speech or Debate Clause, Article I, § 6, also provides that "for any Speech or Debate in either House, they shall not be questioned in any other Place." The Clause protects congressional freedom of speech, debate, and deliberation from executive or judicial intimidation or threat.

   a. *Official legislative duties:* The Speech or Debate Clause absolutely protects members of Congress from executive or judicial inquiry into what they say or do, or into their motivations for their acts, in their respective houses of Congress. The privilege covers all congressional actions that are an integral part of the legislative process, "the deliberative and communicative processes by which Members participate in committee and House proceedings" regarding proposed legislation or other matters the Constitution commits to them. *Gravel v. United States,* 408 U.S. 606 (1972); *United States v. Helstoski,* 442 U.S. 477 (1979). It does not cover political activities, such as constituent service, lobbying administrative agencies, news letters to constituents, or speeches made outside of Congress. *U.S. v. Brewster,* 408 U.S. 501 (1972); *Hutchinson v. Proxmire,* 443 U.S. 111 (1979). It also does not protect a member's *promises* to perform some act in the future, such as a promise to introduce a bill. As promises to take legislative acts are not legislative acts, the government can use evidence of such promises in corruption and bribery prosecutions. *Helstoski, supra.*

   Examples: Members can be prosecuted for acts, such as taking a bribe, which do not require, as a part of the proof, any inquiry into how they spoke, debated, voted, or acted in chamber or committee. *Id.* Similarly, a senator can be prosecuted for arranging for the private publication of secret documents even though he could not be prosecuted for causing the same documents to be published as part of the Senate's public record. *Gravel, supra.*

b. *Legislative aides:* Legislative aides may also invoke the speech and debate privilege regarding their activities which are essential to the legislative process. *Gravel, supra.*

c. *Enjoining congressional subpoenas:* Courts have no power to review the issuance of congressional subpoenas. *Eastland v. United States Servicemen's Fund,* 421 U.S. 491 (1975).

3. ***Executive immunities and privileges:*** For a discussion of this topic, *cf.* Chapter 3, II., *supra.*

E. **Separation of Powers and the Political Question Doctrine:** If the Constitution clearly assigns some particular decision to a specific branch of the government, it has assigned the power to make that decision to that branch. Where this occurs, the judiciary cannot review the decision, for to do so would be to invade the province of another branch. In such cases, the issue is said to involve a "political question" not justiciable for separation-of-powers reasons, and a court must decline to hear the matter. *Baker v. Carr,* 369 U.S. 186 (1962).

1. ***Textually demonstrable constitutional commitment:*** This separation-of-powers strand of the political question doctrine applies only in cases where there is a "textually demonstrable constitutional commitment of the issue to a coordinate political department." *Baker, supra.*

2. ***Limited application:*** The requirement of a "textually demonstrable commitment" is a rather stringent one, for a court must interpret the words of the Constitution to determine exactly what issues it may have committed to a coordinate branch.

Examples: In Article I, § 5, the Constitution provides that "Each House shall be the Judge of [the] Qualifications of its own Members." A surface reading of that provision suggests that each house of Congress has the authority to exclude members that it determines unqualified. Nonetheless, in construing this provision in *Powell v. McCormack,* 395 U.S. 486 (1969), the Supreme Court held that the "Qualifications" referred to were simply those of age, citizenship, and residence. Consequently, the political question doctrine was no bar to judicial review of the House of Representatives' decision to exclude a representative on grounds of wrongful diversion of funds and making false reports. *Id.*

To date, the Supreme Court has recognized few instances of a "textually demonstrable commitment": determination, as between competing state governments, of which was the lawful one, *Luther v. Borden,* 48 U.S. 1 (1849); Senate decision as to which candidate received more lawful votes in an election for Senate, *Roudebush v. Hartke,* 405 U.S. 15 (1972); and congressional authority to create a militia, *Gilligan v. Morgan,* 413 U.S. 1 (1973).

STATE REGULATION AFFECTING COMMERCE, CONTRACTS, AND PRIVATE PROPERTY

▶ CHAPTER SUMMARY

CHAPTER 6: STATE REGULATION AFFECTING COMMERCE, CONTRACTS, AND PRIVATE PROPERTY

Introduction. Several constitutional provisions, including an important inferred provision, the so-called dormant Commerce Clause, restrict state legislative and regulatory action. In addition to the dormant Commerce Clause, there are the Foreign Commerce Clause, the Import-Export Clause, the Contract Clause, and the Takings Clause. Reflecting the relative significance of the Clauses and the volume of decisions concerning them, constitutional law courses often emphasize only the dormant Commerce Clause and the Takings Clause.

6

DORMANT OR "NEGATIVE" COMMERCE CLAUSE

I. **THE DORMANT OR "NEGATIVE" COMMERCE CLAUSE: In the Commerce Clause, Article I, § 8, the Constitution gave Congress broad authority to regulate commerce between the states. The framers' intention behind the Commerce Clause appears to have been to establish a kind of common market or free trade union among the states of the United States. A state, of course, can act in ways inconsistent with free trade by seeking to protect its own commerce and business from competition and discriminating against or burdening commerce moving into the state from other states. If Congress does not adopt legislation to prevent or regulate such practices, the question arises whether the Commerce Clause itself, since it is aimed at creating free trade, does so. The Supreme Court has consistently held that it does and has struck down many state attempts to regulate commerce and economic activity on the basis of this so-called dormant or "negative" Commerce Clause.**

A. **Modern Commerce Clause Cases and the Two-Tier Approach:** While congressional power over interstate commerce is plenary, states can, when Congress has not acted, regulate local matters for health, safety, and welfare purposes even where the regulation affects interstate commerce.

1. *Discriminatory regulation of, or unjustifiable state burdens on, interstate commerce:* In regulating, however, states may not discriminate against interstate commerce. Even where states treat in-state and out-of-state commerce evenhandedly, the Court will invalidate state regulations that unjustifiably burden interstate commerce.

2. *The two-tier approach:* In determining whether to invalidate state regulations in dormant Commerce Clause cases, the Court uses a two-tier approach consisting of a balancing test and a nondiscrimination test.

   a. *Balancing test:* The Court will invalidate state regulations that are not justified by interests outweighing the burdens imposed on interstate commerce. *Pike v. Bruce Church, Inc.,* 397 U.S. 137 (1970).

   b. *The nondiscrimination test:* In appropriate cases, the Court, in addition to the balancing test, also determines whether the subject matter is one concerning which variant and inconsistent regulations from state to state impose a substantial burden on commerce.

B. **Trade Cases:** Because the interstate Commerce Clause evidences a constitutional choice favoring free trade, states may not discriminate against interstate commerce. Thus, where state regulation affecting interstate commerce has a discriminatory purpose, uses discriminatory means, or imposes an unjustifiable burden on interstate commerce, it is unconstitutional.

1. *State protectionism*

   a. *Economic protectionism:* States may not, through regulation of interstate commerce, protect in-state economic interests from out-of-state competition. *Baldwin v. G.A.F. Seelig,* 294 U.S. 511 (1935).

   b. *Out-of-state corporations.* States may not discriminate against out-of-state corporations. They may have different requirements for out of state corporations, but there is a rule of approximate equality of treatment.

      Example. Alabama taxed domestic corporations on the basis of the par value of a corporation's shares. Alabama corporations could set the par value of their shares below book or market value for tax purposes. By contrast, Alabama taxed foreign corporations on the basis of the amount of capital they used in Alabama. This was a facial discrimination that Alabama sought to justify as an offset as foreign corporations did not have to pay a domestic shares tax. But the disparate tax burdens were not even roughly approximate, and foreign corporations paid much higher taxes. Alabama's "compensatory tax" justification therefore failed, and its discriminatory treatment was held unconstitutional. *South Central Bell Telephone Co. v. Alabama*, 526 U.S. 160 (1999).

   c. *Protection of other interests:* A state cannot protect its health, safety, and social welfare interests by discriminating against or burdening interstate commerce – unless the state demonstrates that interstate commerce is the source of the problem which the state seeks to correct and that there are no nondiscriminatory ways available to protect local interests. *Philadelphia v. New Jersey,* 437 U.S. 617 (1978) (ban on disposal, within state, of waste originating out of state, unconstitutional; no showing of any reason, apart from origin, for treating the kinds of waste differently); *Chemical Waste Management v. Hunt,* 112 S. Ct. 2009 (1992) (fee imposed on hazardous waste originating out of state, but not in state, unconstitutional); *Fort Gratiot Sanitary Landfill v. Michigan Dept. of Natural Resources,* 112 S. Ct. 2019 (1992) (state law in effect permitting counties to ban in-county disposal of out-of-county waste unconstitutional).

      (1) Quarantines: States may enact quarantines singling out interstate commerce in specific goods for special treatment, or even banning trade in them altogether, if the commerce is the source of a real and significant harm, and the state cannot otherwise remedy the harm. *Maine v. Taylor,* 477 U.S. 131 (1986) (state law banning importation of out-of-state baitfish upheld because of danger they posed to native species).

   d. *Nonapparent discrimination:* Some state or local actions which, superficially, appear not to discriminate against interstate commerce may nonetheless implicate dormant Commerce Clause concerns. This would occur, for instance, when a state or a local government authorized a ban on both in-state and out-of-state commerce to a locality. The simple fact that a law proscribes both local and interstate commerce does not preclude Commerce Clause invalidation. *Fort Gratiot Sanitary Landfill, supra; Dean Milk Co. v. Madison,* 340 U.S. 349 (1951).

(1) While such bans by applying to both kinds of commerce do not single out interstate commerce for special treatment, they clearly burden interstate commerce nonetheless.

(2) In addition, such bans could be convenient ways for states to circumvent dormant Commerce Clause requirements.

e. *Facial discrimination:* Laws that expressly single out interstate commerce for disparate and negative treatment are per se unconstitutional. *Wyoming v. Oklahoma,* 60 U.S.L.W. (1992) (Oklahoma statute requiring in-state coal-fired power-generating plants to purchase from in-state producers ten percent of coal used to produce power unconstitutional on its face).

2. ***State benefits for in-state economic interests:*** While states may not regulate commerce to advance local interests over outside interests, states may nonetheless provide local interests with some benefits giving them competitive advantage over outsiders.

Example: States may subsidize in-state producers while not providing similar subsidies to nonresidents. *New Energy Co. of Indiana v. Limbach,* 486 U.S. 269 (1988). (For related matter, *cf. D., infra.*)

3. ***State reciprocity requirements:*** States sometimes enact regulations which condition the sale of imported goods on the exporting state's agreement to allow sale of the importing state's similar product in the exporting state. While such requirements seem merely to enforce free and equal trade, they may actually interfere with commerce and be unconstitutional.

Examples: If state *A,* for proper health or safety reasons, bars importation of unsafe milk from state *B,* state *B* cannot in turn bar importation of safe milk from state *A* in order to force state *A* to accept its milk. *A & P Tea Co., Inc. v. Cottrell,* 424 U.S. 366 (1976).

Similarly, a state law requiring reciprocity before permitting transfer of groundwater across the state border is unconstitutional where not shown related to or justified by the state interest in conservation of groundwater. *Sporhase v. Nebraska,* 458 U.S. 941 (1982).

a. *Reciprocity, mutuality of taxation, and subsidies:* Although the net economic effect on competition may be the same, the reciprocity rule treats state efforts to aid in-state business through subsidies differently from state efforts to aid in-state business through taxation, *e.g.,* tax credits.

Example: If state *A* provides its producers with tax credits, it may not condition provision of such credits to state *B* producers selling within state *A* on state *B's* according similar tax credits to state *A* producers selling within state *B. Limbach, supra.* Doing so would impose a discriminatory tax on outside producers.

4. ***State legislation having extraterritorial effect:*** State legislation has extraterritorial effect when it regulates the activities of those outside the state, a result akin to legislating in a sister state.

a. *Direct extraterritorial effect:* On occasion, a state may seek to protect or advance its own economy by extending its laws to outsiders in a way that protects in-state businesses from out-of-state competition. State laws having this kind of extraterritorial effect are unconstitutional. *Baldwin, supra.*

Examples: By statute, a state establishes a minimum price for a product the in-state production and interstate sale of which is critical to the state's economic health. The aim of a minimum price law is to ensure that producers get a sufficient return to stay in business. When the state seeks to apply such minimum price law to out-of-state producers, however, it aims at interstate commerce and destroys any competitive advantage their willingness to accept a lower price confers, thus protecting in-state producers from outside competition. This is an unconstitutional burden on interstate commerce. Thus, New York, in requiring that New York milk dealers pay out-of-state milk producers the same minimum price paid New York producers, violated the Commerce Clause. *Id.*

Similarly, a state law regulating acquisition of shares in corporations having at least ten percent of their capital and surplus in state is unconstitutional as an attempt to regulate nonresident corporations. *Edgar v. Mite Corp.,* 457 U.S. 624 (1982).

b. *Legislation aimed at an in-state market, but having interstate effects:* Laws applicable solely within a state may have effects on interstate commerce.

Example: A law that requires that in-state producers receive a minimum price for their goods effectively requires out-of-state purchasers to pay that price. Such laws, however, apply only in state, are not aimed at interstate commerce, treat it equally rather than discriminate against it, and are thus constitutional. *Parker v. Brown,* 317 U.S. 341 (1943); *Milk Control Bd. v. Eisenberg Farm Prods. Co.,* 306 U.S. 346 (1939).

5. ***Discriminatory effects:*** State statutes or regulations which do not, on their face, discriminate against interstate commerce may nonetheless operate to single out interstate commerce for disadvantageous treatment or otherwise differentially impose burdens on it. State regulation having such discriminatory effects will be upheld only if legitimate, nonprotectionist state interests justify the regulation, and there are no reasonable nondiscriminatory alternatives available to further the state interests. *Dean Milk Co. v. Madison,* 340 U.S. 349 (1951); *Hunt v. Washington Apple Advertising Commission,* 432 U.S. 333 (1977).

Examples: The City of Madison, Wisconsin, passed an ordinance, in the interests of health and safety, barring the sale of pasteurized milk unless it had been processed and bottled at an approved plant located within five miles of central Madison. Madison could have served its interests in wholesome, safe milk by inspecting plants outside the defined radius or by requiring that all milk sold in Madison meet certain uniform standards. The ordinance therefore was an unconstitutional discrimination against interstate commerce. *Dean Milk, supra.*

North Carolina required that containers of apples have only the USDA grade or be marked as not graded. The effect of the requirement was to force Washington State apple growers, who used Washington's superior grading system to alter their marketing practices. This would strip from Washington apple growers the competitive advantage they had because of their grading system, and provide an advantage for local apple growers who marketed under the inferior USDA standards. *Hunt v. Washington State Apple Advertising Comm'n, supra.*

a. *Market configurations:* The Commerce Clause protects interstate dealers or traders from state discrimination designed to insulate in-state competitors, but it does not protect particular configurations or arrangements of the market.

Example: Maryland could forbid producers or refiners of petroleum products, all of whom were out-of-staters, from operating retail service stations in Maryland. The effect of the statute was either to force the out-of-state producers to withdraw from the Maryland market or to divest themselves of their service stations. As all petroleum products were produced and refined outside of Maryland, however, in-state dealers gained no competitive advantage over out-of-state dealers. Furthermore, although the statute might cause some business shift between interstate suppliers, it did not limit the supply of products through interstate commerce. *Exxon Corp. v. Maryland,* 437 U.S. 117 (1978).

b. *Unusual state procedures applied only to out-of-state businesses:* States may require out-of-state businesses to meet reasonable requirements imposed to protect in-staters, *e.g.,* appointment of a resident agent for service of process. Nonetheless, they may not adopt requirements unfairly burdening commerce.

Example: A state statute which tolls the statute of limitations for out-of-state corporations not subject to state court general jurisdiction but nonetheless subject to long-arm jurisdiction is an unreasonable burden on commerce. *Bendix Autolite Corp. v. Midwesco Enterprises, Inc.,* 108 S. Ct. 2218 (1988).

6. ***Reserving the local market to in-staters and other forms of restriction on business entry***

a. *The antiembargo rule:* State regulations designed to curb or limit the export of local products to insure adequate local supplies are unconstitutional. *H.P. Hood & Sons v. Du Mond,* 336 U.S. 525 (1949). Similarly, states may not reserve the sale or use of natural resources to state residents. States, of course, do have conservation interests, but must serve them by means other than discrimination against interstate commerce. *Hughes v. Oklahoma,* 441 U.S. 322 (1979). *New England Power Co. v. New Hampshire,* 455 U.S. 331 (1982).

b. *The antidiscrimination rule:* States must treat out-of-state businesses evenhandedly with in-state businesses, and discrimination against out-of-state businesses is unconstitutional.

Example: A state law which prohibits out-of-state bank holding companies from owning a state business selling investment services discriminates against out-of-state businesses and is unconstitutional. *Lewis v. BT Investment Managers, Inc.,* 447 U.S. 27 (1980).

c. *Regulation of state-organized corporations:* Corporations and the attributes of corporate shares are creations of state law, and a state may, in the interests of shareholders and without violating the Commerce Clause, regulate the acquisition of controlling interests in corporations organized within the state. *CTS Corp. v. Dynamics Corp. of America,* 481 U.S. 69 (1987).

7. ***Requiring in-state processing of exports – the anti-piece-of-the-action rule:*** States, in order to generate business and employment within their borders, have sometimes required that products harvested within the state also be processed or partly processed within the state before being shipped out of state. Such protectionist actions are unconstitutional. *Pike v. Bruce Church, Inc.,* 397 U.S. 137 (1970).

8. ***Transportation cases:*** The transportation cases form a subset of Commerce Clause cases in which states assert transportation safety as an overriding interest justifying state imposition of a burden on interstate commerce. Although the Court asserts that it accords state safety regulations a strong presumption of validity, it in fact appears to follow the balancing approach, giving particular consideration to the problems created for commerce when the various states follow conflicting safety standards.

   a. *The national-local rule and recognition of some state authority to regulate commerce:* The transportation cases have their root in *Cooley v. Board of Wardens,* 53 U.S. 299 (1851). There, the Court in effect held that certain aspects of interstate commerce might demand a uniform rule and consequently exclusive legislation by Congress, but other aspects or matters, because of their local diversity, might, in the absence of congressional legislation, call for local regulation. Safety is one such matter.

   b. *The course of the transportation cases:* The current rule in transportation cases holds that when a state safety regulation seriously conflicts with other states' standards and imposes a heavy burden on commerce, less deference is given to the state legislative judgment and the regulation needs great justification. This was a change from the Court's earlier approach expounded in *South Carolina State Highway Dept. v. Barnwell Bros.,* 303 U.S. 177 (1938), that use of state highways was a local concern and that reasonable state legislative judgments regarding safety measures for state highway use would be upheld.

      Examples: In *Southern Pacific Co. v. Arizona,* 325 U.S. 761 (1945), the Court struck down, as imposing an unjustified burden on commerce regarding a matter where uniform national regulation was needed, a state safety measure limiting train lengths.

      In *Bibb v. Navajo Freight Lines, Inc.,* 359 U.S. 520 (1959), where the record showed that at least forty-five states authorized the use of straight mudguards on trucks and trailers, the Court similarly held invalid an Illinois law requiring the use of contour mudguards.

      Finally, in *Kassel v. Consolidated Freightways Corp.,* 450 U.S. 662 (1981), the Court struck down an Iowa highway ban, having a weak safety justification, on truck-trailer combinations greater than fifty-five feet where other states permitted sixty-five-foot doubles.

C. Market Participant Doctrine: State Actions Not Subject to Dormant Commerce Clause Invalidation

6

1. ***States as market entrepreneurs:*** While states often seek to regulate markets, states can also enter markets as participants, *e.g.,* as traders or manufacturers. When the state acts as a proprietor or entrepreneur, the dormant Commerce Clause is not applied to its activities. Just as a private entrepreneur may decide which parties to deal with, a state acting as entrepreneur may favor its citizens over others. Furthermore, as state citizens pay state taxes and are members of the state's political community, they are entitled to benefit specially from state activities B as long as the state does not, in conferring benefits, effectively regulate outsiders or discriminate against noncitizens in ways inimical to national unity. Acting as a market participant, a state may, without violating the Commerce Clause, do the following:

   a. subsidize the activities of its citizens, *Hughes v. Alexandria Scrap Corp.,* 426 U.S. 794 (1976);

   b. operate a business, not amounting to a monopoly and not involving control over a substantial share of natural resources, in ways favoring citizens over noncitizens, *Reeves, Inc. v. Stake,* 447 U.S. 429 (1980);

      (1) When a state has the good fortune to have within its boundaries some nonreproducible natural resource, the rule may be different, and the state may not be permitted to hoard such resources for its citizens. Doing so, a state might create the kinds of division and hostility that the Commerce Clause, looked upon as a device to create national unity, was intended to prevent.

      (2) Arguments for restraining state entrepreneurial activities through the dormant Commerce Clause may be stronger in cases where the state exercises a genuine monopoly. A monopoly can dictate terms to the parties dealing with it. Laws relating to monopolies often require them to deal with all qualified parties. A state, acting as a market participant, shouldn't have an advantage that a monopolizer wouldn't have.

   c. prefer its own citizens over noncitizens in its purchases, sales, or in the distribution of its goods and properties, or opportunities it has itself created (*e.g.,* employment opportunities).

      Example: A state could choose to purchase office equipment from manufacturers within the state. Similarly, a city undertaking public construction could require its contractors to give a hiring preference to local residents. *White v. Massachusetts Council of Construction Employers,* 460 U.S. 204 (1983).

2. ***Exception to the market participant exception:*** The market participant exception to dominant Commerce Clause restraints applies only to a state's activities in the particular market, narrowly defined, in which it is a participant. A state may not impose conditions, say by contract, that have substantial regulatory effects outside, or "downstream" of the market in which it is participating.

   Example: In *South-Central Timber Dev., Inc. v. Wunnicke,* 467 U.S. 82 (1984), Alaska attempted to require that purchasers of timber from state lands at least partially process the timber in Alaska before shipment outside of Alaska. While

Alaska was participating in the market for the sale of timber, it was also by contract regulating the purchaser's subsequent disposition and therefore violating the dormant Commerce Clause. In general, when a state imposes 'downstream' conditions, *e.g.,* restrictions on resale or use, it no longer acts as a market participant, but as a regulator. By definition, in such a situation, the state is discriminating against interstate commerce, and its action is subject to the Commerce Clause virtual-per-se rule of invalidity.

3. ***Market participant doctrine and foreign commerce:*** The Supreme Court subjects state regulations or activities burdening foreign commerce to a more rigorous and searching scrutiny than those affecting interstate commerce. Consequently, a state's market participant activities affecting foreign commerce are less likely to be upheld. *Wunnicke, supra. Cf. C., infra.*

4. ***The Article IV, § 2, Privileges and Immunities exception to the market participant exception:*** While a state acting as a market participant does not violate the dormant Commerce Clause, it may nonetheless violate some other provision of the Constitution such as Article IV, § 2, Privileges and Immunities.

   a. *Purpose of Privileges and Immunities Clause:* The Article IV, § 2, Privileges and Immunities Clause is a constitutional provision aimed at creating national unity by insuring that states do not discriminate against noncitizens or nonresidents in matters fundamental to interstate harmony. At a minimum, the clause protects the following protected privileges or rights:

      (1) to own, possess, and dispose of property;

      (2) to engage in gainful employment in the private sector;

      (3) to do business on terms of substantial equality with state citizens;

      (4) to travel through and within a state, including the right to change residence from one state to another;

      (5) to be treated equally by justice institutions;

      (6) to seek medical care.

   b. *Rules regarding state discriminations against citizens of other states*

      (1) A state cannot treat a noncitizen differently from a citizen in the exercise of a protected privilege unless the state has a substantial reason for the different treatment. That reason must justify, or bear a substantial relationship to, the difference in treatment.

         (a) There must be no less restrictive means available for dealing with the problem.

         (b) In effect, noncitizens, or their activities, must be shown to be part of the problem the state is attempting to deal with, *e.g.,* demonstrating a sufficient connection with the state to vote or obtain welfare benefits.

(2) If a state discriminates against a noncitizen with respect to a nonprotected interest, to justify its action it need show only that it has not acted arbitrarily.

c. *Examples of unconstitutional discrimination*

(1) State residency requirements for abortions discriminate against women seeking medical care, a protected privilege. *Doe v. Bolton,* 410 U.S. 179 (1973).

(2) State laws requiring private employers to give state residents a hiring preference discriminate against nonresidents in employment, a protected privilege. *Hicklin v. Orbeck,* 437 U.S. 518 (1978).

(3) State laws which condition bar admission on residency also discriminate against nonresidents in choice of occupation. *Supreme Court of New Hampshire v. Piper,* 470 U.S. 274 (1985); *Supreme Court of Virginia v. Friedman,* 487 U.S. 56 (1988).

d. *Examples of constitutional discrimination*

(1) State laws charging higher nonresident than resident fees for nonprivileged activities, *e.g.,* hunting license fees, are constitutional. *Baldwin v. Montana Fish and Game Comm'n,* 436 U.S. 371 (1978).

(2) A state may constitutionally reserve recreational game hunting to state citizens.

e. *Limited application:* The Privileges and Immunities Clause applies to "citizens." Only natural persons can be citizens, and only natural persons born in, or naturalized in, the United States are citizens.

(1) Therefore, the Privileges and Immunities Clause does not apply to corporations or aliens.

(2) Note, however, that other interstate equality principles, *i.e.,* the dormant Commerce Clause or the Fourteenth Amendment Equal Protection Clause would come into play to protect corporations and aliens from state discrimination.

D. **The Twenty-first Amendment As a Limitation on the Dormant Commerce Clause:** The Twenty-first Amendment in effect authorizes states to regulate the importation and use, within the state, of intoxicating liquors. States may, therefore, without violating the Commerce Clause, prohibit the importation of intoxicating liquors or otherwise regulate their importation and use within state borders. *Ziffrin, Inc. v. Reeves,* 308 U.S. 132 (1939).

1. *Limited scope of Twenty-first Amendment:* Presently, the Court takes the view that the Twenty-first Amendment allowed states to address the evils of unrestricted traffic in liquor, but did not allow them to favor local liquor interests over outside interests by imposing competitive disadvantages on them. *Bacchus Imports, Ltd. v. Dias,* 468 U.S. 263 (1984); *Brown-Forman Distillers Corp. v. New York State Liquor Auth.,* 476 U.S. 573 (1986). In other words, the Supreme Court

6

views the Twenty-first Amendment as only partially limiting the effect of the dormant Commerce Clause.

Examples: While a state can ban the importation of intoxicating liquors, it cannot charge a lesser tax on locally produced liquor than on that produced out of state. *Bacchus Imports, supra.*

Similarly, a state cannot require out-of-state distillers to sell at a price within state no higher than prices charged for similar sales in other states. *Brown-Forman Distillers Corp., supra; Healy v. The Beer Institute, Inc.*, 491 U.S. 324 (1989).

2. ***State regulation of the federal government:*** Under the Twenty-first Amendment, states have the authority to control liquor shipments through their territory and to prevent unlawful diversion of liquor. While the federal government is constitutionally immune from state regulation, state liquor transport and labeling regulations regarding liquor sold on federal enclaves within the state fall within state authority under the Twenty-first Amendment. *North Dakota v. United States*, 495 S. Ct. 423 (1990).

3. ***The Twenty-first Amendment and congressional authority under the Commerce Clause.*** Notwithstanding the Twenty-first Amendment, Congress may pass legislation affecting a state's ability to limit liquor consumption, at least where Congress does not directly interfere with the state's authority to regulate the time, place, and manner of liquor importation and sales. *Capital Cities Cable, Inc. v. Crisp,* 467 U.S. 691 (1984) (state liquor advertising ban on out-of-state originating cable television advertising preempted by federal regulatory scheme for cable television).

STATE TAXATION OF INTERSTATE COMMERCE

II. **STATE TAXATION OF INTERSTATE COMMERCE: At one time, the Supreme Court applied a formal rule that states could not impose direct taxes on business activities in interstate commerce. At the same time, the Court accepted the idea that interstate business had to pay its fair share of government costs. The two positions led to some curious law. The Court has now abandoned the formal rule and instead applies a four-part, "practical effect" test to determine the validity of state taxes on interstate commerce. (The test actually derives both from Commerce Clause and Due Process Clause considerations, due process playing a primary role regarding state jurisdiction to tax and the fairness of the taxes imposed. As little of practical import turns on sorting out the respective Due Process Clause and Commerce Clause elements of the test, they are simply treated together.)**

A. **Practical Effect Test:** In order for state taxation of interstate commerce to pass Commerce Clause scrutiny, the tax must be on activity having a substantial nexus with the state, be fairly apportioned, not discriminate against interstate commerce, and be fairly related to services the state provides. *Complete Auto Transit, Inc. v. Brady,* 430 U.S. 274 (1977); *Department of Revenue v. Association of Washington Stevedoring Cos.,* 435 U.S. 734 (1978). The practical effect test takes into account not only the particular taxing statute at issue, but also other tax statutes which help to determine the actual net effect of the taxing statute.

1. ***Substantial nexus:*** Minimum contacts with a state, such as exist when an out-of-state vendor merely uses the mail or a common carrier to facilitate in-state sales,

do not comprise a substantial nexus for Commerce Clause purposes, and a state cannot impose taxes on sales involving such minimum contacts. *Quill Corp. v. North Dakota,* 60 U.S.L.W. 4423 (1992); *National Bellas Hess, Inc. v. Department of Revenue of Ill.,* 386 U.S. 753 (1967).

2. ***Discrimination:*** States must evenhandedly tax commerce originating in state and out of state. Disparate taxation disadvantaging out-of-state commerce is invalid under the Commerce Clause.

Examples: Sales and transfer taxes imposed on in-state events, such as the delivery or transfer of stocks following sale, which are less for in-state sales than for out-of-state sales, in effect, impose a penalty on out-of-state sales and discriminate against them. *Boston Stock Exchange v. State Tax Comm'n,* 429 U.S. 318 (1977).

Maine provided charitable institutions that operated for the benefit of Maine residents with an exemption from real estate and personal property taxes. It did not provide the same exemption for charities operating within Maine that operated principally for the benefit of non-Maine residents. In other words, Maine gave a benefit to charities serving an intrastate clientele and taxed charities serving an interstate clientele. This was a clear discrimination against interstate commerce. *Camps Newfound/Owatonna, Inc. v. Town of Harrison, Maine,* 65 U.S.L.W. 4337 (1997).

a. *Out-of-state impact:* As long as a state tax treats in-staters and out-of-staters the same way, it does not discriminate even if it falls predominantly on out-of-staters. *Commonwealth Edison Co. v. Montana,* 453 U.S. 609 (1981) (Montana severance tax on coal, applied equally to in-state and out-of-state purchasers, constitutional although ninety of coal mined shipped out of state).

b. *Compensating use taxes:* Compensating use taxes which subject imported articles purchased out of state to a tax equal to a sales tax imposed on goods bought within the state are constitutional. Although it is possible to construe such taxes as protective tariffs, they equally tax articles used within a state, whether produced locally or imported. *Henneford v. Silas Mason Co.,* 300 U.S. 577 (1937). While removing some competitive price advantage for goods purchased out of state, such taxes do not advantage in-state producers or sellers by removing all out-of-state advantages.

(1) In-state taxes on mail-order sales: States may not collect sales taxes on items out-of-state vendors sell through mail or telephone orders to in-state purchasers if the vendors' contacts with the state are limited to mail, telephone, or other common carrier. Such contacts do not constitute a substantial nexus, as required by the practical effect test. *Quill Corp., supra; National Bellas Hess, supra.* Without a showing of more substantial contacts with a state, states may not require vendors to pay the tax. *Id.*

c. *Subsidies:* There may be a constitutionally significant difference between a state subsidy and a state tax exemption, although the financial effect may be the same. States may subsidize domestic industries, but a tax that discriminates against interstate commerce amounts to an improper regulation of interstate commerce. *Camps Newfound/Owatonna, Inc., supra.*

d.   *Market analysis:* In determining whether a state action, such as a tax, discriminates against interstate commerce, it is important to examine whether the state is regulating similar interstate and intrastate businesses differentially. If the interstate and intrastate businesses serve different markets and do not compete with one another, the state may be able to justify its differential regulation.

Example: Ohio regulates utilities engaged in local distribution of natural gas. A "local distribution company" (LDC) supplies natural gas to consumers within the state, and Ohio exempts such companies from state and local taxes. Gas sold by LDCs is bundled with certain mandated rights and benefits, *e.g.*, nondiscrimination between customers, backup supplies, and required services to low-income customers. Ohio, however, does not exempt natural gas producers and independent marketers from such taxes. Gas sold by the latter businesses is unbundled, that is, is sold without regulatory rights and benefits. The two different kinds of natural gas suppliers essentially served different markets. LDCs served a captive market of residential consumers, and the producers and marketers served a noncaptive market of resellers and industrial users. As the two served different markets, they were not similarly situated, and the Ohio tax is therefore not discriminatory and is constitutional. *General Motors Corp. v. Tracy, Tax Comm'r of Ohio*, 519 U.S. 278 (1997).

3.   ***Fair apportionment B the three-factor formula:*** Fair apportionment requires that states do not tax interstate businesses (*i.e.*, businesses engaged in interstate commerce in many states and even foreign jurisdictions) beyond their activity in the state.

a.   *Apportionment formula limitation:* Thus, states must devise an apportionment formula which, if applied by every state, would result in taxation of no more than the businesses' overall income. *Container Corp. v. Franchise Tax Bd.*, 463 U.S. 159 (1983).

b.   *The three factors:* A guidepost for fair apportionment is the widely accepted and Supreme Court-approved "three-factor" formula, which takes the average of three percentages: the business's in-state sales divided by its total sales; the business's in-state payroll divided by its total payroll; and the business's in-state property divided by all its property. *Id.; Buder Bros. v. McCoglan,* 315 U.S. 501 (1942).

c.   *Exactness of apportionment:* State apportionment of an interstate business's income attributed to the state must be reasonably related to the business's activities in the state. *Moorman Mfg. Co. v. Bair,* 437 U.S. 267 (1978). If reasonably related, state apportionment formulas which may reach some income not actually earned in the taxing state are not unconstitutional simply because they are imprecise.

d.   *Unitary business principle:* In imposing an income tax, a state may not "tax values earned outside its borders." *ASARCO Inc. v. Idaho State Tax Comm'n,* 458 U.S. 307 (1982). Nonetheless, a state may apportion its taxes to the entirety of an interstate business as long as the business is unitary, that is, when it operates as a functionally integrated enterprise, and when its apportionment formula attributes income to the state in reasonable proportion to the business transacted there.

(1) Rationale: In-state activities of a far-flung enterprise may contribute to creating out-of-state income, and setting precise territorial allocations of value earned is very difficult.

(2) Burden on enterprise

(a) Taxation of extraterritorial value: For an integrated interstate enterprise to establish that some of its income is not subject to an apportioned state tax, it must show that the income was "unrelated" to activities in the state. *United States Steel Corp. v. Multistate Tax Comm'n*, 434 U.S. 452 (1978); *Mobil Oil Corp. v. Commissioner of Taxes*, 445 U.S. 425 (1980). It must show, by clear and cogent evidence, that the state is taxing "extraterritorial" value. *Exxon Corp. v. Wisconsin Dept. of Revenue*, 447 U.S. 207 (1980).

(b) State apportionment formula: The taxpayer also has the burden of proving by "clear and cogent" evidence that the income attributed to the state is in fact, "out of all appropriate proportions to the business transacted . . . in that State." *Hans Rees' Sons, Inc. v. North Carolina ex rel. Maxwell*, 283 U.S. 123 (1931). The Court considers the three-factor apportionment formula noted in F., *supra*, a proper benchmark.

e. *Unfair apportionment:* A tax which unfairly apportions or attributes to the taxing state income an interstate business earns as compared with other venues of earning discriminates against interstate commerce. A state tax unfairly apportions income if the same kind of tax, applied by every state, would significantly interfere with free trade.

Example: In *Armco, Inc. v. Hardesty*, 467 U.S. 638 (1984), West Virginia exempted local manufacturers from its wholesale sales tax while imposing the tax on out-of-state sellers selling in state. The state's justification was that it imposed a larger manufacturer's tax on all products made in the state. Other states, however, might impose a similar manufacturer's tax. In such circumstances, a state sales tax exemption for in-state manufacturers would advantage its manufacturers vis-à-vis out-of-state manufacturers selling in the state. Such an exemption is therefore unconstitutional.

B. **Property Taxes:** State property taxes pose a special problem in state taxation of interstate commerce when the tax is applied to items moving in commerce or to 'instrumentalities' of commerce, such as trucks, trains, or aircraft.

1. *The transit rule:* States cannot impose property taxes on property being shipped through the state. If the rule were otherwise, every state through which the property passed could impose a property tax, and multiple tax burdens on the property would result. *Standard Oil Co. v. Peck*, 341 U.S. 382 (1952).

2. *Property taxes on instrumentalities of commerce:* States can impose a properly apportioned property tax on instrumentalities of commerce which have a taxable situs in the state, that is, sufficient presence or contacts in the state to justify the tax.

Example: In *Braniff Airways, Inc. v. Nebraska State Bd. of Equalization*, 347 U.S. 590 (1954), Braniff aircraft, which traveled interstate, regularly made eighteen stops a day in Nebraska, where Braniff rented ground facilities and bought fuel. The Court upheld a Nebraska property tax on the aircraft apportioned according to the three-factor formula noted *supra*.

3. ***Tax on services:*** A tax on the sale of services is similar to a sales tax on the sale of tangible goods. Taxing the gross receipts for the sale of services having an interstate component, such as transportation between states, and only a partial in-state component, does not violate the Commerce Clause. This is so at least when the service is purchased within the taxing state, and it is highly unlikely that any other state in which the service is also partially performed will have an identical tax for the same sale. *Oklahoma Tax Commission v. Jefferson Lines, Inc.*, 63 U.S.L.W. 4233 (1995) (Oklahoma sales tax on bus tickets sold in Oklahoma for interstate travel originating there constitutional; tax internally consistent as if all states had a similar sales tax; there would be no double taxation; tax externally consistent and not unfair as it was unlikely any other state would impose a different, successive tax on portions of travel outside of Oklahoma).

III. STATE TAXATION OF FOREIGN COMMERCE

A. **Instrumentalities of Commerce:** State taxes on interstate commerce which merely pass muster under the four-part, practical effect test cannot be applied constitutionally to foreign-owned instrumentalities of foreign commerce. *Japan Line, Ltd. v. County of Los Angeles,* 441 U.S. 434 (1979).

1. ***Foreign vs. interstate commerce:*** Commerce Clause analysis respecting state taxation is different depending on whether interstate or foreign commerce is involved.

2. ***More rigorous review of foreign commerce:*** Review is more rigorous in cases involving foreign commerce for two reasons:

   a. *Enhanced risk of multiple taxation:* There is an enhanced risk of multiple taxation, for there is no way to assure correct apportionment when a foreign sovereign may also tax.

   b. *Uniform national rules:* Secondly, taxation of foreign commerce may require uniform national rules, and state taxes might interfere with federal uniformity.

B. **State Taxation of a Domestic Entity's Foreign Income:** States may tax foreign-derived income of unitary business enterprises. *Container Corp. of America v. Franchise Tax Bd.,* 463 U.S. 159 (1983).

1. ***Taxation of income, taxation of property distinguished:*** While the considerations discussed above would appear to apply to a state's taxation of foreign-derived income, the Court takes a rather different view. Taxation of income is different from taxation of property, for property has some situs and can be located. But income, particularly income readily attributed, transferred, or reallocated between affiliated corporations, is much more difficult to locate. In addition, different countries have different tax rules requiring income reallocation between such corporations. For these reasons, it is exceptionally difficult to

determine whether there is serious double taxation when a state applies the unitary business principle to an enterprise and taxes it under an appropriate apportionment formula.

2. ***Less clear foreign policy implications:*** Finally, there are less clear foreign policy implications regarding such state income taxes, particularly because the incidence of the tax falls on the domestic, not the foreign, enterprise.

C. **The Import-Export Clause:** Article I, § 10 of the Constitution provides, "No state shall, without the Consent of the Congress, lay any Imposts or Duties on Imports or Exports, except what may be absolutely necessary for executing its inspection Laws."

1. ***Transit rule:*** The Import-Export Clause prohibits state taxation of foreign commerce while it is in transit. Nondiscriminatory ad valorem property taxes imposed on imported goods no longer in import transit are constitutional. Since such taxes do not select out items to tax because they are imports, they do not constitute imposts or duties. *Michelin Tire Corp. v. Wages,* 423 U.S. 276 (1976).

2. ***Importing-exporting as an activity:*** States may not tax importing or exporting as an activity, for example, by imposing a license tax on importers. *Brown v. Maryland,* 25 U.S. 419 (1827). They may, however, tax the income of importers or exporters, as that is not a tax on the activity itself. *William E. Peck & Co., Inc. v. Lowe,* 247 U.S. 165 (1918).

THE CONTRACT CLAUSE

IV. **THE CONTRACT CLAUSE: The Contract Clause, Article 1, § 10, provides that no state shall pass any "law impairing the Obligation of Contracts." Until this century, the Supreme Court often invoked this clause to invalidate state legislation. Rigid interpretation of the Clause, however, sometimes disabled states from acting in ways essential to the public good. This realization led the modern Court to interpret the Contract Clause in a way that harmonizes it with the authority of states to protect the general welfare of their citizens. Unconstitutional state impairment of a contract has thus come to have a technical meaning. Many state acts effecting changes in contracts to the detriment of contracting parties, in some sense 'impairing' them, are not considered impairments under the Clause.**

A. **Reserved Power Doctrine:** States have some reserved powers that they may exercise in ways effecting constitutionally permissible contract impairments. The scope of this reserved power, however, turns on the parties to the contracts. The rules are different when state acts affect private contracts and when they affect contracts to which the state is a party.

1. ***State contracts:*** The first branch of the reserved powers doctrine holds that states cannot contract away essential state powers. State contracts that in effect do so are invalid.

a. *Essential powers:* States cannot contract away the police power or the power of eminent domain. *United States Trust Co. of New York v. New Jersey,* 431 U.S. 1 (1977).

b. *State financial contracts:* States may enter into financial or debt contracts. When they do so, they may impair them, without violating the Constitution, if the impairment is reasonable and necessary to serve an important public purpose. As states might unnecessarily amend or abrogate their financial obligations in self-serving ways, however, courts scrutinize such actions carefully. *Id.*

2. ***Private contracts:*** Government could hardly operate if private parties were able to insulate themselves from regulation by contract. Governments therefore in effect assert or reserve a general power to act in the public interest without regard to the effect of such actions on private contracts. *Hudson County Water Co. v. McCarter,* 209 U.S. 349 (1908). If the state has a justifying public purpose, it may "[adjust] the rights and responsibilities of contracting parties . . . upon reasonable conditions." *United States Trust Co. v. New Jersey, supra.*

3. ***Impairment:*** There must be a substantial, but not necessarily total, impairment before a court will undertake a Contract Clause analysis.

   a. *Degree of impairment:* The degree or severity of impairment determines the level of justification the state must show to avoid the invalidation of its action under the Contract Clause; the more severe the impairment, the greater the justification required. *Allied Structural Steel Co. v. Spannaus,* 438 U.S. 234 (1978).

   b. *Regulated parties or industries:* In cases involving parties or industries regulated in the past, the fact of prior regulation is taken into account to determine the extent of impairment. *Allied, supra.* In effect, regulated parties or industries are on notice of the possibility of further regulation, and their expectations under existing contracts may not be entirely reasonable.

V. **TAKINGS AND THE JUST COMPENSATION CLAUSE: The Fifth Amendment, among other things, prohibits the governmental taking of private property for public use, without just compensation. Although originally applicable only to the federal government, the Clause has been applied to the states through Fourteenth Amendment due process. (See Chapter 7, *infra.*) As a limitation on government action, its similarity to the Contract Clause calls for its treatment here.**

   A. **Takings and Eminent Domain Distinguished:** Governments have the power of eminent domain and may condemn private property for public use. *Berman v. Parker,* 348 U.S. 26 (1954). But governments provide compensation in such cases, and that satisfies the Just Compensation Clause. Takings cases arise, however, when a government does not exercise eminent domain powers, but instead takes action which arguably injures property rights.

      1. ***Effect of governmental actions:*** Governmental actions short of condemnation in eminent domain can affect private property in many ways. Governments may attempt to take property without payment, may take some portion of an owner's property rights, may restrict property use, or may, without any direct intent to do so, take actions which have the effect of reducing or destroying the value of private property.

      2. ***Effect not necessarily a taking:*** Just as every governmental impairment of a contract does not violate the Contract Clause, not every governmental action affecting the use or value of private property constitutes a taking for purposes

TAKINGS AND THE JUST COMPENSATION CLAUSE

of the *Just Compensation Clause.* In fact, relatively few of them do. In general, governmental regulation of private property for police power purposes – health, welfare, safety – does not amount to a compensable taking even when, as a result, private property loses its value.

B. **Public Use Clause:** Governments may take private property only for public purposes.

1. *Public purposes and private parties:* Even with compensation, a government cannot take property simply in order to give it to another private party. *Pennsylvania Coal Co. v. Mahon,* 260 U.S. 393 (1922). However, to constitute a public use, the use to which the property is put need not be reserved to the general public. Transfer of the taken property to private hands is proper if done for a public purpose.

   Example: In *Hawaii Housing Auth. v. Midkiff,* 467 U.S. 229 (1984), the state appropriately used eminent domain powers to lessen Hawaii land ownership concentration by condemning property of large landowners for later sale to tenant-lessees.

2. *Determination of public use:* As long as the exercise of the power of eminent domain is rationally related to a conceivable public purpose, the Court will not second-guess legislative judgments of what is a public use.

C. **Property:** Property, as protected by the Just Compensation Clause, is defined broadly and includes not only the traditional kinds of property and interests in property recognized at common law, but also modern forms, such as intellectual property. *Ruckelshaus v. Monsanto Co.,* 467 U.S. 986 (1984).

D. **Compensable Takings:** The critical question in takings cases is whether the governmental action affecting private property is a "compensable" taking or whether it is simply a proper exercise of police power. Government regulates the uses to which owners can put private property in many ways, and most of these restrictions do not constitute compensable or "regulatory" takings even when they diminish the value of the property. In some cases, however, governmental regulation goes too far and does amount to a taking. Unfortunately, there is no exact formula to apply in every case to determine when government regulation has gone too far and crossed the line between appropriate exercises of police power and regulatory takings. Instead, the inquiry in alleged regulatory takings cases is generally case specific. In such cases, the Court principally considers the economic impact of the regulation on the property owner, including frustration of reasonable, investment-backed expectations; the invasive character of the government's action; and the public purposes of the regulation. (*Cf.* IV.D., *infra.*) Nonetheless, certain government actions toward, or regulations of, property will constitute a taking per se.

1. *Physical invasion or occupation:* When government, without a justification under nuisance or preexisting property law, undertakes an actual permanent physical appropriation, invasion, occupation, or destruction of private property, its action amounts to a taking and is compensable. *Loretto v. Teleprompter Manhattan,* 458 U.S. 419 (1982); *Babbitt v. Youpee,* 519 U.S. 234 (1997) (Congressional effort to cut off, without compensation, Indians' right to devise fractional interests in allotted real property constitutes a compensable taking).

2. ***Regulation denying all economically beneficial or productive use:*** Where a government regulation, not based on nuisance or preexisting property law, deprives a property owner of all viable uses of the property, there is a regulatory taking.

Example: South Carolina, in order to protect its beaches from erosion, enacted a general ban on construction of habitable structures on beach properties located near an unstable and dangerous "erosion zone." The ban was applied retroactively to Lucas, who had purchased two beach lots when the property was zoned residential, having planned to build on them. Under these circumstances, if Lucas was denied all viable use of his property, there was a regulatory taking. *Lucas v. South Carolina Coastal Council,* 112 S. Ct. 2886 (1992).

   a. *Exception – nuisance abatements or preexisting property law restrictions:* If the viable use to which the owner puts, or seeks to put, her property amounts to a nuisance that the government could abate – or to a use of the property not permitted under law – government regulation ending use does not amount to a taking. *Lucas, supra.*

   b. *Regulation to prevent public harm*

      (1) Permissible regulation: Government can prohibit property uses that comprise nuisances or that exceed those that the owner's title confers on her. Consequently, where government regulation prohibits all economically viable property uses previously permissible under relevant nuisance and property laws, there is a taking. *Id.* In other words, the government must justify total regulatory takings through application of nuisance law or through a determination that the owner did not, under existing property law, have the right to use the property as she used or proposed to use it.

      (2) Impermissible regulation: Under the guise of police power regulation, government cannot sub rosa redefine property rights by declaring certain uses of property inimical to the public interest. There is a danger that government will restrict uses of property in order to force an owner to confer an uncompensated benefit on the public rather than to suppress some harm to the public.

3. ***Appropriation for public functions:*** When the government takes private resources to "facilitate uniquely public functions," such as undertaking military maneuvers or flying government aircraft, its actions may amount to a taking. *Portsmouth Co. v. United States,* 260 U.S. 327 (1922) (military's repeated firing of guns over private land – invasion of airspace – a taking); *Causby v. United States,* 328 U.S. 256 (1946) (government invasions of airspace through overflights of private property, which destroyed property's value as a chicken farm, a taking).

E. **Noncompensable Regulation:** The government generally need not compensate when it takes property for a regulatory purpose. The following are recognized situations:

1. ***Ending public harms:*** The government may, without compensating the property owner, end public harms, that is, terminate nuisances or incompatible uses, caused by the property. *Miller v. Schoene,* 276 U.S. 272 (1928) (destruction of red cedar

trees, which carried a disease affecting apple trees, in vicinity of apple orchards); *Goldblatt v. Town of Hempstead,* 369 U.S. 590 (1962) (safety ordinance banning excavations below water table effectively terminating a sand and gravel mining business).

2. ***Land use regulation:*** Land use regulation which substantially advances state interests and permits an owner an "economically viable use of his land" does not constitute a taking. *Agins v. Tiburon,* 447 U.S. 255 (1980); *Nollan v. California Coastal Comm'n,* 483 U.S. 825 (1987).

   a. *Reciprocity of advantage:* Nondiscriminatory government zoning which creates a "reciprocity of advantage" is not compensable, even if there is a considerable diminution of value and the property cannot be used in the most beneficial or valuable way. *Goldblatt, supra; Agins v. Tiburon, supra.* Although zoning may prevent property from realizing its highest market value, limitations on use of the property can benefit it, *e.g.,* low-density zoning permits amenities unavailable in high-density zoning areas.

   b. *Other noncompensable takings:* In other cases involving zoning or other governmental regulation adversely affecting the value of, or even destroying, a property right, there is no compensable taking if:

     (1) assuming the remaining rights have value, the right affected or destroyed is but one right in the bundle (one "stick") of property rights. *Penn Central Transp. Co. v. City of New York,* 438 U.S. 104 (1978); *Keystone Bituminous Coal Ass'n. v. DeBenedictis,* 480 U.S. 470 (1987);

     (2) on an analysis comparing the property value remaining with the property value lost, it appears that:

       (a) the property retains a reasonable value or, if a business, can continue to earn a reasonable return. *Goldblatt, supra; Penn Central, supra; Keystone Bituminous, supra;*

       (b) the property, or reasonable expectancy, lost is not so great in comparison with the value of the property remaining that the regulation seems "confiscatory." *Penn Central, supra.*

   c. *Historic landmark zoning:* Although historic landmark zoning selectively zones particular parcels rather than areas, it is not discriminatory zoning in the bad sense, and does not for that reason constitute a taking. *Penn Central, supra.*

   d. *Rent control ordinances*

     (1) Rent control as a physical taking: In some circumstances rent control ordinances may have the effect of conferring real property appreciation gains on the tenant rather than the landlord. Such ordinances do not amount to a physical taking. There is a physical taking only when the government forces occupation of an owner's property, depriving the owner of its use.

Example: A mobile home park owner voluntarily rents his land and is under no obligation to continue to do so. Consequently, rent control of his lease prices does not deprive the owner of his right to physical use of his property. *Yee v. City of Escondido,* 112 S. Ct. 1522 (1992).

A tenant may reap the benefit of appreciation in the value of real property when a rent control ordinance prohibits mobile home park owners from raising rents on pads without government approval. In such a case, where law also bars landlords from terminating tenancies, the mobile home owner gains a valuable asset B a mobile home pad rented at a fixed and regulated rate B which she can transfer in the sale of the mobile home. In effect, because of the rent-controlled pad, the mobile home owner can sell her home for a greater price than she could if the pad were not rent-controlled.

(2) Rent control as a regulatory taking: While a rent control ordinance does not comprise a *physical* taking in violation of the Takings Clause, it remains an open question whether such an ordinance constitutes a *regulatory* taking. *Id.*

F. **Nexus Between Public Purpose and Regulation:** The regulatory means that a government chooses to achieve its stated public purpose must reasonably further it. Consequently, while governments may regulate development by imposing permit conditions, the conditions must actually serve the *same* purposes that development regulation aims at. If they do not, they may constitute a taking.

Example: In *Nollan, supra,* the California Coastal Commission's stated public purposes were protecting the public's ability to see the beach, helping the public overcome the psychological barrier to beach use created by shorefront developments, and preventing public beach congestion. To achieve these ends, it conditioned the right of beach property owners to build a house, which would block beach view access, on the owners' granting a public easement across their beachfront property. While the Commission could have prohibited building the house, conditioning permit approval on the grant of an easement did not serve the articulated purposes. Because the condition imposed – an easement – required the owners to relinquish their property right to exclude noninvitees, it constituted a taking.

G. **Remedy for "Temporary" Regulatory Takings:** When government regulation goes too far and constitutes a taking, the remedy, as in other takings cases, is the payment of just compensation and not simply invalidation of the regulation. *First English Evangelical Lutheran Church v. County of Los Angeles,* 482 U.S. 304 (1987). Of course, if the regulation is invalidated or the government chooses to rescind it, compensation is due only for the period that there was a taking.

FOURTEENTH AMENDMENT LIBERTY AND DUE PROCESS

▶ **CHAPTER SUMMARY**

CHAPTER 7: FOURTEENTH AMENDMENT LIBERTY AND DUE PROCESS

Introduction. The Fourteenth Amendment, in its Due Process and Equal Protection Clauses, has been a phenomenal wellspring of constitutional law regarding rights and liberties. The Due Process Clause, which comprises a separate study, reaches fundamental, and difficult, questions regarding constitutional limits on governmental power. Essentially, due process concerns itself with the aims of governmental action and the means, or ways, in which governments choose to act. As interpreted by the U.S. Supreme Court, the Due Process Clause places substantive restraints on the ends of government actions affecting individual liberty or property rights. Indeed, Fourteenth Amendment due process ultimately became the means through which the states of the United States were required to accord their residents the fundamental guarantees found in the Bill of Rights. The study of Fourteenth Amendment due process, however, usually begins with consideration of the Fourteenth Amendment Privileges and Immunities Clause, a failed start in the nationalization of the liberties and protections found in the Bill of Rights.

I. **THE BILL OF RIGHTS AND THE FOURTEENTH AMENDMENT: The Bill of Rights, which comprises the first ten amendments to the Constitution, was added to the Constitution in 1791 in order to provide specific protections for individuals from certain kinds of governmental actions. As originally interpreted, the Bill of Rights applied only to the federal government, not to the states.** *Barron v. Baltimore,* **32 U.S. 243 (1833). As a consequence of the Civil War, however, additional important amendments – the Thirteenth, Fourteenth, and Fifteenth – were added to the Constitution. These amendments were designed to end slavery and the myriad problems of continued unequal and unfair treatment, which the ex-slaves experienced, and to guarantee fair and equal treatment for all citizens. The most doctrinally generative of these amendments, the Fourteenth, protects citizens from state abridgment of their "privileges and immunities." It also prohibits states from depriving "any person of life, liberty, or property, without due process of law" and from denying persons equal protection. As detailed below, the Supreme Court interpreted "privileges and immunities" in a way that made the Clause virtually meaningless. Over time, however, the Fourteenth Amendment Due Process Clause became the vehicle for requiring the states to accord individuals the protections found in virtually all of the specific provisions of the Bill of Rights, together with others not listed there.**

    A. **Fourteenth Amendment Privileges and Immunities of National Citizenship and Article IV, § 2 Interstate Privileges and Immunities Distinguished:** There are two Privileges and Immunities Clauses in the Constitution. The interstate Privileges and Immunities Clause of Article IV, § 2 provides, "The Citizens of each State shall be entitled to all Privileges and Immunities of the Citizens in the several States." Interstate privileges and immunities ensures, for purposes of national harmony, that states treat noncitizens, in matters of fundamental importance, similarly to state citizens. There is also a Privileges and Immunities Clause in the Fourteenth Amendment. It reads differently: "No State shall make or enforce any law which shall abridge the privileges and immunities of citizens of the United States." One obvious reading of the meaning of the latter is that it refers to an unspecified list of fundamental rights of citizenship, which might include the rights listed in the Bill of Rights. But the Supreme Court did not read it so.

        1. *The* **Slaughter-House Cases:** In the *Slaughter-House Cases,* 16 Wall. 36 (1872), the Supreme Court first construed the general import of the Civil War

amendments, taking the position that the intent behind them was to end slavery and the grievances generated by it. Because the Court viewed the states, rather than the federal government, as the guarantor of citizens' civil rights, it was unwilling to read the Fourteenth Amendment Privileges and Immunities Clause as referring to any civil liberties already within state power to accord, secure, and protect.

a. *No federal role in guaranteeing civil liberties:* The Court therefore refused to read the Clause as transferring the function of protecting civil rights to the federal government. It is unclear whether the majority thought that the Clause made Bill of Rights guarantees applicable to the states as well as the federal government. Nevertheless, the *Slaughter-House Cases* have never been taken to support the proposition that the Clause did so, but rather for the reverse, that it *did not.*

b. *Meaning of Fourteenth Amendment Privileges and Immunities:* Having rejected the idea that the Clause federalized civil liberties, the Court was nonetheless obliged to give the Clause some meaning distinct from Article IV, Privileges and Immunities. It stated that Fourteenth Amendment Privileges and Immunities are those which are either specifically designated in the Constitution or necessarily implied from the character of the federal government. As all such rights would be protected even without the Fourteenth Amendment Privileges and Immunities Clause, this reading made it virtually meaningless as a distinctive protection of any civil liberties from state action.

2. ***Rights of national citizenship:*** The Court has on occasion listed some rights of national citizenship the Fourteenth Amendment Privileges and Immunities Clause protects from state actions. These have been stated to be the rights:

a. to travel from state to state,

b. to petition Congress for redress of grievances,

c. to vote for national office,

d. to assemble peaceably,

e. to discuss matters relating to national legislation,

f. to be protected from violence while in the custody of a U.S. Marshall, and

g. to notify federal officials of violations of U.S. laws. *Twining v. New Jersey,* 211 U.S. 78 (1908).

II. **THE MEANING OF FOURTEENTH AMENDMENT "LIBERTY" AND "DUE PROCESS": The concrete meaning of Fourteenth Amendment "liberty" and "due process" has always been something of a puzzle. "Liberty" possibly refers to some undefined set of "natural" rights or perhaps to the freedoms and rights listed in the Bill of Rights, or both. "Process" suggests a procedural focus, and "due" suggests "fair" or "according to some appropriate standard," but both ideas are too vague to decide specific cases.**

THE FOURTEENTH AMENDMENT: LIBERTY AND DUE PROCESS

A. "Incorporation" of the Bill of Rights: To give determinate meaning to Fourteenth Amendment liberty and due process, the Court has referred to some notion of natural rights, to the Bill of Rights, to the general idea of fairness, to history, to tradition, and to general American practice or consensus. Over many cases, Fourteenth Amendment liberty has come to stand for the fundamental freedoms in the Bill of Rights together with a list of implied fundamental rights not expressly stated in the Constitution. "Due process" is taken to mean "fundamental fairness," a fundamental fairness reflected by, but not limited to, most of the protections found in the Bill of Rights. The net result is that the Fourteenth Amendment "incorporates," and therefore makes applicable to the states, most of the freedoms and rights of the Bill of Rights. It also protects from state invasion certain rights, not expressly stated in, but inferred from the Bill of Rights, as well as guaranteeing fundamentally fair treatment.

B. Substantive Due Process: There has always been a natural law undercurrent in American constitutional law – of the idea that there are fundamental rights *not expressly stated* in the Constitution, which governments cannot invade without extraordinary justification. *Cf. Calder v. Bull,* 3 U.S. 386 (1798) (opinion of Chase, J.), *Fletcher v. Peck,* 10 U.S. 87 (1810), *Slaughter-House Cases, supra,* (dissent). Constitutional arguments regarding such fundamental rights have found a home in the Due Process Clause.

If we think of the Due Process Clause as imposing a requirement that the state act toward individuals with fundamental fairness, we can view the requirement in two different ways, procedurally and substantively. A procedural view of due process or fundamental fairness says, in effect, that the state may do anything not expressly forbidden it as long as it does it fairly, that is, in accordance with fair procedures. The substantive view of due process, however, is that there are some things the state cannot do, even if not expressly forbidden it, no matter how fair its procedures. In other words, on this view, due process itself imports implied substantive limits on the power of the state. This is the basic meaning of "substantive due process."

The general problem with the idea of substantive due process is its indeterminateness. "Due process" is a vague term; "fundamental fairness" is not appreciably more specific. When courts use due process critically to review, and sometimes invalidate, governmental action, the questions arise as to how and from where courts derive the schedule of substantive limits on government, usually expressed as "fundamental rights," they use to measure the legitimacy of governmental action. Since such rights are implied, what prevents judges from imposing their own value choices on the country in the guise of a constitutional restraint?

Under the rubric of due process, the Supreme Court has made several controversial forays into the field of substantive due process, recognized some important implied fundamental rights, and issued far-reaching rulings on constitutional law. Reactions to the Court's rulings and the role the judiciary assumed in invalidating legislation by declaring certain implied rights fundamental have deeply shaped current processes and techniques of judicial review in constitutional matters.

1. *Substantive due process and "liberty of contract":* Substantive due process, as a basis for invalidating legislation, made its first successful appearance in the so-called liberty of contract cases. In these cases, the Court construed the liberty protected by the Fourteenth Amendment to include not only physical liberty, but also "the right of the citizen to be free in the enjoyment of all his faculties; to be free

to use them in all lawful ways; to live and work where he will; to earn his livelihood by any lawful calling; to pursue any livelihood or avocation, and for that purpose to enter all contracts which may be proper, necessary and essential to his carrying out [those purposes]." *Allgeyer v. Louisiana,* 165 U.S. 578 (1897).

a. *Judicial review under substantive due process:* The Court coupled its broad reading of liberty, and liberty of contract, with a rigorous standard of judicial review. This standard rejected some legislative ends as being illegitimate, that is, not within the power to the state. It also sometimes required that the means the legislature used to achieve its legitimate ends have some close connection to them.

Example: In the famous, or infamous, case of *Lochner v. New York,* 198 U.S. 45 (1905), the Court declared unconstitutional, on grounds of interference with liberty of contract, a New York law prohibiting bakeries from employing workers for more than ten hours a day or sixty hours a week. The Court implicitly rejected the idea that the state could seek the end of equalizing the bargaining power of employers and employees. Considering the hours limitation as being a means to achieve a health purpose, the Court in effect overruled the legislative judgment that an hour limitation was necessary or appropriate to protect health. Thereafter, the Court used these stricter standards and its views of liberty of contract to invalidate numerous laws regulating prices, labor, and business entry. *See,* for example, *Coppage v. Kansas,* 236 U.S. 1 (1915); *Adkins v. Children's Hosp.,* 261 U.S. 525 (1923); *New State Ice Co. v. Liebmann,* 285 U.S. 262 (1930).

b. *The overthrow of economic substantive due process and pronouncement of the rational basis test:* In a series of cases beginning in 1934, the Court, in response to New Deal legislation and pressures, reversed its course and established the rational basis test, a new noninterventionist principle for constitutional review of governmental regulation of social and economic matters. Today, the Court in applying this test will uphold socioeconomic legislation as long as it has a rational basis. Under this standard as it works in practice, the Court accepts any constitutionally nonforbidden end as legitimate and upholds legislation where "any state of facts either known or which could reasonably be assumed" supports it. *United States v. Carolene Products Co.,* 304 U.S. 144 (1938). In other words, the Court no longer second-guesses legislatures regarding social and economic legislation.

2. ***Noneconomic substantive due process:*** Early substantive due process cases also recognized noneconomic personal liberties as falling within the liberty protected by Fourteenth Amendment due process.

Example: In *Meyer v. Nebraska,* 262 U.S. 390 (1923), the Court added to its *Allgeyer* definition of Fourteenth Amendment liberty the rights "to acquire useful knowledge, to marry, to establish a home and bring up children, to worship God accord to the dictates of . . . conscience, and generally to enjoy those privileges long recognized at common law as essential to the orderly pursuit of happiness by free men." This line of substantive due process cases has survived the overturning of *Lochner* and its liberty-of-contract approach.

a. *Standard of review:* In cases involving noneconomic rights recognized by substantive due process, the Court uses the highest standard of judicial review, that is, strict scrutiny. Under this standard, states, in order to justify action infringing the right, must show a "compelling state interest" and must also show that there is no alternative way of achieving its compelling end that has less impact on an individual's exercise of the right.

b. *Rights of personal liberty or liberty interests:* Substantive due process recognizes the following rights of personal liberty, or so-called liberty interests.

(1) Right of privacy or autonomy: There are specific rights protecting certain kinds of autonomy or private choices and some important kinds of intimate association. While specific, they are often referred to as falling within a right of privacy or autonomy.

There is, however, no general liberty interest in privacy or personal autonomy that covers all basic and intimate personal life choices. The liberty interests the Due Process Clause protects are those that are rooted in the history and traditions of the nation and that can be carefully described and formulated. That many constitutionally protected liberty interests "sound in personal autonomy does not warrant the sweeping conclusion that any and all important, intimate, and personal decisions are so protected." *Washington v. Glucksberg*, 65 U.S.L.W. 3481 (1997).

(a) Within marriage and the traditional family relationships, this right includes the right to create, maintain, or change family relationships: to marry, *Zablocki v. Redhail*, 434 U.S. 374 (1978); to divorce, *Boddie v. Connecticut*, 401 U.S. 371 (1971); *Zablocki, supra;* to procreate, nurture, educate, and control children, *Meyer v. Nebraska, supra; Pierce v. Society of Sisters*, 268 U.S. 510 (1925); *Parham v. J.R.*, 442 U.S. 584 (1979); *Parham v. Hughes*, 441 U.S. 347 (1979) *(but see Planned Parenthood of Missouri v. Danforth*, 428 U.S. 52 (1976), to maintain the parent-child relationship; and to live with family members, *M.L.B. v. S.L.J.*, 519 U.S. 102 (1997); *Moore v. East Cleveland*, 431 U.S. 494 (1977). It appears to include the right to engage in consensual sexual practices within marriage. *Griswold v. Connecticut*, 381 U.S. 479 (1965); *Bowers v. Hardwick*, 478 U.S. 186 (1986) (by implication).

(i) Parents have a due process right to make decisions regarding the rearing of their children, including decisions about third party visitation rights. Without some good reason, beyond a judge's determination that a third party's visitation of a child are in the child's best interests, the state cannot intervene in a fit parent's decision regarding visitation rights. *Troxel v. Granville*, 120 S. Ct. 2054 (2000).

(ii) The family relationship right does not include the right of family members to order the withdrawal of life-sustaining medical treatment for an incompetent family member who has unrecoverably lost all cognitive faculties. *Cruzan v. Director, Missouri Dept. of Health*, 497 U.S. 261 (1990) (states may require "clear and convincing" proof that the affected individual desired termination of life support in such circumstances).

(b) Outside of traditional marriage and family relationships, the reach of the right is more uncertain. It includes the rights to procreate, to nurture, educate, and control children. It may include certain rights of sexual liberty, such as the use of contraceptives, *Eisenstadt v. Baird*, 405 U.S. 438 (1972); *Carey v. Population Services Int'l*, 431 U.S. 678 (1977). It may go so far as the right to engage in consensual heterosexual sexual practices (by implication from *Bowers v. Hardwick, supra; Eisenstadt, supra; Carey, supra;* and *Roe v. Wade, infra, but see Hollenbaugh v. Carnegie Free Libr.*, 439 U.S. 1052 (1978) (refusal to review discharge of public employees for "living together in a state of open adultery"). It apparently does not include the right to live with unrelated persons, *Belle Terre v. Borass*, 412 U.S. 1 (1974). It does not include the right to engage in consensual homosexual sexual practices. *Bowers v. Hardwick, supra.*

(i) A biological father of a child born to a woman married to, and cohabiting with, another man at the time of birth does not have a substantive due process "liberty" right to be declared the natural father with parental rights. *Michael H. v. Gerald D.*, 491 U.S. 110 (1989). Tradition is a test of whether a certain relationship should be viewed as a fundamental right, and our society has not traditionally accorded such a father parental rights. *Id.* (plurality). Similarly, the child of such a natural father has no liberty interest in a legally recognized filial relationship with him. *Id.*

(ii) The right includes the right of a woman to decide whether or not to bear a child. (For extended discussion, *see* § 3., *infra.*)

(c) Refusing unwanted medical treatment: Persons have a liberty interest in refusing involuntary medical treatment. *Washington v. Harper*, 494 U.S. 210 (1990) (administration of antipsychotic drugs); *Vitek v. Jones*, 445 U.S. 480 (1980) (transfer to a mental hospital together with behavior modification); *Cruzan, supra* (right of dying patient to refuse artificial feeding).

(d) Right to die; physician-assisted suicide: Some people with incurable diseases suffer greatly, and even the best of medical care may not be able to alleviate their pain, debilitation, or the burdens they feel their condition places on others. In some cases, such persons may prefer to die rather than continue to suffer, deteriorate, and impose burdens. To die with dignity, they may wish to have a physician assist them to commit suicide, by administering a lethal, but nonpainful, medicine. The history and traditions of the country, however, reveal that it has consistently prohibited assisted suicide, and there is no constitutionally recognized liberty interest in a right to assisted suicide. *Washington v. Glucksberg, supra.* State prohibitions on assisted suicides are rational means to advance state interests in preserving human life, in insuring medical integrity and ethics, and in protecting vulnerable and nonresponsible parties from ill-considered or mistaken decisions about whether to live. *Id.*

(2) Liberty rights while in state custody: Substantive due process guarantees individuals in state custody the rights of personal security and safety,

freedom from unnecessary bodily restraints, and to care and training adequate to ensure freedom from undue restraint. *Youngberg v. Romeo,* 457 U.S. 307 (1982). It does not, however, include a generalized right to treatment or rehabilitation for those institutionalized, and there is considerable judicial deference to professional judgments regarding the disposition of those held in institutionalized settings.

(3) The right of privacy or autonomy and abortion: In the controversial decision, *Roe v. Wade,* 410 U.S. 113 (1973), the Court held that the Constitution implied a fundamental right of privacy which includes within it the right of a woman to decide to end a pregnancy without undue state interference. In *Planned Parenthood v. Casey,* 112 S. Ct. 2791 (1992), a bare majority of the Court strongly reaffirmed this right as a protected liberty under the Fourteenth Amendment. *Casey,* however, changed the framework which the *Roe* Court established to scrutinize abortion regulations. Consequently, in order to understand current constitutional law respecting the woman's right to decide whether or not to bear a child, it is essential first to review *Roe.*

(a) The basic premises and rules of *Roe v. Wade:* In *Roe v. Wade,* the Court, concluding that a fetus was not a person for Fourteenth Amendment purposes. It held that a pregnant woman has a fundamental right of privacy, which included the right to decide, prior to the time her fetus became viable and with the assistance of her physician, not to be pregnant. It also held that the state has interests, some of which, while not compelling during the early stages of a pregnancy, could be compelling in later stages of a pregnancy. These interests are the health of the mother, the interest in potential life, and the interests of third parties. *Casey* reaffirmed these basic premises.

(b) *Roe's* balancing of the woman's fundamental right and state interests: The *Roe* Court devised a formula for balancing the woman's right to choose not to have a child against the states' interests in regulating abortion through a so-called trimester framework. Under this framework, the pregnancy was divided into three three-month stages.

i)   During the first trimester, the Court held that state interests were not compelling, and the state could not interfere with a woman's decision to end a pregnancy. In effect, as confirmed in many subsequent cases, the Court held that it would apply strict scrutiny review to any kind of state regulation affecting a woman's decision during the first trimester of a pregnancy.

ii) During the second trimester, the state interest in the health of the mother became compelling, and the state could regulate abortion procedures to secure the mother's health and safety.

iii) At the third trimester, which is the approximate point at which the fetus becomes viable, the state interest in potential life was compelling. At this point, the state could regulate or prevent abortions, except where necessary to protect the life or health of the prospective mother.

(c) Viability and *Casey's* overthrow of the trimester framework: While reaffirming the right of a woman to decide, previability, whether to end a pregnancy without undue state interference, the *Casey* Court held that the state had an important interest in potential life throughout a pregnancy. In the *Casey* view (dominating plurality), *Roe's* trimester framework, and subsequent cases utilizing it, had undervalued this interest. Under *Casey,* as under *Roe,* the state interest in potential life is compelling at viability, at which point the state may forbid abortions. Prior to viability, however, the state interest in potential life is sufficiently great that it can take some steps to promote and protect potential life as long as it does not impose an "undue burden" on a woman's decision to end a pregnancy. Consequently, in reviewing state regulation of abortion, the essential questions are whether the regulation affects a woman's decision pre- or postviability; and, if previability, whether the regulation unduly burdens her decision. *Casey* thus overturns *Roe's* trimester framework and replaces its strict scrutiny review standard with an undue burden standard of review.

(d) "Undue burden": A state abortion regulation imposes an undue burden on a woman's decision to end a pregnancy when "its purpose or effect is to place a substantial obstacle in the path of a woman seeking an abortion before the fetus attains viability." *Casey, supra.* State laws or regulations having a valid, independent purpose, that incidentally make it more difficult or more expensive for a woman to obtain an abortion, are not necessarily unconstitutional. They are unconstitutional only when they impose an undue burden. *Cf., infra.*

(e) Abortion regulations unduly burdening a woman's decision: State abortion regulations, which substantially affect a woman's decision whether to end a pregnancy are unconstitutional. The Court has decided many cases regarding such regulations, and the Court has effectively defined which previability regulations are permissible. As revised by *Casey,* they are as follows:

(i) State health, safety, and record-keeping provisions

a) Bans on specific abortion procedures; "partial birth abortions." There are two significant second-trimester abortion procedures, each of which have variations: dilation and evacuation (D&E) and dilation and extraction (D&X). It is unclear whether either procedure is safer and under what circumstances one is preferable to the other. Both procedures involve killing the fetus, but differ in how they do so. Without getting into many details, the essential difference is whether the fetus is substantially delivered into the vagina before the killing takes place. In the D&X procedure, that some call "partial birth abortion," the killing takes place after delivery into the vagina. All but the head of the fetus is extracted from the body. Then the head is collapsed and the dead fetus is fully delivered.

All abortion ends the life of the fetus, and the D&E procedure can involve dismemberment of the fetus. Some states, however, have sought to ban the D&X procedure, rather than

7

the D&E procedure, because of the conflation with birth and the fetal killing after an almost completed birth. In *Stenberg v. Carhart,* 120 S. Ct. 2597 (2000), Nebraska sought to outlaw "partial birth abortions", except where necessary to save the mother's life *when physically endangered.* It defined a "partial birth abortion" as partially delivering "vaginally a living unborn child before killing: and further defined that as deliberately and intentionally delivering into the vagina a living unborn child, or a substantial portion thereof...."

The Court held that the Nebraska statute lacked, as constitutionally required, an exception where medical judgment, without the physical endangerment limitation, concluded using the D&X procedure was necessary for the health of the mother. It also held that the statute imposed an undue burden on a woman's decision to end a pregnancy because the statute, as written, was applicable to the D&E procedure as well as the D&X procedure. This was because the wording of the statute – "delivery into the vagina a living unborn child, or a *substantial portion thereof*" (*ital. added*) – reached D&E procedures where a part of the fetus was delivered through the cervix into the vagina before the fetus was killed. *Stenberg v. Carhart, supra.* (The case does not decide whether a more narrowly drawn statute reaching only the D&X procedure would be constitutional. The fact, however, that the state cannot substitute its judgment for a medical judgment about abortion methods protective of the mother's health suggests that states cannot completely outlaw the D&X procedure.)

b) Informed written consent: A state may require that a woman give informed, written consent to an abortion. *Casey, supra; Planned Parenthood of Missouri v. Danforth, supra.* Informed consent is a medicolegal term referring to a voluntary decision to undergo a medical procedure following a physician's statement of the medical and other significant benefits and risks of the procedure.

c) Required preabortion information: As a part of ensuring informed consent, and to promote its interest in potential life, the state may provide a woman with information regarding the medical assistance benefits available for childbirth. It can include information regarding the liability of the father for child support; reading material detailing fetal development and the consequences of abortion on the fetus; and adoption and other services relating to childbirth or child-rearing assistance. *Id.* (This overturns prior case law and is an effect of *Casey's* shift from a strict scrutiny standard to an undue burden standard.)

d) State preference for childbirth: As a part of its informed consent information package, the state may include efforts to persuade a woman to choose childbirth over abortion. As long as the information the state provides is truthful, nonmisleading, and does not impose an undue burden, providing a woman with such information is constitutional. *Id.* (To the degree that this holding suggests that some state efforts to persuade a woman contemplating an abortion to prefer childbirth do not impose an undue burden, it changes prior law.)

e) Physician counseling: A state may require that only a physician counsel and obtain informed consent. *Id.* (Overturning prior law.)

f) Delay: Although delay in obtaining an abortion may make an abortion more difficult or expensive (*e.g.,* through repeated visits to a physician and lodging costs), a state may require that a woman wait twenty-four hours after preabortion counseling before obtaining an abortion. *Id.* (Overturning prior law.)

g) Place of abortion: While the state has an important interest in maternal health, it may not impose health or safety regulations which place a substantial obstacle in a woman's path to an abortion, but are not reasonably necessary for health and safety. Thus, a state may not require that all midstage abortions be performed in a hospital. *Akron v. Akron Center for Reproductive Health,* 462 U.S. 416 (1983) (as reinterpreted through *Casey*).

h) Record-keeping: As long as it protects the woman's privacy and confidentiality, the state may require the keeping, for statistical and health purposes, of abortion health-related information. *Casey, supra; Danforth, supra.* Such information can include the names of the physician and facility; the woman's age and number of prior pregnancies and abortions; the type of procedure, the basis for determining the abortion was medically necessary, and the gestational age and weight of the fetus; marital status of the woman; and the like.

ii) State regulation in the interests of third parties and minors

a) Spousal consent or notification: The legal decision whether to end a pregnancy is the woman's, and the male responsible for conception cannot legally prevent an abortion. Although both sexes have a fundamental right to procreate, as she bears the burden of birth and child rearing, the woman has the sole right to decide whether to abort. Spousal consent and notification requirements are unconstitutional. *Casey, supra; Danforth, supra.*

b) Minors and parental consent; judicial bypass: The Court has sought to balance the pregnant minor's right to decide whether to end a pregnancy against concerns about her ability to decide maturely and intelligently and against legitimate parental and familial interests. At the same time, the Court has attempted to ensure that parents will not be able to veto abortions or interfere unduly in the minor's decision whether to end a pregnancy. It has therefore held that a state may impose a parental consent requirement when it provides a pregnant minor with an alternative way to get approval for an abortion if a parent cannot or does not consent or, for some good reason, should not be notified. *Casey, supra; Bellotti v. Baird,* 443 U.S. 622 (1979). That alternative way is a fast and anonymous judicial determination, now called a "judicial bypass." States may not require the consent of both parents, which might be difficult or impossible to obtain when the parents are divorced or separated or where there is an abusive or vindictive parent. *Hodgson v. Minnesota,* 497 U.S. 417 (1990).

c) Parental notification requirements: While parental notice requirements differ from consent requirements in not giving parents a veto over a minor's decision to have an abortion, they present similar problems when they prohibit an abortion without notice. A pregnant minor, however, may have good reasons for not wishing to notify a parent, for example, when the parent has abused her physically or sexually. Parental notification statutes having a judicial bypass procedure to accommodate such cases are constitutional. *Casey, supra. Ohio v. Akron Center for Reproductive Health,* 497 U.S. 502 (1990).

d) Judicial bypass procedure: A state must provide judicial bypass procedures, in which a judge may authorize a minor to obtain an abortion, where the minor is unable, or unwilling, for good reason, to obtain parental consent or give parental notification. To be constitutional, such procedures must allow the minor to show she has the information and maturity to make her abortion decision. Alternatively, if she cannot make the decision herself, the procedures must permit a showing that the abortion or a failure to give parental notification would be in her best interests. Procedures must ensure the minor's anonymity; and, because delay may increase the physical risks associated with abortion, be sufficiently swift to allow the minor an effective opportunity to have an abortion. *Lambert v. Wicklund,* 520 U.S. 292 (1997); *Bellotti, supra; Akron Center, supra.*

iii) State viability regulations

a) Physician requirement: A state may restrict the performance of abortions to physicians. *Mazurek v. Armstrong,* 65 U.S.L.W. 3524 (1997). In postviability abortions, except in those situations where the health of the woman might be endangered while waiting for the arrival of a second physician, the state may require that two physicians attend the abortion. One physician would attend to the woman and the other to the fetus on the chance that it might be delivered alive. *Planned Parenthood Ass'n of Kansas City v. Ashcroft,* 462 U.S. 476 (1983).

b) Determination of viability: The state may not determine when a particular fetus is viable, even using objective factors, but must leave that for the attending physician. *Colautti v. Franklin,* 439 U.S. 379 (1979). The state, however, may require a physician, prior to performing an abortion, to conduct viability tests on a fetus when it is possible that the fetus is viable. *Webster v. Reproductive Health Services,* 492 U.S. 490 (1989).

c) Method of abortion: A state may not, in the interests of the fetus, dictate a method of abortion less dangerous to the fetus, but more dangerous to the woman.

d) Prohibition: A state may prohibit abortions of viable fetuses, but may neither question a doctor's decision that the health of a woman carrying a viable fetus requires that she have an abortion nor decide whether a particular fetus is viable. *Colautti, supra.*

(f) Abortion funding: Governments have no constitutional obligation to provide welfare benefits, and none to fund abortions, even medically necessary abortions, and even where governments fund childbirth. *Maher v. Roe,* 432 U.S. 464 (1977); *Harris v. McRae,* 448 U.S. 297 (1980).

i) The *Roe v. Wade* right is *not* the right to have an abortion, but a right that the state not unduly interfere with a woman's decision whether or not to have an abortion. There is a difference between state interference and state encouragement, and states have greater authority to encourage activities, such as conception and childbirth, as a matter of public policy than they have to interfere. Refusal to fund abortions is not an interference with a decision whether or not to have an abortion.

ii) States may refuse to allow public employees to perform abortions in public hospital facilities, and neither private physicians nor their patients have any constitutional right of access to public facilities for the performance of abortions. *Webster, supra.*

iii) States may forbid the use of public funds for, or public employee participation in, encouraging or counseling abortions. *Webster, supra.*

(g) Refusal to fund abortion counseling: Under the due process clauses, government has no duty to provide persons with aid, even if such aid is necessary to secure life, liberty, or property. Except in certain contexts, *e.g.,* criminal trials, the government has no obligation to subsidize the exercise of constitutional rights. Therefore, the government's refusal to fund abortion counseling does not violate a woman's right to choose whether or not to have a child. *Rust v. Sullivan,* 111 S. Ct. 1759 (1991).

c. *Property rights – excessive penalties:* While the Constitution provides some specific protections for property rights, *e.g.,* the Takings, Just Compensation, and Contract Clauses, substantive due process also provides some protection. Specifically, substantive due process protects against state imposition of fines "so grossly excessive as to amount to a deprivation of property without due process of law." *Waters-Pierce Oil Co. v. Texas (No. 1),* 212 U.S. 86, 111 (1909). There may be procedural due process problems as well. In the case of punitive damage awards, an award may be so disproportionate to misconduct that possible tort-feasors cannot be said to have had notice of the sanctions that might be imposed on them. *BMW of North America, Inc. v. Gore,* 517 U.S. 559 (1996).

(1) Punitive damages: Where there are appropriate procedural safeguards, a jury award of punitive damages does not per se violate substantive due process. As jury punitive damage awards became prominent and controversial, business and insurance interests complained that the awards were often extreme, *i.e.,* so disproportionate as to bear no relationship to the actual misconduct of defendants. The Court originally rejected these criticisms, but has recently changed course.

Example: In *Pacific Mutual Life Ins. Co. v. Haslip,* 499 U.S. 1 (1991), the defendant challenged the American common law system of awarding punitive damages. Under that system, juries, under general instructions from trial judges, have large discretion to determine the amount of punitive damage awards. The defendant's general complaint was that the system allowed juries such unbridled discretion that awards were essentially arbitrary and often resulted from prejudice against large, wealthy, and out-of-state interests. The Court held, however, that common law methods of assessing punitive damages did not per se violate substantive due process. Where there are appropriate procedural protections, the system itself is constitutional. For example, where the trial judge gives juries adequate guidance through instructions on punitive damages and there is adequate post-verdict review of awards, taking into account such factors as the extremity of the wrong, retribution, deterrence, the extent of wrongful gain, and the like.

(2) Excessive punitive damages: In particular cases, jury punitive damage awards in litigation may be so excessive as to amount to a denial of substantive due process. *Haslip, supra; TXO Production Corp. v. Alliance Resources Corp.,* 61 U.S.L.W. 4466 (1993).

(3) Excessive punitive damages – standard of review: No Court majority has agreed on a clear standard for reviewing punitive damage awards to determine whether they are excessive. The Court has rejected both a rational basis standard and heightened scrutiny. *TXO Production Corp., supra.* A plurality of the Court, however, considers excessive penalty claims as follows. Assuming that the trial jury was adequately instructed and followed fair procedures, and there was adequate postverdict review, the jury's award is entitled to a strong presumption of validity. Given that

presumption, the question then is whether, taking into account all factors that may rationally affect punitive awards, the award was reasonable. *Id.*

Example: In *TXO Production,* a jury awarded the plaintiff $19,000 in actual damages and $10 million in punitive damages, a punishment 526 times actual damages. A plurality of the Court held that, taking into account the potential harm of TXO's actions, its malicious and fraudulent actions, and the need to deter it from such actions in the future, the $10 million award was not so unreasonable or arbitrary as to be grossly excessive in violation of substantive due process.

Recently, the Court has articulated some of the matters to be taken into account in determining whether a punitive damages award is excessive. These are the degree of reprehensibility of the conduct, the ratio between the punitive damages award and actual damages, and state civil and criminal sanctions for comparable misconduct. *BMW of North America, Inc. v. Gore, supra.* In *BMW,* the Court held that, without aggravating factors suggesting particularly reprehensible conduct, a punitive damages award of $2 million in a case involving actual damages of $4,000 – a ratio of 500 to 1 and an award seriously out of line with civil or criminal penalties for similar misconduct – was grossly excessive.

(4) Excessive punitive damages – out-of-state activity: While states have considerable latitude in determining the level of punitive damages allowable, they may not impose such damages in order to change tort-feasors, lawful conduct in other states. *BMW of North America, Inc. v. Gore, supra* (conduct in conjunction with auto sales deemed fraudulent in Alabama, but lawful in other states).

C. Procedural Due Process

1. *Procedural due process in criminal cases – incorporation of the criminal procedural protections of the Bill of Rights:* On a case-by-case basis, the Court has decided that the states must accord suspected or accused persons virtually all the criminal procedural protections of the Bill of Rights. While the details of constitutional law relating to criminal procedure are beyond the scope of this outline, the following is of general importance:

a. *Differing state and federal standards regarding Bill of Rights protections:* Once having decided that Fourteenth Amendment due process required the states to abide by a specific provision of the Bill of Rights, the Court had to determine what a due process application of the specific provision required of the states. This problem arose because, in many cases, the content or meaning of specific provisions of the Bill of Rights was not fully defined. In addition, prior federal case law interpreting specific provisions of the Bill of Rights did not always distinguish between what was constitutionally required and what federal courts may have added from common law or their authority to supervise the administration of criminal justice. This forced the Court to reassess what was "fundamental" to the specific provision. The result, in some cases, was that the states were not required to abide by the federal rules regarding the specific provision.

Example: The Sixth Amendment provides for the right of jury trial in criminal cases. According to federal law, juries in criminal cases must have twelve persons and must return unanimous verdicts. In *Duncan v. Louisiana,* 391 U.S. 145 (1968), the Court decided that the Due Process Clause required selective incorporation of the jury trial right against the states. In *Williams v. Florida,* 399 U.S. 78 (1970), however, the Court decided that the twelve-person requirement was not "fundamental" to the jury trial right and that states therefore need not provide twelve-person juries in criminal cases. Thereafter, in *Apodaca v. Oregon,* 406 U.S. 404 (1971), it decided that states, unlike the federal government, did not have to provide unanimous juries.

2. ***Procedural due process in civil matters:*** Both the Fifth and the Fourteenth Amendments proscribe the state from taking life, liberty, or property without due process of law. The prohibition is both substantive and procedural. It is substantive in that the state would violate due process if it took life, liberty, or property without a legitimate reason for doing so. It is procedural in that the state can take life, liberty, or property for the right reasons if it does so in the right way, *i.e.,* according to fair procedures.

   a. *Life, liberty, and property interests entitled to protection:* The Supreme Court has defined life, liberty, and property interests narrowly and legalistically rather than in accordance with what might be common understandings.

      (1) Life and liberty interests generally: Curiously, the "life" interest protected by procedural due process is ill-defined, and there is little Supreme Court jurisprudence directly treating it in that context. Instead, the "life" interest features prominently in constitutional criminal procedure decisions, and there, overwhelmingly in death penalty cases. Similarly, the "liberty" interests involved in a person's being free of improper incarceration are also subjects of many criminal procedure decisions. (The Constitution, in the Fourth, Fifth, Sixth, and Eighth Amendments, provided specific procedural protections for criminal defendants, and the Court has used these to articulate the procedural protections the Constitution accords the accused. Constitutional criminal procedure protections are fully explored in criminal procedure courses, and this outline focuses instead on civil procedural protections.)

      (2) Liberty interests: The Court has acknowledged the following liberty interests:

         (a) Liberties contained in the Bill of Rights, and other Court-defined fundamental liberties: These rights include the rights of privacy or autonomy and the family relationship rights the Court has held protected under substantive due process.

            Example: Where a state seeks to remove a child from its parents on the grounds of their unfitness, it must prove unfitness by clear and convincing evidence. *Santosky v. Kramer,* 455 U.S. 745 (1982).

         (b) State law-defined liberties: Liberties which a state grants under its own law (state constitutional law, statutory law, or common law) are liberty interests protected under the procedural due process provisions of the federal Constitution. "[A] State creates a protected liberty interest by placing substantive limits on its official discretion." *Olim v. Wakinakona*, 461 U.S. 238, 249 (1983).

Example: Suppose a state provides by statute that juries shall sentence in felony criminal cases. Following conviction of a felon, but before sentencing, the trial judge mistakenly discharges the jury. To remedy his error, he sentences the felon. The felon would have a federal constitutional claim that he was deprived of his liberty interest in jury sentencing. On the other hand, if a state gives prison officials completely unfettered discretion to transfer prisoners between prisons, a prisoner has no state-defined liberty interest in not being transferred. *Meachum v. Fano*, 427 U.S. 215 (1976).

(c) "Federal" liberties: This is a vague, ill-defined category composed of "liberties" the Court has defined ad hoc, roughly describable as certain freedoms of action or freedoms from governmental restraint. This category includes the physical liberty to be free of improper governmental punishments or restraints, such as institutionalization for mental illness without a fair determination of the necessity for doing so. It also includes the right to contract, to engage in the common occupations of life, to engage in activities or retain licenses essential to modern life, and reputational interests.

Examples: In *Addington v. Texas*, 441 U.S. 418 (1979), the Court held that a state cannot involuntarily commit a person to a mental institution without clear and convincing evidence that the person is dangerous to himself or another.

The government must accord a hearing if it seeks to terminate an individual's license to practice a profession, *In re Ruffalo*, 390 U.S. 544 (1968), or if it seeks to terminate an individual's automobile driver's license, *Bell v. Burson*, 402 U.S. 535 (1971).

In *Wisconsin v. Constantineau,* 400 U.S. 433 (1971), state law authorized the police chief to post in liquor stores the names of excessive drinkers, which posting would proscribe them from buying liquor for a year. The posting, if efficacious, would have limited the freedom of action of those named, and the Court held this was the deprivation of a liberty interest which required a hearing.

In two cases, the Court addressed the issue of prison transfers. In *Meachum v. Fano, supra,* the Court held that administrative transfer of a prisoner from one prison to another did not involve a liberty interest. In other words, unless state law otherwise provides, convicted prisoners generally have no liberty interest in any particular level or place of confinement. In *Vitek v. Jones,* 445 U.S. 480 (1980), however, the Court held that a prisoner has a liberty interest which protects her from summary transfers from a prison to a prison mental institution. The difference between the two cases lies in the facts that transfer to a mental institution requires a factual finding of mental illness. The transfer, which would have involved a behavior modification program utilizing the drug prolixin, constituted a major change in conditions of confinement, unlike the transfer in *Meachum, supra.*

b. *The following property interests are protected:*

(1) State defined property: "Property" certainly includes the common law forms of property and includes all other kinds of state law defined property. For instance, wages are certainly property, as are a debtor's interests in items a creditor has seized.

(2) Entitlements: In the era of the social welfare state, many persons receive statutory benefits, such as welfare or disability payments, and can obtain various kinds of statutory licenses or privileges, such as a driver's license or a medical technician's certification. The Court has acknowledged that such statutory "entitlements" constitute cognizable "property" interests.

Examples: The circumstances under which persons are entitled to receive welfare benefits are statutorily defined. If an individual qualifies under the provision of such a statute, he is "entitled" to receive the benefit. The benefits qualify as "property" and may not be terminated without an appropriate hearing. *Goldberg v. Kelly,* 397 U.S. 254 (1970).

In the past, many states had laws which required revocation of the license of an uninsured driver involved in an accident unless the driver posted a bond for alleged damages. In *Bell v. Burson,* 402 U.S. 535 (1971), the Court held that a driver's license is a "property" interest calling for due process protections.

c. *Expectations:* The Court has also recognized that contract provisions, or even mutual understandings, can confer a "property" interest, although certainly not all will do so.

Examples: In *Perry v. Sindermann,* 408 U.S. 593 (1972), the Court found a property interest where the nontenured college teacher had been employed for ten years and alleged the college had a de facto tenure policy but had failed to rehire him in violation of that policy.

In *Board of Regents of State Colleges v. Roth,* 408 U.S. 564 (1972), however, Roth had only a one-year teacher's contract and there was no policy or understanding regarding renewal. At the expiration of a year, his contract was not renewed. He had no property interest as his contract was for one year, and that had ended.

d. *The relationship between substantive property rights and procedure*

(1) State-defined procedures as affecting the substantive property right: For a time, the Court flirted with the idea that state procedures for taking a property interest determined what the substantive property interest was.

Example: In *Bishop v. Wood,* 426 U.S. 341 (1976), a police officer classified as a permanent employee was dismissed without a hearing. The relevant ordinance called for a "for cause" dismissal, that is, for performance failures, negligence, unfitness, etc. The ordinance, however, did not provide for judicial review of the city manager's decision to discharge. The Court viewed this "procedural" provision (no review) as qualifying or negating the substantive job right of employment until termination for cause. Consequently, the officer in reality had a job without security of employment and therefore no property interest.

(2) Substantive and procedural rights distinct: This foregoing view was rejected in *Cleveland Bd. of Educ. v. Loudermill,* 470 U.S. 532 (1985). Loudermill, a security guard, was discharged when it was discovered that he had been convicted of a felony. He was not given a pretermination opportunity to contest the charge of dishonesty or to challenge the dismissal. Under Ohio law, he could be discharged only for misfeasance, malfeasance, or nonfeasance in office. The relevant statute further provided, however, that he could be discharged without a pretermination hearing. His only recourse was posttermination administrative review of a written appeal. The Court held that substantive rights and procedural rights are distinct and that procedural rights do not define substantive rights. If the state confers a property right to employment, it cannot terminate that right without adequate procedures.

e. *Deliberate deprivation:* Due process protects life, liberty, and property interests only from *deliberate* deprivation, not from *negligent* deprivation. *Daniels v. Williams,* 474 U.S. 327 (1986).

f. *State tort cases:* The state, by making its courts available for tort suits against state officials and thus providing an elaborate set of procedures for handling such claims, satisfies all appropriate procedural due process requirements, albeit postdeprivation. *Ingraham v. Wright,* 430 U.S. 651 (1977); *Parratt v. Taylor,* 451 U.S. 527 (1981).

(1) This approach to state tort cases avoids a constitutional dilemma, which would otherwise arise in a special class of cases involving certain kinds of liberty or property takings, such as where a state official acts tortiously, and negligently or intentionally destroys someone's property. Since a state official was involved, normal application of procedural due process doctrines would impel a conclusion that such a taking was unconstitutional because it had been done without notice, hearing, opportunity to be heard, etc.

(2) But such a conclusion would mean that every claim against a state official, which would be a tort claim under state law, would become a federal constitutional claim for which an action could be brought in federal court. Federal courts would displace state courts in all tort claims involving state officials as defendants.

3. *Figuring out what procedures procedural due process requires in any given case:* In speaking of procedural protections accorded when the state seeks to take or terminate an individual's life, liberty, or property interests, we refer to various devices used to ensure that such state actions are timed correctly and that they are fair and accurate. While there is probably a limitless range of attention and care the state could give to such actions, there are three factors which, balanced against one another in a cost-benefit way, determine the procedural design

appropriate to a given type of case. These are: (1) the private interest affected; (2) the risk of error inherent in the given procedure as opposed to alternative procedures; and (3) the interest the government is seeking to protect and further, together with the fiscal and administrative burdens of alternative procedures. *Matthews v. Eldridge,* 424 U.S. 319 (1976).

a. *Using the factors:* Using factors 1 and 3, *supra,* is fairly easy. One just has to determine the significance and relative importance of the interests involved. As the importance of the individual interest increases, one would normally enhance the procedures leading to a taking or termination decision, so that they become more careful and refined. As the government's interest becomes more significant or pressing, and as costs of procedures become an important factor, one would incline toward making procedural moves, which would facilitate the government's aims and reduce costs. But it isn't possible to consider factors 1 and 3 in isolation from factor 2, which consists of the actual and hypothetical procedures used to make a final decision.

b. *The importance of the interest and the risk of error in the procedures followed:* In our legal system, the paradigm model of a decision procedure most error- or risk-free is the criminal trial and appeal system. Its principal procedural features are:

   (1)   specific notice of charges so that the defendant knows what she is accused of and can prepare to defend against;

   (2)   an opportunity, at an adversary trial, for the defendant to hear the witnesses against her so that she knows what the case against her actually is;

   (3)   an opportunity to confront and cross-examine those witnesses so that the defendant can test their veracity, ability to observe, etc., and otherwise test the case against her;

   (4)   an opportunity for the defendant to present witnesses and evidence in her own behalf;

   (5)   the assistance of counsel to prepare and present a defense and to test the government's case;

   (6)   rules of evidence limiting or prohibiting the use of certain kinds of evidence as untrustworthy or inflammatory;

   (7)   an impartial judge to referee the proceedings;

   (8)   a decision by a jury based upon the facts and evidence presented at trial;

   (9)   a transcribed record of the proceedings; and

   (10) an appeal on the law or facts on the basis of the record.

c. *Important interests:* The more important the individual interest the government seeks to take or terminate, the more the procedures due process requires will tend toward the criminal trial paradigm. Where the state seeks to take or terminate any truly important liberty or property interest, and the decision turns on significant factual questions or complicated questions of law, there are minimum procedural due process requirements. These are notice, an oral hearing, presentation of evidence before an impartial decision-maker, an opportunity to confront and cross-examine witnesses, counsel, and a decision on the basis of the record adduced at the hearing.

d. *Lesser interests:* As the importance of the individual interest decreases, the procedural requirements become less rigid and formal.

Example: In *Goss v. Lopez,* 419 U.S. 565 (1975), a public school student was accused of a rule infraction which resulted in a temporary, short-term suspension. Concerning the student interest not to be suspended for a short time, the Court held that notice, an explanation of the evidence, and an opportunity for the student to present her side of the story were sufficient procedural protections to satisfy procedural due process requirements.

e. *Timing of procedural protections: pre- or postdeprivation hearings:* Aside from the question of just exactly what procedures should be accorded, there is the question of when they should be accorded. Otherwise put, this is the issue whether there must be a predeprivation hearing or whether a postdeprivation hearing will do. Here again balancing is the key, but the principal factors to be considered are the irreparability of the injury to, or the seriousness of the impairment of, the individual interest as opposed to the need for the government to act expeditiously.

(1) If the government takes or terminates someone's interest *before* she can contest the action, that person could suffer grievously.

Example: Suppose, as in *Goldberg v. Kelly, supra,* that the government terminates an individual's welfare benefits without a hearing, but provides a delayed administrative review process which could restore those benefits. If that review process takes very long, a person dependent on welfare benefits to provide the basic necessities of life could be evicted, go seriously hungry, possibly have to relinquish children, lose essential health care, etc., before restoration of benefits. The situation demands a prior hearing.

(2) There are cases where a postdeprivation hearing is either necessary or will do. This might occur when there is a need for quick action, when it isn't possible to provide meaningful predeprivation process, or where the harm is reversible. These situations would include emergencies (destruction of diseased animals, burning forest land or homes, etc.); cases involving unpredictable, intentional, but unauthorized acts of state employees; cases involving *de minimis* interests (*e.g.,* your right to a parking validation sticker on campus); and cases where there are adequate substitutes for a prior hearing.

(a) Suspensions without pay; presuspension hearings: Where there are reasonable grounds to support a job suspension without pay – for example, a grand jury indictment or prosecutor's information – and the state provides for a prompt postsuspension hearing, due process does not require a presuspension hearing. *Gilbert, President, East Stroudsberg Univ. v. Homar*, 65 U.S.L.W. 4442 (1997).

f. *Debtors' property interests:* At one time, government often privileged creditors over debtors in disputes over property. For example, attachment statutes often allowed creditors to "attach" a debtor's property, disabling the debtor from using it or disposing of it, on the simple filing of an action. Similarly, states have allowed creditors to "garnish" or appropriate a debtor's wages. The Court has held that where such statutes operate prior to trial, the debtor has a procedural due process right to some kind of notice and a prior hearing to determine whether the creditor should be allowed to take such prejudgment action. *Sniadach v. Family Finance Corp.*, 395 U.S. 337 (1969); *Fuentes v. Shevin*, 407 U.S. 67 (1972); *North Georgia Finishing, Inc. v. Di-Chem, Inc.*, 419 U.S. 601 (1975). In such cases, involving prejudgment replevins, attachments, or garnishments, procedural due process minimally requires the creditor's posting of a bond, an affidavit establishing a prima facie case, a neutral magistrate, and a prompt postattachment hearing. *Di-Chem, supra.*

D. **The Conclusive Presumption Doctrine or Shell Game**

1. ***The problem and initial resolution:*** We can conceptualize regulatory classifications in three ways: (1) as rules of substantive law; (2) as rough classifications intended to achieve some other purpose; (3) as rules of evidence. When regulatory statutes do not call for individualized hearings or fact determinations, but instead use classifications as a proxy, they are often overinclusive or underinclusive. That is, such statutes use some general trait or characteristic as a proxy for selecting out a desired class, but the proxy doesn't select exactly.

   Example: The voting age qualification that one be eighteen years old or older to vote can be thought of either as just a substantive rule or as a proxy for the voting qualifications of maturity, ability to understand issues, and the like. As a proxy, however, it is both overinclusive and underinclusive: not all those eighteen years and older have the desired characteristics, and some persons under eighteen probably do have them. If we look at such a proxy as a rule of evidence, however, we can see that it operates to create a conclusive or irrebuttable presumption about the persons classified. Looked at this way, in the voting example, the law creates an irrebuttable presumption that persons under eighteen are incompetent to vote, no matter what their personal knowledge, understanding, or interest in politics. In general, virtually any statute or regulation which prohibits an individualized fact determination can be viewed as a rule of evidence and be said to create a conclusive presumption. Where the actual facts are different from those conclusively presumed, however, such a presumption can be viewed as denying procedural due process, *i.e.,* by denying a person an opportunity to show otherwise.

   Example: In *Stanley v. Illinois,* 405 U.S. 645 (1972), state law provided that if the mother of a child died and the natural father was not married, the child would become a ward of the state. The father was not entitled to a hearing of any kind. This statute can be read as establishing a conclusive presumption that a natural father is an unfit parent. The Court so held and required individualized hearings. Such hearings effectively convert a conclusive presumption into a permissive inference.

2. ***Conclusive presumptions after* Stanley:** After *Stanley,* the conclusive presumption doctrine enjoyed a constitutional vogue for a time. Under its aegis, the Court struck down an almost unsatisfiable state-residency-for-state-tuition-purposes-statute, *Vlandis v. Kline,* 412 U.S. 441 (1973); and a mandatory pregnancy leave rule for women schoolteachers, *Cleveland Bd. of Educ. v. LaFleur,* 414 U.S. 632 (1974).

3. ***Conclusive presumption doctrine reconsidered:*** The major problem with the conclusive presumption doctrine is that it calls for individualized hearings whenever a regulatory statute can be viewed as creating a conclusive presumption. But this view would invalidate even those statutes involving social and economic regulation where the Court has acknowledged legislatures are free to legislate as they wish as long as the legislative action taken is rational. A legislative choice not to have individualized hearings in order to save money or increase administrative efficiency is, of course, quite rational.

   a. *Alternative of established doctrines:* Beyond this, it is easy to see how the Court could have used other established doctrines to reach the same results, *i.e.,* treat the cases as involving state classifications affecting fundamental rights or, additionally, in *LaFleur,* handle the case as a gender discrimination case. *Cf.* Chapter 8, I.A., *infra.*

   b. *Doctrine in disguise:* What this consideration suggests is that the conclusive presumption doctrine is really a fundamental rights-substantive due process doctrine in disguise. Under the rubric of requiring individualized hearings, the Court was just substituting its judgment about what the underlying *substantive* rule of law should be. Calling the state law a conclusive presumption and then striking it down simply hides the implicit strict scrutiny which the Court, in effect, has given the statute. This is the conclusive presumption shell game.

4. ***Limitation of conclusive presumption doctrine to important liberties:*** Recognizing the foregoing, the Court called a halt to the march of conclusive presumption doctrine in *Weinberger v. Salfi,* 422 U.S. 749 (1975). Consequently, this whole minor body of law can be taken to stand for the proposition that due process requires individualized hearings when a statute or regulation purports adversely to affect an important liberty interest recognized in constitutional law, but fails to provide for such a hearing.

   Example: *Salfi* involved a Social Security Act regulation limiting survivor's benefits to survivors married to the decedent at least nine months before decedent's death. The rule was intended to prevent sham marriages entered into for the sake of survivor's benefits. Had the Court followed the conclusive presumption doctrine, it would have had to invalidate the rule, but it did not do so. It did not overrule *Stanley* and *LaFleur,* but distinguished them on the ground that they involved the constitutionally protected status of parenthood. *Salfi,* by contrast, involved economic and social regulation, and the Court applied a rational basis test to review the rule, thus upholding it. *Cf.* Chapter 8, I., *infra.*

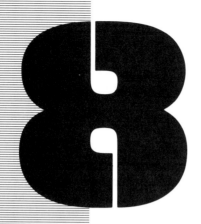

EQUAL PROTECTION (I)

▶ **CHAPTER SUMMARY**

CHAPTER 8: EQUAL PROTECTION (I)

Introduction. The Fourteenth Amendment guarantees that no state shall deny any person the equal protection of the laws. The Supreme Court has interpreted the Fifth Amendment Due Process Clause, which applies only to the federal government, to require the federal government to accord equal protection as well. Consequently, all governments in the United States must accord individuals equal protection.

The meaning of equal protection, however, is not transparent. Obviously governments cannot treat all individuals the same in all respects. Indeed, the nature and problems of government require that governments differentiate between persons and situations in order to accomplish proper and worthy governmental goals. On the other hand, governments cannot do just anything they choose to do and cannot use any means, no matter what its consequences, to accomplish their aims. Two important and related premises of American constitutional law are that government's powers are limited and that government cannot transgress on the rights the Constitution guarantees individuals. We must therefore understand the meaning of equal protection to lie somewhere between these constraints.

I. **OVERVIEW: When the Supreme Court reviews state actions to determine whether they have denied equal protection, it is essentially deciding whether the state had an appropriate justification for differentiating between persons. What is an "appropriate" justification depends very much on what the state is seeking to do (how important its goal is), and how it seeks to achieve its goal (what means it uses). For example, it should take a pretty powerful justification to permit the state to inhibit someone's exercise of a constitutional right. On the other hand, if the state deems it useful to raise taxes on alcohol to provide additional public money for prenatal and infant health care, it's hard to question either the purpose or the means.**

To these considerations we must add one further factor, that of institutional competence. In a representative democracy, as long as the legislature acts within its powers, its judgment about means and ends should normally have great weight. After all, unlike a court, a legislature can explore all aspects of a problem, including necessary political tradeoffs, and is therefore better positioned to know how best to tackle it. Still, it is the nature of democratic politics – and the legislature is the chief arena of politics in the United States – to reflect majoritarian will, and that can mean neglect, even invasions, of the interests and rights of minorities. In our society, the courts, by and large, comprise the branch of government that, for constitutional reasons, has taken on itself the role of protecting minority rights. Consequently, while the legislature has the greatest institutional competence to make most governmental ends-means decisions, there are limits legislatures cannot constitutionally exceed.

All these considerations play themselves out in equal protection doctrines and rules. They are reflected primarily in the doctrine of three levels of judicial review in equal protection cases. The levels, or intensities, of judicial review really amount to questions of how much deference courts should give to legislative and executive judgment about governmental ends and means selected to achieve particular ends. Current equal protection doctrine holds that the level of judicial deference depends very much on what government seeks to do, how it seeks to do it, and the substantive consequences, for individuals, of what it seeks to do.

A. Levels of Judicial Review Under the Equal Protection Clause: In equal protection cases, the Supreme Court scrutinizes or reviews state action with one of three levels of intensity. These are (1) rational basis review; (2) intermediate review; and (3) strict scrutiny review. Some members of the Court, with justification, dispute that there is a three-tier scheme of categorizing and analyzing equal protection cases (*e.g., City of Cleburne v. Cleburne Living Center,* 473 U.S. 432 (1985), (Stevens, J., concurring)). Notwithstanding, the three-level system of review does best reflect what the Court does and says it does. The close student of constitutional law should understand, however, that the Court sometimes applies its equal protection review standards flexibly, as noted more fully below.

1. *Rational basis review:* When applying rational basis review, the Court accepts any conceivable, legitimate goal as an appropriate legislative purpose. It also accepts any rational means the legislature determines is useful or necessary to reach its goal. Obviously, in carrying out this form of review, the Court is highly deferential to the legislature, and rational basis review is the weakest form of judicial review.

2. *Intermediate review:* When undertaking intermediate level review, the Court requires that the legislature have some "substantial and important" goal and that the means the legislature uses to reach its goal serve it well. Less deferential than rational basis review, intermediate review nonetheless permits the legislature some latitude.

3. *Strict scrutiny:* Strict scrutiny review is the most stringent form of judicial review. Under strict scrutiny review, the Court requires the state to justify its actions by showing that it has a "compelling interest" and that the means the state chooses to realize its interest infringes as little as possible on the exercise of individual rights.

B. Classifications and Equal Protection: Most statutes and administrative regulations classify persons or situations in order to regulate. Classification has the effect of differentiating between persons and situations. In examining governmental actions – whether statutes, regulations, or applications of them – to determine whether they deny equal protection, it is necessary to examine the way they classify individuals and the justifications offered for the classifications. In working with equal protection analysis of classifications, it is important to understand the following terms and distinctions.

1. *Formal characteristics of classifications*

a. *Rational:* Classifications are rational if they tend, within broad limits, to serve the purposes for which they were designed.

Example: Take the following statute: "All businesses operating in buildings not fireproofed to state standards as found in the Health and Safety Code shall undergo fire safety inspections, and no such business shall operate without a fire safety permit issued after inspection." This statute classifies businesses in accordance with a defined standard of fireproofing. Assuming the state standards provide some meaningful level of fire protection, the statute is rational for it requires permits and inspections of only those businesses in buildings below the standard.

b. *Irrational*

Example: "All businesses operating in buildings found to be fireproof under the fire safety standards found in the Health and Safety Code, and no others, shall have fire safety inspections, and no such business shall operate without a fire safety permit issued after inspection." Assuming there is no defect in the fire safety standard which the legislature is trying to correct, this statute is perfectly irrational, for it requires a fire inspection for only those businesses which do not need it.

c. *Underinclusive:* A classification is underinclusive if it reaches only some, but not all, of the instances of the problem that the classifying body is seeking to treat.

Example: "All businesses operated in wooden buildings and owned by persons over age forty shall have fire safety inspections." Granting that wooden buildings present fire safety hazards other buildings do not, the fire safety aim is proper. Nonetheless, the classification does not include all businesses operated in all wooden buildings, but only a subset of them. This classification is underinclusive.

d. *Overinclusive:* A classification is overinclusive if it reaches both instances of the problem that the classifier is seeking to treat together with instances in which the problem does not occur.

Example: "Alcoholism is a serious disease. All persons who drink alcoholic beverages must undergo treatment for alcoholism." This statute aims to treat alcoholism. The classification, however, sweeps well beyond the group of those who are alcoholics to include others who are not. It is therefore overinclusive.

e. *Overinclusive and underinclusive:* Classifications can be overinclusive and underinclusive at the same time.

Example: Assume the following statute is intended to ensure that only those who can drive competently shall be licensed to drive. "All persons aged sixteen and over who have 20-20 uncorrected vision shall be entitled to drive." Obviously, some persons aged sixteen and over with 20-20 vision are perfectly competent to drive. However, not all such persons are. Similarly, undoubtedly many people sixteen and over who do not have 20-20 vision are competent to drive. The classification thus is both overinclusive and underinclusive.

2. ***Fit, tailoring, underinclusion, and overinclusion:*** The underinclusiveness or overinclusiveness of a classification is essentially a question of a means-end fit. The classifier classifies situations or persons in order to address some problem or to achieve some end. If a classification selects out exactly the instances of a problem the classifier is seeking to address, and all of them, then the classification is perfectly tailored to the problem. If the classification is broadly underinclusive or overinclusive, the means-end fit is poor and the tailoring loose. If the classification is only somewhat, but not significantly, underinclusive or overinclusive, the means-end fit and tailoring are fair or good.

a. *Importance of the fitness or tailoring distinctions:* The three broad types of underinclusion and overinclusion are important, for different levels of equal protection review require different degrees of fitness or tailoring in the means-end relationship. Rational basis review is satisfied with a loose fit or broad tailoring. Intermediate review requires a good fit or tailoring. Strict scrutiny review requires the most exact fit or tailoring possible.

3. *Categories of classification traits:* Classifications do their work through the use of criteria or traits that distinguish between persons or situations. It is possible, and useful, to categorize classification criteria or traits, for different levels of equal protection review are associated with different kinds of classifications.

a. *Suspect classifications:* Classifications based on race, religion, national origin, alienage, and ethnicity are suspect. They are "suspect" because, although possible to use for proper ends, they have been used historically to disadvantage a minority group. The Supreme Court accords strict scrutiny review to suspect classifications.

b. *Classifications impinging on a fundamental right:* Government bodies sometimes seek to achieve their ends in ways that adversely affect individuals' exercise of constitutionally protected fundamental rights. For example, a state statute that seeks to limit the number of poor people in a state by prohibiting the immigration of poor persons into the state infringes their fundamental right to travel in the United States. Classifications affecting fundamental rights receive strict scrutiny review.

c. *Questionable or quasi-suspect classifications:* There are some classification criteria – gender and mental or social status, and birth status – which are useful for many legitimate purposes, but which depend on stereotyped thinking and have, in the past, often been used to disadvantage a group. Such classifications are subject to intermediate review.

d. *All other classifications:* If a classification is not based on suspect criteria, does not impinge on the exercise of a fundamental right, or is not based on questionable or quasi-suspect criteria, it is subject to rational basis review.

C. **Equal Protection Matrix:** Current equal protection doctrine is broadly formula-dependent and operates through categorizing situations and assigning specific levels of judicial review or scrutiny to assess them. While the close student of constitutional law will realize there is more latitude or flex in equal protection doctrine and analysis than the formulas suggest, the formulas nonetheless create the basic frame of analysis. In any case, the following matrix is a useful tool in approaching equal protection issues.

*RATIONAL
BASIS
REVIEW*

8

STRICT SCRUTINY REVIEW

(Suspect Classifications and Invasions of Fundamental Rights)

		Means-End Fit		
		Narrow, Exact	Good	Poor
PURPOSE OR INTEREST	Compelling	Const.	Unconst.	Unconst.
	Important	Unconst.	Unconst.	Unconst.
	Legitimate	Unconst.	Unconst.	Unconst.

INTERMEDIATE SCRUTINY REVIEW

(Questionable or Quasi-suspect Classifications)

		Means-End Fit		
		Narrow, Exact	Good	Poor
PURPOSE OR INTEREST	Compelling	Const.	Const.	Unconst.
	Important	Const.	Const.	Unconst.
	Legitimate	Unconst.	Unconst.	Unconst.

RATIONAL BASIS REVIEW

		Means-End Fit		
		Narrow, Exact	Good	Poor
PURPOSE OR INTEREST	Compelling	Const.	Const.	Const.
	Important	Const.	Const.	Const.
	Legitimate	Const.	Const.	Const.

II. RATIONAL BASIS REVIEW

A. Basic Principles

1. ***Applicable to cases involving social and economic regulation:*** The Court applies rational basis review in cases involving social and economic regulation where there is no suspect or quasi-suspect classification nor a classification affecting the exercise of fundamental rights. *Dandridge v. Williams,* 397 U.S. 471 (1970).

   a. *Equal protection and taxation:* The rational basis standard of review is especially deferential regarding tax law classifications, and states have great latitude in creating taxation schemes and distinctions. *Williams v. Vermont,* 472 U.S. 13 (1985). A state tax law classification having some rational relationship to a plausible policy justification is constitutional. Notwithstanding this deferential standard, however, tax law classifications can be so unrelated to their justification as to be arbitrary or irrational.

      (1) Real property taxes: Where a state requires assessment of all real property, for property tax purposes, at *current market value,* a tax assessor's practice of assessing recently purchased property on the basis of its purchase price and other real property at older values denies equal protection. *Allegheny Pittsburgh Coal Co. v. Webster County,* 488 U.S. 336 (1989). In such a case, the assessor's practice is not rationally related to the goal of uniform assessment at true current value. Where a state requires real property assessment based on value at the time of purchase (acquisition value), the classification scheme, while producing widely discrepant property taxes for comparable properties, is constitutional. Assuming a rise in real property values, an acquisition value assessment scheme favors old owners over new owners. But such a scheme protects existing owners from unpredictable, market-driven property tax increases and promotes home retention, or stability in homeownership. *Nordlinger v. Hahn,* 60 U.S.L.W. 4563 (1992).

2. ***Overinclusive and underinclusive classifications***

   a. *General run of cases:* The Equal Protection Clause protects against arbitrary, unreasonable, and irrational classifications. However, in the normal case, regulations that are overinclusive or underinclusive do not for that reason violate the Equal Protection Clause. Legislatures may seek to remedy problems one step at a time, *Williamson v. Lee Optical Co.,* 348 U.S. 483 (1955), and, consequently, underinclusiveness by itself does not invalidate regulation. Overinclusive statutes may work some unfairness or inequality, but legislatures may experiment and seek efficient ways to deal with problems and are not required to hit the mark exactly in their classifications.

   b. *Truly exceptional cases:* On occasion, a law may be so broad, when one attempts to justify it in terms of its asserted, specific goals, that it must be deemed irrational.

   Example: Equal protection contemplates "that government and each of its parts remain open on impartial terms to all who seek its assistance". Laws that, without a rational basis, single out a certain class of citizens and make it more difficult for them to seek government aid than it is for others violate equal protection. *Romer v. Evans*, 517 U.S. 620 (1996). In *Romer v. Evans*, Colorado citizens passed an initiative to amend the Colorado Constitution. The initiative had two effects. It repealed all laws and policies, at any level of government, that barred discrimination based on sexual orientation, and, short of a new constitutional amendment, it prohibited any governmental entity from adopting similar rules in the future. The disability imposed reached so far beyond any rational justification offered in support that its only real purpose appeared to be to impose a status-based disability on homosexuals because they were homosexuals. [As Justice Scalia pointed out in dissent, there is some tension between this case and *Bowers v. Hardwick, supra,* where the Court upheld the criminalization of homosexual conduct. If it is rational to make homosexual conduct criminal, it must be rational to pass laws disfavoring homosexuality. But the Colorado amendment aimed at disempowering homosexuals politically, with respect to sexual orientation laws, rather than proscribing homosexual conduct or protecting others from such conduct. The electoral disability imposed on homosexuals is the key to the case.]

3. ***Irrational and arbitrary classifications:*** As the foregoing subsection demonstrates, a classification can be so unlikely to lead to any discernable and understandable legitimate purpose that it must be deemed irrational and therefore arbitrary. Classifications can also be irrational and arbitrary when they regulate similarly situated parties differently, but without a demonstrably good reason for the differential treatment.

Example: In *City of Cleburne v. Cleburne Living Center,* 473 U.S. 432 (1985), the city required, and on application denied, a special use permit for the operation of a group home for the mentally retarded. The city did not require permits for apartment houses, boarding and lodging houses, fraternities and sororities, dormitories, hospitals, sanitariums, and nursing homes for convalescents or the aged. The existence of a group home for the mentally retarded would have raised no problems or concerns different from those presented by the facilities not requiring permits except for fear of, and bias against, the mentally retarded. The Court held that the city had not shown it was rational to treat the retarded differently and held the city's action denied equal protection.

On the other hand, one must be careful in comparing differently classified parties seemingly similarly situated. What may seem to be similar cases may in fact involve differences justifying differential treatment.

Example: In *Cruzan v. Director, Missouri Dept. of Health,* 497 U.S. 261 (1990), the Supreme Court assumed there was a constitutional right to refuse unwanted medical treatment. This right included the decision of a terminally ill patient to refuse life-sustaining treatment, even though that refusal would result in death. There are persons, also terminally ill, such as an individual with an incurable cancer, who may not be receiving life support, but who wish to die and need assistance in dying, *e.g.*, fatal medication. For constitutional purposes, is there a difference between choosing to die by refusing medical treatment and choosing to die with physician assistance? Arguably there is no difference because in each case a physician helps a willing, terminally ill patient die, in the one case by removing life support; in the other, by administering a drug. There are, however, relevant differences which justify treating the cases differently. In the case of death resulting from withdrawal of life-sustaining treatment, the cause of death is the underlying disease or medical problem. In the case of physician administered lethal medication, the drug kills. There is also a difference in intent. A physician who withdraws life-support measures intends to respect the patient's wishes; one who administers a lethal drug intends death. For these reasons, the distinction between laws permitting withdrawing life support and laws prohibiting assisted suicide are rational, and legislatures may constitutionally permit the former and prohibit the latter. *Vacco, Atty Gen'l of New York v. Quill*, 65 U.S.L.W. 3481 (1997).

4. *Hypothetical purposes:* To be rational, a statutory classification or differentiation must serve the purpose underlying the statute. There are cases, however, where there is no clear or obvious legislative purpose or where the statutory classification does not appear to serve the apparent legislative purpose. Under rational basis review, the Court indulges a rebuttable presumption that a legislature has acted constitutionally in enacting legislation. Essentially what this means is that, in cases of uncertain or poorly served legislative purpose, the Court will uphold a statutory classification if *any conceivable* grounds justify it. In other words, the Court will postulate hypothetical purposes the statute might serve, and if the classification is in some way relevant to achieving the postulated purpose, it will uphold it. *McDonald v. Board of Election,* 394 U.S. 802 (1969); *McGowan v. Maryland,* 366 U.S. 420 (1961).

Example: In *Railway Express Agency v. New York,* 336 U.S. 106 (1949), New York City forbade advertising on vehicles, except business delivery vehicles advertising the business of the owner. In other words, the City banned the selling or leasing of advertising space on vehicles. The apparent aim of the ban was to reduce the distractions that vehicle advertising presented to pedestrians and drivers of other vehicles. The regulatory classification, which differentiates between owner and nonowner advertising, doesn't appear to serve that purpose as ownership of the advertising appears irrelevant to the distracting character of advertising. The Court, however, speculated that City authorities may have concluded that those who advertise their own business on their own vehicles may advertise in sufficiently different ways as to present a lesser traffic problem than nonowner advertising. On this supposition, weak as it appears, the Court upheld the regulation.

B. **Inconsistency in Rationality Review:** The Court has not been completely consistent in its application of the rational basis standard of equal protection review. As usually described and applied, the standard is an extremely deferential form of review, and the Court will uphold all but the most irrational or arbitrary of classifications. On occasion, however, the Court has been more rigorous in applying the standard and has overturned statutory classifications on the ground that they were irrational. *U.S. Dept. of Agric. v. Moreno,* 413 U.S. 528 (1973); *Jimenez v. Weinberger,* 417 U.S. 628 (1974). When one compares these cases with others in which the Court upheld statutory classifications as rational, it is necessary to conclude that the Court, while claiming to apply the same standard, is, in fact, applying different standards of rationality. This suggests there is some flex in the standard. The use of classifications, not amounting to suspect or quasi-suspect classifications, which reflect unreasoned fears, hatred, or prejudice against a discrete and relatively defenseless minority, may sometimes trigger more rigorous rationality review.

STRICT SCRUTINY REVIEW

Example: See *City of Cleburne v. Cleburne Living Center* example, *supra.*

Counterexample: In *Heller v. Doe,* 61 U.S.L.W. 4728 (1993), the Court reviewed state statutes providing differential standards for commitment of the mentally retarded and the mentally ill. The statutes provided for mental retardation commitment on clear and convincing evidence, while mental illness commitment was based on proof beyond a reasonable doubt. The Court declined to apply a heightened standard of review on the ground that the standard issue had not been properly presented below and instead applied rational basis review. A bare majority applied two rationales to uphold the differential standards as rational. The first was that it was easier to diagnose mental retardation than mental illness, and thus less risk of error in making retardation commitments. The second was that mental retardation treatment on commitment was "less intrusive" than that accorded mental illness commitments. The holding thus endorses lesser protections from commitment for the mentally retarded than for the mentally ill. In its opinion, the majority also strongly reaffirmed the weakest form of rational basis review.

C. **The Debate over Enhanced Rationality Review:** There is a debate, within the Court, over the rigor of rationality review. A strong minority of justices have opined that the Court should not invent purposes that legislative classifications might serve. Instead, the Court should judge legislative classifications by articulated, readily identifiable, or reasonably presumed purposes. *U.S. Railroad Retirement Bd. v. Fritz,* 449 U.S. 166 (1980) (Stevens, J., concurring; Brennan, J., and Marshall, J., dissenting); *Schweiker v. Wilson,* 450 U.S. 221 (1981) (Powell, J., dissenting). A corollary to this position is that where there is no indication of legislative purpose, the Court will not uphold a classification that serves a hypothecated purpose unless it bears a "fair and substantial relation" to that purpose. *Id.* These changes would make the rational basis standard more difficult to satisfy in cases where legislative purpose was indeterminable.

Example: In the federal Supplementary Security Income program, Congress provides subsistence funds for the needy aged, blind, and disabled unless such persons are in public mental institutions, the presumption there being that most of their needs are taken care of. In *Schweiker, supra,* Congress provided "comfort allowances" for this latter group, that is, $25 a month, which permitted them to buy items not institutionally provided. However, Congress also provided that these needy could receive such payments only if they resided in institutions receiving Medicaid payments on their behalf. In effect, this made the institutionalized needy between the ages of twenty-one to sixty-five ineligible to receive comfort allowances unless they were mental patients in public mental hospitals or *private* mental institutions. There was no stated or clearly inferable congressional purpose in treating this group differently from the Medicaid group or those in medical or private mental hospitals. Applying the rational basis test, the Court speculated that Congress's intention was to further traditional state responsibility for those in public mental institutions and upheld the classification. The dissenters, however, observed that as this was a hypothecated purpose, the classification had to bear a "fair and substantial relation" to that purpose. There the classification failed, for the residence of the needy person bore no relationship to her need.

Recently, however, a bare Court majority has rejected the minority efforts by strongly endorsing weak rational basis review, even in cases involving classifications based on mental disability or illness. *Heller v. Doe, supra.* According to this latest articulation, classifications that are neither suspect nor involve fundamental rights receive a strong presumption of validity. There is no requirement that some articulated legislative purpose or rationale support such classifications. Nor need a state provide evidence to support a classification's rationality. A court should uphold such classifications if "any reasonably conceivable state of facts could provide a rational basis," and classifications will fail rational basis review only when based on grounds "wholly irrelevant" to the state's objectives. *Id.,* at 4730. (*Cf. Federal Communications Commission v. Beach Communications,* 508 U.S. 307 (1993), for an even stronger statement upholding minimum rationality review in cases involving social and economic legislation and legislation regulating line drawing.)

III. **STRICT SCRUTINY REVIEW – SUSPECT CLASSIFICATIONS: Suspect classifications differentiate between persons on bases almost always irrelevant to legitimate state interests. Historically, such classifications were expressions of prejudice, bias, or hatred of minorities, and legislatures and officials used such classifications to discriminate against minorities. Suspect classifications also classify on the basis of characteristics, such as skin color, which are impossible for the persons affected to change. Finally, since suspect classifications strike at discrete and insular minorities, the affected groups are unable to obtain redress from the legislatures, which reflect majority will and prejudices. To protect minorities, courts review official use of such classifications with the greatest strictness and care.**

A. **Classifications Based on Race, Ethnicity, or National Origin:** The Equal Protection Clause bans discrimination on the basis of race, color, ethnicity, *Strauder v. West Virginia,* 100 U.S. 303 (1880), and national origin, *cf. City of Cleburne v. Cleburne Living Center,* 473 U.S. 432 (1985). This does not mean that states may never use such classifications, but rather that the Court subjects them to strict scrutiny review and that only a compelling interest, such as military necessity, can justify such classifications. *Korematsu v. United States,* 323 U.S. 214 (1944) (military exclusion order, during World War II, of persons of Japanese ancestry from certain West Coast areas held justified).

   1. *Interracial marriage:* States may not ban interracial marriages. *Loving v. Virginia,* 388 U.S. 1 (1967).

   2. *Racial classifications facilitating racial prejudice:* As a forbidden ground of classification, the state may not classify on the basis of race. This is so whether the effect of doing so is to make it possible for racial prejudice to operate or whether the intent behind such classification is to inhibit racial or social prejudice.

      Examples: In *Anderson v. Martin,* 375 U.S. 399 (1964), the state required that the race of candidates for election to public office appear on the ballot. The Court overturned the law on the ground that by highlighting race, the state made it an important consideration for voters and opened the door to racial prejudice in voting.

      In *Palmore v. Sidoti,* 466 U.S. 429 (1984), a state court judge divested a white mother of custody of her child because of her remarriage to an African-American man. Citing the best interests of the child as reason for his decision, the judge took the view that the child would suffer prejudice and social stigmatization if allowed to remain with the mother. The Court overturned the order, reasoning that a court, as an arm of government, could not give effect to private racial prejudice.

3. ***Prison security:*** While racial tension in prisons exists, and authorities may on occasion have to take it into account in maintaining security, discipline, and good order, the possibility of racial tension does not justify a general requirement for racial segregation in prisons. *Lee v. Washington,* 390 U.S. 333 (1968).

4. ***Differential heavier burdens in the political process***

   a. *Electoral discrimination; differential heavier burdens in the political process:* Laws making it more difficult for members of a race, or other protected minority, to succeed in enacting laws, are unconstitutional.

      Example: In *Hunter v. Erickson,* 393 U.S. 385 (1969), the Akron City Charter provided that most ordinances adopted by the City Council would be effective, within a short period of time, subject, however, to repeal by referendum called by ten percent of the voters. Subsequently, the public amended the Charter to provide for an automatic referendum with respect to any ordinance that regulated real estate transactions "on the basis of race, color, religion, national origin or ancestry." The amendment contained a clear racial classification and made it more difficult to pass ordinances relating to certain kinds of housing discrimination than other kinds of ordinances, and was therefore unconstitutional.

   b. *Irrational electoral discrimination.* Note that, even under rational basis review, electoral discrimination may be unconstitutional even when directed at an unprotected minority. In *Romer v. Evans, supra,* II. A. 2., the electoral disability Colorado imposed on homosexuals was so broad, and so unrelated to any specific, legitimate legislative purpose that it was deemed irrational.

5. ***Petit jury selection and peremptory challenges:*** Racial discrimination in jury selection violates equal protection, and a pattern of peremptory strikes of minority race members, whether by prosecutor or defense counsel, gives rise to an inference of racial discrimination. A potential juror's race is unrelated to his or her fitness to serve as a juror. Once a party makes a prima facie showing that the other party discriminatorily used peremptory challenges, the latter must provide satisfactory, neutral, nonracial explanations for the challenges in order to sustain them. *Batson v. Kentucky,* 476 U.S. 79 (1986) (prosecution); *Georgia v. McCollum,* 60 U.S.L.W. 4574 (1992) (defense).

B. **Racial Segregation in Public Schools:** In *Plessy v. Ferguson,* 163 U.S. 537 (1896) the Supreme Court legitimated state-enforced racial segregation. There, in sustaining a law that required "equal but separate accommodations" for white and black railroad passengers, the Court held that the Equal Protection Clause was satisfied when the state treated members of different races equally. This meant that the state could segregate them as long as it provided equally for the segregated groups. Although in practice, given the reality of racial prejudice, the facilities and services provided blacks were greatly inferior to those provided whites, eventually *Plessy* led to a requirement that states provide blacks educational services and benefits equal to those provided whites. *Missouri ex rel. Gaines v. Canada,* 305 U.S. 337 (1938); *Sipuel v. Board of Regents,* 332 U.S. 631 (1948); *Sweatt v. Painter,* 339 U.S. 629 (1950); *McLaurin v. Oklahoma State Regents,* 339 U.S. 637 (1950). Then came *Brown v. Board of Educ.,* 347 U.S. 483 (1954), which overturned *Plessy,* worked a revolutionary change in the legal conception of what equal protection required in racial matters, ultimately required desegregation in all public facilities, and marked profound changes in public education.

1. ***Separate is inherently unequal:*** In *Brown, supra,* the Court held that racial segregation in state public schools denied equal protection to the minority, segregated children, even if their schools were equal to those of whites. Segregation denotes racial inferiority and retards the children's educational and mental development. In *Bolling v. Sharpe,* 347 U.S. 497 (1954), the Court applied the same rule to the federal government, interpreting the Fifth Amendment Due Process Clause as proscribing the deprivation of liberty imposed by segregation. Thereafter, in a series of cases, through *per curiam* orders, the Court ordered desegregation of all public facilities.

2. ***Desegregation "with all deliberate speed":*** In the second *Brown* case, *Brown v. Board of Educ.,* 349 U.S. 294 (1955), the Court addressed the question of implementation of the original *Brown* decision. Ending the system of racially segregated schools posed immense practical, social, and financial problems. Among other things, there was no central authority to oversee the integration of segregated schools, for school systems in the United States were traditionally governed by local school boards. The Court determined that local school authorities, overseen by federal district courts, should have the primary responsibility for resolving the problems desegregation posed. Federal courts were to use their broad and extensive equity powers to shape flexible remedies needed to realistically desegregate schools and adjust and reconcile local needs. The courts were authorized to issue orders relating to school administration, physical facilities, transportation, personnel, attendance areas, and even to the revision of local laws and regulations. Finally, they were to maintain oversight of desegregation to ensure compliance and to move the process forward "with all deliberate speed."

3. ***Essential concepts:*** In order to understand the school desegregation cases, it is essential to have in hand a few concepts and distinctions.

   a. De jure *and* de facto *segregation; state action: De jure* means "by law or of law," and the term *de jure segregation* refers to official segregation in some way ordered or implemented by governmental authority or public officials. In the American south, although not exclusively there, there was a regime of legally imposed segregation. *De facto* segregation refers to segregation existing without the backing authority of law, as might arise from private racial discrimination, residential segregation not imposed by law, and the like. The distinction between *de jure* and *de facto* segregation is important, for Fourteenth Amendment equal protection prohibits the *states* or governmental authorities generally, and not private parties, from denying equal protection. Consequently, the Equal Protection Clause, of its own force, reaches only what is referred to as "state action," that is, governmental activity.

   b. *Intentional segregation:* Since equal protection forbids only state action denying equal protection, a finding of official, intentional segregation is a predicate for a desegregation order. The Equal Protection Clause does not apply to private discrimination or to segregation arising de facto.

4. ***Desegregation of southern schools***

a. *"Freedom of choice" plans:* Many districts required to desegregate their schools resisted greatly, and some adopted plans which had the effect of continuing school segregation, albeit without direct state sanction. One such plan was the "freedom of choice" plan. Under freedom of choice plans, school officials permit parents and school children to select the school they wish to attend. Freedom of choice plans do not segregate officially, for officials do not make the decision regarding which schoolchildren shall attend. They are therefore not unconstitutional *per se*. In many situations, however, freedom of choice plans would not lead to racially desegregated schools, but would maintain them. This might occur, for example, where there was de facto residential segregation, for parents would naturally incline to send their children to schools nearest their homes. In *Green v. County School Board,* 391 U.S. 430 (1968), the Court addressed this issue. It effectively held that where there was a finding that there had been official school segregation, there was an obligation to create a *unitary* school system in which there was no racial discrimination. Consequently, where there had been state-compelled school segregation, officials could not rely on desegregation plans which, although no longer requiring official segregation, did not result in unitary school system. Therefore, if a freedom of choice plan had the effect of continuing a racially dual system of education, it was unconstitutional.

5. ***Remedies for school segregation:*** In *Swann v. Charlotte-Mecklenburg Board of Educ.,* 402 U.S. 1 (1971), and subsequent cases, the Court revisited questions of the remedial powers of federal district courts in desegregation cases and discussed the remedies these courts could use to create unitary school systems.

a. *Role of the federal district courts:* While federal district courts have broad remedial powers in school desegregation cases, local school boards have the responsibility to devise school desegregation plans in the first instance. If such plans are unacceptable, the courts may amend them. While these plans must remedy the constitutional violation, they can, if the school board so desires, go beyond what the Constitution requires.

b. *Facially neutral standards and attendance zones:* If a neutral pupil school assignment plan perpetuates a racially dual school system, it is unconstitutional. Although having neighborhood schools serves important values and assigning pupils to schools in their neighborhoods is a facially neutral assignment standard, it is improper to use such a scheme where it continues a dual system.

c. *Racial balancing:* The Equal Protection Clause does not require racial balancing, but a federal court may use racial population ratios as guidelines to test the effectiveness of alternative integration plans.

d. *One-race schools:* One-race schools are not per se unconstitutional. But where there is a history of de jure segregation, there is a presumption that any one-race schools remaining after an integration plan are the result of discriminatory intent. The burden is on the school board to prove otherwise.

e. *Busing:* Busing is an appropriate remedy where a dual school system would continue to exist but for the busing of children from one part of a school district to another.

f. *Reasonableness:* Reasonableness is *not* a test of school desegregation remedies. A school integration plan is reasonable not because it is not overly burdensome, but because it works to end a dual system.

g. *Judicially ordered tax levies:* If necessary as a remedy to finance appropriate desegregation plans, a district court may direct local governments to levy taxes and may enjoin the operation of laws limiting, or setting a cap on, such taxation where necessary to make the levy effective. *Missouri v. Jenkins,* 58 U.S.L.W. 4480 (1990).

6. **De jure *and* de facto *school segregation in the same school system:*** A finding of *de jure* segregation with regard to some schools in a school system, but not others, may justify a system-wide desegregation remedy, as opposed to a remedy directed solely at the segregated schools. A finding of segregatory intent in one part of a system is relevant to such a finding in other parts of the system. If intentional segregation in a meaningful part of a system has a substantial reciprocal segregative effect on other parts of the system, then a court may find the system officially segregated and order a system-wide remedy. *Keyes v. School District,* 413 U.S. 189 (1973).

7. ***Combining minorities:*** For purposes of determining whether or not there was official segregation, a district court should combine racial minorities. In other words, when looking at any particular school in a district, it might not appear segregated if its minority populations are considered in isolation.

Example: A school described as having forty black students may not appear segregated, but if it turns out that another minority, say Hispanic students, comprise another forty-five of the same school's population, the school is in fact an overwhelmingly minority race school. *Keyes, supra.*

8. ***Original intentional segregation and current segregative effect:*** School districts that officially segregated prior to the *Brown* decision have a constitutional duty to remedy that segregation. A post-*Brown* failure to meet that obligation, whether intentional or unintentional, is a continuing constitutional violation. In other words, if a school district intentionally segregated prior to *Brown,* and there remains a current segregative impact from the original segregation, the district must remedy the current segregative impact. *Columbus Board of Educ. v. Penick,* 443 U.S. 449 (1979); *Dayton Board of Educ. v. Brinkman,* 443 U.S. 526 (1979). Of course, school districts must also remedy any official intentional segregation arising after the *Brown* decision.

a. *Legacies of* de jure *discrimination affecting student college choice:* Although a state adopts race-neutral college admissions policies, and students are relatively free to choose which state college or university they wish to attend, other state policies may so affect student choice as to continue a racially dual system of education. Where current state educational policies are traceable to policies of de jure segregation, and have current segregative effects, a state has a duty to eradicate or remedy them. *United States v. Fordice,* 112 S. Ct. 2727 (1992).

Example: Mississippi's *de jure* system of segregation in higher education secured certain state colleges as white schools and other schools as black schools. The admissions standards at the schools were adopted, at least in part, for segregatory purposes. Notwithstanding desegregation and present policies of race-neutral admissions, the automatic admissions standards at Mississippi schools were traceable to the segregatory standards. Although students not qualifying automatically might still gain admission, the standards had the effect of discouraging student applications and led to the continued existence of racially identifiable colleges. Similarly, under *de jure* school segregation, Mississippi's white universities were flagship schools with broad institutional missions, while schools designated black had much more limited missions. Notwithstanding the end of *de jure* segregation, the relative missions of the schools did not change. As a school's mission will affect student choices whether to attend a school and student choices at the school, the policy of perpetuating the school missions following desegregation — without an independent, present, sound educational justification — is a traceable current effect of prior segregation which the state must remedy. *Fordice, supra.*

9. ***State efforts to limit busing as a desegregation remedy:*** States may not amend their political processes in ways that make it more difficult for racial minorities, than for other members of the political community, to effect political change. Consequently, a statewide initiative that prohibited local school boards from voluntarily using criteria other than geographical proximity to assign students was unconstitutional. *Washington v. Seattle School Dist. No. 1,* 458 U.S. 457 (1982). On the other hand, a state initiative that limits state courts' authority to order busing or pupil assignments to only those cases where a federal court would be permitted to do so under the Equal Protection Clause is constitutional. *Crawford v. Los Angeles Board of Educ.,* 458 U.S. 527 (1982). These cases appear somewhat inconsistent, but perhaps may be reconciled on the theory that in the former, the effect of the initiative was to take away local decision-making on a particular topic of great importance to minorities, thus making it more difficult for minorities to effect voluntary change.

10. ***Satisfactory compliance with desegregation orders:*** Local control of public education remains the norm. Once a school district has successfully complied with a school desegregation decree, a federal district court can enter an order ending the case and its jurisdiction. In other words, once a federal court has terminated a desegregation case because of compliance, a school district may act without further judicial supervision. Of course, the district cannot engage in intentionally segregatory acts, but that would be a new case. *Board of Educ. of Oklahoma City Pub. Schools v. Dowell,* 498 U.S. 237 (1991).

11. ***Partial compliance:*** In certain circumstances, a federal district court has authority *incrementally* to terminate supervision and control of school districts under de segregation orders. A court may do so where a school district has succeeded in creating a unitary system in some functional areas, *e.g.,* attendance zones, but not in others, *e.g.,* teacher assignments; and continued overall supervision is unnecessary to secure compliance in areas remaining dual. *Freeman v. Pitts,* 112 S. Ct. 1430 (1992).

12. ***Racial balance:*** Once a school district has remedied prior school segregation, it has no constitutional obligation to ensure racial balance in schools where the student population has become racially imbalanced because of population shifts in school attendance zones. ("Racial balance is not to be achieved for its own sake. It is to be pursued when racial imbalance has been caused by a constitutional

violation. Once the racial imbalance due to the de jure violation has been remedied, the school district is under no duty to remedy imbalance that is caused by demographic factors.") *Freeman v. Pitts, supra. Cf. Pasadena City Bd. of Educ. v. Spangler,* 423 U.S. 424 (1976).

8

13. ***Limits on power to remedy*** **de jure** ***segregation:*** The population of some school districts, mostly urban, is overwhelmingly minority. In some cases, this has come about because of "white flight" and that in part because of efforts to desegregate schools within a district. In such districts, it may be virtually impossible to create a racially integrated school system because the number of nonminority students within the district is too small. In attempting to end officially segregated schools in such districts, courts have sometimes tried to get nonminority students from outside the district to attend schools within the district. This could be done by including other school districts, where nonminority students reside, in the desegregation plan. Another way is to make schools within the segregated district so attractive that nonresident, nonminority students will attend them voluntarily. Both of these methods of integrating schools raise constitutional problems.

   a. *Remedies outside of district:* The extent of the constitutional violation limits the scope of the desegregation remedy. Consequently, where there has been official segregation only within a district, not causally related to segregation in other districts, it is improper for a court to order a remedy involving the other districts. In other words, a court may not order *inter*district remedies for *intra*district violations. This is so even where, because of racial residential patterns, it is impossible to create racially integrated schools within the district found to have been officially segregated. *Milliken v. Bradley,* 418 U.S. 717 (1974).

   b. *Interdistrict "desegregative attractiveness" remedies:* One remedy courts have used to create integrated schools is to create so-called magnet schools. A magnet school is a high-quality school that usually has extraordinary facilities and resources, superb teachers, and rich programs and course offerings. Magnet schools attract students who attend voluntarily and thus avoid some of the problems associated with mandatory attendance zones, residential segregation, and court-ordered busing. While creating a magnet school is an appropriate remedy to end intradistrict segregation, a court may not order increased school expenditures simply in order to attract nonminority students from outside the district to attend district schools. This is, in effect, an *inter*district remedy for an *intra*district violation, and a court may not order it without proof of an *inter*district violation. *Missouri v. Jenkins (II),* 63 U.S.L.W. 4486 (1995) (district court order for salary increases and for state funding of quality education programs to improve desegregative attractiveness held unconstitutional).

C. **Proving Purposeful Discrimination**

   1. ***Disproportionate or disparate impact:*** An action is said to have a "disproportionate" or "disparate" impact when it affects one distinctive group more heavily than another. For example, a facially neutral law that required all brown-eyed people to have a special test to obtain a driver's license would proportionally impact much more heavily on blacks than on whites. In other words, in application, seemingly neutral criteria can select for race or other characteristics in statistically significant ways. The use of such criteria can be intentional; that is, officials could

use facially neutral criteria known to select disproportionately for race, *in order to screen selection based on race.* Officials can also use such criteria in good faith, not seeking to select for race, but inadvertently or unintentionally doing so because the selection criteria in practice has a disproportionate and negative impact on a particular race. The official use of facially neutral criteria to implement some program, therefore, is no guarantee that there is no racially discriminatory motive operating. Similarly, the fact that neutral criteria in application have a disproportionate impact does not, of itself, dispositively prove a racially discriminatory motive or intent behind the use of such criteria.

Discriminatory effects: "Discriminatory effects" are the detrimental effects of a statute, action, or practice falling disproportionately more upon one distinct group than another. In that sense the terms *discriminatory effects* and *disproportionate effects* or *impacts* are equivalent.

3. ***The sophisticated discriminator problem:*** It is possible to frame statutes or decisions intended to have discriminatory effects in nondiscriminatory or facially neutral terms. Not all facially neutral statutes having discriminatory effects, however, are intended to discriminate.

   Example: Suppose a state adopts a literacy test for voting or a public employer adopts a standard language test for job qualification. In a particular jurisdiction, either test may disproportionately select out certain minorities as having failed. Although neither test is framed in terms of racial criteria, in application they have a strong racial impact. Knowing this, a sophisticated discriminator could choose to use such tests in order to discriminate. On the other hand, parties not wishing to discriminate might also use such tests, in each case because they believe the test screens out unqualified persons without regard to race.

4. ***General rule – discriminatory intent necessary:*** In order to establish a violation of the Equal Protection Clause, one who claims discrimination on the basis of a suspect classification must prove there was a discriminatory intent or purpose. A showing of disproportionate or discriminatory effect alone generally will not establish discriminatory intent. *Washington v. Davis,* 426 U.S. 229 (1976).

   Example: Language-based exercises of peremptories. Language-based juror strikes, even when disproportionately impacting members of a particular minority, do not violate equal protection unless based on race. *Hernandez v. New York,* 500 U.S. 352 (1991). (Prosecutor struck Hispanic jurors out of fear their knowledge of Spanish would compromise their ability to rely on the official translation of testimony of Spanish-speaking witnesses.)

   a. *Exceptions:* There are a few exceptions to the foregoing rule.

      (1) In extreme cases, where discriminatory effect is so great as to admit of no other conclusion than discriminatory purpose, *Yick Wo v. Hopkins,* 118 U.S. 356 (1886); *Gomillion v. Lightfoot,* 364 U.S. 339 (1960).

      Example: In *Yick Wo, supra,* a San Francisco City ordinance prohibited operating a laundry in wooden buildings without the consent of the Board of Supervisors. In administering the provision, the Board granted permits to operate laundries in wooden buildings to none of the some 200 Chinese applicants but to virtually all non-Chinese applicants. The neutral provision was clearly administered with discriminatory intent and was unconstitutionally applied.

(2) In jury selection cases, where the law imposes a community cross-sectional representation requirement, and there is a showing of substantial discriminatory effect, *Casteneda v. Partida,* 430 U.S. 482 (1977).

(3) In school desegregation cases, where there is an affirmative duty to remedy prior purposeful discrimination and there is a showing of current segregative effect from such prior discrimination.

8

5. *Mixed-motivation cases:* Cases will arise where a decision-maker has mixed motives in making a decision. For example, in a multimember body, it is possible for some members to vote for a measure because, although framed in terms of neutral criteria, it will have a desired discriminatory effect, while others voting for it have no such intention. In such mixed-motivation cases, a plaintiff need not show that all decision-makers had a discriminatory motive nor that all motives were discriminatory. Instead, the plaintiff need only prove that a discriminatory motive played a role in the decision taken. If a plaintiff can prove that discrimination was a substantial or motivating factor in the decision, then the burden of proof shifts to respondents to show that the same action would have been taken absent the discriminatory motive. *Arlington Heights v. Metropolitan Housing Corp.,* 429 U.S. 252 (1977); *Mt. Healthy City Board of Educ. v. Doyle,* 429 U.S. 274 (1977).

Example: In the *Arlington Heights case, supra,* a zoning commission met to consider a request to rezone a fifteen-acre parcel from single family to multifamily housing in order to build racially integrated low-income housing. At the meeting, some speakers spoke out against the requested change on racial grounds; others opposed it for other reasons. The zoning commissioners denied the requested change and could justify the denial on legitimate criteria the commission regularly used, and themselves expressed no racial motives for their decision. Under these circumstances, there was no showing that racial motivation played a role in the commission decision, and their decision was subject to rational basis review rather than strict scrutiny.

HEIGHTENED SCRUTINY BASED ON GENDER, ALIENAGE, AND ILLEGITIMACY CLASSIFICATIONS

6. *Neutral criteria adopted with a discriminatory purpose*

a. *Discriminatory effect and intent:* Neutral criteria shown to have a discriminatory effect and adopted with discriminatory intent violate the Equal Protection Clause. *Hunter v. Underwood,* 471 U.S. 222 (1985).

Example: In *Hunter, supra,* the Alabama Constitutional Convention of 1901 adopted a state constitutional provision disenfranchising persons convicted of any crime of moral turpitude, including within the list of crimes misdemeanors not punishable by imprisonment in state prison. Substantial evidence demonstrated that a major aim of the convention was to disenfranchise blacks, and that this particular provision was part of that effort. In fact, the provision operated to disenfranchise far more blacks than whites. On this showing, the provision was held unconstitutional as applied to persons convicted of misdemeanors.

b. *No discriminatory effect:* Neutral criteria adopted with a discriminatory intent, but having no discriminatory effect, do not violate equal protection. *Palmer v. Thompson,* 403 U.S. 217 (1971).

Example: In *Palmer, supra,* a city closed its public swimming pools when they were ordered desegregated. Although one motivation for closure was discriminatory, there was no discriminatory effect as the decision closed the pool to members of all races.

7. ***Neutral criteria maintained for a discriminatory purpose:*** In some cases, sophisticated discriminators could use neutral criteria, originally adopted without a racially discriminatory purpose, in order to discriminate presently. If the criteria have a discriminatory impact, the intent to maintain them *because of* their discriminatory impact is purposeful discriminatory intent sufficient to establish a violation of the Equal Protection Clause. *Rogers v. Lodge,* 458 U.S. 613 (1982).

Example: *Rogers v. Lodge, supra,* dealt with at-large election systems. In at-large systems, every voter in a geographical unit, such as a county, votes for a candidate for every seat, say on a five-person county board of directors. Such systems are facially neutral but can have disproportionate impact. Because of such factors as voter polarization by race, low black voter registration, travel distance to voting sites (which may be affected by residential segregation), poverty, lack of education, and the like, African-Americans in such a system may not be able to elect members to the board. This is so even when they are numerically in a majority as in *Rogers.* These factors, even considered together, do not amount to discriminatory purpose. However, maintaining this system because it has a discriminatory effect does constitute a discriminatory purpose. *Rogers, supra.*

8. ***Foreseeability:*** When someone can foresee that one result, among others, will flow from some action, he or she can yet choose to do the action not desiring the result, but for reasons unrelated to it. In other words, one can do an act "in spite of" an undesired consequence rather than "because of" it. For this reason, in equal protection cases, the fact that one can foresee that a certain discriminatory effect will follow, subsequent action having a discriminatory effect does not of itself establish discriminatory intent. Foreseeability is merely evidence of discriminatory intent. *Personnel Admin. of Mass. v. Feeney,* 442 U.S. 256 (1979).

Example: In *Feeney, supra,* plaintiffs attacked a Massachusetts statute granting veterans a job preference in competitions for state civil service positions on grounds of a denial of equal protection for women, as virtually all Massachusetts veterans were male. Although the discriminatory impact of the preference was quite great, it did not of itself demonstrate a discriminatory purpose in its adoption. Furthermore, nothing else in the record demonstrated the preference was adopted in order to discriminate against women, and the preference was upheld despite its effect on women's job opportunities.

9. ***Discriminatory effect in death penalty cases:*** There is good statistical evidence, at least in some jurisdictions, that capital case jurors are more likely to return a death sentence in cases involving African-American defendants and white victims. Such statistical proof, however, does not establish discriminatory intent in a particular case, nor that racial discrimination is the cause of any particular death

sentence, which generally can be attributed to other factors in capital cases. *McKleskey v. Kemp,* 481 U.S. 279 (1987).

IV. **HEIGHTENED SCRUTINY FOR CERTAIN OTHER CLASSIFICATIONS. THE COURT APPLIES SOME FORM OF HEIGHTENED SCRUTINY TO CLASSIFI-CATIONS BASED ON GENDER, ALIENAGE, AND ILLEGITIMACY: After an uncertain start, the Court has settled on intermediate scrutiny for gender classifications; a dual scheme of scrutiny – strict scrutiny in some cases and deferential scrutiny in others – for alienage classifications; and some form of intermediate scrutiny in illegitimacy cases.**

8

A. **Gender Classifications:** Prior to 1971, the Court applied rational basis review to classifications based on sex or gender. Since then, the Court has applied a more stringent level of review, finally settling on intermediate review as the appropriate standard in gender classification cases.

1. *General considerations:* Unlike classifications based on race or ethnicity, for which, generally, there is no legitimate purpose, classifications based on gender sometimes do have valid purposes and may be useful or essential for regulation. Gender classifications, however, have for the most part been based on stereotyped, rather than realistic, thinking about sex roles and the abilities, strengths, weaknesses, and needs of the respective sexes. Historically, governments have often classified on the basis of gender in ways detrimental to women, excluding them from opportunities available to men or otherwise imposing disabilities on them constraining their freedom. But there is stereotyped thinking regarding men's nature and roles as well, and gender classifications sometimes, although not nearly as often, work to men's disadvantage. In this context, the essential work of the intermediate standard of review is to force governments to assess the position of men and women realistically rather than on the basis of myths or long-held, but untrue, assumptions about the nature of men and women.

2. *Intermediate review standard regarding gender classifications:* In its latest version of the intermediate standard of review in cases involving gender classifications, the Court requires that the government provide an "exceedingly persuasive" justification for using a gender classification. In reviewing the use of such classifications, the Court will not consider hypothetical objectives, as it does under rational basis review. The burden of justification rests on the state, and a reviewing court should consider as justifications only purposes that the legislature actually intended to realize. The government must have important objectives for using the classification, and the classification must substantially relate to the achievement of those objectives — that is, must make some really significant contribution to realizing the government purposes. *United States v. Virginia,* 518 U.S. 515 (1996); *J.E.B. v. Alabama ex rel. T.B.,* 511 U.S. 127 (1994); *Mississippi University for Women v. Hogan,* 458 U.S. 718 (1982).

3. *Classifications involving gender stereotypes*

a. *Statutes presuming greater male competency:* Statutes which presume a greater competency in men than women or which accord men greater, or special, rights to control or dispose of property are unconstitutional. *Reed v. Reed,* 404 U.S. 71 (1971); *Kirchberg v. Feenstra,* 450 U.S. 455 (1981).

Examples: In *Reed, supra,* the Court struck down an Idaho statute that gave a preference to men over women in appointments to administer estates.

In *Kirchberg, supra,* the Court struck down a Louisiana property law which gave a husband unilateral authority to dispose of community property.

b. *Statutes presuming dependency in women:* Statutes that presume that women are dependent and simultaneously presume male nondependence or require men to prove dependency are unconstitutional. *Frontiero v. Richardson,* 411 U.S. 677 (1973); *Weinberger v. Weisenfield,* 420 U.S. 636 (1975); *Califano v. Goldfarb,* 430 U.S. 199 (1977); *Orr v. Orr,* 440 U.S. 268 (1979); *Wengler v. Druggists Mutual Ins. Co.,* 446 U.S. 142 (1980).

Examples: In *Frontiero, supra,* the Court invalidated a federal law granting the wife of a serviceman an automatic dependency allowance, but requiring that a servicewoman prove her husband's dependency to obtain a similar allowance for him.

In *Weisenfield, supra,* the Court found unconstitutional gender discrimination in a Social Security survivor's benefits provision. The law gave benefits to the surviving widow and minor children when the husband died but provided support for only minor children, not the widower, when the wife died. The articulated purpose of the statute was childcare, with parental benefits tied to childcare. The classification between male and female surviving spouses was not substantially related to this purpose, as widowers were denied benefits. The apparent stereotyped assumption behind the statute was that males support families financially while females do not.

In *Orr, supra,* Alabama law authorized its courts to require alimony of husbands, but not wives. The state objectives of supporting needy women and compensating women for discrimination during marriage were important, but the classification did not serve those objectives well. Not all divorcing wives are needy, and the state, in its divorce proceedings, held individualized hearings regarding the parties' financial circumstances. In this situation, a gender-neutral classification would have served the state's objectives as well, or better than, its gender-based classification.

c. *Statutes assuming gender-based bias; peremptory challenges:* Occasionally, a statute or practice may be based on the idea that gender has an impact on attitudes and decision-making. Trial attorneys have often taken this view in their exercise of peremptory challenges, particularly in cases involving gender-related issues, such as paternity, rape, or sexual harassment cases. In *J.E.B. v. Alabama ex rel. T.B., supra,* the court held that the state use of peremptory challenges to strike male jurors in a paternity case was unconstitutional sex discrimination. The Court reasoned that such use of peremptory challenge was based on the stereotype that gender alone was an accurate predictor of juror attitudes.

4. ***Classifications based on alleged or real differences between the sexes:*** There are cases where the state seeks to justify a gender classification based on asserted real differences between the sexes or on the related idea that the sexes are "dissimilarly situated" with regard to the problem the state is seeking to solve. The question in such cases is whether gender is an appropriate proxy for the state to use in its regulation or whether some other classification would better serve its

purpose. The Court's decisions in this area are difficult to reconcile because the Court has been inconsistent in the rigor of its review. The most recent trend, however, as evidenced by *United States v. Virginia, supra*, has been toward quite rigorous review, approaching, but not quite reaching, strict scrutiny.

8

a.   *Gender differences in drinking behavior:* In *Craig v. Boren,* 429 U.S. 190 (1976), Oklahoma, in the interests of traffic safety, prohibited sale of 3.2% beer to males under twenty-one and to females under eighteen. The state claimed that males between the ages of seventeen and twenty-one had more alcohol-related arrests and more serious traffic accidents than females and were more likely to drink and drive than females. The Court held, however, that the relationship between male gender and traffic safety was too tenuous to support use of the classification. While there were statistics showing that two percent of males in the relevant age group were arrested for drinking and driving, the proscription applied to all males and thus was wildly overinclusive. In addition, the state barred sale of beer to young men, not their drinking of it. Consequently, this means of ensuring enhanced traffic safety did not clearly lead to it.

b.   *Statutory rape:* In *Michael M. v. Superior Court,* 450 U.S. 464 (1981), the Court sustained California's statutory rape law, which made intercourse with a female under age eighteen, even with consent, criminal. The law was gender-based in punishing the male but not the female. The Court sustained the classification on the ground that males and females were not similarly situated with regard to the problem the state was seeking to address, which was to prevent pregnancy. Only females get pregnant, and while that may deter them from intercourse, there is no similar deterrent for males. In addition, if the law punished the female as well as the male, the female would not likely report instances of statutory rape, thus frustrating enforcement of the statute.

c.   *Draft registration:* In *Rostker v. Goldberg,* 453 U.S. 57 (1981), the Court upheld a congressional statute requiring males, but not females, to register for a potential military draft. Other law made women ineligible for combat positions in the military. The issue in *Rostker,* therefore, was whether, *under that assumption,* excluding women from registration closely served the congressional purpose. The Court plurality questionably concluded that one of Congress' major purposes was to create a list of draft-eligibles who could all serve as combat troops if necessary. Since women were not combat-eligible, men and women were not similarly situated with respect to the draft registration requirement.

d.   *Single-sex education and gender-segregated educational opportunities:* While the constitutionality of single-sex education remains to be decided, state provision of unique educational opportunities to one gender, but not the other, is unconstitutional. *United States v. Virginia, supra.*

In *United States v. Virginia,* Virginia operated a famous military college, the Virginia Military Institute, for men only, and had no comparable institution for women. Virginia claimed that it had two purposes in educating only men at VMI: diversity in educational opportunities in the state and differences between the sexes. Regarding the latter, Virginia claimed that VMI provided "adversative" education, and that if women were admitted, it would have to change its educational methods. The Court viewed the diversity rationale as a postrationalization and not a real reason for the differential treatment. With regard to adversative training, it was clear that some women could meet all of VMI's standards and could handle, and profit from, such training. As Virginia was denying these women a unique educational opportunity solely on the basis of their gender, VMI's male-only admissions policy was unconstitutional.

In *Mississippi U. for Women, supra,* Mississippi denied a registered male nurse admission to the nurse's baccalaureate program at its all-female School of Nursing. Mississippi claimed that its purpose in restricting admission to females was to compensate for discrimination against women in the field of nursing. The evidence completely belied the state's claim, however, for there was no showing of any employment discrimination against women in nursing – indeed, the evidence was to the contrary. The state therefore failed to establish an actual, legitimate purpose for the gender discrimination. The state, however, made the second claim that the presence of men in its nursing classes adversely affected the education of women. As the state permitted men to audit nursing classes at the school, however, its male-gender admission exclusion didn't achieve the asserted goal.

e. *Pregnancy disability benefits:* In *Geduldig v. Aiello,* 417 U.S. 484 (1974), the Court upheld a California workers' disability insurance program which covered virtually all disabilities but short-term disabilities of less than eight days and normal pregnancies. The pregnancy exclusion was attacked as a gender-based discrimination as only women can be pregnant. Aside from the pregnancy exclusion, however, the program covered disabilities unique to women as well as disabilities unique to men, for example, disabilities stemming from hysterectomies and abnormal disabilities stemming from pregnancy. The discrimination, therefore, was not against women as such, but against women with normal pregnancies. Since there was no gender discrimination, the Court applied the rational basis standard of review. As the program was supported through workers' contributions, the Court viewed the pregnancy exclusion as based on a certain kind of actuarial risk and its potential program cost and therefore justified.

f. *Gender discrimination against fathers of illegitimates*

(1) Conclusive presumption of unfitness: States may not conclusively presume that, on the death of the mother, an unmarried father is unfit to raise a surviving child. While such a presumption denies due process, it also violates equal protection because only unmarried fathers fail to receive a hearing on fitness to be a parent. *Stanley v. Illinois,* 405 U.S. 645 (1972).

(2) Paternal consent to adoption: Some states have statutes requiring that natural mothers consent to the adoption of their children but do not similarly require the natural fathers' consent. In many cases, this is efficient and facilitates adoption as the natural father is either unknown or unfindable and has had no relationship with the child. On the other hand, where the natural father is known and has had a relationship, such laws operate to cut off parental rights without consent. Where the known father has had a substantial relationship with his child, he is, for adoption consent

purposes, in a situation similar to the mother's, and laws denying him the right to consent to adoption discriminate against him on the basis of gender. *Caban v. Mohammed,* 441 U.S. 380 (1979). Where the father has had no significant relationship with the child, however, the mother and father are differently situated, and the state may provide for adoption on the mother's consent alone. *Quilloin v. Wolcott,* 434 U.S. 246 (1978); *Lehr v. Robertson,* 463 U.S. 248 (1983).

(3) Paternal wrongful death actions: Some states provide that natural fathers, but not natural mothers, can legitimate their children. In such states, statutes that deny a natural father the right to sue for the wrongful death of his child unless he has legitimated the child do not deny equal protection. Such statutes do not discriminate against natural fathers as a class, but against those who have not legitimated their children. *Parham v. Hughes,* 441 U.S. 347 (1979) (plurality). (Query, however, whether, proof of paternity problems aside, there is not a gender-based discrimination between unmarried mothers and fathers as the mothers need not legitimate their children to sue in wrongful death.)

B. Alienage Classifications

1. *Congressional regulation:* Under the Constitution, Congress has plenary authority to regulate immigration and nationalization. Therefore, Congress's determinations respecting aliens are subject to rational basis review.

   a. *Unauthorized administrative regulation of immigration:* Only Congress has the authority to set the terms for the admission of aliens and the conditions of their stay in the United States.

      Example: In *Hampton v. Mow Sun Wong,* 426 U.S 88 (1976), the Court considered federal civil service regulations which barred aliens from most federal civil service positions. The Civil Service Commission argued its goals were to create an incentive for naturalization; to give the president a bargaining chip in foreign affairs; and to ensure loyalty in sensitive government positions. The Court held that while these were laudable goals, only Congress had the authority to set terms of admission. Congress had not barred aliens from federal civil service and had not authorized the Commission to do so, and the regulations were therefore invalid.

   b. *Denial of benefits:* As long as it acts rationally, Congress can deny benefits to those admitted for permanent residence in the country.

      Example: In *Matthews v. Diaz,* 462 U.S. 67 (1976), Congress conditioned aliens' receipt of medical benefits on admission for permanent residence and continuous residence for five years. Two aliens lawfully admitted as refugees, one of whom was admitted for permanent residence but did not meet the five-year residency requirement, claimed a denial of equal protection. The Court applied the rational basis standard and held the permanent and five-year residency requirements rationally related to establishing affinity and protecting the public fisc.

2. *State regulation:* The states have no constitutional role in immigration and nationalization, and once Congress has determined who may lawfully enter the

country, states may not act to discourage or burden lawful immigration. Furthermore, while states may regulate social welfare matters, they may not, with one significant exception, use alienage classifications. The Equal Protection Clause refers to persons, not citizens, and therefore protects aliens. As aliens are a discrete and insular minority, state classifications based on alienage are inherently suspect and subject to strict scrutiny.

a. *Benefits cases*

   (1) Unless authorized by Congress or justified by a compelling interest, state laws excluding permanent resident aliens from receipt of welfare benefits through imposition of long-term residency or citizenship requirements are unconstitutional. *Graham v. Richardson,* 403 U.S. 365 (1971).

   (2) Unless authorized by Congress, states may not disqualify resident aliens from receiving state financial assistance offered or given to state citizens or residents. *Nyquist v. Mauclet,* 432 U.S. 1 (1977).

b. *Employment and licensing cases; political function — political community exception:* The Court generally applies strict scrutiny to review state denials of public employment or licenses to aliens. If, however, the employment or license involves a position where the holder performs policy formulation, execution, or review functions going to the heart of representative democracy, and therefore justifying a citizenship requirement, the Court applies rational basis review.

   (1) Common occupations of the community: States cannot prefer citizens over noncitizens for employment in common occupations or trades. *Sugarman v. Dougall,* 413 U.S. 634 (1973).

   Examples: States cannot require citizenship for positions such as administrative assistant, clerk-typist, or assistant counselor, *Sugarman, supra,* as a condition for state bar membership, *In re Griffiths,* 413 U.S. 717 (1973), to be a licensed civil engineer, *Examining Bd. of Engineers, etc. v. Flores de Otero,* 426 U.S. 572 (1976), or to be a notary public, *Bernal v. Fainter,* 476 U.S. 216 (1984).

   (2) Political-function exception: A state may require citizenship as a condition of employment for those who participate in the formulation and execution of governmental policy, whose allegiance to the state, and not to foreign powers, may be important. The state may thus certainly require that its high officers – governor, legislators, judges, agency heads – be citizens. A citizenship requirement for other state employees may be more questionable. While it is difficult to state exactly how far down the public employment scale the political-function exception reaches, the Court has indicated that it also covers public positions involving discretionary decision-making, authority to use force, and training others for citizenship.

   Examples: Police officers exercise considerable discretion in law enforcement and have the authority to use force on behalf of the state. Their position therefore falls within the political-function exception, and the state may require citizenship of police officers. *Foley v. Connelie,* 435 U.S. 291 (1978).

A significant part of public education involves training for citizenship, and public school teachers are important citizenship role models. Public teaching therefore falls within the political-function exception. *Ambach v. Norwick,* 441 U.S. 68 (1979).

Deputy probation officers exercise considerable discretion in carrying out their duties of supervising those who are placed on probation, and the state may require that they be citizens. *Cabell v. Chavez-Salido,* 454 U.S. 432 (1982).

C. **Illegitimacy as a Classification:** Classification of children based on the nonmarital status of parents reflects an enduring, if declining, social discrimination. Most would now agree that it is wrong to punish or disadvantage a child because his parents were not married. The child has no responsibility for the legal character of his birth, and a state should not authorize unequal treatment of a child because he is considered illegitimate.

On the other hand, in our society, we tie the provision of support and inheritance rights to biological relationship to a parent. We usually know who the mother of a child is, but, at least until the advent of genetic testing, have not had the same certainty regarding the father. For children born out of marriage, we generally require proof of paternity in order to make an alleged father financially responsible and similarly require paternity proofs in cases involving claims on estates. Once a child or an alleged father is dead, it may be much harder to prove paternity.

Furthermore, we generally link the provision of other children's benefits or compensatory awards, such as wrongful death awards, insurance, social security, or workers' compensation, to a child's establishing dependency, presumed or actual, on a covered individual. This is so because the benefits are intended to provide some of the support lost by death or accident. The marital status of parents is not conclusive on the issue of a child's dependency, but as generalizations go, it is at least arguably reasonable to suppose that fewer nonmarital fathers support their children than marital. Nonmarital fathers have no legal obligation to support until they either legally acknowledge children as theirs or there is a court order of support. Consequently, when a nonmarital father dies without an established legal obligation to support, it is natural for a state to demand a demonstration of actual dependency to avoid fraudulent claims.

For the foregoing reasons, it is not always irrational or irrelevant to use a child's legal birth status for some purposes. Furthermore, illegitimacy as a classification does not have all the features which make the use of suspect classifications unacceptable. Illegitimate children do not comprise a readily identifiable group and are not subjected to pervasive societal discrimination, although they have been at certain times and places in history. Finally, birth status is not an unalterable trait. Parents can legitimate an illegitimate child. Consequently, illegitimacy does not appear to qualify as a suspect certification. On the other hand, it is one of those classifications that has often been used to punish a helpless minority for the sins of their parents or to deny them benefits because of a thoughtless social prejudice.

The Court's illegitimacy decisions reflect all these tensions and considerations regarding illegitimacy as a classification, sometimes upholding its use, but more often not. The best that can be said is that the Court, over a series of illegitimacy decisions, wavered in the search for an appropriate standard, but finally settled on intermediate review.

1. *Qualification for awards or benefits*

   a. *Wrongful death actions:* States may not, in order to discourage people from having children out of wedlock, provide that only legitimate children may be entitled to recover in a wrongful death action for the death of a parent. As a classification, illegitimacy has no relationship to the wrong committed against the deceased parent nor to the actual dependency of the surviving children. Furthermore, the classification does not serve its intended purpose of discouraging illegitimacy for it is not rational to assume that persons would decline to have children because the children could not receive an award following their wrongful death. *Levy v. Louisiana,* 391 U.S. 68 (1968); *Glona v. American Guaranty & Liability Ins. Co.,* 391 U.S. 73 (1968).

   b. *Workers' compensation awards:* The state interest in protecting legitimate family relationships does not justify giving legitimate children a priority over illegitimate children in the receipt of workers' compensation death benefits. It is not reasonable to assume that people have children, whether legitimately or illegitimately, so that the children will receive compensation on the death of a parent. *Weber v. Aetna Casualty,* 406 U.S. 164 (1972).

   c. *Social Security survivor's benefits:* Under the Social Security Act, children dependent on a parent at the time of the parent's death are entitled to survivor's benefits. Children are dependent if living with the parent at time of death or if the parent was contributing to their support. For administrative convenience, the statute presumes dependency for those children entitled to inherit under state law and for illegitimate children whose parents had married before death, whose parents had acknowledged in them in writing, or whom a court had decreed to be a particular parent's child. In effect, the statute requires certain illegitimate children, but not all, to present proof of dependency. The statute, therefore, does not discriminate against illegitimate children as such, but against a subclass of illegitimate children. The Court held the classification was substantially related to the congressional purposes of requiring dependency and administrative convenience and was therefore justified. *Matthews v. Lucas,* 427 U.S. 495 (1976).

   d. *Parental support:* States cannot deny illegitimate children rights to support. *Gomez v. Perez,* 409 U.S. 535 (1973).

   e. *Paternity suit statutes of limitations:* Some states, while imposing no time limits on the right of a legitimate child to sue for support, do require that illegitimate children bring their action within a certain period of time after birth. Proof of paternity distinguishes support suits by illegitimates, and states do have an interest in restricting the prosecution of stale or fraudulent claims. Nonetheless, unrealistically short statutes of limitations periods deny equal protection. States must allow sufficient time for those interested in an illegitimate child to bring a paternity suit on his behalf, and any time limitations must be substantially related to avoiding stale or fraudulent claims. *Mills v. Habluetzel,* 456 U.S. 91 (1982). Paternity suit limitation periods of one year, *Mills, supra,* and two years, *Pickett v. Brown,* 462 U.S. 1 (1983), and six years, *Clark v. Jeter,* 486 U.S. 456 (1988), are clearly too short.

2. *Intestate inheritance:* A number of states, in their intestate inheritance provisions, subordinate illegitimate children to legitimate children and, sometimes, other relatives of the deceased. While the Court's decisions in this category are not consistent – because of a shift in standards applied over time – the Court now applies intermediate scrutiny.

Examples: In *Labine v. Vincent,* 401 U.S. 532 (1971), Louisiana subordinated the inheritance rights of illegitimate children to all other relatives of the deceased. The Court, applying a rational basis standard of review, held that the state interest in having an orderly method for directing the disposition of intestate property at death justified the classification. The Court thought it particularly important to give deference to state rules regarding the disposition of property.

In *Trimble v. Gordon,* 430 U.S. 762 (1977), Illinois provided that illegitimate children could inherit intestate only from their mother. The state purposes, in addition to promoting legitimate family relationships, were to regulate the disposition of property and to preclude difficult proof problems respecting paternity. The Court applied intermediate scrutiny and struck down the provision. The purpose of promoting legitimacy was thought tenuous and disregarded. While solving proof of paternity problems was a substantial state interest, barring all illegitimate children claimants was extreme because it denied all possibility of a valid claim. As the bar excluded forms of proof not compromising the state's interest in precluding spurious claims, the Court ruled the classification did not substantially contribute to the articulated purpose.

In *Lalli v. Lalli,* 439 U.S. 259 (1978), New York required that before intestates could inherit from an intestate father, they had to produce a court order of filiation, issued sometime during the life of the father, as proof of paternity. The classification did not discriminate against illegitimates per se since any illegitimate with a filiation order could inherit. Unlike *Trimble,* the provision did not operate as a total bar to illegitimates inheriting from their fathers. In addition, the period of time in which a filiation order had to be obtained was not unreasonably short or burdensome. The Court, applying intermediate scrutiny, held that the classification bore a substantial relation to the state purpose of avoiding spurious claims.

D. **Other Classifications as Possible Suspect or Quasi-suspect Classifications:** Race, ethnicity, national origin, and state, as opposed to federal, alienage classifications comprise the list of suspect classifications; gender and illegitimacy the list of quasi-suspect classifications. The Court has rejected arguments that additional classifications, such as age or mental retardation, should be considered as suspect or quasi-suspect classifications. Both age and mental retardation lack the characteristics of suspect classifications. While there has been some historical discrimination on the basis of age or mental retardation, legislatures have also acted positively to assist people having problems because of age or mental retardation. In addition, age and mental retardation are often useful grounds of classification, highly relevant to legitimate state aims. For these reasons, the Court reviews state use of such classifications under the rational basis standard. *Massachusetts Bd. of Retirement v. Murgia,* 427 U.S. 307 (1976) (age); *City of Cleburne v. Cleburne Living Center,* 473 U.S. 432 (1985) (mental retardation).

Note: While the Court has refused to hold that mental retardation is a quasi-suspect classification, its application of the rational basis standard of review to this classification reveals a more careful and searching review than the standard generally calls for. This suggests that those cases where a classification, albeit neither suspect nor quasi-suspect, disadvantages often disfavored, despised, or feared minorities, the Court will scrutinize the relationship between the classification and its asserted aims with special care.

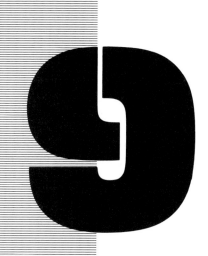

EQUAL PROTECTION (II)

▶ **CHAPTER SUMMARY**

CHAPTER 9: EQUAL PROTECTION (II)

Introduction. This chapter discusses two major equal protection topics, affirmative action and classifications adversely affecting fundamental rights. In the past, governments have used state power and authority to discriminate against minorities and women. While governments may no longer do this, at least as a matter of constitutional law, the ending of official discrimination has not delivered practical equality. Relatively speaking, minorities, and to a lesser extent, women, remain disadvantaged in employment, educational, and entrepreneurial opportunities. To deal with continuing disadvantage, governments have sought to use otherwise forbidden or questionable classifications to provide special assistance to members of historically disadvantaged groups. The constitutional issues are whether, and in what circumstances, governments may do so, and Part I of this chapter treats those issues.

"BENIGN" SUSPECT OR QUASI-SUSPECT CLASSIFICA-TIONS

Part II principally deals with the rather different issue of classifications adversely affecting the implied fundamental rights to vote, to travel within the United States, and access to the courts. Of these, the right to vote is most significant, for Court decisions under that rubric have profoundly shaped the political process in this country. The right to travel, actually a bundle of several rights, deals with rights to movement, migration, and equal treatment. The right of access to the courts takes up the issue of fundamental fairness to the poor in adjudication. The chapter concludes with a brief discussion of other candidate fundamental rights, such as a proposed right to the basic necessities of life and a right to education.

I. "BENIGN" SUSPECT OR QUASI-SUSPECT CLASSIFICATIONS

A. **"Benign" Racial Classifications:** The Court subjects racial classifications to strict scrutiny review, requiring a compelling state interest and a classificatory sweep as narrow as possible. The long and terrible history of slavery, state-imposed racial disadvantage, and racial discrimination, however, worked its way deep into American life. Although official state discrimination has ended, greatly disproportionate numbers of racial minority members remain disadvantaged in employment, educational opportunities, and other ways, when compared with whites. Their continued disadvantage and denial of opportunity have prompted legislative and other official efforts to overcome disadvantages and open opportunities. As the problems are specifically racial, governments and state agencies have used racial classifications to target remedies thought necessary or desirable. Given the structure of the constitutional law of racial discrimination, however, strict scrutiny review of racial classifications is a barrier to their use in many circumstances.

1. *Constitutional limits on the use of race-conscious remedies:* The constitutional law of racial discrimination distinguishes strongly between intentional discrimination and societal discrimination, perceived to be the result of individual, as opposed to state, choices. As seen in the school desegregation cases, when there is a finding of official state racial discrimination, courts may, often must, impose race-conscious remedies. The Court has held, however, that when there is no finding of prior or current discrimination against an identifiable group of victims —no finding of an equal protection violation — then neither courts or the government may use race-conscious remedies. *Adarand Constructors Inc. v. Pena,* 63 U.S.L.W. 4523 (1995); *City of Richmond v. J.A. Croson,* 488 U.S. 469 (1989); *Wygant v. Jackson Board of Educ.,* 476 U.S. 267 (1986); *cf. Regents of the University of California v. Bakke,* 438 U.S. 265 (1978).

    a. *Constitutional arguments for race-conscious remedies:* A strong minority of the Court has argued that state action favoring racial minorities is quite different from state action disadvantaging minorities. When the state acts to favor minorities to remedy the widespread effects of societal discrimination, not shown to be caused by any particular acts of discrimination against an identified group of victims, the white majority is, in effect, burdening itself. There is no history of discrimination against the white majority, and no stigma would attach to whites because of the classification. The benign use of racial classifications, therefore, does not entail one of the major evils of suspect classifications. That evil is, of course, a majority victimizing a minority, unable, because it is a minority, to help itself through use of state power. Nonetheless, given the potential misuse of racial classifications, there is a need to scrutinize them carefully. Consequently, these justices would apply intermediate scrutiny review to positive race-conscious classifications. *Bakke, supra* (Brennan, J., White, J., Marshall, J., Blackmun, J., concurring in judgment in part and dissenting).

b. *Arguments against race-conscious remedies not tied to intentional discrimination: "color-blind" theory:* The argument against race-conscious remedies is that the Equal Protection Clause prohibits the state from denying equal protection to any person, and that the ban on using race as a classification applies regardless of which race the classification benefits or burdens. Although racial classifications benefiting minorities unable to demonstrate they have suffered from specific discrimination may seem nonharmful, in fact they carry a danger of "stigmatic" harm. Because "benign" classifications are thought to advantage minorities over whites on the basis of race, not competitive merit considerations, minorities may suffer the harm of being branded as members of an inferior race needing governmental advantaging. Such advantaging could also lead to extremely hostile and divisive racial politics, where race determines who wins and who loses in the use of political power. Therefore, all racial classifications, whether seemingly harmful or seemingly beneficial, must receive strict scrutiny review. Only the compelling need to remedy demonstrated discrimination impacting on an identifiable group justifies the use of racial classifications. A majority of the Court now accepts this position. *Croson, supra.*

2. ***Diversity in education as a compelling state interest:*** In *Bakke, supra,* the Court, in an unusual alignment, overturned a special medical school admissions program involving a quota for minority students. Four members of the Court, applying intermediate scrutiny, voted to uphold the program. Four members of the Court, applying strict scrutiny, voted to overturn the program. The last member of the Court, Justice Powell, who wrote the opinion, also applied strict scrutiny and voted to overturn the program in its quota form. However, he was of the view that, in an educational setting, diversity of the student body — racial, ethnic, geographical, class, talent, and the like — was a compelling state interest. In a democratic, multiracial society, learning from, with, and about others from diverse backgrounds is essential. He therefore agreed with the four dissenters that public universities could take race into account in their admissions policies, but — and here he parted company with the dissenters — only as an aspect of diversity. Consequently, racial admission quotas, which make race solely determinative, are unconstitutional. Public universities, however, may use race as one factor, among other factors, to help them compose a diverse student body. This, of course, means that public universities may use race consciously as a classification for this narrow purpose.

3. ***Congressional use of race-based classifications — strict scrutiny:*** The Fourteenth Amendment itself gives Congress the power to enact legislation to enforce equal protection of the laws. Congress certainly has the power to define situations it believes threaten equality and to adopt laws which further and protect it. *Katzenbach v. Morgan,* 384 U.S. 641 (1966), (O'Connor, J.); *cf.* § C, *infra,* and Chapter 10, II.A., *infra.* The Court, however, has been sharply divided over the question of whether Congress's use of "benign" race-conscious classifications is subject to strict scrutiny review or intermediate scrutiny review. In other words, may Congress use race-conscious classifications to further important, rather than compelling, governmental objectives? *Cf. Metro Broadcasting, Inc. v. F.C.C.,* 497 U.S. 547 (1990). Most recently, the Court has held that congressional use of race-conscious classifications is subject to strict scrutiny review. *Adarand Constructors Inc. v. Pena,* 63 U.S.L.W. 4523 (1995).

Example*: Adarand Constructors* involved a federal Small Business Administration, governmental contracts minority set-aside program. The government awarded a highway construction contract to a prime contractor, which in turn awarded subcontracts for parts of the construction. The prime contract provided that the contractor would receive a premium for awarding subcontracts to "socially and economically disadvantaged individuals." Members of certain minority groups were presumed to fall within that class. *Adarand,* which did not fall into this class, submitted the low bid for highway guardrail construction but was denied the subcontract in favor of a minority-owned business. In reviewing Adarand's equal protection challenge to this program, the lower court applied intermediate scrutiny review. The Supreme Court reversed, stating that the correct standard to apply in such cases was strict scrutiny. To justify a program using such race-based classifications, the government must establish a compelling interest and show that the program is narrowly tailored to meet that interest. The latter includes establishing that race-neutral means would not achieve the same goals and that the program will not "last longer than the discriminatory effects it is designed to eliminate."

History: In *Fullilove v. Klutznick,* 448 U.S. 448 (1980), a deeply divided Court, in a plurality opinion, upheld a congressional minority business set-aside program. In the Public Works Employment Act of 1977, Congress, to alleviate unemployment, stimulate the economy, and provide work in the construction industry, provided funds to state and local governments for public works projects. One provision of the Act, passed with virtually no debate, was a "minority set-aside" program. The set-aside required state and local grantees to award ten percent of their contracts to minority business enterprises, defined as businesses owned at least by fifty-percent minority group members. Minority group members were defined as U.S. citizens who were "Negroes, Spanish-speaking, Orientals, Indians, Eskimos and Aleuts." Five members of the Court, for quite different reasons, agreed that Congress could use a racial classification in this way to remedy the effects of racial discrimination in the construction industry. The Court, however, left unclear whether strict or intermediate scrutiny was to apply to such classifications.

In *Metro Broadcasting, supra,* a bare majority of the Court, using intermediate scrutiny, upheld congressionally approved Federal Communications Rules giving a preference to minorities in comparative proceedings for new licenses and giving minorities an advantage in purchasing licenses of owners threatened with revocation hearings and wishing to sell. The Rules promoted programming diversity, an important governmental objective. Further, minority ownership was substantially related to that end because the FCC and Congress have drawn the empirical conclusion that minority participation in the ownership and management of broadcast facilities led to more diverse programming. In *Adarand Constructors, supra*, the Court overruled *Metro Broadcasting* on the question of applying intermediate scrutiny to congressional use of benign racial classifications.

4. ***State and local race-based policy decisions:*** Without a substantiated conclusion — a strong basis in evidence — that specific remedies are required to redress prior or current discrimination, state and local government bodies may not use race classifications in furtherance of affirmative action programs. *Croson, supra; Wygant, supra.*

   Examples: In *Croson, supra,* the City of Richmond adopted a minority set-aside program modeled on the congressional program upheld in *Fullilove, supra.* The program required prime contractors on city construction contracts to subcontract at least thirty-percent of the contract to minority business enterprises, defined as in *Fullilove.* Five members of the Court applied strict scrutiny and concurred that the program was unconstitutional. A majority of the Court held that the race-conscious remedy had not been justified by a showing of any identified discrimination in the Richmond construction industry. Therefore, there was no compelling interest in apportioning public contracts on the basis of race, and the 30% set-aside was clearly not narrowly tailored to remedy discrimination.

   In *Wygant, supra,* a local board of education and a local union provided, in a collective-bargaining agreement, that minority employees would be insulated against layoffs. During a layoff, the effect of the provision was to permit the laying off of nonminority teachers while requiring the retention of minority teachers with less seniority. The board attempted to justify its action as an attempt to alleviate societal discrimination and to ensure that its minority students would have minority role models. A Court majority viewed the action as a violation of the Equal Protection Clause. Common to the various opinions of justices voting to overturn the action were the views that neither societal discrimination nor the need to have minority role models were compelling interests justifying the layoff policy, which discriminated against nonminority teachers.

   Indigenous peoples: As a part of the U.S. population, many Native American tribes exist as quasi-sovereigns under U.S. laws. There is a long-recognized special trust relationship between the federal government and the tribes, ad the Federal Bureau of Indian Affairs administers many programs for Native American peoples. Given this special relationship and the obligations the U.S. has towards Native Americans and other indigenous peoples, Congress must enact legislation that singles them out for special treatment. Although such legislation is ethnic, race, or ancestrally based, it usually presents no constitutional problem. *Morton v. Mancari,* 417 U.S. 535 (1975).

   a. Ethnic, race based, or ancestral voting qualifications: Although Congress can delegate its special authority to states, where a state conducts a state election relating to the administration of state generated funds, the state may not use a race-based classification to determine who may vote in the election. *Rice v. Cayetano,* 120 S.Ct. 1044 (2000). In *Rice,* Hawaii created a state agency to administer programs for the benefit of native Hawaiians and descendants of

1778 inhabitants of Hawaii. The Hawaii constitution and law limited the right to vote for trustees of the agency to the beneficiaries of the state trust. This was an ancestrally based classification, and in effect a proxy for race. Under the Fifteenth Amendment, states may not abridge or deny the right to vote on the basis of race.

B. **"Benign" Use of Gender Classifications**

1. *Affirmative governmental use of quasi-suspect classifications:* In cases involving racial classifications, strict scrutiny and the need to demonstrate discrimination greatly limit the use of affirmative action remedies. In gender classification cases, however, where the Court applies intermediate review, governments may more readily undertake affirmative action. This is simply because the Court recognizes that governments can sometimes use the quasi-suspect classifications, gender and illegitimacy, to achieve legitimate ends. As intermediate review requires only an important, as opposed to a compelling, governmental aim and a classification "substantially related" to that aim, the test is easier to meet than strict scrutiny. Consequently, government can use gender-based classifications in either of the following two general situations:

   a. *Sexes dissimilarly situated:* The government may use gender-based classifications when the sexes are truly differently situated with respect to a problem the government is seeking to solve and the classification is reasonably well-tailored to reflect that difference. The perception that the sexes are differently situated must be based on a realistic assessment rather than on stereotyped or traditional thinking about sex roles.

   b. *Ameliorating sex-based discrimination:* The government may also use gender-based classifications when it seeks to correct a significant sex-based discrimination. The discrimination must disadvantage one sex with regard to opportunities available to the other. Again reflecting the need for a realistic governmental assessment, as opposed to stereotyped thinking about sex roles, the discrimination must also be one that genuine gender differences cannot justify.

   Examples: In *Schlesinger v. Ballard,* 419 U.S. 498 (1975), the Court sustained a United States Navy promotion regulation which treated men and women differentially. The rule provided for a mandatory discharge for officers who had been passed over twice – not promoted on two consecutive promotion reviews. In the case of men, a failure to be promoted within nine years resulted in the discharge. In the case of women, a failure to be promoted within thirteen years resulted in discharge. In giving women a longer promotion window, it gave them a kind of preferential treatment. The justification for the different treatment, however, was that, as women were not then permitted to go to sea, they were denied the same promotion opportunities as men, for sea duty was an important determinant of Navy promotion. On this basis, the Court upheld the gender-based regulation.

   The amount a beneficiary receives in Social Security old-age insurance benefits is based on a formula dependent in part on the number of years of employment. The formula is based on the highest average monthly wage over the period, and beneficiaries are entitled to exclude a certain number of lower-earning years from the calculation. In *Califano v. Webster,* 430 U.S. 313 (1977), the Court considered the differential way the formula was used to calculate benefits for men and women. In order to enhance their benefits, women were permitted to exclude three more lower-earning years from the calculation than similarly situated men. The Court concluded that Congress had instituted the differential formula to compensate female wage earners for past employment discrimination against women and upheld it as well tailored to that end.

Note: For additional examples, where the Court upheld or overturned gender-based classifications, see Chapter 8, IV.A., *supra.*

C. Affirmative Action Under Title VII

1. ***Title VII:*** In Title VII of the Civil Rights Act of 1964, Congress, which may reach beyond simple constitutional requirements to end discrimination, extended civil rights protections in public and private employment. In general, Title VII bans employment discrimination based on race, color, religion, sex, or national origin.

   Note: Title VII cases are complex cases involving several interlocking layers of analysis. Given that Congress may in some sense outlaw discriminations the Constitution itself does not forbid, the major question in Title VII cases is the statutory construction question: with constitutional requirements and limits as background, just exactly what was it Congress intended to do? This, of course, depends on a close reading of statutory language. While the Court has held that Title VII permits both private and public employers to undertake voluntary race and gender-based affirmative action plans, a strong minority asserts that the Constitution forbids such discriminations *and that* Congress did not intend to authorize them in Title VII. To this point in Title VII jurisprudence, however, the basic issue in any given case has been the intended scope or reach of Title VII. The Court has not yet resolved the issue of whether the Constitution permits Congress to authorize the use of race or gender-conscious classifications in the ways in which the Court has construed Title VII.

2. ***The reach of Title VII:*** The Court has construed congressional power to permit the banning of discriminatory effects that of themselves do not violate equal protection. Title VII addresses such effects in employment. The Court has also construed Title VII to authorize the use of race-based and gender-based classifications to correct imbalances in traditionally segregated job categories.

   a. *Discriminatory impact or effect:* While the Constitution requires discriminatory intent to establish an equal protection violation, Congress may, and in Title VII did, ban the use of neutral employment criteria or discretionary hiring and promotion practices which have a discriminatory or disproportionate impact or effect. *Griggs v. Duke Power Co.,* 401 U.S. 424 (1971); *Watson v. Fort Worth Bank and Trust,* 487 U.S. 977 (1988).

      Example: In *Griggs, supra,* the company, which once had openly discriminated racially in hiring and job assignment, used a general intelligence and mechanical comprehension test to screen applicants for hiring or transfer into certain departments. While the test was neutral on its face, it had a significant discriminatory impact in that proportionately many more blacks than whites failed the test. As there was no business necessity for the test, that is, no demonstrable relationship between the jobs and the skills the test screened, the Court held that the use of the test violated Title VII because of its discriminatory impact alone.

b. *Proof of discriminatory impact:* In order to establish a disparate impact claim under Title VII, plaintiffs often use statistical proofs to show that minorities have proportionately fewer job positions than their numbers in the labor force warrant. To make out a prima facie case of disparate impact on the basis of statistical comparisons, the relevant comparison is between the racial composition of the group holding the contested jobs and the racial composition of the group of persons in the labor market qualified to hold those jobs. This narrow test precludes proofs based on simple comparisons of the racial composition of the general labor market and those holding contested jobs. In addition, plaintiffs must show that the disparate impact they demonstrate is due to the employment practice they challenge. *Wards Cove Packing Co., Inc. v. Atonio,* 490 U.S. 642 (1989).

c. *Affirmative action plans in employment:* While Title VII forbids discrimination on the basis of race or sex and is subject to a "color-blind" reading, the Court nonetheless has construed it to permit voluntary affirmative action employment plans classifying on the basis of race or sex. Title VII is now read to permit voluntary affirmative action plans which: (1) have a clear remedial purpose to correct manifest imbalances in "traditionally segregated job categories"; (2) do not unduly burden the rights or interests of other employees; (3) and end when there is no longer a manifest imbalance. *United Steelworkers v. Weber,* 443 U.S. 193 (1979); *Johnson v. Transportation Agency, Santa Clara County,* 480 U.S. 616 (1987). Such plans may benefit persons who themselves were not actual victims of discrimination, *Firefighters v. Cleveland,* 478 U.S. 501 (1986). Similarly, courts may order race-conscious relief which includes nonvictims where there has been "persistent or egregious discrimination, or where necessary to dissipate the lingering effects of pervasive discrimination." *Local 28 Sheet Metal Workers v. EEOC,* 478 U.S. 421 (1986).

Examples: In *Weber, supra,* the Court upheld a collective bargaining agreement between a private employer and a union. The agreement reserved fifty percent of the openings in a craft-training program for black employees until the percentage of black craftworkers in the plant was comparable to their percentage in the local labor force. There was a manifest racial imbalance in the craftworkers job category. The plan did not require discharge of white workers or deny them too large a number of training opportunities. Finally, the plan was temporary and ended when the percentage of skilled black workers approximated the percentage of blacks in the local labor force.

A county transportation agency unilaterally adopted an affirmative action plan addressing employee promotion. The plan authorized the consideration of sex as one factor in making promotions to positions "within a traditionally segregated job classification in which women have been significantly underrepresented." Applying the *Weber* criteria, the Court upheld the promotion, to the position of road dispatcher, of a female employee over a male employee, although the male employee had scored somewhat higher in a promotion interview. *Johnson, supra.*

9

Note: As the *Johnson* decision involved a public employer, it has particular significance. Since equal protection applies only to state actors, until *Johnson*, it was possible to argue that Title VII did not authorize public employers to use race or gender-conscious classifications. The argument was that equal protection applies only to state actors. As private employers have no equal protection obligations, Congress could authorize them to use race or gender. But it could not equally authorize public employers to do so, for that would breach the equal protection barrier on state action. Because the Court has construed Title VII to allow public employers to use race or sex-conscious remedies, the stage is now set for a constitutional challenge, notwithstanding the holding of *Metro Broadcasting, supra.*

II. **FUNDAMENTAL RIGHTS AND EQUAL PROTECTION:** The Court subjects classifications impinging on fundamental rights to rigorous review, but in practice something less than complete strict scrutiny review. Essentially the Court balances important interests the state offers for regulation against the impact of the regulation on the exercise of the rights. Where a regulation severely restricts the exercise of a fundamental right, it must be narrowly tailored to meet a compelling state interest.

A. **The List of Fundamental Rights:** There are three categories of fundamental rights. The first comprises those rights listed in the Bill of Rights which the Court has held the Fourteenth Amendment Due Process Clause incorporates, and therefore must be accorded by states as well as the federal government. The second category is composed of substantive due process rights, such as the rights to marry, procreate, raise a family, educate children, and to privacy, which the Court has held the Constitution necessarily implies. The final category is made up of the rights to vote, to travel – or, more properly, the right to migrate interstate – and to have meaningful access to the courts, also implied from the Constitution. As other constitutional doctrine deals with the first two categories, the fundamental rights branch of equal protection doctrine deals primarily with the last category.

B. **The Right to Vote:** Voting is a fundamental political right "because preservative of all rights," *Yick Wo v. Hopkins,* 118 U.S. 356 (1886). To ensure fair and orderly elections, however, governments must structure and regulate them. Strict scrutiny review of state electoral provisions is therefore inappropriate, and the Court instead balances the asserted injury to voting rights against the precise interests the state seeks to advance with its rules. *Burdick v. Takushi, Director of Elections of Hawaii,* 504 U.S. 428 (1992). Where the state regulation severely restricts voting rights, the regulation must be narrowly drawn to advance a compelling state interest. Where voting rights are not severely restricted, but subject only to reasonable, nondiscriminatory restrictions, important state regulatory interests will suffice. *Id.*

Governments have a compelling interest in securing to voters the right to vote freely and effectively, and thus in preventing voter intimidation and election fraud. *Burson v. Freeman,* 504 U.S. 191 (1992). In securing this right to vote, governments may sometimes have to enact laws which in some sense impinge on other fundamental rights, *e.g.,* the right to free speech. *Id.* (content-based ban on political speech within 100 feet of a polling place justified to protect right to vote).

Example: Hawaii bans write-in voting, but otherwise provides relatively easy candidate access to the ballot. Hawaii's interests in winnowing out candidates avoiding "unrestrained factionalism" at general elections, and party-raiding to manipulate the outcome of another party's election, justify the slight burden on the right to vote and associate that the write-in-voting ban imposes. *Burdick, supra.*

1. ***Voting qualifications or restrictions***

   a. *Poll taxes:* States may not impose a poll tax on the right to vote, barring those unable or unwilling to pay it from voting. The ability to pay a tax bears no relationship to voting qualifications. *Harper v. Virginia Dep't of Taxation,* 61 U.S.L.W. 4664 (1993).

   b. *General interest elections:* States sometimes provide for "special district" elections and attempt to limit the franchise in those elections to persons having certain defined qualifications.

      Examples: A state might provide that those who vote in elections involving public school issues own property within the school district or that only those who receive water from a water irrigation district vote in that district's elections. Classifications that so distribute or restrict the franchise must be narrowly tailored so that all those who are substantially affected and have a direct interest in the election may participate in it. *Kramer v. Union Free School District No. 15,* 395 U.S. 621 (1969).

      In *Kramer, supra,* New York provided that in school district elections, only district residents who owned or leased taxable property or had children enrolled in local public schools could vote. The classification does not well serve the end of ensuring that citizens primarily interested in school matters, and no others, are entitled to vote. Under the law, an apartment renter, without children, and who directly paid no taxes could vote, while a grown adult living with his parents could not.

      Louisiana law granted only property taxpayers the right to vote in elections called to approve the issuance of municipal utility revenue bonds. The bonds, however, were to be financed from utility operations and not by a property tax. Since the issuance of such bonds would affect many citizens beyond the group of property taxpayers, for example, in the provision of services and in utility rates, the classification disenfranchised persons substantially affected by, and directly interested in, the election. *Cipriano v. Houma,* 395 U.S. 701 (1969).

      In *Phoenix v. Kolodziejski,* 399 U.S. 204 (1970), the city permitted only real property taxpayers to vote in elections on general obligation bonds which were serviced with property tax revenues. Although the burden of payment fell essentially on property owners, the issuance of such bonds would undoubtedly substantially affect other citizens, for example, through creation or not of new city facilities.

   c. *Limited interest elections:* In elections for special limited purposes which are removed from the core of the general governmental powers, duties, and activities and which have a disproportionate effect on a certain group, the state may limit the franchise to that group.

      Example: In *Salyer Land Co. v. Tulare Lake Basin Water Storage District,* 410 U.S. 719 (1973), the Court upheld a restricted franchise in elections for a water storage district. The district was created to provide water for farming, and its costs were apportioned to land on the basis of water received. The election enfranchised only landowners and apportioned their votes according to their land's assessed valuation. *Cf. Ball v. James,* 451 U.S. 355 (1981).

d. *Durational residency requirements:* In order to protect against voting fraud and to give time for officials to verify voter lists, states do have some interest in imposing some residency requirement as a qualification for voting, but residency requirements of one year are not necessary to serve the state interest. *Dunn v. Blumstein,* 405 U.S. 330 (1972). On the other hand, the Court has sustained fifty-day residency requirements. *Marston v. Lewis,* 410 U.S. 679 (1973); *Burns v. Fortson,* 410 U.S. 686 (1973).

e. *Conviction of a felony:* Section 2 of the Fourteenth Amendment acknowledges that states may abridge the right to vote on the basis of a criminal conviction. Consequently, the Court has held that states may deny the franchise to ex-felons. *Richardson v. Ramirez,* 418 U.S. 24 (1974).

f. *Party affiliation:* States have a legitimate interest in prohibiting primary crossover voting or party "raiding" where voters of one party declare themselves members of another party so they can vote in the latter's primary to influence its results. However, a voter's rights to vote and association secure the right to change party affiliations. Therefore, while states may provide that a voter registered with one party may not change her affiliation and vote in the new party's primary except after some waiting period, that period cannot be unreasonably long. *Kusper v. Pontikes,* 414 U.S. 51 (1973) (twenty-three months, too long); *Rosario v. Rockefeller,* 410 U.S. 752 (1973) (eleven months, not too long).

2. **Vote dilution**

a. *Apportionment: one person–one vote:* The nature of representative government requires that, insofar as is possible, the government treat each person's vote equally. Consequently, electoral schemes that accord greater weight to the votes of some than the votes of others are unconstitutional unless justified by an important state interest. *Reynolds v. Sims,* 377 U.S. 533 (1964).

Example: State legislature apportionment plans which assign legislative seats to districts other than on a strict population basis – for example, by giving rural or farm districts proportionately more seats than their population justifies – are unconstitutional.

(1) *De minimis* deviations: Mathematical exactness may be impossible to achieve in apportioning electoral districts by population, and some deviations are permissible.

(a) State elections: The Court has permitted some apportionment population deviation in state elections because states may have legitimate reasons for attempting to maintain traditional political subdivisions such as counties. For state elections, the Court has established a ten-percent deviation as presumptively *de minimis.* Greater deviations may be acceptable if specially justified. *Brown v. Thompson,* 462 U.S. 835 (1983).

(b) Federal congressional elections: In federal elections, virtually no deviation is small enough to be considered *de minimis*. In federal elections, there is no justification for drawing congressional districts along lines of state political subdivisions. The Court, therefore, has held that states should seek precise mathematical equality in congressional electoral district apportionment and has rejected deviations under one percent. *Karcher v. Daggett,* 462 U.S. 725 (1983).

b. *Supermajority requirements:* As long as a supermajority requirement does not discriminate against any identifiable class, it is permissible.

Examples: A state could require that bond measures that may subject citizens to tax increase must be passed by sixty percent of the voters. On the other hand, a state could not provide that only measures relating to racially integrated housing must be passed by sixty percent of the voters. The latter imposes special, and unequal, burdens on an identifiable group seeking change through the political process.

3. *Voting rights, vote dilution, and gerrymandering*

   a. *Definitions*

      (1) Gerrymander: the drawing of voting district lines in a winner-take-all district voting system so as to maximize the number of seats won by a given party or group. Conferring possible enormous political advantages, gerrymandering and gerrymanders are sometimes referred to as a "pathology of democracy."

      (2) Racial gerrymander: a gerrymander, intended or having the effect of diluting or strengthening the voting or elective power of a racial group. Generally, if the gerrymander strengthens a racial group's elective power, we would refer to it as an "affirmative" racial gerrymander.

      (3) Proportional representation: a system of voting and election in which each group of voters receives the same proportion of the seats in the legislative body as the number of voters in the group is to the number of the total electorate.

      (4) Stacking: a common form of gerrymander by creating a few districts with an overwhelming majority for one party and many districts with a thin majority for the other. Stacking dilutes the voting strength of the party with the overwhelming majority as all its votes beyond a simple majority are wasted.

   b. *Common gerrymandering methods*

      (1) Packing voting strength to ensure lopsided majorities;

      (2) Fragmenting voting strength to ensure that a political group will be in a minority;

      (3) Joining the districts of two incumbents of the same party;

(4) Dividing an incumbent from her constituency;

(5) Preserving old districts for dominant party incumbents while creating new districts for members of the other party;

(6) Disregarding natural communities, cities, towns, and other customary political subdivisions;

(7) In drawing district lines, departing from standards of compactness and contiguity in order to sweep in or exclude constituencies.

9

c. *Gerrymandering as vote dilution:* Obviously, gerrymandering can dilute the right to vote. On the other hand, the gerrymandering problem is a difficult one for redistricting is essential. Election district lines have to be drawn somewhere, and even good faith line drawing can result in voting inequities. It is simply not possible to conclude there has been invidious gerrymandering whenever a party receiving a minority of the total votes attains a majority in a legislature. That effect can arise simply from the winner-take-all system even when there has been no effort to draw district lines for political advantage.

d. *Unconstitutional gerrymandering:* Gerrymanders that intentionally dilute votes are unconstitutional. Gerrymanders that intentionally segregate voters, without sufficient justification, solely on the basis of race are also unconstitutional. The two are distinct, however, and it is not necessary to show vote dilution to establish the latter.

(1) Vote dilution: Gerrymandering constitutes unconstitutional voting discrimination by dilution when the electoral system is arranged in a manner that will *consistently* degrade voters' or a group of voters' influence on the political process. *Davis v. Bandemer,* 478 U.S. 109 (1986) (plurality). (Since, in a winner-take-all system, there will always be deviations from proportional representation, evidence from a single election is generally insufficient to establish a constitutional violation.)

(a) Establishing unconstitutional vote dilution: To establish a claim of unconstitutional gerrymander resulting in vote dilution, the plaintiff must show both intentional discrimination, that is, an intent to dilute voting rights; and actual discriminatory effect, that is, some actual vote dilution. *Id. United Jewish Organizations of Williamsburgh, Inc. v. Carey,* 430 U.S. 144 (1977).

(b) Proving discriminatory effect: To prove actual vote dilution, plaintiffs must show that "the political processes . . . were not equally open to participation by the group in question – that its members had less opportunity than did other residents in the district to participate in the political process and to elect legislators of their choice." *White v. Regester,* 412 U.S. 755, 766 (1973).

(2) Racial gerrymanders: When done for the right reasons, taking race into account in settling electoral district lines is constitutional. When done for no reason other than to segregate by race, however, it is unconstitutional.

(a) Inevitable, required, or permissible uses of race in electoral districting: It is inevitable that electoral districting and reapportionment will take race into account. Legislators, always concerned with future electoral results, will be aware of all the various demographic factors that will affect such results, and will attempt to create districts that maximize the results they want. Race-conscious districting is also sometimes necessary, as, for example, when used as a remedy for prior racial discrimination in voting. Furthermore, the Voting Rights Act of 1965, as amended, 42 U.S.C. § 1973, often requires legislators to take race into account in electoral districting and reapportionment plans. To satisfy Voting Rights Act requirements, legislators must sometimes create majority-minority districts to secure minority-voting rights. As long as legislators do not deliberately dilute others' voting rights in doing so, such districting is constitutional. *United Jewish Organizations v. Carey, supra.*

(b) Impermissible uses of race in electoral districting: Where a reapportionment plan, although race-neutral on its face, deliberately segregates voters into separate districts predominantly on the basis of race, without a compelling interest, it is unconstitutional. *Miller v. Johnson,* 515 U.S. 900 (1995). The constitutional harm in such a case is simply the improper use of a racial classification, and plaintiffs need not show that their own voting rights are diluted. *Shaw v. Reno,* 61 U.S.L.W. 4818 (1993).

   i) Bizarre shape, explicable only on racial grounds: Where a legislature completely disregards appropriate and traditional districting principles, while creating a district so bizarre in shape that it can be understood only as an effort to separate voters on the basis of race, the districting is subject to strict scrutiny review. *Id.*

   Example: In *Shaw, supra,* North Carolina devised an electoral district stretching 160 miles along a major interstate highway. It was alleged that for much of its length, the district was little wider than the interstate corridor. It was not compact, did not respect natural or established political boundaries, but did contain a majority of Afro-Americans. The district's shape, therefore, provided strong circumstantial evidence that the district had been drawn as it had *solely* for racial reasons. While the state, in establishing the district, was attempting to meet Voting Rights Act requirements by creating a new majority-minority district — and had to take race into account — it apparently could have created a more compact and less "grossly contorted" district than it did. As the only explanation for the district's odd shape was race, the districting was challengeable under equal protection.

   ii) Factors other than shape: Even where a district's shape is not so bizarre as to support a conclusion of racial gerrymandering, other factors may do so. Where a legislature, in drawing electoral districts, *subordinates* traditional race-neutral districting principles – such as compactness, contiguity, and respect for political subdivisions or communities defined by actual shared interests – to racial considerations, the districting is unconstitutional. In other words, while legislatures may take race into account in districting — indeed, must do so, particularly when meeting Voting Act requirements — they may not make race determinative.

Example: In *Miller v. Johnson, supra*, Georgia, in response to U.S. Justice Department pressure, changed its original reapportionment plan to create an additional majority-minority district. Evidence regarding the district's shape and demographics, as well as direct evidence of legislative purpose, showed that race was the predominant factor in assigning voters to the challenged district, and the districting was therefore unconstitutional.

(3) Voting Rights Act — majority-minority districts

    (a) Voting Act requirements: A state's need to satisfy the requirements of the Voting Rights Act and remedy racial discrimination may constitute a compelling state interest justifying the use of race in drawing district lines. Nonetheless, the district drawn must be narrowly tailored. This means that in drawing district lines on the basis of race, the legislature may not subordinate traditional districting principles to race more than is reasonably necessary. *Bush v. Vera*, 517 U.S. 952 (1996); *Shaw v. Hunt*, 517 U.S. 899 (1996). Compliance with the Voting Rights Act does not require states to create districts that are not reasonably compact. *Abrams v. Johnson*, 117 S. Ct. 1925 (1997). In general, bizarreness of district shape and noncompactness suggest a use of race more than reasonably necessary. *Id.* Districts with *Gingles* shapes, that is, geographically compact districts where the minority group is sufficiently large and politically cohesive to elect candidates, appear to be presumptively constitutional. (*See* subsection 4.B.2.b.(1)(b) *infra*.)

    (b) Justice Department pressure: Mere pressure from the U.S. Justice Department, using its preclearance authority, to create additional majority-minority districts does not justify drawing districts on the basis of race. *Abrams v. Johnson, supra*.

Mixed-motive cases: In legislative redistricting, legislatures usually have multiple goals. These include incumbency protection, aligning communities of interest, and satisfying Voting Rights Act requirements and Department of Justice preclearance review. In addition, in redistricting, legislatures must satisfy the one-person, one-vote requirement of *Reynolds v. Sims, supra*. Furthermore, under Supreme Court rulings, where a legislature neglects traditional districting criteria, such as compactness, regular shape, and community of interest, and has created majority-minority districts, a suspicion of racial gerrymandering arises. Finally, under *Shaw* and *Miller*, if race was a predominate reason for drawing particular district lines, then the so-called racially gerrymandered districts will be subject to strict scrutiny review and will likely fail to pass scrutiny. All of these together create serious constraints on a legislature's ability to draw electoral district lines.

When a legislature does create irregular majority-minority districts, in order to sustain its action against constitutional attack, it will have to demonstrate that nonracial motivations explain the majority-minority district lines it draws. If race was a consideration, it must show that it was not a predominate factor in drawing the lines. This can be quite difficult because there is a considerable overlap between incumbency protection, communities of interest, and racial demographics. But it can be done, if done in the right way.

Where political affiliation correlates with race, using political affiliation to draw district lines, even if it also draws racial lines, is constitutional. That is simply a political gerrymander and doesn't involve a racial classification. On the other hand, using race as a proxy for political affiliation involves using a racial stereotype and calls for strict scrutiny review. *Bush v. Vera,* 65 U.S.L.W. 2109 (1997). Using race as a proxy for incumbency protection is, therefore, unconstitutional unless justified by a compelling state interest and utilizing narrowly tailored means. *Id.*

Example: In *Bush v. Vera, supra,* Texas, for congressional redistricting purposes, created three majority-minority districts of quite irregular shape. For one of these districts, the evidence disclosed that the district was composed on a block-by-block level, had split voter tabulation districts, and that even individual streets in the district had been split. The districting software program that the state used to draw district lines provided only racial data at the block level. While the resulting district shape maximized minority population, it did not maximize party voting strength. This was strong evidence that racial considerations took precedence over political considerations, and the district was unconstitutionally drawn on the basis of race.

(c) Voting Rights Act and noncovered jurisdictions: While some states are not covered jurisdictions under the Voting Rights Act, some political subdivisions of those states may be covered. Normally, a noncovered state would not have to preclear electoral changes in accordance with Voting Rights Act procedures. However, as a matter of statutory construction, where a noncovered state enacts general legislation calling for electoral changes in its subdivisions, covered subdivisions must preclear the changes. *Lopez v. Monterey County,* 525 U.S. 266 (1999). The preclearance requirement is not an unconstitutional invasion of states' rights because Congress can, under the Enforcement Clause of the Fifteenth Amendment, enact deterrent or remedial legislation that reaches state conduct not itself unconstitutional. *Id.*

4. ***Vote dilution through racial bloc voting:*** In *Reynolds v. Sims, supra,* the Court said, "fair and effective representation of all citizens" was "the basic aim of legislative apportionment." Even aside from gerrymandering, however, the American system of winner-take-all district voting has the result that those voting in the minority in the election will not be represented by the candidate of their choice. There is thus a tension between one person, one vote and "fair and effective representation": between the right to an *equally weighted vote* and the right to an *equally powerful vote.* Proportional representation electoral systems would solve this problem, but, in general, the United States does not use them. The majority vote, winner-take-all system, however, has resulted in serious problems of minority

political representation and power. In this regard, the problem of racial bloc voting has been particularly acute. For a long time, in many places in the country, significant racial minorities had been unable to obtain any political power, influence, access to candidate slating, and also unable to elect candidates of their choice because the white majority consistently outvoted them. This often occurred in winner-take-all, at-large systems of voting (also called multimember electoral systems) in districts having an overall majority of whites. Where there is racially polarized voting, and the white majority votes as a racial bloc, that is, uses race as the dominant factor in deciding which candidates to vote for, minorities in multimember electoral districts will be unable to elect their own candidates. As is readily imaginable, such racially polarized at-large systems would often be highly insensitive to minority interests or needs. In such circumstances, an obvious remedy would be to create single-member electoral districts, where the racial minority had a voting majority (so-called majority-minority districts) and could elect its preferred candidates. The constitutional problem, however, was to demonstrate that the inability of minorities to elect their preferred candidates arose from constitutionally remediable discrimination. This was exceptionally difficult, and in the upshot, Congress solved the problem through amendments to the Voting Rights Act of 1965, 42 U.S.C. § 1973.

a. *Constitutional requirement of discriminatory intent:* In *Mobile v. Borden,* 446 U.S. 55 (1980), a plurality of the Court held that a showing of mere voting dilution for minority group members resulting from a particular electoral scheme does not establish an equal protection violation. Instead, it is necessary to show that the electoral system was designed or maintained in order to discriminate racially.

b. *Voting Rights Act amendment and discriminatory effect:* In response to *Mobile v. Borden,* Congress amended the Voting Rights Act to provide that plaintiffs could establish a violation of § 2 of the Act through a showing of discriminatory effect alone. Where minorities are sufficiently numerous to elect candidates, the absence of minorities in elected bodies may be a discriminatory effect of racially polarized voting and white racial bloc voting. On the other hand, the absence may result from the fact that minorities actually preferred other candidates, and the mere showing of a failure to win an election does not establish remediable vote dilution.

(1) To successfully challenge electoral devices, such as at-large, multimember electoral systems, minority plaintiffs must show that, under the totality of the circumstances, the device reduces or precludes their ability to elect their preferred candidates.

(a) A minority group's demonstration that it lacks proportional representation in the group of elected officials is, by itself, insufficient to establish a violation of § 2 of the Voting Rights Act. A lack of proportional representation could occur simply because minorities preferred white over minority candidates.

(b) In order to show a violation of § 2 of the Voting Rights Act, minority plaintiffs must show that, in the absence of the challenged electoral structures, they have the potential to elect their own candidates. They may prove this by showing that:

(1) the minority group is: "sufficiently large and geographically compact to constitute a majority in a single-member district";

(2) the group is also politically cohesive; and

(3) "the white majority votes sufficiently as a bloc to enable it . . . to defeat the minority's preferred candidate." *Thornburg v. Gingles,* 478 U.S. 30, 50 (1986).

5. ***Ballot access restrictions:*** Although the Court, of late, has turned to analyzing ballot access problems as First Amendment associational problems, its initial decisions in this area were resolved at least in part as equal protection cases. Ballot access problems arise when a state seeks to restrict the access of candidates or parties, particularly nonmainstream candidates and minority and new parties, to a place on the election ballot. Such restrictions have an obvious impact on associational rights but also impair voters' rights to cast their votes effectively, for without a place on the ballot, they may not be able to vote for the candidate or party of their choice. States, however, seek to justify such restrictions on the grounds that they ensure political stability and prevent voter confusion and deception by excluding candidates or parties lacking a significant modicum of support.

   a. *Strict scrutiny:* The Court has applied strict scrutiny to ballot access restrictions. *Williams v. Rhodes,* 393 U.S. 23 (1968); *Storer v. Brown,* 415 U.S. 724 (1974); *American Party of Texas v. White,* 415 U.S. 767 (1974); *Illinois Elections Bd. v. Socialist Workers Party,* 440 U.S. 173 (1979).

   Examples: In *Williams v. Rhodes, supra,* the Court examined an Ohio law which distinguished between major, established parties and those newly seeking access to the ballot. Major parties were placed on the presidential ballot if they received ten percent of the votes in the prior election for governor. Other parties seeking to gain access to the presidential ballot had to file, quite early, petitions signed by a number of people equal to fifteen percent of the total number of ballots cast in the last governor's election. In addition, the parties seeking access for the first time had to create a complicated party structure and had to conduct primaries. These requirements, in addition to conferring a significant advantage on the major parties, could plainly be very burdensome and prevent even parties with many members from finding a place on the ballot. The Court held that state interests of promoting compromise and political stability – in effect, by forcing persons to ally with the major parties – were not compelling.

   In *Socialist Worker's Party, supra,* Illinois imposed a greater barrier to ballot access for Chicago elections than for statewide elections, requiring a greater number of voter signatures to qualify. As the requirement curtailed political expression, it was an overbroad means of serving the state interests of screening out frivolous candidates and avoiding overloaded ballots. In other words, the requirement did not in any way distinguish between parties and candidates with serious messages to communicate and those that did not. Finally, the state failed to provide any reason why there should be a greater ballot access requirement for Chicago elections than for statewide elections.

   While states may require new political parties to demonstrate some support before granting them access to the ballot, they may not require such parties to make a greater showing in state political subdivisions than statewide. *Norman*

v. *Reed,* 502 U.S. 279 (1992) (Requirement of 25,000 supporters for each subdivision in a multidistrict subdivision while requiring only 25,000 supporters overall for statewide elections is unconstitutional).

b. *Acceptable ballot access restrictions:* State interests in political stability and avoiding ballot confusion can, however, justify certain ballot access restrictions. As long as access requirements afford minority parties and candidates "a real and substantially equal opportunity" to qualify, and alternative requirements would not serve the state interests in significantly less burdensome ways, the state may impose them. *Storer, supra; American Party, supra; Jenness v. Fortson,* 403 U.S. 431 (1971).

Example: In *Jenness, supra,* Georgia allowed independents to appear on ballots without party endorsement if they filed nominating petitions signed by five percent of those eligible to vote in the last election. There were neither early filing nor complex primary election requirements. While the Georgia scheme did treat the established parties differently, it did not significantly inhibit access to the ballot for others. The state interest in avoiding ballot confusion and deception justified its requirement of a showing of a modest level of support as a condition of ballot access.

c. *Fusion candidates:* Fusion candidates are those who appear on a ballot as a candidate of more than one party. Many states bar fusion candidacies to avoid intraparty discord and party splintering in order to maintain a stable political system, and to promote candidate competition. Arguably, if a state bars fusion candidacies, it burdens the association rights of political parties: they are unable to place on the ballot, as their party's choice, a candidate appearing on the ballot as another party's choice. But antifusion laws do not prevent a party or its members from endorsing, supporting, or voting for anyone. Fusion candidacies could stimulate the development of multiple political parties, formed around narrow interests, but advancing a particular popular candidate to capitalize on a candidate's popularity rather than the party's own voter appeal. As these interests are substantial, and the burden a fusion ban imposes on a party is not severe, fusion bans are constitutional. *Timmons v. Twin Cities Area New Party,* 65 U.S.L.W. 4273 (1997).

d. *Financial and other candidate ballot access restrictions:* The Court has invalidated both very large candidate filing fees, *Bullock v. Carter,* 405 U.S. 134 (1972), and candidate filing fee requirements completely barring indigent candidates from access to a position on the ballot, *Lubin v. Panish,* 415 U.S. 709 (1974). On the other hand, the Court has upheld requirements that limited the ability of public officials to run for other public offices, either by requiring them to serve out their current term before becoming a candidate or by treating an announced candidacy as an "automatic" resignation from the current office. A Court plurality opined that the state interest in ensuring that an officeholder would not abuse or neglect her position justified the requirements. *Clements v. Fashing,* 457 U.S. 957 (1982).

C. **The Indigent's Right of Fair Treatment in State Adjudication Processes:** Court adjudication of disputes, traditionally a public function, costs money. While the state provides courts and pays the costs of facilities and court personnel, the state has always imposed certain litigation costs on the parties. Thus, parties generally must pay filing fees, jury, witness, and attorney fees, and must also purchase transcripts of proceedings essential to appeals. In a criminal case, inability to pay attorney, witness, or transcript costs can mean an unwarranted conviction. In a civil case, inability to pay necessary court costs may mean loss of a legitimate claim, inability to resolve one's legal problems or status, or an inability to defend against actions. The requirement to pay court fees, however, is in effect a classification based on ability to pay, a so-called wealth classification. In a series of cases dealing first with criminal prosecutions, and then with some civil matters, the Court determined that, in some situations, the requirement that an indigent litigant pay certain litigation or court costs denied equal protection as well as due process. Most properly viewed, these cases are due process cases in equal protection dress, for the underlying question in them is whether it is fair for the state to make poverty a determining factor in the search for justice. The net result of these cases is that while the state must provide certain resources to indigents compelled to litigate, it need not equalize completely and make an indigent as able to litigate as one who can afford to pay. The key here is the state's satisfaction of some minimum standard of fair treatment.

1. ***Criminal cases:*** In criminal trials, the state cannot discriminate on the basis of poverty where doing so would deny the indigent the opportunity of a fair adjudication of his guilt or innocence. *Griffin v. Illinois,* 351 U.S. 12 (1956); *Douglas v. California,* 372 U.S. 353 (1963); *cf. Ake v. Oklahoma,* 470 U.S. 68 (1975). Consequently, where the state permits criminal appeals as of right, it must provide without charge to indigent criminal appellants the criminal trial transcripts necessary to appeal, *Griffin, supra,* and appellate counsel. *Douglas v. California, supra.* (In related due process decisions, the Court held that the state must provide indigent defendants trial counsel, *Gideon v. Wainwright,* 372 U.S. 335 (1963); *Argersinger v. Hamlin,* 407 U.S. 25 (1972), and the services of a psychiatrist when preparing and presenting a mental defense, *Ake, supra.*) On the other hand, where the state has provided one appeal as of right, with counsel, it need not provide counsel for discretionary appeals or petitions to the Supreme Court permitted thereafter. *Ross v. Moffitt,* 417 U.S. 600 (1974). One reason for this is that discretionary appeals or petitions for writs of certiorari do not serve the same functions as ordinary appeals. The former are more concerned with the appropriate functioning of the legal system while the latter more concerned with the provision of individual justice.

2. ***Imprisonment for inability to pay fines:*** States may not discriminate against indigent criminals unable to pay fines by imprisoning them, in lieu of payment, for a period of imprisonment beyond that authorized by the statute under which the indigent was convicted. *Williams v. Illinois,* 399 U.S. 235 (1970); *Tate v. Short,* 401 U.S. 395 (1971). Imprisonment for nonpayment of fines may be constitutional where there are no adequate, alternative forms of punishment, and, despite good efforts, the defendant is unable, over time, to pay the fines. *Bearden v. Georgia,* 461 U.S. 660 (1983); *Tate, supra.*

3. ***Civil cases:*** In a related line of civil cases, the Court treated the court access issue as one involving due process rather than equal protection.

   a. *Required subsidy or waiver of fees:* Where the state forces persons to settle their claims or obligations regarding some fundamental interest through the judicial process, it must give them a meaningful opportunity to be heard. *Boddie v. Connecticut,* 401 U.S. 371 (1971); *Little v. Streater,* 452 U.S. 1 (1981).

(1) Divorce: As only the state may grant legal divorces, and divorce proceedings involve the right to adjust marital status, an aspect of the fundamental right to marry, the state must waive divorce filing fees for indigents unable to pay them. *Boddie, supra.*

(2) Paternity actions: Similarly, as the state is deeply involved and interested in paternity actions, which are quasi-criminal in nature, due process requires the state to subsidize blood-grouping tests for indigent paternity action defendants. *Little, supra.*

(3) Terminating parental rights: Where the state provides appeals from actions terminating parental rights, it may not condition an indigent parent's appeal on prepayment of transcript preparation fees. *M.L.B. v. S.L.J.,* 519 U.S. 102 (1997). The parent-child relationship is a fundamental liberty interest protected by the Fourteenth Amendment. In cases where the state terminates the parental interest, it must provide an indigent parent with a record sufficiently complete to permit proper appellate review. *Id.*

b. *Court access in cases not involving fundamental interests:* The Court has rather strictly limited the right of meaningful access to courts in civil cases to *Boddie-Little* situations involving either some fundamental interest or state monopoly of remedy, or both. Thus it has held that the government need not waive bankruptcy filing fees for indigents. *United States v. Kras,* 409 U.S. 434 (1973). Similarly it has held that states need not waive filing fee requirements for indigents in cases involving judicial review of administrative denials of welfare benefits. *Ortwein v. Schwab,* 410 U.S. 656 (1973).

D. The "Right to Travel": The Court has implied a fundamental right to travel from the Constitution. As states rarely impose barriers to travel as such, but rather sometimes impose disabilities for having moved into the state from another place, the migration aspect of travel is prominent in Court cases involving the so-called right to travel. The nature of the federal union is such that states cannot bar persons from immigrating into, and taking up residence in, the state, or penalize them because they've done so. States, however, sometimes do have legitimate reasons for imposing durational or other residency requirements as a condition of receiving state benefits or preferences. The cases under this heading deal primarily with the issue of when a state may constitutionally impose such residency requirements.

1. *State purpose to deter immigration:* In order to save state funds, prevent fraudulent claims, and deter out-of-state indigents from immigrating, states have sometimes imposed durational residency requirements, for example, a one-year waiting period after arrival in the state, as a condition of receiving welfare and other kinds of state assistance. The Court has held that states may not adopt residency requirements in order to deter the immigration of indigents. *Edward v. California,* 314 U.S. 160 (1941); *Shapiro v. Thompson,* 394 U.S. 618 (1969).

2. *Durational residency requirements*

a. *Basic necessities of life – welfare and other indigent assistance:* When the effect of a state residency requirement is to penalize individuals who have traveled or moved into the state by denying them the basic necessities of life, the Court applies strict scrutiny review. In such cases, a state must demonstrate a compelling interest. The state interests of saving money, administrative efficiency, and deterring fraudulent claims do not justify a one-year waiting period as a condition of receiving welfare, *Shapiro, supra,* or free medical assistance, *Memorial Hosp. v. Maricopa County,* 415 U.S. 250 (1974), both basic necessities of life for poor persons.

b. *Divorce:* States may impose durational residency requirements as a condition for obtaining an in-state divorce. Such requirements serve a state's interests in not involving itself in matters in which another state has a much greater interest and in protecting its divorce decrees from collateral attack on the basis of lack of jurisdiction. *Sosna v. Iowa,* 419 U.S. 393 (1975).

3. ***Apportionment of state benefits on the basis of length of residence:*** States may not apportion the benefits they give to bona fide residents on the basis of length of residence. *Zobel v. Williams,* 457 U.S. 55 (1982).

Example: In *Zobel, supra,* Alaska, which received a bonanza in petroleum revenues from oil reserves located on state lands, decided to distribute some of its earnings to the state's adult residents in amounts directly proportional to length of residence. The Court held this scheme to constitute an unconstitutional differentiation between residents.

Preferences based on residency: States may not distinguish between *bona fide* residents by according preferences to some based on the date they became residents. *Attorney Gen. of New York v. Soto-Lopez,* 476 U.S. 898 (1986); *Hooper v. Bernalillo County Assessor,* 472 U.S. 612 (1985). Thus, a state may not give a preference to veterans in civil service examinations on the basis of state residency on entry into military service. *Soto-Lopez, supra.*

New Developments: In *Saenz v. Roe,* 526 U.S. 489 (1999), the Court decided that the Privileges and Immunities Clauses of the Constitution protects various aspects of the right to travel. As the Court elaborated, the right to travel has three facets. These are the right of citizens of a state to enter and leave other states'; the right of citizens of another state to be treated as visitors rather than as aliens; and, on changing residence from one state to another, the right to be treated like other citizens of that state.

The first of these rights is a consequence of national union. The second derives from Art. II, Sec. 2, Privileges and Immunities. The last from the Fourteenth Amendment Privileges and Immunities Clause. This last aspect of the right to travel calls for equal treatment. Except where a state has legitimate residency requirements that recent resident citizens haven't met, states may not treat such residents differently than similarly situated state citizens.

Example: A California law that limited, for one year, the welfare benefits of recent residents to the amount they would have received in their state of origin was unconstitutional. *Saenz, supra.* The California law in effect created many classifications among state citizens dependent on the states from which they came, thus denying them equal treatment with state citizens.

E. **Other Fundamental Rights:** The Court has limited the fundamental rights branch of equal protection to the foregoing rights, expressly declining to hold that the importance of an interest to an individual or to society should determine whether the Court should subject state classifications regarding it to strict scrutiny review.

1. ***Basic necessities of life:*** Individuals have no fundamental constitutional right to the basic necessities of life that would require the state to meet strict scrutiny review in welfare benefits legislation. Welfare legislation is a matter of social and economic regulation and, as such, subject to rational basis review. *Dandridge v. Williams,* 397 U.S. 471 (1970).

   Examples: In *Dandridge, supra,* Maryland provided welfare assistance to poor persons based on need, but imposed a maximum grant limit of $250 per family on poor families with dependent children. In larger families, the effect was to reduce the amount of grant per child, as the same amount had to provide for a greater number of children. Although the state provided proportionately less to larger families, thus, in a sense, refusing to provide sufficient funds for the basic necessities of life, the Court sustained the scheme.

   In *Lindsey v. Normet,* 405 U.S. 56 (1972), the Court refused to hold that there was a fundamental interest in the "need for decent shelter" which called for any kind of stringent review of eviction statutes.

2. ***Education***

   a. *Education as a fundamental right:* Even though education may be fundamental to success or effective functioning in modern society, there is no fundamental constitutional right to education. *San Antonio Ind. School Dist. v. Rodriguez,* 411 U.S. 1 (1973). Consequently, equal protection does not require states to ensure that equivalent financial resources are devoted to the education of each child. Specifically, states can rely on public school financing schemes based on property taxes, even where some school districts, because they have a richer property tax base, are able to invest more in education per child than poorer districts. *Id.* There are indications, however, that the Court would view a complete denial of education differently.

   b. *Deprivation of education for children of a disfavored group:* While there is no fundamental right to education, the Court has recognized the importance of basic education for children and has held that a state may not deny a public education to undocumented alien children. *Plyler v. Doe,* 457 U.S. 202 (1982). *Plyler* is an example of the Court's application of heightened scrutiny in cases involving despised, feared, abused, or neglected minorities.

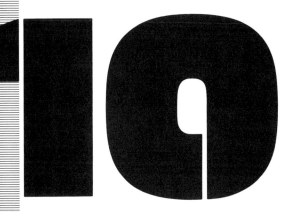

STATE ACTION AND CONGRESSIONAL AUTHORITY TO REACH PRIVATE ACTION TO PROTECT CIVIL RIGHTS

 CHAPTER SUMMARY

**CHAPTER 10: STATE ACTION AND CONGRESSIONAL AUTHORITY
TO REACH PRIVATE ACTION TO PROTECT CIVIL RIGHTS**

Introduction. The Civil War Amendments form principal bases of civil rights protection. The Thirteenth Amendment outlaws slavery and involuntary servitude. The Fourteenth Amendment defines American citizenship and ensures due process and equal protection. The Fifteenth Amendment guarantees citizens the right to vote without regard "to race, color, or previous condition of servitude." Each of these amendments has a direct force of its own, enforceable through a court. In addition, each amendment also has a provision giving Congress power to enforce it by appropriate legislation. There is an important difference between the amendments, however. The Thirteenth Amendment bans slavery completely, whether the result of official and public, or private, acts. By contrast the Fourteenth and Fifteenth Amendments prohibit the states, respectively, from denying due process and equal protection, and the right to vote. The latter amendments, of their own force, do not proscribe private action denying these rights. Similarly, although Congress has the power to enforce the Fourteenth and Fifteenth Amendments, Congress arguably must use that power to address only acts of the state denying these rights, satisfying the so-called state action requirement.

STATE ACTION

I. **STATE ACTION: In the enforcement of civil rights, state action presents a problem only in those cases in which the state itself, through its action or its officials, does not directly deprive or infringe civil rights. In the difficult cases, the principal actors depriving civil rights are private parties. A showing of "state action," however, generally forms a predicate for enforcing the Fourteenth and Fifteenth Amendments, and congressional civil legislation based on them. To support an action against private parties for infringement of Fourteenth or Fifteenth Amendment-based civil rights, it is therefore usually necessary to show some kind of state involvement or responsibility. Otherwise, the action cannot stand as a civil rights action, but is simply a private wrong pursuable only through ordinary state remedies. "Civil rights, such as are guaranteed by the Constitution against state aggression, cannot be impaired by the wrongful acts of individuals, unsupported by state authority in the shape of laws, customs, or judicial or executive proceedings."** *Civil Rights Cases,* **109 U.S. 3 (1883). Consequently, the principal question in state action cases is when may we attribute actions of private parties to the state for purposes of enforcing civil rights.**

A. **State Action through the Undertaking of Public Functions:** When private parties exercise powers traditionally exclusively reserved to the state, there is state action. *Flagg Bros., Inc. v. Brooks,* 436 U.S. 149 (1978); *Jackson v. Metropolitan Edison Co.,* 419 U.S. 345 (1974); *Marsh v. Alabama,* 326 U.S. 501 (1946).

1. *Narrow reading:* In modern society, the presence of the state is felt everywhere, and the state is involved, through regulation and funding, in a vast number of private party activities. For this reason, a broad reading of the public-function strand of state action doctrine risks converting much of what many would consider to be purely private activity into state action for the purposes of civil rights actions. To avoid this, the Court has read the public-function doctrine narrowly. It refuses to find state action simply because the state in some sense regulates or funds private parties, or involves them in, or permits them to undertake, activities the state has taken on or could undertake if it chose.

2. **Functions exclusively reserved to the state**

   a. *Company town:* When a private company owns and operates a town, having the facilities and functions of ordinary towns, it has taken on a public function, and its action is state action. *Marsh, supra.*

      Note: The Court has refused to extend the public-function state action rationale to shopping centers and malls. *Hudgens v. NLRB,* 424 U.S. 507 (1976); *cf. Lloyd Corp. v. Tanner,* 407 U.S. 551 (1972).

   b. *Election primaries:* States generally make party primaries a part of the state election machinery. For that reason, party primaries are so closely related to, or intertwined with, electoral schemes that, even though controlled by private political parties, their processes and procedures constitute state action. *Smith v. Allwright,* 321 U.S. 649 (1944); *Terry v. Adams,* 345 U.S. 461 (1953).

3. **Functions not exclusively reserved to the state**

   a. *Public utilities:* Public utilities, while state licensed and heavily state regulated, do not provide services traditionally the exclusive prerogative of the state. The actions of a privately owned public utility in terminating service, without notice and a hearing, therefore, do not constitute state action. *Jackson, supra.*

   b. *State-authorized remedies without state involvement:* The action of a private warehouseman, without state involvement and without notice and a prior hearing, in selling entrusted goods for nonpayment of storage fees, pursuant to provisions of a state Uniform Commercial Code, does not constitute state action. *Flagg Bros., supra.* Dispute resolution, while a traditional function of the state, is not an *exclusive* function of the state.

B. **State Action Through State Involvement:** Although the state itself does not initiate a particular violation of civil rights, there is, nonetheless, state action when there is "significant state involvement" in the conduct alleged to violate civil rights. In order to establish significant involvement, the plaintiff must show a close nexus between the private party and state participation in, or responsibility for, the activity that caused plaintiff's injury. Private party receipt of state benefits alone, without other indicia of state responsibility, does not establish state action.

   1. **State enforcement of racially restrictive covenants:** A private party's use of state courts to enforce a racially restrictive covenant, either by way of a suit for injunction, divestment, or damages, constitutes state action. *Shelley v. Kraemer,* 334 U.S. 1 (1948); *Barrows v. Jackson,* 346 U.S. 249 (1953).

      Note: The Constitution permits private discrimination, and in their private activities and premises, members of the various races and other minorities need not associate if they do not so desire. The *Shelley* rule, therefore, should not be read too broadly. For example, one could take *Shelley* to stand for the proposition that whenever anyone sought to use state power to enforce a private arrangement, there was state action. Any private party litigation, even an action in trespass, could then form the predicate for state action. Perhaps *Shelley* should simply be taken as an instance of the rule that the state may not ally itself with the enforcement of a racial classification that has the effect of discriminating.

2. ***State enforcement of racially motivated decisions that do not discriminate:*** At least in some circumstances, state enforcement of a private, racially motivated decision which does not have the effect of actually discriminating does not constitute discriminatory state action. *Evans v. Abney,* 396 U.S. 435 (1970).

Example: In *Evans, supra,* Senator Bacon by will conveyed property in trust to Macon, Georgia, for use as a park for whites only. In 1966, the Court held that the city could not discriminate racially in operating the park. Subsequently, the state court ruled that the testator's express intention had become impossible to fulfill, and that therefore, under state law, the land reverted to the heirs. Enforcing the testator's reverter intention had the effect of closing the park entirely to all, whites and blacks alike. In that sense, the state action was nondiscriminatory.

3. ***State partnership, sponsorship, or association:*** Even where the state itself does not act directly to infringe civil rights, the state failure to act when a private party with which it is closely associated infringes civil rights constitutes state action. *Burton v. Wilmington Parking Authority,* 365 U.S. 715 (1961).

Example: In *Burton, supra,* the state leased a portion of a publicly owned parking building to a private restaurant. The building, which the state shared with the lessee, was identified as a public building, and the state obtained revenues from the restaurant lessee. In its lease, however, the state did not require that the restaurant open its facilities nondiscriminatorily, nor did it adopt other rules or regulations having the same effect. Under these circumstances, the Court held that the state had sufficiently involved itself with the restaurant that the restaurant's action of discriminating on the basis of race was attributable to the state. In other words, under the circumstances, it was fair to hold the state responsible for the private discrimination.

4. ***State participation:*** Where a state actor actually participates in private party action which a state rule or procedure authorizes, there is state action.

   a. *Prejudgment attachment procedures:* States have sometimes authorized parties to replevin, attach, or sequester property, or to garnish wages *ex parte,* on the basis of filing an action or appropriate affidavit, before any hearing on the party's right to the property. Where the state authorizes such prejudgment attachment and the creditor uses state assistance to seize or sequester the property, *e.g.,* by way of a sheriff's writ of attachment or a court's prejudgment garnishment order, there is state action. In such cases, the state has both authorized the action and participated in it. *Lugar v. Edmondson Oil Co.,* 457 U.S. 922 (1982).

   b. *Passive state authorization without participation:* Where the state passively authorizes a creditor to undertake a self-help remedy, but does not in any way participate in carrying it out, there is no state action. *Flagg Bros., Inc., supra.*

   Example: In *Flagg Bros., Inc., supra,* the state Uniform Commercial Code permitted warehousemen who stored goods to sell them, without invoking state assistance in any way, on nonpayment of storage fees. The Court found no state action in this simple authorization.

5. ***State licensing:*** State licensing of private activities on private premises, such as liquor licensing for private clubs, of itself does not constitute state action. *Moose Lodge No. 107 v. Irvis,* 407 U.S. 163 (1972).

6. ***State funding:*** State funding contracts with private parties do not of themselves constitute state action sufficient to hold the state responsible for those private parties' violations of civil rights. *Rendell-Baker v. Kohn,* 457 U.S. 830 (1982); *Blum v. Yaretsky,* 457 U.S. 991 (1982). Even the extensive state regulation associated with certain state programs, such as Medicaid, will not convert the actions of private parties administering them into state action. *Blum, supra.* There must be additional state activity that makes it fair to say that the state is *responsible* for the challenged action.

   Examples: In *Rendell-Baker, supra,* employees of a private school funded almost entirely by public funds brought a federal civil rights action claiming they were discharged for exercising rights of free speech and without procedural due process. The Court held there was no state action.

   In *Blum, supra,* Medicaid patients residing in privately owned nursing homes alleged they were transferred from higher grade to lower grade facilities without procedural due process protections. Private physicians and nursing home administrators made the decisions to transfer. While the state funded the homes and regulated them heavily through Medicaid, it was not involved in the decisions to transfer and neither encouraged nor commanded them. Consequently, even though the state acquiesced in the decisions after the fact, it was not responsible for them.

C. **State Authorization or Encouragement:** Affirmative state acts, designed to authorize or encourage private violations of civil rights, constitute sufficient state action to make the state responsible for the actions of private parties.

   Example: In *Reitman v. Mulkey,* 387 U.S. 369 (1967), California voters passed a state constitutional amendment denying the state any power to regulate the sale, lease, or rental of any real property to any person the owner chose. The context of the amendment's passage made it clear that it was designed to overturn and prohibit state laws which limited the ability of property owners to discriminate on the basis of race. Passage of the amendment amounted to legislative action by the people of the state that authorized and encouraged a right to engage in racial discrimination in housing. The Court invalidated the state constitutional amendment as constituting state action violative of the federal Constitution.

   1. ***State approval of regulated utilities' practices and procedures:*** Public utility companies are often private monopolies regulated in the public interest. Heavy state regulation of a public utility, however, even general approval of its tariffs, does not convert its ordinary business practices into state action. In other words, what a business is privately permitted to do does not become state action because the state regulates the business.

      Example: In *Jackson, supra,* a public utility terminated service to an individual, without a hearing, for nonpayment. The practice of terminating service for nonpayment was longstanding and had been presented, along with other matters, to the state in tariffs filed for approval. The state approved a new tariff having the same provision but never considered this particular item. The Court held there was no state action.

2. ***State actor's compliance with private actor's demands:*** State authorization of, or participation in, a private actor's demands – in the sense of complying with them – will not necessarily convert the private action into state action which meets the state action requirement. State "complicity" in private action would not convert the private action into state action when the state actor chooses, for its own reasons, to comply with a private actor's demands. In *NCAA v. Tarkanian*, 488 U.S. 179 (1988), the National Collegiate Athletic Association, a private association which establishes and enforces standards that member colleges and universities agree to follow in competitive athletic programs, threatened to sanction the University of Nevada at Las Vegas unless it suspended its basketball coach, Tarkanian. UNLV vigorously fought the threatened suspension in protracted adversary proceedings, but finally agreed to the NCAA's demands. Because the state actor was not cooperating with the private actor, although it acquiesced after a long struggle, the private actor's demand for suspension was not attributable to the state. Tarkanian's suit against the NCAA for deprivation of liberty and property without due process therefore failed, as the NCAA was not a state actor.

State legislation as approval or authorization. A change in state law that allows private insurers to withhold payment for disputed medical services, pending a final determination, where formerly they could not do so, does not constitute state action. Such changes or modifications of legal remedies are normal in the legislative process and are not to be considered state authorization or encouragement. *American Mfrs. Mutal Insurance Co. v. Sullivan*, 526 U.S. 40 (1999).

D. **Private Actors Operating Under State Statutes:** Private actors sometimes exercise state-granted authority in ways that would clearly be thought to deny someone a constitutional right if the actor were a state actor. Whether the private actor should be deemed a state actor depends on (1) the extent of the actor's reliance on governmental assistance and benefits; (2) whether the function the actor performs is a traditional government function; and (3) whether the apparent exercise of state authority uniquely aggravates the injury. *Lugar v. Edmondson; Edmondson v. Leesville Concrete Co.*, 500 U.S. 614 (1991).

Example: Civil litigants' discriminatory use of race-based peremptory challenges: Civil juries are bodies carrying out a traditional governmental function. States create and regulate civil litigation systems, including the jury, and create and administer, through the trial judge, peremptory challenge systems. Therefore a private civil litigant's use of peremptory challenge authority to strike potential jurors on the basis of race is state action. *Edmondson v. Leesville Concrete Co., supra.*

E. **State Inaction:** State inaction, where there is no constitutional duty to act and no state responsibility for private action, cannot constitute state action. *DeShaney v. Winnebago County Dept. of Soc. Services*, 489 U.S. 189 (1989).

Example: In *DeShaney*, a tragic case, state social workers and local officials were aware that a young boy's father was seriously abusing him physically. Eventually, the father beat the boy so badly that he suffered severe brain damage. The Court held that Fourteenth Amendment due process prohibits the government from denying life,

CONGRESSIONAL
AUTHORITY
TO REACH
PRIVATE
ACTION
INFRINGING
CIVIL RIGHTS

liberty, or property without due process but does not require the government to protect private parties from one another. As the government has no federal constitutional duty to act to protect persons from harm by others, the state cannot be held responsible, in a suit for denial of civil rights, for the harm.

II. CONGRESSIONAL AUTHORITY TO REACH PRIVATE ACTION INFRINGING CIVIL RIGHTS

A. **The Civil Rights Statutes:** The Civil Rights Statutes provide for criminal and civil remedies for private interferences with the exercise of federally protected civil rights. There is a considerable body of case law construing these statutes and dealing with the complex problems individual statutes and particular language in them pose.

1. *Criminal civil rights legislation:* There are two principal criminal civil rights statutes: a conspiracy provision, 18 U.S.C. § 241, which prohibits conspiracies against the rights of citizens; and a substantive provision, 18 U.S.C. § 242, which criminalizes the deprivation of federally protected rights "under color of law."

   a. *Importance:* The criminal civil rights statutes are important for two reasons. They provide federal criminal sanctions for invasions of federally protected rights. They also provide a federal forum for the prosecution of racially motivated crimes, a feature which was of special significance during the early desegregation and integration efforts when state and local authorities refused to prosecute crimes committed against blacks and civil rights workers. While it may seem strange to prosecute a racially motivated murder as a deprivation of life without due process of law rather than as a murder, the fact that states sometimes did not prosecute them as murders left violations of the federal civil rights statutes as the only prosecutable offenses.

   b. *Problems of interpretation:* There are many difficulties in the interpretation of the criminal civil rights statutes. In addition to the usual problems attending the interpretation of statutes, these statutes posed special criminal void-for-vagueness issues and issues generated by the state action requirement. If the conspiracy or deprivation of rights alleged involved Fourteenth or Fifteenth Amendment rights, then the prosecutions had to meet the state action requirement.

   c. *Conspiracies against the rights of citizens:* In a series of cases, *Screws v. United States*, 321 U.S. 91 (1945); *Williams v. United States*, 341 U.S. 97 (1951); *United States v. Guest*, 383 U.S. 745 (1966); and *United States v. Price*, 383 U.S. 787 (1966), the Court construed the criminal civil rights conspiracy provision, 18 U.S.C. § 241 as follows:

      (1) Reach: Section 241 protects Fourteenth Amendment rights as well as Thirteenth Amendment rights and the rights of national citizenship, which depend on no amendment.

      (2) State action requirement: Whether or not the government must establish state action in § 241 prosecutions depends on the rights alleged violated. If the rights are Fourteenth or Fifteenth Amendment rights, as these are protected only against state, and not private, action, the government must allege and show state action. If the rights alleged violated are rights of

national citizenship, such as the right to travel, or Thirteenth Amendment rights, then there is no state action requirement. Congress can, and did, proscribe *private* infringements of those rights.

(3) Conspiracy prosecutions of private parties: Where there is a state action requirement for the rights allegedly violated, such as violations of Fourteenth Amendment rights, private parties can be prosecuted when they have conspired with state officers. Agreement with a state official to violate civil rights satisfies the state action requirement.

(4) Vagueness: Section 241 is not unconstitutionally vague in proscribing conspiracies against rights of citizens, as the crime of conspiracy requires specific intent.

d. *The substantive offense of deprivation of rights under color of law:* The Court construed 18 U.S.C. § 242, the substantive criminal civil rights provision, as follows:

(1) Color of law: The "color of law" language of § 242 is a state action requirement. That requirement is met when the government shows that

(a) the wrongdoer was *clothed* with the authority of the state, whether or not the state actually gave him the authority; or

(b) the wrongdoer with an "actual semblance" of state authority acted through it, and not just in the role of a private party; or

(c) the wrongdoer willingly participated in joint activity with the state or its agents.

(2) Vagueness: As federally protected rights are susceptible to Supreme Court construction and reinterpretation, they can hardly be said to be definite. This raises a criminal law vagueness problem, for criminal statutes are required to give reasonable notice of what they proscribe. To avoid the vagueness problem, the Supreme Court has construed § 242 to have a strict *scienter* requirement. To prove a violation of the substantive criminal civil rights provision, the government must show that the defendant had a specific intent to deprive a victim of a federal right made definite by decision or other rule of law.

2. **Civil rights statutes with civil sanctions:** There is a civil conspiracy civil rights statute, 42 U.S.C. § 1985(c), which is the counterpart of the criminal conspiracy statute, and which provides civil remedies for conspiracies to deny "equal protection of the laws, or of equal privileges and immunities under the laws." Similarly, there is a civil substantive counterpart to the substantive offense of deprivation of federal rights, 42 U.S.C. § 1983, which provides civil remedies for deprivation of rights "under color of law." The Court has interpreted the civil conspiracy provision to require a discriminatory intent and to reach private conspiracies directed at Thirteenth Amendment rights or rights of national citizenship such as the right to travel. *Griffin v. Breckenridge,* 403 U.S. 88 (1971); *Carpenters v. Scott,* 463 U.S. 825 (1983).

B. Congressional Power Under the Thirteenth Amendment: The Thirteenth Amendment bans all slavery and involuntary servitude in the United States, whether public or private, and has no state action requirement. Under the Enabling Clause of the Thirteenth Amendment, Congress is empowered to pass any law that may be necessary to abolish all badges of and incidents of slavery. *Civil Rights Cases, supra.*

1. *Private discrimination in housing:* Congress therefore has the power to ban, as it did in 42 U.S.C. § 1982, all racial discrimination, private as well as public, in the sale or rental of property. *Jones v. Alfred H. Mayer Co.,* 392 U.S. 409 (1968).

2. *Private discrimination in making and enforcing contracts:* Similarly, Congress has the power, under the Thirteenth Amendment, to forbid private, as well as public, discrimination in the making and enforcement of contracts. Congress banned such discrimination in 42 U.S.C. § 1981. *Runyon v. McCrary,* 427 U.S. 160 (1976). While § 1981 reaches discrimination in contract formation, and thus would include the making of an employment contract, the Court has nonetheless held that it does not ban discrimination arising in the employment relationship. *Patterson v. McLean Credit Union,* 493 U.S. 164 (1989).

C. Congressional Power Under the Enabling Clauses of the Fourteenth and Fifteenth Amendments

1. *Congressional "remedial" power*

   a. *Scope:* The enabling clauses of the Fourteenth and Fifteenth Amendments give Congress greater powers to remedy violations of those amendments than courts have. Thus, Congress can provide remedies for state actions, which courts would find violate the amendments, which courts themselves are unable to provide. *South Carolina v. Katzenbach,* 383 U.S. 301 (1966). As long as Congress uses rational means to effect the constitutional prohibitions against discrimination, the Court will uphold its action.

   Example: In investigating voting discrimination in the southern states, Congress found that, historically, southern states and communities had used literacy tests and other voting qualifications tests discriminatorily to prevent blacks from voting. Such action would, of course, violate the Fifteenth Amendment. Congress also found that case-by-case enforcement of the Fifteenth Amendment through litigation was not effective in ending such discrimination. In the Voting Rights Act of 1965, Congress suspended the use of literacy tests in areas of the country where it found the most serious racial discrimination in voting. It suspended the tests even in localities within the covered jurisdictions where the courts had not found voting discrimination through the use of literacy tests. The Court held that the congressional action was a rational means of remedying the problem of voting discrimination. As case-by-case adjudication was not an effective means of ending voting discrimination, Congress was not limited to remedies that depended on a prior adjudication. It could also, as a court could not, shift the burden of proof to covered jurisdictions to show they were not using designated tests and devices to perpetuate discrimination. *South Carolina v. Katzenbach, supra.*

   b. *Remedies for discriminatory effects:* Under the enabling clauses, Congress has the power to prohibit state action which, while not itself violative of the

Fourteenth or Fifteenth Amendments, nonetheless perpetuates the effects of past intentional discrimination. *South Carolina v. Katzenbach, supra.*

c. *Prophylactic remedies:* Where there has been a history of intentional racial discrimination, Congress may forbid state actions which, although neutral, have a discriminatory impact and create a risk of purposeful discrimination. *Rome v. United States,* 446 U.S. 156 (1980); *Katzenbach v. Morgan,* 384 U.S. 641 (1966).

Example: In the Voting Rights Act of 1965, Congress devised a federal administrative structure which required covered jurisdictions to "preclear" with the attorney general of the United States any proposed changes in their voting qualifications or practices. The covered jurisdictions were those where Congress had found there was a history of serious racial discrimination in voting, and the preclearance requirement prohibited changes unless the attorney general gave prior approval. The city of Rome, Georgia, pursuant to state law, changed its electoral system to an at-large system and annexed surrounding territory. The annexations, of course, would have had the effect of increasing and changing the composition of Rome's voting population. As the annexations might have had the effect of diluting the black vote in the city, the attorney general refused to preclear them. Although there was no showing that the city desired annexation in order to discriminate, the annexation clearly had a discriminatory impact. The Court held the action of Congress in prohibiting electoral system changes which had a discriminatory impact and which risked being used for a discriminatory purpose constitutional. *Rome v. United States, supra.*

2. ***The controversy over the scope of congressional power under the Enabling Clauses:*** There is no question that Congress has very broad remedial powers under the Fourteenth and Fifteenth Amendments. Simply put, Congress can do far more than courts could do in situations where they would find a violation of the prohibitions of those amendments. There is a major issue, however, whether Congress has "substantive" as well as "remedial" power under the Enabling Clauses. In other words, can Congress define Fourteenth or Fifteenth Amendment violations? If Congress can do so, and can do so where the Court has found there is no constitutional violation, then Congress would, in effect, replace the Court as final arbiter of the meaning of the Constitution. The possibility was raised by Justice Brennan's opinion for the Court in *Katzenbach v. Morgan, supra,* and the issues presented are explored below.

a. *Congressional power to define constitutional violations:* In *Lassiter v. Northampton Election Bd.,* 360 U.S. 45 (1959), the Court, while acknowledging that states could possibly use literacy tests discriminatorily, held that English language literacy tests for voting did not violate the Constitution. In the Voting Rights Act of 1965, however, Congress banned the use of an English language literacy test as a voting qualification for any person who had successfully completed the sixth grade in an American-flag school in Puerto Rico. The basic effect of this provision was to enfranchise many Spanish-only speaking Puerto Ricans living in New York City, which otherwise had an English language literacy test. The Court upheld the ban on two different theories. The first was that the ban was a remedy intended to ensure nondiscriminatory treatment for Puerto Ricans living in New York. This theory was in accord with other case law and presented no problem. The other theory was that Congress could have determined that New York's application of its literacy test was intentionally discriminatory. In effect, this theory holds that Congress may itself make determinations of constitutional violations, and that as long as the Court can perceive a rational basis on which Congress could base its conclusions, the Court would uphold them.

b. *The* Morgan *ratchet:* The *Morgan* theory that Congress has the power under the Enabling Clauses to make findings of substantive violations of the Constitution, subject only to deferential review, was a bit startling given the Court's traditional role and posed an immediate obvious problem. If Congress, as well as the Court, could define constitutional violations, then perhaps Congress could in effect overrule Court determinations of what constituted constitutional violations. Congress could conclude, for example – as many have urged it to – that equal protection required the states to protect the rights of fetuses in ways that prohibited a woman from having a free choice in deciding whether or not to bear a child. To avoid such a possibility, Justice Brennan noted, in footnote 1 in *Morgan,* that the Enabling Clause of the Fourteenth Amendment gave Congress the power to expand, but not contract, Court definitions of equal protection and due process. The Court has subsequently reaffirmed the position that the Enabling Clauses give Congress "no power to restrict, abrogate, or dilute these guarantees." *Mississippi U. for Women v. Hogan,* 458 U.S. 718 (1982).

c. Morgan *issue resolved:* The issue raised in *Morgan* has now been settled. Congressional power under the Fourteenth Amendment Enabling Clause is limited to remedial or preventive legislation. *City of Boerne v. Flores, Archbishop of San Antonio,* 521 U.S. 507 (1997). (Congress's attempt in Religious Freedom Restoration Act to impose compelling state interest test in court review of neutral government laws arguably burdening free exercise unconstitutional). Congress has only the power to enforce the Fourteenth Amendment, not the substantive power to determine what constitutes a substantive violation. Congress therefore does not have the authority to enact legislation expanding the rights recognized under the Fourteenth Amendment. *Id.* In effect, there is no *Morgan* ratchet.

Congruence and proportionality test. In determining whether Congress used its Section 5 power to remedy or prevent rights violations, the Court examines whether there is "congruence and proportionality between the injury to be prevents or remedied and the means adopted to that end." *City of Boerne, supra,* at 520. Essentially this means examining the legislative record for evidence of rights abuses or potential abuses that Congress was seeking to remedy. If there is little evidence of rights problems, the Court will find an "inappropriate" use of Section 5 power.

Examples: An attempt by Congress to override state sovereign immunity from suits for age discrimination in employment failed because the Age Discrimination in Employment Act (ADEA) was not appropriate legislation under Section 5 of the Fourteenth Amendment. This Act extended protection beyond the requirements of the Equal Protection Clause. Under Court holdings, age classifications for employment do not generally violate the Clause. Given that states can make rational use of age classifications, and that there was no showing of any pattern of state age discriminations, the ADEA could not constitute remedial or preventive legislation in support of Fourteenth Amendment rights. *Kimel v. Florida Board of Regents,* 120 S.Ct. 631 (2000).

The Federal Violence Against Women Act of 1994 provides for a federal civil rights remedy for crimes of violence motivated, at least in part, by gender animus. In *United States v. Morrison,* 120 S.Ct. 1740 (2000), the Court held that, insofar as the Act was adopted under Section 5 of the Fourteenth Amendment, it was unconstitutional. The Fourteenth Amendment prohibits only state action, but the Act did not aim at proscribing discrimination by state officials or other state actors. Instead, it targeted private parties who committed gender motivated acts of criminal violence. Furthermore, although Congress had evidence of state justice system bias against victims of gender-motivated violence, the evidence did not show that the bias existed in all or most states. However, Congress imposed a national remedy notwithstanding that the problem was not demonstrably national. The remedy therefore lacked "congruence and proportionality."

The Court has not had occasion to follow the second *Morgan* theory, and there has been sufficient criticism of it, by some justices and other commentators, that its current status is unclear. In *Oregon v. Mitchell,* 400 U.S. 112 (1970), the Court upheld a national congressional ban on the use of literacy tests. However, a majority also voted that Congress could not force states to permit eighteen-year-olds to vote in state elections. As Congress could have, in some way, determined that state failure to permit eighteen-year-old voting rights in state elections denied equal protection, the refusal to uphold the provision suggests that a Court majority would impose limits on *Morgan.*

(1) *Morgan* as a theory of fact-finding competence: In *Mitchell, supra,* Justice Brennan, the author of the *Morgan* theory, argued that *Morgan* stands for the idea that Congress has a fact-finding ability superior to that of courts. While courts are required to defer to state legislative findings if rational, Congress need not. Congress could thus factually find that certain state laws or practices, neutral on their face and rationally supportable, were nonetheless adopted or applied with a discriminatory purpose.

(2) *Morgan* as limited to cases involving discrete and insular minorities: Other justices in the same case also argued that *Morgan* does not permit Congress to overrule the Court's determination of what the Constitution requires. Instead, it simply recognizes that Congress, in seeking to protect a minority, could override state laws that it found were used to discriminate, even if a court would not so find. As *Mitchell* did not deal with discrete and insular minorities, but with eighteen-year-olds, these justices thought *Morgan* not controlling.

(3) Narrow *Morgan* reading: A majority of the Court how holds that Congress cannot revise or expand Court constitutional decisions. A majority also agrees that Congress can use its Enabling Clause power to remedy actual violations of the Fourteenth and Fifteenth Amendments. It is unclear, however, whether a majority continues to think that Congress can, in seeking to enforce the Fourteenth or Fifteenth Amendments, invalidate neutral state laws without a showing, acceptable to a court, that such laws screened intentional discrimination.

3. ***No-clear-statement rule:*** As the various Voting Rights Act cases reveal, Congress can use its Enabling Clause powers to enforce constitutional rights in ways extraordinarily disruptive of traditionally accepted spheres of state power. In those cases, the Court sustained, in certain circumstances, congressional power to limit, or even take away, states' power over their own electoral processes. The potential scope of this kind of intrusion into traditional state authority prompted the Court to suggest, in dicta, that it would not infer a congressional intent to do so without an express statement that Congress was exercising its Enabling Clause powers. In other words, the Court would not construe a congressional statute to work major incursions into state authority unless Congress made clear it so intended in order to protect constitutional rights. *Pennhurst State School v. Halderman,* 451 U.S. 1 (1981). Subsequently, however, the Court held that it requires no such express statement and would continue to construe congressional legislation as it always had done. *EEOC v. Wyoming,* 460 U.S. 226 (1983).

10

FREEDOM OF SPEECH (I)

▶ **CHAPTER SUMMARY**

11

CHAPTER 11: FREEDOM OF SPEECH (I)

Introduction. The First Amendment provides that Congress shall make no law abridging the freedom of speech, or of the press. The Amendment is not taken literally, however, for there are permissible laws abridging some kinds of speech, for example, laws punishing or prohibiting libel, incitement, blackmail, obscenity, solicitation, or contempt of court. Such laws may be valid because we do not consider them to reach the kinds of speech or the freedom of speech that the First Amendment protects. In order to distinguish between what is protected speech and what is not, we need some theory or theories of what the First Amendment Freedom of Speech Clause is meant to do.

I. THEORIES OF THE FIRST AMENDMENT

A. Instrumental Theories: The following instrumental theories of the First Amendment view free speech as a means to achieve some other good.

1. *Self-government:* Freedom of speech is required to ensure that the government remains open, responsive, and democratic. The strongest form of this view would hold that freedom of speech is a form of self-government. There is always the danger that the governors will govern in their self-interest rather than in the interests of the governed. In a diverse society such as ours, with many different creeds, beliefs, and group identifications, free speech is necessary to ensure that all views are heard. Under this view, the clause protects only political speech, defined broadly, and the clause is therefore meant only to prevent the government from suppressing political speech.

    This position has inherent difficulties. The first is that we must define what speech counts as political speech. This is hard to do since, whether or not politically intended, much "nonpolitical" speech may have an ultimate political effect. For example, obscene speech might be deemed political because it conceivably undermines a regime of obscenity laws meant to repress sexuality. More importantly, the Court has never so limited the free speech guarantee, and it is difficult to find a reason why it should do so. If only political speech is protected, then Congress could outlaw mathematical equations, poems, etc. Most of us would react strongly to such a suggestion, and this indicates there is some root value beyond the merely political which freedom of speech protects.

2. *Progress or the "marketplace-of-ideas" theory:* Under the marketplace-of-ideas theory, the regime of free speech is analogized to the economic marketplace and depends on similar "invisible hand" thinking. The idea here is that we are all better off when the truth of anything is known, or when the "best" wins out. The basic idea is that speech is free so that there will be a fair contest of ideas – no idea wins simply because some counteridea is suppressed – ultimately leading to the success of ideas which are true or more valuable or in some sense better. This is a historically important view, doubtless true to a certain degree, which still forms an important part of free-speech rationale. But there is also good reason to doubt that true or "better" ideas will always win out in the marketplace. It may be just as likely that the dominant view, the view most money supports, or the view the media promotes will win.

3. *Toleration theory:* A society such as ours, composed of people of immensely different backgrounds, beliefs, commitments, and ideals must be strongly tolerant

of diversity in order to survive, work effectively, and prosper. Freedom of speech is required not only so that each person can have a chance to partake of the society, but also for its symbolic value. We need a strong free speech principle, tolerant of even extreme and despised views, to model tolerance as a general operating principle in society.

B. Free Speech and Self-expression: Speech as an End in Itself: The theory of free speech as self-expression holds that self-expression is an important part of what it means to be human and therefore an ultimate value or a good in itself. Self-expression is also instrumentally essential to self-development, to autonomy, and to the pursuit of happiness and the good life.

Obviously this view is related to, and has historical roots in, freedom of religious beliefs, but it extends well beyond expression related to religious belief. If we focus on expression as a root value, then we will be led not to suppress speech even in those cases where it is not obviously a means to reach some other goal we prize. Furthermore, when free-speech rationale focuses on self-expression rather than on some other end, we can read the Free Speech Clause rather easily to protect expression which we do not normally think of as speech, *i.e.,* art, pictures, dance, music, even some kinds of behavior or conduct.

C. Freedom of Speech as a Default Principle: A final theory proposes that free speech is a kind of default principle that we resort to because we are unable to devise a fair and trustworthy mechanism for regulating speech. Suppose we say that there are ideas or kinds of speech that should not be tolerated. We are immediately faced with the problem of identifying what those are. Moreover, once we have identified them, we must create some kind of enforcement mechanism that will ensure the prohibition or proscription of the condemned speech. Obviously, in a society like ours, government would be entrusted with these tasks. But we do not have confidence that government is capable of accurately separating truth from falsehood, of deciding whether ideas are harmful or good, of being neutral and not reflecting simply the beliefs, attitudes, predilections, or needs of the government officials themselves. Otherwise put, we are incapable of creating an appropriate and fair system of regulating speech. Rather than trust government officials with such a job, we would prefer that the job not be done at all.

II. THE FIRST AMENDMENT AND "DANGEROUS" SPEECH HAVING SOCIAL OR POLITICAL AIMS

A. Historical Background: It is not at all clear how the founders felt about free speech as it related to advocacy to commit some unlawful act. It appears most likely that they intended the First Amendment simply to outlaw prior restraints on publications, that is, any form of censorship that prohibited publication until the material to be published was *first* reviewed and officially approved. Given early congressional legislation as evidence, the founders probably thought that the First Amendment did not prohibit laws punishing seditious libel. That is, did not reach speech against the government, its major officials, or branches, made with an intent to defame or to bring into contempt or disrepute, or to stir up sedition or opposition to the law.

Throughout American history, Congress, and, on occasion, the president has acted to suppress and punish speech thought harmful to government interests. The Alien and Sedition Acts of 1798, Lincoln's detention of 38,000 persons by executive arrest during

THE FIRST AMENDMENT AND "DANGEROUS" SPEECH

the Civil War, and the World War I and antisyndicalism and anticommunist statutes discussed below are also examples.

Modern free speech law begins in the era of World War I and the years following it. It is hard to return to the mentality of that time, but attitudes were distinctly different then from now and were such that there was establishment fear of so-called radical ideas. The late 1800s and early 1900s saw great struggles between capital and labor in this country, and there was a fear of labor organizing. In addition, the early 1900s saw a vast immigration of Southern European peasants to the United States. There was a xenophobic and competitive reaction, as there always is, to these foreigners in our midst. In addition, many of these immigrants either became union members or were ripe for unionization. Others of them brought radical ideas from Europe – socialism, communism, and anarchism. Finally, in 1917 in Russia, during the First World War, a small group of disciplined communists succeeded in taking over the Russian Revolution. The United States had become a belligerent force in World War I, against strong opposition from German-Americans, and the War loosed strong patriotic feelings of the kind always conducive to the suppression of contrary views.

The forces of patriotism, capitalism, and order commanded the day, and Congress passed various kinds of legislation proscribing certain acts or effects thought dangerous to the war effort or to the fragile public order. Many prosecutions were brought under these statutes, and it was out of these prosecutions, mostly lost by the defendants, that modern free speech consciousness was born. Inauspiciously begun, it is ultimately a wonderful story, showing the maturing of a nation, a growing confidence in the strength of basic institutions, and our ability to tolerate dissent, as well as a growing understanding of the importance of free speech.

B. **Unlawful or Subversive Advocacy Directed at the State or Major State Goals**

1. ***Advocacy of unlawful action:*** There are two principal reasons why the state may seek to prohibit or punish speech that advocates unlawful action. These are to reach speech which *causes* or improperly encourages unlawful action, *e.g.,* solicitation to murder; and to prevent speech the legislature deems inherently dangerous, *e.g.,* speech which advocates violent overthrow of the government.

2. ***Constructive intent:*** In early cases involving speech alleged to cause or to attempt to cause unlawful action, federal courts treated speech just as they treated any action alleged to cause crime or other wrongful acts. Under criminal law principles, persons are presumed to intend the natural and probable consequences of their acts. If a speech might lead to a proscribed harm (that is, it had a bad tendency), a jury could also find the speaker intended the harm (constructive intent).

   Example: In a prosecution arising during World War I, a federal court upheld a conviction for obstructing the recruiting service through publication of a book deriding patriotism and stating that the war against Germany was wrong. *Shaffer v. United States,* 255 F. 886 (9th Cir. 1919).

   Clear and present danger: In *Schenck v. United States,* 249 U.S. 47 (1919), Justice Holmes reformulated the "bad tendency" test as a proximity test. Words constituted a criminal attempt to bring about a proscribed harm when they were "used in such circumstances and [were] of such a nature as to create a clear and present danger" that they would bring about the harm.

a. *Problems with the initial clear and present danger test:* As originally formulated and applied, the clear and present danger test was used to *uphold* convictions for speech activities alleged to interfere with the war effort. While the test purported to distinguish between normal and "dangerous" political criticism, it did so by focusing more on the context of the speech than on its content. This meant the government could sometimes punish ordinary critique of its acts or policies. In addition, the clear and present danger test was vague on the question of what constituted a "clear and present danger" and made that an issue for the jury to decide. As a consequence, the Court upheld convictions in the following:

   (1) In *Schenck, supra,* the defendant printed and circulated to draftees a document quoting the Thirteenth Amendment and statements of well-known public men, and claimed the Constitution was violated when someone refused to recognize the right to assert opposition to the draft.

   (2) In *Frohwerk v. United States,* 249 U.S. 204 (1919), the defendant helped print and publish a newspaper, of small circulation and not directed to men of draft age, which opposed the war against Germany, was critical of the draft, and sympathetic to draft resisters.

   (3) In *Debs v. United States,* 249 U.S. 211 (1919), Debs gave a speech, to an audience where there were persons possibly subject to the draft, which discussed socialism and which expressed admiration for three persons convicted for aiding and abetting another to fail to register for the draft.

b. *The clear and present danger test given new content:* In *Abrams v. United States,* 250 U.S. 616 (1919), the Court upheld a conviction of five Russian immigrants for printing and distributing circulars which criticized American intervention in Russia during the First World War. In his famous dissent, Justice Holmes infused the clear and present danger test with new meaning.

   (1) Attempting to cause harm by speech: Justice Holmes first noted that the attempt crimes were *specific intent* crimes. Defendants were charged with attempting, by speech, to hinder the American war effort in Germany. As their intent was instead to support the Russian Revolution, they could not be guilty of an attempt to hinder.

   (2) Imminence and immediacy: Justice Holmes then effectively stated that the Constitution recognized the special value of free speech and that suppression or punishment of speech was an extraordinary act that needed virtual overwhelming justification. The government should not "check the expression of opinions . . . unless they so imminently threaten immediate interference with the lawful and pressing purposes of the law that an immediate check is required to save the country."

4. ***Advocating overthrow of the government by force or violence:*** A speaker may possibly cause harm by influencing or persuading others to undertake unlawful acts. But a legislature may also decide that certain ideas or doctrines are themselves so harmful that speakers cannot speak or promote them, regardless of whether they cause some specific harm. Consequently, early in this century, some legislatures enacted statutes forbidding the teaching or advocacy of certain

doctrines – generally, anarchist, "syndicalist," or communist doctrines – which advocated the overthrow of government by force or violence or by what we might now call terrorist acts. They also forbade organizing associations to teach such doctrine and criminalized membership in them.

a. *The early cases and the clear and present danger test*

    (1) In *Gitlow v. New York*, 268 U.S. 652 (1925), the Court upheld a New York statute which outlawed the doctrine of criminal anarchy, as applied to an individual who published a manifesto advocating mass industrial revolts and political strikes to overthrow the state. The Court said legislatures could outlaw doctrines advocating overthrow of government by unlawful means and that the clear and present danger test did not apply when the legislature had done so.

    (2) In *Whitney v. California*, 274 U.S. 357 (1927), the Court upheld, as not violating any right of speech, assembly, or association, an organizing and membership conviction. The woman convicted had participated in a meeting which formed a Communist Labor Party and which adopted, over her protest and without her agreement, an extremist overthrow platform.

    (3) In *De Jonge v. Oregon*, 299 U.S. 353 (1937), however, the Court overturned a state conviction, under a criminal syndicalism law, of a person who assisted a Communist Party-sponsored meeting not involving illegal advocacy. The Court recognized peaceful assembly as a fundamental First Amendment right and held that "peaceable assembly for lawful discussion cannot be made a crime."

b. *The Communist Party cases:* In a series of complicated cases dealing with Smith Act prosecutions of Communist Party leaders and members, the Court refined the clear and present danger test. It also defined more sharply what kind of teaching or advocacy the legislature could proscribe; defined prohibitable membership or association; and made clear what kind of evidence would support forbidden advocacy convictions.

    (1) Clear and present danger test as applied to advocacy of violent overthrow: In cases involving the Communist Party and its members, a highly trained and disciplined group prepared to take violent action when directed, the question is "whether the gravity of the 'evil,' discounted by its improbability, justifies such invasion of free speech as is necessary to avoid the danger." *Dennis v. United States*, 341 U.S. 494 (1951) (plurality). In other words, if the danger is truly great, the likelihood of its occurrence need not be.

    (2) Ancillary rules

        (a) Whether there is a clear and present danger is a question of law, to be decided by a judge, not a jury. *Dennis, supra.*

        (b) To avoid constitutional problems, the Court will narrowly construe statutes seeking to, or having the effect of, regulating the freedoms of speech or association. *Yates v. United States*, 354 U.S. 298 (1957).

(3) Rules distinguishing between lawful and unlawful advocacy

    (a) Congress has the power to prohibit acts intended to overthrow the government by force and violence. *In some circumstances,* Congress can proscribe or punish advocacy of violent overthrow. *(Dennis, supra,* as interpreted by *Yates, supra.)*

    (b) Congress cannot proscribe simple advocacy of doctrine, even where the doctrine teaches forcible overthrow.

        i) Congress can proscribe advocacy of action directed at, or creating a danger of, *immediate* overthrow.

        ii) Congress can proscribe the advocacy involved in the creation and indoctrination of a disciplined group prepared to take violent action when the time is ripe.

    (c) Organization and membership rules *(Scales v. United States,* 367 U.S. 203 (1961); *Noto v. United States,* 367 U.S. 290 (1961)):

        i) Congress can proscribe organizations advocating violent overthrow where the organization advocates illegal action, either immediately or in the future when the opportunity arises.

        ii) Mere membership in such an organization, however, without anything else, is protected associational activity.

        iii) Knowing or active membership, on the other hand, that is, membership *with knowledge and specific intent* to further the illegal aims of the organization, is not constitutionally protected association.

    (d) Evidentiary rules. *(Yates, supra; Scales, supra).* The following evidence establishes such illegal advocacy:

        i) the teaching of forceful overthrow, together with specific directions or instruction regarding illegal action to be taken in the future;

        ii) the teaching of forceful overthrow, together with present action, even legal, specifically aimed at making later illegal action effective;

        iii) convicting someone on the basis of membership in the Communist Party requires evidence of present advocacy of violent overthrow, now or in the future. An intent to advocate in the future or a conspiracy to advocate once groundwork is laid, is insufficient.

C. Incitement: Incitement involves a speaker's urging someone or a group to engage in unlawful action.

    1. *Likely to cause harmful action:* The problem in incitement cases, as in the early free-speech cases, is in drawing the line between speech which expresses opinions, no matter how unpopular or how intemperately stated, and speech which is a trigger to action and thus likely to cause real harm. Put more strongly, the First Amendment concern is to find a rule that does not permit suppressing disagreeable or belief-threatening speech but does allow punishing speech likely to cause harmful action. The Court has placed the line close to the latter.

2. ***Intent required:*** Government can forbid or proscribe advocacy of force or illegal action only when the speaker intends to incite or produce imminent lawless action and is likely to do so. *Brandenburg v. Ohio,* 395 U.S. 444 (1969).

3. ***Limited application of Brandenburg test:*** The *Brandenburg* test is not an all-purpose test but appears to apply only to those situations in which a speaker arguably urges illegal action either in opposition to government or government policies or against private parties.

   Example: The Court would not use *Brandenburg* to determine whether Congress can proscribe a genuine, noninciting threat to kill the president. *Watts v. United States,* 394 U.S. 705 (1969).

D. **Fighting Words:** "Fighting words" are direct personal insults likely to cause the hearer to react violently.

1. ***Injurious insults not protected:*** In *Chaplinsky v. New Hampshire,* 315 U.S. 568 (1942), the Court upheld a conviction under a state statute prohibiting a speaker from addressing "offensive, derisive, or annoying" words to another in a public place. The speaker called a police officer a "God-damned racketeer" and "a damned Fascist." The Court held that insulting words "which by their very utterance inflict injury or tend to incite an immediate breach of the peace" were not protected speech. In other words, the abstract character of words as insults as opposed to their *actual effect* under the circumstances determines whether they are protected or punishable.

2. ***Other solutions:*** Subsequent developments, such as the protection of emotive or offensive speech likely to trigger adverse reaction, and the move away from categorizing or defining certain kinds of speech as unprotected have undermined the vitality of the fighting words doctrine. Further, other doctrines, such as the *Brandenburg* incitement rule, may adequately solve the problem the fighting words doctrine addresses.

E. **Group Libel:** Group libel consists of false and derogatory statements, tending to produce hate or prejudice, made about a group.

1. ***Depravity:*** Assertions that a certain race, creed or religion is depraved constitute group libel.

2. ***Current status:*** In *Beauharnais v. Illinois,* 343 U.S. 250 (1952), the Court held that group libel was not constitutionally protected speech and that states could make group libel a criminal offense. *Beauharnais* has never been overruled, and it is uncertain whether it survives subsequent developments in free speech law, particularly the *Brandenburg* rule and current defamation law.

F. Defamation of Government Officials, Public Figures, and Private Parties

1. ***Actual malice required:*** In *New York Times v. Sullivan*, 376 U.S. 254 (1964), the Court held that in order for a public official to recover for libelous false statements regarding her official conduct, the official had to prove the statements were made with "actual malice," that is, made with knowledge of falsity or in reckless disregard of the truth.

   a. *Evolution of libel rule:* The *New York Times* rule changed the common law libel rule, which provided that false statements were libelous and that truth was the only defense in a libel action. The Court reasoned that the constitutional protection of speech does not depend on the truth or acceptability of ideas expressed. The First Amendment assumes wide-open public debate, and erroneous statements are inevitable. In addition, given their position of public trust, as a matter of accountability and responsiveness, public officials should be subject to criticism, even if it injures their official reputations.

   b. *Clear and convincing evidence:* The *New York Times* actual malice standard is an even stronger standard than first appears, as it must be established by clear and convincing evidence, as opposed to a preponderance of the evidence.

   c. *Reckless disregard:* To establish publication in reckless disregard of the truth, the plaintiff must show that the defendant in fact entertained serious doubts as to the truth of the statement, yet nonetheless published it. *St. Amant v. Thompson*, 390 U.S. 727 (1968).

   d. *Public officials:* Public officials are governmental functionaries or employees who either have or appear to have substantial responsibility for or control over the conduct of governmental affairs.

   e. *Official conduct:* Official conduct has been interpreted to mean "anything that might touch on an official's fitness for office." *Garrison v. State of Louisiana,* 379 U.S. 64 (1964). Consequently, the actual malice standard applies not only to false statements made regarding conduct in office, it also extends false statements regarding matters of personal life or habits which in some way are relevant to public thinking about that person in her office.

2. ***Public figures:*** The *New York Times* rule applies to public figures as well as public officials. *Curtis Publishing Co. v. Butts,* 388 U.S. 130 (1967); *Associated Press v. Walker,* 388 U.S. 130 (1967). Public figures are those who are famous, are celebrities, or who have thrust themselves into the public spotlight.

3. ***Fact and opinion:*** The *New York Times* rule applies to false statements of fact and to opinions on matters of public concern where a reasonable person could interpret the opinion as having been based on facts. In other words, an individual can sue in libel for statements of opinion impliedly based on facts that are knowingly false or made in reckless disregard of the truth. *Milkovich v. Lorain Journal,* 497 U.S. 1 (1990). On the other hand, opinions not reasonably interpretable as stating or implying actual facts about an individual are not actionable. *Id.*

   Example: Suppose someone says, "I've been with Mayor White at any number of private meetings and parties and have watched his behavior carefully. It is my opinion that he is a narcotics user." The statement implies possible observations of drug use, a fact. If the fact is knowingly false or made in reckless disregard of the truth, the statement is actionable as libel. Contrast the foregoing with the following statement: "Mayor White is a scum-sucking pig." No one could reasonably view the latter statement of opinion as implying any particular, actual facts about the Mayor, and would not, by itself, be actionable.

4. ***Inaccurate, distorted, or fabricated quotations:*** A reporter's deliberate alteration of a speaker's words may or may not constitute libel. If changing the words does not change the meaning of what the speaker said, there is no actual malice for libel purposes. Therefore, a public figure claiming libel through falsely attributed quotations must show that the attributed quotation materially changes the meaning of what the plaintiff actually said. *Masson v. New Yorker,* 501 U.S. 496 (1991).

5. ***Private persons:*** Following *New York Times,* the Court also changed common law libel rules regarding defamation of private persons.

   a. *Private persons involved in public issues:* Persons who, although not generally known, place themselves into a particular public controversy may become public figures for a limited range of issues. Whether such a person is a public person for *New York Times* purposes is a factual question turning on the nature and extent of her involvement in the controversy giving rise to the libel. Voluntary involvement, an attempt to gain public attention, or an attempt to influence the outcome of a public controversy all suggest the person has become a public figure in that controversy.

   b. *Private persons:* The *New York Times* rule does not apply to private persons not involved in public issues nor to private persons involuntarily caught up in public issues. *Gertz v. Robert Welch, Inc.,* 418 U.S 323 (1974).

   c. *Negligence standard regarding matters of public interest:* At a minimum, the First Amendment requires that a private party suing a defendant for a false and defamatory statement concerning the plaintiff's involvement in a matter of public interest show that the statement was negligently made. States may adopt higher standards if they wish, *i.e.,* gross negligence or actual malice.

   d. *Damages:* Damages for negligent defamation of a private party involved in a matter of public interest are limited to compensation for actual injury, which includes not only out-of-pocket loss, but also impairment of reputation, humiliation, mental anguish, and suffering. Punitive damages may be permissible on a showing of actual malice. *Cf. Dun and Bradstreet v. Greenmoss Builders,* 472 U.S. 749 (1985) *(Gertz* damage limitations apply only in cases involving matters of public interest.)

G. **Invasion of Privacy:** There are some torts actions, which like libel, involve statements or disclosures about a person. It is unclear whether the *New York Times* rule and its corollaries apply to them.

   1. ***Privacy cases:*** In invasion of privacy cases, the issue is not the falsity of published information, but the fact that it was published. The objection is to the publication of true information that may be embarrassing or otherwise damaging and which an individual has a right not to have disclosed. While there are no cases in point, the *New York Times* rationale appears to apply, at least insofar as the disclosures

involve public officials or figures and are relevant to their positions. The harder question is whether the public interest in information can always override a private person's interest in privacy. The Court has not resolved this question, but there are suggestions that if the revelation involves material of legitimate concern to the public, then the private party cannot recover in a privacy action for disclosure of truthful information. This would constitute a sort of "First Amendment easement" over a person's right of privacy.

2. ***"False light" privacy cases:*** False light cases are cases in which facts published are true but are misleading, perhaps because not completely true or because not all the facts are published, thus giving a false impression. False light cases have two aspects: an invasion of privacy aspect through the disclosure of true facts someone desires kept private; and a harm to reputation aspect stemming from the false impression. These separate aspects should be analyzed separately.

   Example: *Time, Inc. v. Hill,* 385 U.S. 374 (1967), was an unusual false light case. *Life* magazine reported that a play based on a hostage incident was true, but while the event had occurred, the play substantially distorted what actually happened. The New York privacy statute, under which suit was brought, made truth a defense, but permitted a "newsworthy person" to recover when a report was substantially falsified. The Court applied the *New York Times* actual malice standard. It is doubtful that *Time, Inc.* survives the *Gertz, supra,* rule.

3. ***Disclosure of private information in the public record:*** No invasion of privacy action will lie for disclosure of information in the public record. *Cox Broadcasting Corp. v. Cohn,* 420 U.S. 469 (1975) (father suing for broadcasting of fact that his daughter was a rape victim, a fact learned from official court records).

4. ***Appropriation of information:*** The First Amendment does not protect the media from liability for appropriating "proprietary" information. *Zacchini v. Scripps-Howard Broadcasting Co.,* 433 U.S. 562 (1977) (television station broadcast "human cannonball's" entire performance).

III. EROTIC, OBSCENE, AND PORNOGRAPHIC EXPRESSION

A. Definitions

1. ***Erotica:*** Erotica refers to expression devoted to or tending to arouse sexual love or desire.

2. ***Obscenity:*** Obscenity is that aspect or character of expression about sex which is disgusting, offensive, filthy, foul, loathsome, or repulsive. The First Amendment does not protect obscene expression. *Roth v. United States / Alberts v. California,* 354 U.S. 476 (1957). For the constitutional test for what comprises obscenity, *see* B., *infra.*

3. ***Pornography:*** Pornography is the depiction of erotic or sexual behavior intended to cause sexual excitement.

   a. *Pornography is usually divided into categories of soft-core and hard-core pornography:* The distinguishing features between the two are primarily the offensiveness and explicitness of the sexual depiction. Hard-core pornography involves the depiction of explicit, physical, sexual conduct – ultimate sexual acts – or lewd exhibition of the genitals. Generally speaking, under current constitutional tests for obscenity, hard-core pornography is obscene.

    b.   An alternative definition of pornography, proposed by some feminists, is that pornography consists of sexual depictions in which one party dominates another (usually a man dominating a woman) or which portray one party as sexually inferior or subservient to the other (usually women portrayed as inferior and subservient). *(Cf.* I., *infra.)*

B. **Attempts to Restrict Censorship:** The First Amendment problem in obscenity cases is essentially the creation of a test which is clear enough to prevent the repression of ideas or expressions having erotic or sexual content or effect yet able to condemn works having no value other than sexual stimulation. Given the range of beliefs about sexual matters, and the history of censorship regarding them, this is an exceptionally difficult problem. The ordinary administration of obscenity laws complicates the problem, for it generally criminalizes the publication of obscene materials and makes questions of obscenity jury questions. There is a great risk that untutored jurors – and unsophisticated judges for that matter – will condemn as obscene works whose sexually tied message may offend but which is nonetheless integral to the overall expression of ideas. Consequently, the Court has devised a set of rules that, while not easy to apply or completely discriminating, greatly restrict the likelihood of repression or censorship through obscenity laws.

    1. *Initial solution:* The Court initially tried to solve the problem broad obscenity laws present by defining what speech was obscene. This, however, was not completely satisfactory, for it did not clarify the First Amendment value of sexually oriented or sexually explicit speech and failed to define what state interests justified the regulation of such speech.

    2. *Works of serious value protected:* The Court eventually made it clear that the First Amendment protects works of *"serious* literary, artistic, political, or scientific value" and that states could not use obscenity laws to suppress them *no matter what their sexual content. Miller v. California,* 413 U.S. 15 (1973).

    3. *State interests:* The Court has also held that legitimate state interests in order, safety, and morality justify obscenity laws. *Paris Adult Theatre v. Slaton,* 413 U.S. 49 (1973). More specifically, these are the prevention of sex crimes and antisocial behavior, and the protection of the unwilling public from offensive displays or depictions, from degradation of the public environment and from moral debasement in sexual matters. *Id.*

C. **Three-Part Test:** For First Amendment purposes, expression is obscene if (1) to the average person, applying contemporary community standards, the *dominant theme* of the material taken as a whole appeals to the *prurient interest, and* (2) the work depicts or describes, in a *patently* offensive way, sexual conduct specifically defined by statute as unlawful to portray, *and* (3) the work taken as a whole lacks serious literary, artistic, political, or scientific value. *Miller v. California, supra.*

    1. *Material taken as a whole:* A work cannot be condemned as obscene because of isolated obscene passages.

    2. *Average person:* The fact-finder must determine whether the average person would find the appeal directed to prurient interest, and not whether it appealed to the average person.

3. ***Prurient interest:*** "Prurient interest" is a "shameful or morbid interest in nudity, sex, or excretion." Model Penal Code § 207.10(2) Tentative Draft No. 6, 1957. Material appealing to the prurient interest may attract or repel but must be sexually stimulating – in the sense of exciting lustful thoughts – and not merely immoral or offensive because of the use of sexual terms.

   a. *Appeal to a subgroup sufficient:* Sexually explicit material may portray matters not appealing or sexually stimulating to the general public, *e.g.,* bestiality, coprophilia, necrophilia, sadomasochism. Nonetheless, if, taken as a whole, the material appeals to the prurient interest of a sexual subgroup or a deviant sexual group, it meets the prurient interest requirement. *Pinkus v. United States,* 436 U.S. 293 (1978).

   b. *Pandering may qualify:* In a close case, evidence of *pandering* can support a finding that material is obscene. *Ginzburg v. United States,* 383 U.S. 463 (1966); *Splawn v. California,* 431 U.S. 595 (1977). One who through advertising and promotion stimulates a reader to accept materials not technically obscene under *Miller* as prurient can be convicted for distributing obscene materials. *Id.*

   c. *Advocacy of sexual immorality:* Works advocating sexual immorality, *e.g.,* adultery, are not, for *that* reason, obscene. *Kingsley Int'l Pictures Corp. v. Regents,* 360 U.S. 684 (1959).

4. ***Patently offensive:*** Material which is patently offensive is material which describes or depicts sexual matters in ways substantially beyond customary limits of candor or affronting current community standards of decency. *Jacobellis v. Ohio,* 378 U.S. 184 (1964).

   Example: Representations or descriptions of ultimate sex acts, normal or perverted, actual or simulated; masturbation; excretory functions; and lewd exhibition of the genitals are patently offensive. *Miller, supra.*

   a. *Statutes prohibiting obscene material must describe in specific detail what depictions are prohibited:* Statutes which simply proscribe material that corrupts the public morals or stimulates lust are insufficient.

5. ***Average person:*** The *Miller* formulation directs jurors to take the position of the "average person" in assessing allegedly obscene material. This gives jurors an objective focus and is meant to avoid the problem of considering material from the point of view of the especially sensitive or insensitive.

6. ***Contemporary community standards:*** The *Miller* rule also directs the jurors to apply contemporary community standards, another objective focus. The jury must itself determine what the community standards are; the legislature cannot define them nor is expert evidence regarding them necessary. *Pinkus, supra; Paris Adult Theatre v. Slaton, supra.*

   a. *The relevant community:* The relevant community is the local adult community, even in a federal prosecution, and the trial judge need not define the community for the jury. *Pinkus, supra.* States can define the relevant community under state law, however, making it the whole state or something less. *Miller, supra; Jenkins v. Georgia,* 418 U.S. 153 (1974); *Hamling v. United States,* 418 U.S. 87 (1974).

    b. *Not applicable to value:* Community standards apply only to two of the *Miller* elements, prurient appeal and patent offensiveness. Those standards do not apply to the element of the work's value.

7. *Value:* In assessing the artistic, literary, political, or scientific value of a work, the jury is to apply an objective, reasonable person standard, not limiting itself to community standards. *Pope v. Illinois,* 481 U.S. 497 (1987).

8. *Judicially reviewable:* Although all the foregoing issues are jury questions, what is obscene is ultimately a question of law. *Jenkins v. Georgia, supra* (film *Carnal Knowledge* not obscene notwithstanding jury obscenity finding). Courts may review jury determinations of obscenity.

D. **Obscenity and Privacy:** As a matter of the right to the privacy of one's own home, the state cannot make it a crime to possess obscene material there. *Stanley v. Georgia,* 394 U.S. 557 (1969).

1. *The right of privacy does not include access to obscene materials from outside the home:* Congress may therefore prohibit the use of the mails for commercial distribution of obscene materials, *United States v. Reidel,* 402 U.S. 351 (1971), and may prohibit the interstate transmission of obscene commercial telephone messages ("dial-a-porn"). *Sable Communications v. F.C.C.,* 492 U.S. 115 (1989).

2. *Transporting is actionable:* Although the state cannot punish someone for possessing obscene materials in her home, she has neither a right to buy them nor receive them. Consequently the state can prosecute individuals for bringing obscene materials into the country and for transporting them, even if intended for personal use. *Reidel, supra.*

E. **Dealing in or Distributing Obscene Materials:** The state may prosecute those who create, deal in, distribute, sell, or exhibit obscene materials. *Paris Adult Theatre v. Slaton, supra.*

1. *Consent irrelevant:* There is thus no right of "consenting adults" to see obscene materials in a theater.

2. *Intent required:* In order to convict dealers, distributors, or exhibitors, as opposed to authors or publishers, however, due process requires *scienter*. Those defendants need not know that the material was obscene in the legal sense, but they must have knowledge of the contents or character of the material.

3. *Child pornography distinguished:* As states have a compelling interest in protecting children from being used as subjects of pornographic materials, they may penalize those who possess or view such materials in order to reduce demand. Consequently, they may prohibit possession of such materials in the home. *Osborne v. Ohio,* 495 U.S. 103 (1990).

F. **Child Pornography:** A state's interest in "safeguarding the physical and psychological well being" of minors is compelling. States may therefore proscribe live performances or recorded live performances of sexual activity involving children, *New York v. Ferber,* 458 U.S. 747 (1982). Unlike obscenity cases involving adult sexual conduct, in which the *Miller* standard applies, in child pornography cases the *Miller* standard is modified in important ways. In such cases, the trier of fact need not find that the material appeals to the average person's prurient interest, the portrayal of child sexual conduct need not be patently offensive, and the material need not be considered as a whole.

G. **Juvenile Obscenity:** The states may regulate children's access to nonobscene but sexually stimulating material. They may outlaw for sale or distribution to minors works whose predominant appeal is to the prurient interest of minors, which are patently offensive to community standards regarding materials suitable for minors, and which are without redeeming value for minors. *Ginsberg v. New York,* 390 U.S. 629 (1969).

H. **Sexually Violent and Degrading Expression:** Some, but not all, pornographic material is sexually violent, and there is some evidence that there is a causal relationship between exposure to sexually violent pornography and aggressive and sexually violent behavior toward women. There is also some evidence, more tenuous yet, which suggests a similar causal relationship for sexual expression degrading women by depicting them as existing solely to satisfy men sexually. *Report of the Attorney General's Commission on Pornography* (1986). Consequently, the Attorney General's Commission recommended increased enforcement of existing obscenity laws against sexually violent and sexually degrading expression, declining a suggestion that the state cease attempting to regulate obscene expression. As not all sexually violent or degrading expression is obscene under *Miller,* this strategy would not reach all such material, but only that which had no content other than sexual stimulation.

I. **Pornography as Discrimination against Women through Explicit Sexual Subordination:** Recently, there have been efforts to redefine pornography as a systematic practice of sexual exploitation and subordination of women. This definition ties into an attempt to treat pornography as a practice of discrimination against women, violative of their civil rights. As the key feature of this definition is the idea of sexual subordination, it defines obscenity quite differently from the *Miller* standard and would proscribe sexually explicit speech not obscene under *Miller.* On the other hand, the new definition would not forbid sexually explicit speech "premised on equality" even if obscene under *Miller.* A federal circuit court has held such a definition unconstitutional as restricting expression because of its message, contrary to the First Amendment premise of a completely open "marketplace of ideas." *American Booksellers Assn., Inc. v. Hudnut,* 771 F.2d 323 (7th Cir. 1985), *judgment aff'd,* 475 U.S. 1001 (1986).

IV. INDECENT AND OFFENSIVE SPEECH

A. **Words Not Per Se Proscribable:** There are no words which can be forbidden per se, not even words generally thought taboo or offensive. Absent a showing of direct personal insult or provocation of a group, the state may not punish the use of nonobscene but indecent or offensive words expressed in a public place where speech is not legitimately restricted. *Cohen v. California,* 403 U.S. 15 (1971) ("Fuck the draft" sign worn on jacket in a courthouse).

1. *Outside a few established exceptions, the government cannot proscribe the form or content of expression:* Without evidence of concrete harm, the state

cannot, by punishing their utterance, in effect remove certain "offensive" words from the public vocabulary.

2. ***The emotive, as well as cognitive, features of words carry their messages, and the shock value of an offensive word may be an important part of its message:*** There is a significant risk that the censorship of particular words – excising them from the public discourse – will disguise a governmental ban on the expression of an unpopular message conjoined with the use of offensive words.

B. **Offensive Displays:** At least in public areas where unwilling recipients can turn away to avoid exposure, the First Amendment strictly limits government's ability to ban offensive expression on the basis of its content. *Erznoznik v. Jacksonville,* 422 U.S. 295 (1975) (ordinance prohibiting drive-in theaters from showing films with nudity on screens visible from public streets held unconstitutional).

C. **Zoning and Offensive Expression:** As long as the effect is not to regulate content or restrict access in any significant way, governments may limit, for substantial land use regulation reasons, the display of sexually explicit materials to certain areas of a community. *Young v. American Mini Theatres,* 427 U.S. 50 (1976); *City of Renton v. Playtime Theatres, Inc.,* 475 U.S. 41 (1986). Absent adequate alternative expressive outlets, however, a government cannot ban protected forms of expression from a community without demonstrating a good zoning reason for doing so. *Schad v. Mt. Ephraim,* 452 U.S. 61 (1981) (city ordinance completely barring live entertainment, including nude dancing, from city held unconstitutional).

D. **Content Neutrality:** One hallmark of much First Amendment jurisprudence is "content neutrality," that is, the requirement that the state not regulate expression on the basis of its content. The content-neutrality requirement can be viewed as a kind of anticensorship rule – the state has no business favoring or disfavoring ideas or expressions of one kind or another – or as a kind of equal protection for all kinds of expression.

E. **Content Neutrality and Secondary Effects of Speech:** Government regulation of speech is completely content neutral when it treats all kinds of speech similarly, *e.g.,* political, erotic, literary, sexually explicit, or offensive speech. The government may, however, treat different kinds of speech differently *because* of regulable matters associated with a particular kind of speech.

1. ***Zoning may apply to sexually explicit speech:*** As in *Young,* the government may have zoning rules specially applicable to sexually explicit but nonobscene speech. Such regulation is not completely content neutral, for it must take the content of the speech into account in order to regulate.

2. ***Secondary effects:*** The Court has held that governments may treat at least some different kinds of protected speech differently, as long as the regulation is not based on the message of the expression, but on its "secondary effects" instead. *City of Renton, supra.*

   Example: "Adult" theaters showing explicitly sexual films may be associated with higher levels of neighborhood crime or other externalities. Zoning of "adult" theaters to mitigate their undesirable externalities is a regulation of the "secondary effects" of the kind of expression taking place there. In this example, the government regulation is speech content related in the sense that the externalities the government seeks to regulate are associated with a particular kind of speech. It is, in the view of the Court, however, also content neutral – in the sense that the government is not seeking to regulate the content of the expression or any of its direct impacts on viewers or listeners. It is unclear whether the secondary effects rule applies to speech other than sexually explicit expression.

3. ***Regulation is not censorship:*** "Secondary effects" theory, first applied in the context of zoning regulation of sexually explicit speech, holds that regulations directed to the social ills that the existence of a certain kind of speech creates are not to be viewed as efforts to regulate speech content or the direct effects of the message on the audience.

4. ***Ambiguity of secondary effects theory***

   a. *Applicability:* There is some question as to the reach of the "secondary effects" theory: specifically, is it limited to sexually explicit speech, or is it a theory of general applicability? Some justices, *e.g.,* Justice O'Connor, apparently would apply secondary effects theory to any kind of speech. *Cf. Boos v. Barry,* 485 U.S. 312 (1988). This view has not commanded a majority, however, and it would appear the theory should be limited to sexually explicit or other "lower-value" speech.). *Cf. City of Erie v. PAP'S A.M.* 120 S.Ct. 1382 (2000).

   b. *Scope:* In *Boos, supra,* Justice O'Connor opined that the state may regulate the secondary effects of speech whenever its regulation was content neutral. She defined regulation as content neutral when its justification had nothing to do with the specific content of the expression and the regulation was unconcerned with listeners' reactions to it. This view of content neutrality effectively transforms content neutrality into viewpoint neutrality, for secondary effects regulation, while unconcerned with viewpoint, must depend on the subject matter of the expression. So construed, secondary effects theory would permit indirect regulation of speech on the basis of its subject matter content. There is no majority for this view. (For further discussion, *see* Chapter 12, § I.C., *infra*.)). *Cf. City of Erie v. PAPS A.M.* 120 S.Ct. 1382 (2000).

F. **Regulation of Offensive Speech According to Context**

   1. ***Broadcast media:***

      a. *Indecent broadcasts:* Because of the reach of the broadcast media into American lives and the privacy of the home and because children are often a part of broadcast audiences, the F.C.C. may regulate nonobscene, indecent, and offensive broadcasts by channeling them to certain times to limit offensive exposure. *F.C.C. v. Pacifica Foundation,* 438 U.S. 726 (1978).

      b. *Cable television; prohibit, segregate, and block:* Under federal law, cable operators are required to reserve some channels for commercial lease. These are channels they own and would otherwise use for their own purposes. Cable agreements with cities usually also require them to reserve channels for public and governmental access. Unlike leased access channels, these are not channels over which the cable operator ever had a right of editorial control. In the Cable Television Consumer Protection and Competition Act, Congress authorized cable operators to refuse to broadcast material on leased and public access channels that the operator "reasonably believes describes or depicts sexual or excretory activities or organs in a patently offensive manner." If the operator did not prohibit such broadcasts, the operator had to "segregate" and "block," that is, provide a separate sex-dedicated channel and to block its showing without a written request. On receiving a written request to unblock, the cable provider had thirty days to comply.

In *Denver Area Educational Telecommunications Consortium, Inc. v. F.C.C.*, 518 U.S. 727 (1996) (in divided plurality opinions), the Court upheld the prohibition on leased access channels, but invalidated the segregate and block requirements. With regard to the prohibition for leased access channels, a plurality argued that the problem was similar to that which arose in *Pacifica*. In addition, protecting children from exposure to patently offensive sexual displays, and accommodating the countervailing First Amendment interests of cable operators in editing what appeared on their own channels lead to the conclusion that the prohibition was an appropriately tailored response to a serious problem.

The balance was different for public access channels. Cable operators never exercised editorial rights over them, and therefore there was no countervailing First Amendment interest to accommodate, and prohibition for public access channels was unconstitutional.

A plurality also concluded that the segregate and block provisions were unconstitutional as not being the least restrictive alternatives. It is possible for a cable operator to block single programs on the basis of a telephone request. Therefore, blocking an entire channel, imposing a burden of a written request, and permitting blocking for up to thirty days following a request hardly seems the least speech restrictive means available to meet the government's child protective goals.

c. *Indecent telephone recordings:* As there are less restrictive means of ensuring that children do not gain access to indecent telephone recordings, a total governmental ban on such commercial services is unconstitutional. *Sable Communications v. F.C.C., supra.*

d. *Internet transmissions:* Laws prohibiting knowing electronic transmission of obscene, indecent, or patently offensive messages or displays to persons under eighteen years of age are content-based regulations of speech. Insofar as they are vague, reach transmission of protected material to adults, and do not meet the *Miller* standards for defining obscenity, they are unconstitutional. *Reno v. American Civil Liberties Union*, 521 U.S. 844 (1997). It is impossible to "cyberzone" the internet. Parties sending messages over the Internet cannot segregate the messages by the age of the recipient; and there is no way to prevent minors from obtaining access to Internet communications without also denying access to adults. *Id.*

G. **Uncertainty over the Status of Offensive or Other Low-Value Speech:** There is a division in the Court over the constitutional status of certain kinds of speech, such as offensive speech. Justice Stevens, whose views represent one bloc of justices, thinks that offensive speech is "low-value" speech whose content is entitled to less constitutional protection than higher-value speech such as political speech. In this view, offensive words may be protected *in some* contexts but not in others. This is because their capacity to offend and their social value vary with context and circumstances. Applying this understanding, judges would have to decide the First Amendment value of speech falling into the low-value category on a case-by-case basis. Other justices take the view that there is no such category of low-value speech and that all protected speech must be treated alike. Others, while seeming to accord full constitutional protection to all protected speech, nonetheless appear to balance constitutional speech interests against the interests served by the regulation.

V. COMMERCIAL SPEECH

A. Definitions

1. ***The core meaning of "commercial speech" is any speech that does no more than propose commercial transaction, e.g., an offer to sell:*** Commercial speech, however, is not limited to proposals for commercial transactions and includes some speech aimed at promoting products or services.

2. ***Promotion:*** "Promotional advertising" is advertising which promotes a product or service or which provides ideas or information in some way beneficial to the economic interests of the speaker. Some, but not *all* promotional advertising is commercial speech.

3. ***Motivation:*** "Commercially or economically motivated speech" is speech which although motivated by money-making does not propose any commercial transaction, *e.g.,* a public relations speech aimed at creating good will for a company or a corporation-supported informational public interest announcement.

4. ***Requires all three factors:*** The fact that speech advertises or refers to a specific product or is economically motivated does not compel a conclusion that it is commercial speech. All three of these factors together, however, will support a conclusion that speech is commercial speech.

B. The First Amendment Protects Truthful Commercial Speech concerning Lawful Activities: Truthful commercial speech provides information or ideas that help consumers make choices about products and services. It may also help them form intelligent opinions about the operation of the free enterprise system.

1. ***Paternalism not permitted:*** The First Amendment takes freedom and an informed people as premises, and governments may not, as a general rule, suppress the spread of truthful commercial information and ideas. In other words, governments may not keep people ignorant, for the paternalistic reason that people may make wrong and harmful choices if provided with truthful information. *Cf. Linmark Associates, Inc. v. Willingboro,* 431 U.S. 85 (1977) (town cannot prohibit posting of real estate "for sale" or "sold" signs to help stem "white flight"). *But see Posadas de Puerto Rico Associates v. Tourism Company of Puerto Rico,* 478 U.S. 328 (1986), noted in C., *infra.*

2. ***Because of its special characteristics, the government may regulate commercial speech on the basis of its content to ensure its truthfulness:*** These characteristics are the commercial speaker's access to truthful product or

service information, and the profit motive, which means government regulation is unlikely to deter commercial speech.

3. ***Illegal activity:*** In order to ensure that commercial speech is not false, misleading, deceptive, or that it does not lead to illegality, the government may ban forms of communication which are likely to deceive or which are related to illegal activity. It may, if necessary, require the publisher to submit proposed commercial speech for examination prior to publication and to add information or warnings and disclaimers.

   a. *Use of trade names:* The use of trade names, at least until such names acquire meaningful associations in the public's mind, provides no information about a product or service but creates possibilities for deception or for misleading the public, *e.g.,* by failing to identify ownership. Consequently, states may prohibit trade names where their use is deceptive or misleading.

C. ***Level of Scrutiny:*** Where commercial speech concerns lawful activity and is not misleading, government can regulate it only when seeking to serve some substantial state interest. The regulation must directly advance that state interest and cannot suppress information when it could serve its interest as well in other ways. If it must regulate commercial speech, the state must adopt that regulation which, while achieving its purposes, limits speech the least. *Central Hudson Gas v. Public Service Comm'n,* 447 U.S. 557 (1980).

   1. ***Regulation permitted:*** Note that this test for the constitutionality of state regulation of lawful, nonmisleading commercial speech *permits* the state to regulate truthful commercial speech. The state cannot regulate other kinds of protected speech on such a showing. Truthful commercial speech therefore is thought to have *less* First Amendment value than other kinds of speech and is *less* protected. The lesser protection accorded truthful commercial speech therefore makes the determination that certain speech is commercial speech critical.

      a. *Advertising lawful but harmful products:* Unquestionably, governments can prohibit the sale of certain products or the undertaking of certain activities because they are harmful. When a government chooses not to prohibit, however, the issue arises whether it may instead seek to reduce demand through advertising restrictions. The cases on this point are in tension, as the examples below illustrate, but a majority of the Court now applies a reasonably rigorous form of the *Central Hudson* test, *supra,* to resolve this problem. This gives rise to the answer: it depends. It depends on whether there are other alternative, equally effective ways for the state to achieve its goals without restricting speech.

      In *44 Liquormart, Inc. v. Rhode Island,* 517 U.S. 102 (1997), Rhode Island prohibited retail price advertising of alcoholic beverages. It claimed that its aim was to reduce consumption of alcohol, but there was no evidence that the prohibition on price advertising had any effect on market-wide consumption. Other forms of regulation, not involving any speech restriction, such as a tax on liquor sales or an educational campaign focused on the problems of drinking alcohol, would likely have been more effective. The Court concluded that the ban on advertising truthful, nonmisleading commercial speech did not pass the *Central Hudson* test and invalidated the ban.

11

In an earlier case, however, *Posadas de Puerto Rico Associates v. Tourism Company of Puerto Rico,* 478 U.S. 328 (1986), the Court held that a prohibition on casino gambling advertising directed at Puerto Rico residents was constitutional. The Court reasoned that as Puerto Rico could have banned gambling altogether, it could take the "lesser step" of prohibiting gambling advertising. It is doubtful that the *Posadas* reasoning and handling of the issue survives *44 Liquormart,* which did not overturn *Posadas,* as there were but four votes to do so. More important, a majority of the Court in *44 Liquormart* made it clear that the Court now reviews state bans on truthful advertising of "harmful" products more rigorously than it had done in *Posadas.* It apparently also does not endorse the theory that if the state can ban particular conduct, it can take the "lesser" restriction of banning advertising for the conduct when it chooses not to ban the conduct itself.

Example: Congress may constitutionally prohibit lottery broadcasting by broadcasters licensed in states not allowing lotteries while permitting lottery broadcasting by broadcasters licensed in states allowing lotteries. Even though the broadcasts can be heard across state lines, Congress was attempting to support the policies of both lottery and nonlottery states. Each state's stations will have an audience in their home state, so the regulation directly and reasonably advances the federal interest of promoting the policy of the home state. *FCC v. Edge Broadcasting Company,* 509 U.S. 418 (1993).

New developments. The Court has continued to apply the Central Hudson test rigorously, and appears to have finally concluded that Congress' efforts to regulate commercial broadcast advertising for gambling is fatally flawed. In the Federal Communications Act or 1934, Congress forbade radio and television broadcasting of advertisements or information concerning lotteries. Since then it has narrowed the scope of the prohibition and has provided for exemptions, particularly for state lotteries and tribal-run gambling. Nonetheless, Congress continued to prohibit advertising for gaming at private, for-profit casinos. Where lawful, such gaming could be advertised in-state, but the advertising could not be broadcast to states where private casino gambling was unlawful. Given Congress' policies both for and against gambling and gambling advertisement, the continued prohibition does not directly and materially serve the government's interest in reducing both the demand for casino gambling and compulsive gambling. This is particularly true as Congress itself approved the promotion of kinds of gambling, indistinguishable in terms of the government's interests, from the kinds of gambling it sought to discourage. *Greater New Orleans Broadcasting Assn., Inc. v. United States,* 527 U.S. 173 (1999).

D. **Lawyers and Commercial Speech:** In *Bates v. State Bar of Arizona,* 433 U.S. 350 (1977), the Court held that the commercial speech doctrine protects truthful attorney advertising concerning routine legal services. The nature of lawyer services is such, however, that states may regulate some lawyer business promotion activities and advertising to protect consumers from undue influence or overreaching and to ensure that lawyer advertising is not misleading or deceptive, for example, advertising regarding the quality of legal services.

1. *Solicitation rules*

   a. Because face-to-face lawyer solicitation of clients creates real possibilities of pressuring clients and unduly influencing their decisions, states can regulate lawyer in-person solicitation for business gain without a specific showing of actual harm. *Ohralik v. Ohio State Bar Association,* 436 U.S. 447 (1978).

   b. The First Amendment freedom of association, however, protects organizations that provide legal assistance to individuals as a way of furthering organizational political and ideological goals. Consequently, the commercial speech doctrine does not apply to attorneys advising potential clients on behalf of such organizations, and states may not punish the attorneys for such activity without actual harm shown. *In re Primus,* 436 U.S. 412 (1978).

2. *Advertising rules*

   a. To ensure that attorney advertising is not misleading or deceptive, states may require attorneys to make mandatory disclosures in their advertisements, for example, informing clients in contingent fee cases of the client's responsibility for costs. *Zauderer v. Office of Disciplinary Counsel,* 471 U.S. 626 (1985).

   b. As a primary state interest in regulating commercial advertising is to ensure truthful advertising, states cannot suppress attorney advertising simply because it is indecorous, embarrassing, or offensive. *Id.*

   c. Attorney direct-mail solicitation of targeted individuals does not pose the overreaching and undue influence problems of face-to-face solicitation. Consequently, a state cannot prohibit direct-mail solicitation; but may, to prevent possible abuse or mistake, require prior review of direct-mail solicitation letters. *Shapero v. Kentucky Bar Association,* 486 U.S. 466 (1988).

      (1) On a substantial showing of harm, however, a state may ban immediate postaccident or postdisaster lawyer direct-mail solicitation of victims and their relatives. A bar rule – justified on the basis of protecting the substantial interests of victim, relative privacy and tranquility, and preventing a loss of public confidence in the legal profession – banning such solicitations for thirty days after an accident or disaster is a constitutional regulation of lawyer commercial speech.

NON-COMMERCIAL SOLICITATION

VI. **NONCOMMERCIAL SOLICITATION**

   A. **Charitable and Interest Group Solicitation:** Types of solicitors include those who solicit contributions for charitable, political, or social causes, whether by mail, street encounter, or door-to-door; present information and ideas; propagate views; advocate; and seek to persuade. Such solicitations, even in residential neighborhoods, are protected First Amendment activity. *Village of Schaumburg v. Citizens for Better Environment,* 444 U.S. 620 (1980).

   B. **Narrow Tailoring:** In regulating solicitation in the interests of protecting people from the crime, fraud, or annoyance which might be associated with solicitation, governments may not ban on-the-street or door-to-door solicitation and must narrowly tailor other regulations to ensure that protected speech is not infringed. *Schaumburg, supra.*

1. ***Percentage requirements:*** Because some legitimate soliciting organizations may seek to raise money in order to provide information to a broader public and to advocate, governments may not require that solicitors demonstrate that a certain percentage of their receipts be spent on charity. *Id., Secretary of State v. J.H. Munson Co.,* 468 U.S. 947 (1984); *Riley v. National Fed'n of The Blind of North Carolina, Inc.,* 487 U.S. 781 (1988).

2. ***Compelled disclosure:*** Compelling professional fundraisers to disclose to potential donors the amount of funds retained from previous solicitations violates the First Amendment. Such disclosure might discriminate against small or unpopular charities, for their fundraising costs might be great, and such information might dissuade potential donors from contributing. *Riley, supra.*

C. **Door-to-Door Canvassing:** Governments may not, in the interests of residents' repose or to prevent crime, ban door-to-door canvassing or handbilling. Such regulation is not the least restrictive means of achieving the goal, for residents may and should determine for themselves whom they wish to exclude. *Martin v. Struthers,* 319 U.S. 141 (1943).

11

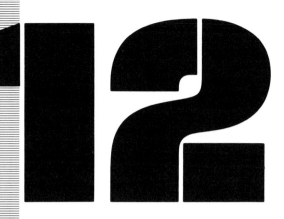

FREEDOM OF SPEECH (II)

▶ ## CHAPTER SUMMARY

CHAPTER 12: FREEDOM OF SPEECH (II)

Introduction. Some important First Amendment doctrines deal with issues likely to be found in many free speech cases. Generally speaking, these doctrines are highly sensitive to the possible effects that governmental regulation, often undertaken for nonspeech purposes, may have on speech and expressive activities. Consequently, these doctrines deal with the form and permissible scope of governmental regulation, which in some way affects free speech. These doctrines and related concepts – prior restraint; overbreadth and vagueness; excessive discretion; content-neutrality; the speech-conduct distinction and symbolic speech; time, place, and manner regulation; and public forum doctrine – are conceptually and practically linked. Consequently, they are, and should be, used to analyze and resolve many First Amendment cases. Note, also, that in many cases, each, or many, of these doctrines can apply.

I. FIRST AMENDMENT VARIABLES

A. **Prior Restraint:** The First Amendment forbids censorship. There is a very strong presumption against any form of prior restraint on publication, and when the government seeks to prevent or censor a publication, it must meet a great burden of justification.

　　1. *Prior restraint possible:* Freedom from prior restraint is not an absolute, however, and there are cases where the governmental interest is sufficiently compelling to justify a restraint on publication.

　　　　a. *National security interests:* On an appropriate showing, concrete national security interests may warrant a restraint on publication. For example, the government could restrain publication of information regarding ship sailings or secret troop movements during wartime. *Cf. Near v. Minnesota ex rel. Olson,* 283 U.S. 697 (1931). Nonetheless, simple assertions of a need to protect national security interests, without a convincing demonstration of a direct, immediate, and irreparable harm flowing from publication, will not do. *New York Times Co. v. United States [The Pentagon Papers Case],* 403 U.S. 713 (1971).

　　　　b. *Interest in ensuring a fair trial:* Both the government and criminal defendants have a great interest in ensuring fair criminal trials. In high-profile cases, press coverage of pretrial and trial events may adversely and unfairly influence or bias potential jurors or those selected to serve on the jury. Restraining the press from publishing reports regarding the offender and proceedings would prevent that particular harm. Nonetheless, the presumption against prior restraints prohibits such press "gagging" without a convincing showing that other alternatives, such as a change of venue, trial postponement, juror screening, sequestration, jury instructions, and gag orders on trial participants, would not ensure a fair trial. *Nebraska Press Ass'n v. Stuart,* 427 U.S. 539 (1976).

　　2. *Procedural requirements for injunction:* With the exception of allegedly obscene materials and where time is of the essence, even when justified, restraints against publications may issue only after an adversary hearing. *Carrol v. Princess Anne County,* 393 U.S. 175 (1969). In other words, they should not, except perhaps in the most extraordinary circumstances, issue *ex parte.* In addition, to ensure that improperly issued restraints are quickly overturned and speech restrained as little as possible, states authorizing such injunctions must either provide for immediate

appellate review or allow a stay of the injunction pending review. *National Socialist Party v. Village of Skokie,* 432 U.S. 43 (1977).

3. ***No bar to action after publication:*** The rule against prior restraints does not bar governmental action after publication, however. Suppose a newspaper obtains and publishes classified information, disclosure of which would not harm national security, and that there is a law making knowing publication of classified information a crime. While the government could not restrain the publication, it could bring a prosecution against the newspaper after publication.

    a. *Publication of truthful information:* Without a compelling interest, states may not bar or punish the publication of lawfully obtained truthful information about a matter of public importance. *Butterworth v. Smith,* 494 U.S. 624 (1990); *Smith v. Daily Mail Publishing Co.,* 443 U.S. 97 (1979); *The Florida Star v. B.J.F.,* 491 U.S. 524 (1989).

4. ***Prior restraints and nonprotected speech:*** The no-prior-restraint rule bars restraints on speech, which the First Amendment protects. As the First Amendment does not protect obscene, inciting, or libelous speech, or "fighting" words, the rule is technically inapplicable in such cases. Practically speaking, however, in many situations involving inciting speech or fighting words, there is no advance notice of the character of the speech to come and, thus, no opportunity to apply a prior restraint. Further, given the constitutional free speech rules regarding libel, it is virtually impossible to determine in advance whether allegedly libelous speech is nonprotected and therefore restrainable. Obscene speech, however, forms a special category.

    a. *Presumptive protection and the* Freedman *procedural safeguards in obscenity cases:* Because of the danger of restraining protected speech in cases involving arguably unprotected speech, the rule has evolved that all speech is presumptively protected. There are, nonetheless, cases, such as publication of obscene materials or films, where the state might wish to prevent publication and therefore wishes to make a determination of obscenity prior to publication. State licensing or censorship schemes calling for prepublication submission and review of allegedly obscene films, and possibly other nonprotected materials, are valid if they provide the following minimum procedural protections designed to obviate the dangers of censorship.

        (1) The state bears the burden of showing that the expression is unprotected speech;

        (2) The delay in publication caused by the review procedure must be brief;

        (3) Following review, the censor must either issue a license or go to court to obtain an order restraining publication;

        (4) Any judicial restraint imposed to maintain the status quo pending a judicial determination must be for the shortest period possible; and

        (5) The procedure must assure a prompt, final judicial resolution. *Freedman v. Maryland,* 380 U.S. 51 (1965).

b. *Interim restraints on speech and the collateral bar rule:* The *Freedman* rules allow courts to enter temporary injunctions against publication of films, and perhaps other materials, and this is a form of permissible prior restraint. The collateral bar rule provides that court orders must be obeyed and that one who refuses to abide by a court order may be punished, even if it is later determined that the disobeyed court order was unconstitutional.

(1) Consequently, a publisher who publishes in the face of a temporary injunction against publication may be punished for publishing even if it is later determined that the published material was protected speech and not suppressible.

(2) Exceptions: There are some exceptions to the collateral bar rule, however. One is not barred from raising a defense to a charge of violating a court order in the following cases. 1) The court order was a sham; (2) time was of the essence in that, for some reason, action after judicial determination would not be effective; or, (3) judicial relief procedures from improperly entered court orders are illusory.

5. *Licensing and permit systems as prior restraints:* Governments sometimes adopt licensing or permit systems to regulate certain kinds of activity, *e.g.,* permits to engage in door-to-door soliciting, permits to parade, permits to operate sound amplifiers. Such licensing or permit systems are constitutional when aimed at regulating, for public health, safety, welfare, or convenience purposes, the nonexpressive activities involved. For example, a parade licensing requirement meant to notify police for public regulation purposes, and to ensure noninterference with other normal uses of the streets, is constitutional. But licensing systems aimed at forbidding speech or regulating it for its content are unconstitutional as forms of prior restraint. *Lovell v. Griffin,* 303 U.S. 444 (1938); *cf.* G., *infra.*

a. *Standards for licensing and permit systems:* Because licensing and permit systems can be misused to restrain speech, they are constitutional if they provide clearly defined, relevant standards for issuance and do not accord officials such discretion that they could deny permission due to the content or viewpoint of the expression or the identity of the speaker. *Cox v. New Hampshire,* 312 U.S. 569 (1941).

b. *Facially void permit schemes:* When licensing officials have such broad discretion that they could effectively suppress legitimate speech, the permit scheme is "void on its face," and speakers need not comply with it by seeking a permit. *Staub v. Baxley,* 355 U.S. 313 (1958); *Shuttlesworth v. Birmingham,* 394 U.S. 147 (1969).

c. *Facially valid schemes:* Where licensing schemes provide clear standards for issuance, speakers must seek a permit and, if refused – even improperly – must seek judicial or administrative relief rather than speak without permission. *Poulos v. New Hampshire,* 345 U.S. 395 (1953).

6. *Seizure as a prior restraint:* States sometimes criminalize the production and sale of obscene materials. When this is so, such materials constitute evidence of a crime and may be seized on probable cause. Search and seizure warrants, however, issue ex parte, without a prior adversary hearing and the other procedural

protections required before an obscenity determination. Large-scale seizures of allegedly obscene books, magazines, and films block their distribution or exhibition and therefore amount to a prior restraint. For these reasons, such confiscations of allegedly obscene materials are unconstitutional. *Fort Wayne Books, Inc. v. Indiana,* 489 U.S. 46 (1989); *Marcus v. Search Warrant,* 367 U.S. 717 (1961). Seizure of a single copy of allegedly obscene material to preserve as evidence, however, does not take the material out of circulation and is therefore constitutional. *Heller v. New York,* 413 U.S. 483 (1973).

7. ***Forfeitures as prior restraints:*** As a part of the punishment for the crime, persons convicted of racketeering under RICO statutes are subject not only to imprisonment and fine, but also to forfeiture of assets relating to racketeering activity. When the assets subject to forfeiture include protected materials such as books or films, or bookstores or theaters, the question arises whether requiring their forfeiture amounts to a prior restraint. The Court has held that forfeitures imposed following racketeering convictions are subsequent punishments rather than prior restraints. *Alexander v. United States,* 61 U.S.L.W. 4796 (1993). RICO forfeiture provisions are directed at assets of any kind and neither target nor prohibit expressive activity, and assets involving expressive materials, *even if they have not been adjudicated unprotected,* receive no special protection under the First Amendment.

Example: In *Alexander,* defendant was convicted of obscenity and racketeering. He was ordered to forfeit approximately $9 million and his many wholesale and retail businesses, some of which – bookstores and theaters – purveyed expressive materials, which had not been adjudicated obscene or otherwise, unprotected. The Court upheld the order.

B. Overbreadth and Vagueness

1. ***Overbreadth:*** A statute or regulation is overbroad if it regulates or purports to regulate both matters which the state can regulate and matters which it cannot. Overbroad statutes purporting to proscribe or punish speech are of particular concern because they may reach speech which the state cannot regulate.

   a. *Facial overbreadth:* When a statute or regulation as written applies to both protected and unprotected speech, it is said to be facially overbroad. To save such statutes from constitutional objection, courts sometimes – if it is possible to do so – construe them narrowly so that they do not reach protected First Amendment activity or reach as little of it as possible, given the language of the statute.

   b. *Overbroad as applied:* When a statute or regulation does not, as written, apply to protected speech but is applied to reach protected speech, it is said to be overbroad as applied.

   Examples: Suppose a statute provides that "any person who shall, without provocation, use to or of another person opprobrious words or abusive language, tending to cause a breach of the peace" is guilty of a misdemeanor. Such a statute is facially overbroad for in its terms it reaches speech not prescribable under the "fighting words" doctrine of *Chaplinsky* or under the *Brandenburg* incitement doctrine. In this example, if the statute is applied or construed to reach only unprotected speech, *e.g.*, "fighting words," or *Brandenburg* incitements, then the statute, although facially overbroad, is not overbroad as applied. *Cf. Gooding v. Wilson*, 405 U.S. 518 (1972).

Suppose a statute permits conviction, as a disorderly person, of one who uses "indecent" or "offensive" language in public places. The statute is interpreted to apply to words that are "likely to incite the hearer to an immediate breach of the peace or to be likely, in the light of the gender and age of the listener and the setting of the utterance, to affect the sensibilities of a hearer." This statute is overbroad. *Cf. Rosenfeld v. New Jersey*, 408 U.S. 901 (1972).

Assume that the fighting words doctrine is good law and that a statute provides that "one who actually incites another to violence by using offensive, derisive words as a direct personal insult is guilty of a misdemeanor." Suppose further that the statute is applied to one who inadvertently started a fight by saying "Salman Rushdie is a good novelist" to another person who turned out to be deeply offended by the remark. While the statute in its terms applies only to unprotected speech that the government can punish, as applied it punishes protected speech. It is therefore overbroad as applied or construed.

    c.   *Facially overbroad statutes and "chilling effect":* Facially overbroad statutes, unless construed to apply only to speech that the government can proscribe or regulate, may deter protected speech. Persons who want to engage in the protected speech may conclude that an overbroad statute will be applied to their speech and therefore decline to speak. This is sometimes referred to as a "chilling effect."

    d.   *Standing rules and facially overbroad statutes:* The normal rule of standing is that one who seeks to challenge the constitutionality of a statute must show that the statute infringes his own rights. In First Amendment cases involving alleged facially overbroad statutes, however, the challenger may attack the statute simply on the ground that it can be applied to protected speech, *even if his own speech was not protected.* In other words, in facial overbreadth cases, the challenger may assert the rights of third parties. The fact that the statute may be constitutional *as applied* to him is irrelevant.

        (1) The facial overbreadth standing rule, which allows someone whose speech is unprotected to challenge on the basis of third parties' protected speech rights, in effect, rewards the unprotected speaker. The "chilling" or deterrent effect that overbroad statutes have on protected speakers means such speakers are unlikely to challenge them.

        (2) Under original overbreadth doctrine, when a statute is found to be facially overbroad, it cannot be enforced *at all* unless its overbroad portions are effectively excised by a limiting construction or a partial invalidation.

    e.   *Problems with the overbreadth rules:* Suspending enforcement of overbroad statutes disables states from applying them to reach unprotected speech or conduct which they have every right, and perhaps need, to regulate. In such circumstances, a legislature might have to enact a new statute before it can reach unprotected speech or conduct. Furthermore, it is problematic to reward someone whose conduct is clearly unlawful for helping to uncover statutes that could be used to reach protected speech. Finally, striking down statutes for their potential applications is hypothetical and abstract. Such considerations lead to the counterview that statutes not overbroad as applied should not be overturned on grounds of facial overbreadth. If facially overbroad statutes are not overturned, however, because not overbroad as applied, they continue to have some chilling effect. To resolve this problem, the Court modified the basic overbreadth rule so that facially overbroad statutes will be overturned only when "substantially overbroad." Consequently, in overbreadth cases it is necessary first to determine whether the law being challenged reaches a substantial amount of constitutionally protected conduct. *Village of Hoffman Estates v. Flipside,* 455 U.S. 489 (1982).

12

f. *Substantial overbreadth:* Typically, allegedly overbroad statutes reach both speech and conduct. The current overbreadth rule is that particularly where a statute reaches conduct as well as possibly reaching protected speech, it will not be held unconstitutional on its face unless it is *substantially overbroad, Broadrick v. Oklahoma,* 413 U.S. 601 (1973), that is, has a "substantial number of impermissible applications." *New York v. Ferber, supra.*

   (1) The notion of "substantial overbreadth" is not clear. But the basic idea is that the Court will consider facial overbreadth challenges only when there is a "realistic danger," as opposed to a possibility, that a statute will have a "chilling" or deterrent effect on the First Amendment rights of parties not before the Court. *Los Angeles City Council v. Taxpayers for Vincent,* 466 U.S. 789 (1984). *Cf. Houston v. Hill,* 482 U.S. 451 (1987) (criminal statutes making "unlawful a substantial amount of constitutionally protected conduct may be held facially invalid even if they also have a legitimate application").

   (2) If a statute is not substantially overbroad, but nonetheless capable of application to protected speech, that overbreadth should be handled on a case-by-case basis. *Broadrick, supra.*

   (3) If a statute is not substantially overbroad and constitutionally applies to the challenger's speech or conduct, then the challenger has no standing to attack it. In other words, a litigant whose speech or action is clearly and constitutionally covered by a statute can challenge its facial overbreadth only if it is substantially overbroad.

2. **Vagueness:** A statute is vague if "persons of common intelligence must necessarily guess at its meaning and differ as to its application." *Connally v. General Construction Co.* 269 U.S. 385 (1926).

   Example: The following statutes are vague:

   "Any person found wandering in the streets without apparent destination and without visible means of support is guilty of a misdemeanor."

   "It shall be a misdemeanor to be a member of a gang."

   a. *Due process vagueness:* Vague statutes violate due process by failing to give notice of what conduct is proscribed.

b. *First Amendment vagueness:* Vague statutes that can be used to reach expression may deter protected First Amendment activity. In failing to give notice that only they will be applied to reach only unprotected speech, they may induce self-censorship.

3. ***First Amendment vagueness and excess discretion:*** Because vague statutes give no discernible guides as to what is proscribed or how they will be enforced, they also effectively vest standardless discretion in officials: the law is what they say it is.

Example: In *Lakewood v. Plain Dealer Publishing Co.,* 486 U.S. 750 (1988), a city ordinance allowed the placing of newspaper racks on public property, but only on receipt of a permit which might be denied or granted, among other things, on "terms and conditions deemed necessary and reasonable by the Mayor." The ordinance, which fails to delineate standards the mayor is to apply, confers excess discretion.

Example: A city ordinance that allows police officers to arrest, on refusal to follow a police order to disperse, persons identified as "loitering" gang members and associates – where loitering is defined as "remain[ing] in any one place with no apparent purpose – is vague. The law, which requires no harmful purpose, gives police officers virtually absolute discretion to determine whether a person's conduct constitutes loitering. *Chicago v. Morales,* 527 U.S. 41 (1999).

4. ***The relationship between overbreadth and vagueness:*** An overbroad statute can be clear and precise or vague.

Examples: The statute "No one shall make any speech which uses the words, 'you should overthrow the government by force and violence'" is overbroad. It is not vague because it proscribes precisely the use of certain words. It is overbroad, however, because it reaches constitutionally protected speech. An overbroad statute can, however, be vague. The statute "Whoever shall use opprobrious, abusive, or derisive words to or of another, tending to cause a breach of the peace is guilty of a misdemeanor" is both overbroad and vague.

a. *A vague statute, if construable to reach protected First Amendment activities, is of necessity overbroad:* If it is uncertain, then it is susceptible to being applied to protected speech or conduct.

5. ***Vagueness and standing***

a. *Overbreadth rules applicable to standing:* To the degree that a vague statute is overbroad, the standing rules relating to overbreadth, *i.e.,* requiring substantial overbreadth, apply to vagueness challenges.

b. *Licensing laws:* Facial challenges to vague licensing laws are proper when the laws relate to expression and confer enough official or agency discretion to permit discrimination against disfavored speech or speakers because of content or viewpoint. *Lakewood v. Plain Dealer, supra.* To withstand a facial challenge, such laws must be administered in accordance with neutral criteria that ensure that licensing decisions are not based upon the content or viewpoint of speech.

C. **Content-based Restrictions on Speech and Content Neutrality**

1. ***Content neutrality:*** As they relate to the exercise of free speech, laws or regulations are said to be content neutral if they do not distinguish between kinds of speech on the basis of what the speech is about.

   Example: A law that provides that no one shall use a sound truck to broadcast messages in a residential district is a content-neutral law for it does not regulate on the basis of what the speech says. Content-based laws and regulations, on the other hand, do attempt to regulate speech based on its subject, as the law would do in the sound truck example if it were directed only at religious or political communications.

2. ***Viewpoint neutrality:*** Content-based regulations of speech can be either viewpoint neutral or viewpoint based. They are viewpoint neutral when they regulate an entire subject matter or topic of speech, regardless of the opinions or views expressed on that topic.

   Example: A regulation that provides that there shall be no political speech in the park is content based, but viewpoint neutral. By contrast, the regulation would be viewpoint based if it sought not to regulate the subject matter but the speaker's particular position or point of view with regard to her subject. A law providing that no one shall advocate free love or communist ideas is both content and viewpoint based.

3. ***General rule:*** The First Amendment generally prohibits governmental regulation of speech based on its content or the speaker's point of view, and the Court subjects such speech discriminations to strict scrutiny. *Police Dept. of Chicago v. Mosley,* 408 U.S. 92 (1972) (law barring all picketing, except labor picketing, within 150 feet of a school, unconstitutional). *Carey v. Brown,* 447 U.S. 455 (1980). *Widmar v. Vincent,* 454 U.S. 263 (1981).

   Example: In *Metromedia, Inc. v. San Diego,* 453 U.S. 490 (1981), San Diego, in the interests of curbing visual pollution and eliminating distractions for pedestrians and motorists, adopted an ordinance regulating billboards located on private property. The City permitted the billboards to carry commercial advertising for products or services offered at the property where the billboard was located. With some exceptions, such as religious symbols, it forbade on-site noncommercial advertising. The ordinance in effect made two content-based discriminations – one involving the commercial-noncommercial advertising distinction, the other involving the distinction between permitted and nonpermitted on-site noncommercial advertising – and was held unconstitutional.

   a. *Content neutrality in perspective:* Content neutrality, as used in First Amendment analysis, is a term of art. In a sense, First Amendment doctrine does permit content-based regulation of some speech. For example, laws regulating obscenity, libel, fighting words, or commercial speech clearly regulate on the basis of content. To avoid a seeming contradiction regarding regulation of such material, the Court has sometimes said that the proscribed material either was not speech or was not speech protected within the freedom of speech. This is a manner of speaking, however, and it is best to think in terms of categories of protected and unprotected speech. The content-neutrality rule then applies primarily to the category of protected speech.

12

(1) Content neutrality and unprotected speech – hate speech: In an extraordinary recent opinion, *R.A.V. v. St. Paul, Minn.*, 60 U.S.L.W. 4667 (1992), the Court applied the content-neutrality rule to unprotected speech. In that case, the Court reviewed a city ordinance that punished what is called "hate" speech. The ordinance proscribed speech knowingly made to arouse "anger, alarm or resentment in others on the basis of race, color, creed, religion, or gender." In order to save the ordinance from failing constitutionally because of overbreadth, the state supreme court construed it to apply only to fighting words. As fighting words amount to a category of speech unprotected by the First Amendment, one would normally assume that the content-neutrality rule would not come into play.

In *R.A.V.*, the Court devised a new content-neutrality doctrine. *To ensure there is no possibility that the government is suppressing speech because of the ideas it contains, when the government proscribes unprotected speech, it must proscribe it for the reason such speech is unprotected.* Thus, while the fighting words doctrine permits proscription of speech which inflicts injury or tends to incite to immediate violence, the St. Paul ordinance did not punish hate speech for that reason, but because it was bias-motivated speech. As the majority opinion put it, "the power to proscribe speech on the basis of one content element [*i.e.,* the quality of speech as fighting words] does not entail the power to proscribe it on the basis of other content elements [*i.e.,* the hate message]." *Id.* at 4670. In effect, St. Paul regulated fighting words because of their subject matter and not simply because they were fighting words. Unprotected speech is unprotected for some reason relating to its content, and the government must regulate unprotected speech for its *objectionable* content and not simply because it is generally thought unprotected. Consequently, depending on the content of the features of unprotected speech government seeks to reach, *some speech falling within the category of unprotected speech may be protected.*

Wondrous to contemplate, there now appears to be a category of *protected unprotected speech,* but it remains to be seen whether this is a doctrine widely applicable to future cases or rather limited to an *R.A.V.* situation. The *R.A.V.* holding in effect requires governments to proscribe entire categories of unprotected speech rather than subsets of them. Thus, St. Paul may reenact its ordinance if it includes within it a proscription on all fighting words for whatever motivation. In this sense, what the opinion seems designed to do is to provide a basis for striking down enactments of speech rules designed to protect minorities and groups thought to need special protections in discourse. We can thus expect the Court to use it in cases involving university hate speech codes and the like, and possibly in cases involving pornography-as-violence-toward-women ordinances or statutes.

b. *Variable fees for permits to speak, parade, or assemble:* Governments, in order to manage public fora to accommodate competing uses, may require those undertaking First Amendment activity in them to obtain a permit. (*Cf.* B.5, *supra* and G., *infra.*) They may not, however, set permit fees based on the cost of maintaining public order for the specific proposed First Amendment activity, even if the fee is only nominal. Under such schemes, an administrator must examine the content of the message and predict the likely public response to it in order to set a fee. This amounts to content-based regulation of speech and is unconstitutional. *Forsyth County v. Nationalist Movement,* 60 U.S.L.W 4597 (1992).

4. ***Justified content-based regulation of protected speech:*** Government can regulate protected speech on the basis of its content in those rare cases where it can demonstrate it has a compelling interest to do so and that its means of regulation are necessary.

    Example: In *Burson v. Freeman,* 504 U.S. 191 (1992), Tennessee prohibited solicitation of voters and distribution of campaign materials within 100 feet of a polling place. Governments generally have a compelling interest in securing to voters the right to vote freely and effectively, and thus in preventing voter intimidation and election fraud. The ban on solicitation and distribution was, in effect, a ban on political speech, and not other forms of speech such as commercial speech, and was thus content based. Nonetheless, recognizing the state's compelling interests, the Court upheld the statute. Given the compelling interests in preventing voter intimidation and election fraud, the only question in the case was whether the 100-foot boundary was a necessary means to secure those ends. One might question any kind of line drawing, but as the 100-foot boundary did not work any "significant impingement" on a speaker's First Amendment rights, the Court upheld it as reasonable.

5. ***Viewpoint discrimination and government funding of expression:*** Government can choose to favor childbirth over abortion, and it can decline to fund the promotion or encouragement of abortion. When government funds programs promoting certain activities, such as childbirth, it need not fund other programs promoting contrary aims, such as abortion programs. In such cases, the government's choice to favor one set of activities over another is not to be deemed viewpoint discrimination. *Rust v. Sullivan,* 500 U.S. 173 (1991).

6. ***Taxes or other state-imposed financial burdens on the media or speakers:*** In general, the First Amendment prohibits the government from imposing taxes or financial burdens on speakers because of the content of their speech.

    a. *Noncontent-based differential taxation:* Differential taxation of speakers does not violate the First Amendment "unless the tax is directed at, or presents the danger of, suppressing particular ideas." *Leathers v. Medlock,* 499 U.S. 439 (1991). That danger exists when a tax targets a relatively small number of speakers because it risks affecting a limited range of views. When a tax affects a large segment of the media, and is not in any sense content or viewpoint based, it is constitutional. *Id.* (Generally applicable goods and services sales tax applied to cable television services, but exempting newspapers, magazines, and satellite broadcast services, constitutional.)

    b. *Compensating crime victims:* Laws appropriating the publication earnings of accused or convicted criminals, who publish accounts of their crimes, in order to compensate victims comprise unconstitutional content-based legislation. Compensating crime victims and ensuring that criminals do not profit from their crimes are compelling state interests. However, compensating victims solely out of proceeds attributable to the wrongdoer's speech places a burden on that speech that is not narrowly tailored to reach the goal. *Simon & Schuster, Inc. v. New York State Crime Victims Board,* 112 S. Ct. 501 (1991).

D. **The Speech/Conduct Distinction:** While government cannot regulate speech, it can regulate conduct. As long as its aim in regulating conduct is not to regulate the speech associated with it, its regulation is reasonably tailored to reach the conduct harms that concern it, and the regulation does not unduly burden speech, it will be upheld. The rules regarding "symbolic" speech, § F., *infra;* time, place, and manner regulation, G., *infra;* and the regulation of the "secondary effects" of sexually explicit material, Chapter 11, IV.D., *supra,* are all instances of the speech/conduct distinction.

E. **Conduct and Symbolic Speech:** Humans communicate meaning through means other than speech or writing, and often with greater effect. Consider that, in an appropriate context, burning or trampling an American flag can passionately convey contempt for the United States or its policies. The flag itself is a symbol freighted with meaning, customarily treated with reverence and ritual respect. For some, the shock value of breaking the social barriers or mores regarding the flag can appear an effective way to express their point of view. On the other hand, as expressive beings, humans can invest anything with meaning, and a rule which allowed treating any and all actions as protected First Amendment expression could dissolve all distinctions between speech and action and potentially subject all regulation of action to strict scrutiny analysis. Consequently, we need tests to help us distinguish between expressive and nonexpressive conduct and to validate appropriate governmental regulation of conduct which may have expressive value.

1. *Expressive conduct:* For purposes of the First Amendment, conduct is expressive when undertaken in order to convey a particularized message and when the audience at whom it is directed is highly likely to understand the message. *Spence v. Washington,* 418 U.S. 405 (1974). Wearing black armbands in school to protest the Vietnam War, *Tinker v. Des Moines School District,* 393 U.S. 503 (1969), desegregation sit-ins, *Brown v. Louisiana,* 383 U.S. 131 (1966), and attaching a peace sign to an American flag, *Spence, supra,* have all been held to be expressive conduct.

2. *Regulation of expressive conduct – the* **O'Brien** *two-tier test:* In *United States v. O'Brien,* 391 U.S. 367 (1968), a case involving draft card burning to influence others to adopt antiwar beliefs and to question the propriety of the draft, the Court adopted a two-track test to analyze involving speech and symbolic speech or expressive conduct.

    a. When the government seeks to regulate expression as expression, the Court subjects the regulation to strict scrutiny analysis and upholds such regulations only on a showing of a compelling governmental interest justifying the regulation and a lack of other regulatory means less injurious to expression.

    b. If the government has an important aim unrelated to suppressing expression, but its regulation of action or conduct incidentally affects expression, then the Court uses a balancing test in which the government's interest in, and its mode of, regulating are balanced against their impact on expression.

    Examples: In *Texas v. Johnson,* 491 U.S. 397 (1989), Johnson was convicted under a flag desecration statute, the aim of which was clearly to reach any message intentionally associated with destroying an American flag. As the state's aim was to suppress expression, the Court applied strict scrutiny review and overturned the conviction and statute.

In *O'Brien, supra,* the government's aim in prohibiting draft card destruction was not to suppress expression but to ensure the effectiveness of the selective service system. Balancing this governmental interest against the prohibition's effect on expression, the Court upheld O'Brien's conviction for draft card destruction.

In *Clark v. Community for Creative Non-Violence,* 468 U.S. 288 (1984), the National Park Service, under regulations prohibiting national park camping in other than designated campgrounds, forbade a group of demonstrators from sleeping in tent cities outside of campgrounds. The intent of the sleep-in was to demonstrate the plight of the homeless. The anticamping regulation was not aimed at expressive conduct, but was simply a time, place, and manner regulation intended to conserve park property. Applying the *O'Brien* balancing test, the Court upheld the ban.

In *Turner Broadcasting System, Inc. v. FCC,* 520 U.S. 351 (1997), the Court used *O'Brien* to uphold "must carry requirements" for cable television. The federal Cable Television Consumer Protection and Competition Act required cable television systems to carry local television broadcast stations. The government's interest in these content neutral requirements were to preserve free, over-the-air local broadcast television, to promote dissemination of information from various sources, and to promote competition in the television programming market.

(1) *O'Brien* as a general utility test: The Court now uses the *O'Brien* test in cases involving government regulations of conduct that may affect speech other than symbolic speech.

Examples: In *Los Angeles City Council v. Taxpayers for Vincent,* 466 U.S. 789 (1984), the Court used *O'Brien* to analyze governmental authority to control secondary effects of communications. There a group of a candidate's supporters had political signs attached to public utility poles, in violation of an ordinance prohibiting posting of signs on public property. The City banned signs to help reduce visual clutter and improve the appearance of its streets, a substantial aesthetic interest unrelated to suppressing ideas. The ban, tailored exactly to the evil, was upheld.

In *Turner Broadcasting System, Inc. v. FCC,* 65 U.S.L.W. 4209 (1997), the Court used O'Brien to uphold "must carry requirements" for cable television. The federal Cable Television Consumer Protection and Competition Act required cable television systems to carry local television broadcast stations. The government's interest in these content neutral requirements were to preserve free, over-the-air local broadcast television, to promote dissemination of information from a variety of sources, and to promote competition in the television programming market.

c. *Public nudity and nude dancing:* Nude dancing is expressive activity protected by the First Amendment. In the interests of morality, public order, and decency, however, where a state does not seek to suppress expression, a state may ban public nudity. The state may also apply such a general ban to prohibit nude dancing. *Barnes v. Glen Theatres,* 501 U.S. 560 (1991). *Cf. City of Erie v. PAP'S A.M.* 120 S.Ct. 1382 (2000).

F. Discriminatory Motivations for Conduct: While the First Amendment protects expression and beliefs, it does not protect bias-motivated conduct. The state may therefore take motivation into account in regulating and punishing conduct. *Wisconsin v. Mitchell,* 61 U.S.L.W. 4575 (1993). The state, however, may not punish a person for beliefs not, in some sense, generating proscribed conduct. *Dawson v. Delaware,* 503 U.S. 159 (1992).

1. *Hate conduct crimes:* Violent crimes, based on discriminatory animus or bias, appear to be on the rise in the United States. Some states have responded by adding penalty-enhancement provisions for bias-motivated crimes. Under such statutes, where the state proves that an accused committed a crime against a person or property because of a prejudice based on race, religion, ethnicity, or similar discriminatory motivation, the punishment for the underlying crime is enhanced. Criminal statutes generally use intent or motive as a sentencing factor. The First Amendment does not prohibit sentence enhancements based on discriminatory motivations, nor does it prohibit the evidentiary use of an accused speech or expressions of belief to prove motive or intent. *Mitchell, supra. (Cf. § D.3.a.(1)* for the Court's distinctive treatment of hate speech crimes.)

G. Time, Place, and Manner Regulations

1. *Regulation permitted:* Although there may be some effect on expression, the state may reasonably regulate the time, place, and manner of access to, or uses of, public fora for expressive purposes. A city, for example, may, for traffic flow and control purposes, legitimately require that those who wish to parade on busy city streets obtain a permit. Similarly, a city could prohibit the use of loudspeakers on the streets in residential districts at night. *Kovacs v. Cooper,* 336 U.S. 77 (1949).

2. *Requirements for time, place, and manner regulations:* Time, place, and manner regulations must be content neutral; must serve significant governmental health, safety, aesthetic, welfare, and similar purposes; be reasonably well-tailored to serve those purposes; and leave open ample alternative channels of communication. The means the government uses to achieve its interests, however, need not be the least restrictive means of doing so. Instead, any means which serves the government's interests better than nonregulation and which are not substantially overbroad are constitutional. *Ward v. Rock Against Racism,* 491 U.S. 781 (1989).

   a. *Recent developments in viewpoint discrimination law:* In an important recent case involving a clash between Free Speech Clause and Establishment Clause jurisprudence, the Court shifted the meaning of viewpoint discrimination. *Rosenberger v. Rector and Visitors of the University of Virginia,* 63 U.S.L.W. 4703 (1995). In that case, the University, using moneys from mandatory student fees collected to support student activities, supported student organization activities related to the University's educational purpose. The supported activities had to involve student news, information, opinion, entertainment, and academic communication media groups. Excluded from such support were religious, philanthropic, electioneering, and lobbying activities and a few other general categories. The University defined religious activity as any activity "that *primarily* promotes or manifests a particular belief in or about a deity or an ultimate reality." [Emphasis added.]

On the basis of the exclusion and this definition, the University refused to fund the printing of a student magazine, *Wide Awake*, dedicated to publishing matter from a Christian viewpoint. The University's objection was not that the magazine promoted a Christian viewpoint but that it was a religious activity. The University would have equally refused to support publications primarily expressing the views of other religions as well, *e.g.*, Islam, Buddhism, Taoism, and even antireligions such as atheism. In other words, the University, in order to avoid providing public support for religion, was refusing to fund publications primarily devoted to discussions aimed at promoting religions of any kind, pro or con, from any religious point of view. This is normally what we would think of as a subject matter discrimination, a kind of discrimination proper in the limited public forum the University had created. *Cf.* § I, *infra*. The University was not choosing between specific religious viewpoints, supporting one or another to the exclusion of others. Of course, one might claim that the University was favoring nonreligious over religious views on particular matters, but that is not accurate. The University was refusing to fund expression *primarily* aimed at promoting a particular religious belief, not religiously generated viewpoints on secular matters. Nonetheless, the Court held that the University was engaged in viewpoint discrimination because it precluded discussions from a religious perspective while allowing discussions from other perspectives.

[Addendum, for those wishing to grapple with the implications of *Rosenberger:* Treating all religious views, whatever they may be, as a viewpoint confounds the distinction between subject matter discrimination and viewpoint discrimination and confuses existing law regarding limited public fora. *Cf.* § I, *infra*. At present, it is unclear whether this step of equating subject matter discrimination and viewpoint discrimination applies only to expression aimed at promoting or opposing religion or whether it applies more broadly. For example, the Court has upheld exclusion of political speech from some limited fora, which is a subject matter exclusion. Should we now regard political speech as constituting a particular perspective on the way the world operates and therefore deem such speech nonexcludable from a limited forum? This seems doubtful, but it is difficult to discern a line of limitation.]

The distinction, if there is one, may lie in two facts. The student organization that published *Wide Awake* was not itself a religious organization. Further, the student publications in question, in addition to carrying religious articles, included articles on secular matters — *e.g.*, racism, crisis pregnancy, homosexuality, eating disorders — addressed from a Christian, evangelistic viewpoint. In that sense, when the University refused to fund the publications, it was excluding a specific Christian viewpoint on secular issues. What this may amount to, however, is a sub rosa determination that the University was wrong in deciding that the publications were primarily aimed at *promoting* a religious belief, as opposed to *expressing* such a belief. This is a fine line, indeed, and one which tracks into Establishment Clause considerations. *Cf.* Chapter 14, § I, *infra*.

H. The Captive Audience Problem: The Court has generally recognized the government's interest in securing individual privacy by protecting persons from unwanted intrusions and, on occasion, from material that might offend their sensibilities. How far the government may go depends on the expectations of privacy persons may have in any given place, the ease of avoiding the unwanted or offensive information or display, and the existence of special audiences, such as children, requiring special protection.

1. ***Audiences in the traditional public fora:*** In general, in the traditional public gathering places – the streets, parks, public monuments, and the like – people can expect unwanted expression to be thrust at them and may either avoid it or turn away. In that sense, the audience is not "captive" or involuntarily subjected to inescapable unwanted expression. The government consequently has little authority to protect potential audiences in such arenas. *Terminiello v. Chicago,* 337 U.S. 1 (1949); *Cohen v. California, supra.*

2. ***Constrained public areas and the home:*** In other places, such as on public transportation, which people need to use for personal reasons, individuals cannot easily avoid unwanted or offensive expression, and government may protect them by limiting expression there. *Lehman v. Shaker Heights,* 418 U.S. 298 (1974) (plurality). Government obviously has most authority to protect privacy in the home, the place most private and from which one should not be forced to retreat.

   Example: It may, therefore, ban residential picketing focused on a single home. *Frisby v. Schultz,* 487 U.S. 474 (1988). To protect children in the home, it may limit media broadcasts of offensive expression to hours when children are unlikely to hear or see it. *F.C.C. v. Pacifica Foundation,* 438 U.S. 726 (1978). On the other hand, where the householder can easily reject undesired intrusions, for example, by turning away visitors or canvassers or by posting, governmental bans on door-to-door canvassing or solicitations are improper. *Lovell v. Griffin,* 303 U.S. 444 (1938); *Schneider v. New Jersey,* 308 U.S. 147 (1939).

I. **Public Forum Doctrine:** Public forum doctrine deals with the questions whether and to what degree the First Amendment requires the opening of certain public places to assembly, debate, discussion, and other expressive activities (guaranteed access. It also considers whether those places must be open to all expressive activities (equal access); and what limits the government can place on "speech" in public places.

   1. *Definitions and distinctions*

      a. A "public forum" is a publicly owned place or property open to First Amendment activities.

      b. A "traditional public forum" is public property, such as a street, park, or monument, that "has as a principal purpose . . . the free exchange of ideas," as evidenced by a long-standing public practice or historic tradition of openly permitted speech activities. *International Society for Krishna Consciousness v. Lee,* 112 S. Ct. 2701 (1992). For a time, it was unclear whether the Court followed a "categorical" or objective and analytical approach to determining whether public property was a traditional public forum. Under a categorical approach, the Court relies primarily on history and tradition to determine whether public property is a traditional public forum. The categorical approach is closed-ended and delivers a limited list of traditional public fora. Under an objective approach, which is open-ended, the Court analyzes the principal uses and character of the property to determine whether opening the property fully to First Amendment activities is compatible with the property. Most recently, a bare majority of the Court has adopted the categorical approach. *Id.*

c. A "public forum by designation" is a nontraditional place or channel for expression transformed into a forum when the government intentionally opens it to expressive activities such as assembly or speech, or for the discussion of certain subjects, *e.g.,* advertising space on public transportation, governmental office communication systems made open to nonofficial messages.

d. A "limited public forum," a kind of forum by designation, is a place in some sense open to the public, but having a limited or specialized use, *e.g.,* a theater, a zoo, a school, a school board meeting. Such places, while intended to be open to certain kinds of public communication, are not open to any and all kinds of communication. The public purpose of this kind of forum is paramount, and the government has a stronger interest in ensuring that only the kinds of speech compatible with the underlying purpose of the forum take place there.

e. A "nonpublic forum," or more properly a nonforum public place or property, is a publicly owned place or channel of communication where specialized public business is conducted but not otherwise generally open to the public, *e.g.,* courts, jails, power plants, military bases, mail boxes. Obviously, there is communicative activity in nonpublic fora, and the government may even open such fora to some expressive activity beyond that essential to conduct normal public business. Such opening, however, does not, of itself, convert a nonpublic forum into a public forum by designation.

f. The government's provision for limited discourse in a nontraditional place or channel does not, of itself, convert it to a public forum by designation. *Cornelius v. NAACP Legal Defense and Educational Fund, Inc.,* 473 U.S. 788 (1985). In such a case, if the normal use of the public property is incompatible with generalized expressive activity, the Court will not infer that the government intended to create a public forum by designation.

2. ***Constitutional review standards for the different fora:*** The distinction between public and nonpublic fora is critical, for different constitutional tests apply to governmental regulation of First Amendment activities in these different types of places. The forum-by-designation distinction is also important, and such a forum can best be viewed as a subcategory of public fora where the purpose behind establishing the forum is overriding. Consequently, in designated forum cases, the governmental interest can justify restricting expressive activities to those for which the forum was established.

a. *Standard for traditional public fora:* The Court applies a strict scrutiny – a less restrictive alternatives analysis – to content-based regulations in the public forum.

    Example: In *Boos v. Barry,* 485 U.S. 312 (1988), the Court held unconstitutional a District of Columbia Code provision prohibiting the display, within 500 feet of a foreign embassy, any sign tending "to bring that foreign government into 'public odium' or 'public disrepute.'" This was clearly a content-based restriction of political speech in a traditional public forum.

b. *Standard for fora by designation:* The standard of review applied to fora by designation depends on the particular character of the forum and what its designation is. The government could, for example, completely open a forum to all expressive activities. Were it to do so, the forum would have the same status as a traditional public forum and the same review standard would apply. By contrast, if the government creates a limited public forum, it may restrict speech uses to those compatible with the forum.

c. *Time, place, and manner regulation:* Traditional public fora are generally assumed open to First Amendment activities. The government opens public fora by designation to such activities. Because both traditional public fora and designated fora are used for purposes other than First Amendment activities, however, use of them for expressive activities is subject to compatibility regulations usually referred to as reasonable time, place, and manner regulations. To be constitutional, such regulations must:

   (1) Be content neutral, that is, not regulate expression on the basis of its content;

   (2) Further a significant governmental interest such as traffic control, safety, protection of privacy, protection of unwilling audiences unable to protect themselves, and the like;

   (3) Further the governmental interest, in ways not substantially overbroad;

   (4) Not, because there are no ample alternative fora for the expressive activities, have the effect of suppressing speech.

d. *Speech limitation in the nonpublic forum:* By contrast, where the government has opened a nonpublic forum to some speakers or to limited discourse on some subjects, it can deny other speakers access and need not open the forum to discourse on other subject matters. To justify opening a nonpublic forum in a limited way, the government need show only that the distinctions it draws between speakers and subject matters are reasonable, given the underlying purpose of the forum, and viewpoint neutral. *Cornelius, supra; Perry Ed. Ass'n v. Perry Local Educators' Ass'n,* 460 U.S. 37 (1983).

3. ***Principal fora cases***

a. *Traditional fora:* Public streets, even residential streets, parks, and monuments, are the traditional public fora open to free speech activities. *Hague v. CIO,* 307 U.S. 496 (1939); *Frisby v. Schultz,* 487 U.S. 474 (1988). Note, however, that not all streets and sidewalks are, for that reason, necessarily traditional public fora. Some sidewalks, for example, may be associated with such a limited range of activities they cannot be considered public fora. In *United States v. Kokinda,* 497 U.S. 720 (1990) (plurality), the government located an isolated post office in a freestanding building, with its own parking lot and adjacent sidewalk, on a major highway. The sidewalk was used only for access to the post office, not as a general utility sidewalk. Under these circumstances, the Court held this particular sidewalk was not a traditional public forum and therefore was not generally open to First Amendment activities.

   (1) Handbilling or leafletting: Use of traditional fora is subject to reasonable time, place, and manner regulations or legitimate permit requirements. These restrictions, however, may not be applied to bar handbilling or leafletting, *Lovell v. Griffin,* 303 U.S. 444 (1938); nor may such activities be

banned outright even in order to prevent littering. *Schneider v. State,* 308 U.S. 147 (1939).

(2) Expression of unpopular views; the hostile audience and the abusive speaker: Government may criminalize the peaceful expression of unpopular views. *Edwards v. South Carolina,* 272 U.S. 229 (1963); *Terminiello v. Chicago,* 337 U.S. 1 (1949). While this much is clear, it is unclear whether the government may restrain a speaker inciting an audience hostile to him or must instead seek to restrain the crowd and protect the speaker's right to speak. In *Feiner v. New York,* 340 U.S. 315 (1951), the Court, using a clear and present danger test, upheld the disorderly conduct conviction of a speaker who refused police requests to stop speaking to a crowd he was angering. *Terminiello, supra,* however, suggests that speakers have some First Amendment right to anger or disturb an audience. As the clear and present danger test is now somewhat discredited, or at least considerably refined, perhaps the best resolution of this issue would be to treat it as a *Brandenburg* situation. *Cf.* Chapter 11, § II.C.

(3) Religious speech in public fora: Although the state may not endorse religion, the state also may not ban private religious speech in a traditional public forum. *Capital Square Review and Advisory Board v. Pinette*r, 515 U.S. 753 (1995) (Review board for large state-owned plaza, a traditional public forum surrounding the statehouse, denied Ku Klux Klan permission to erect a cross during Christmas holiday season). Freedom of speech fully protects private religious speech, and rules against governmental content-based distinctions on speech in traditional public fora dictate its opening to all protected speech.

b. *Mass demonstrations in the traditional public fora:* Mass demonstrations, particularly those involving patrolling, marching, and picketing, pose order, safety, and traffic problems different from those posed by wholly speech communications, and the conduct element in them may be regulated even though entwined with speech. Nevertheless, whether or not such activities could be prohibited altogether for such reasons, permission to engage in them cannot depend on unbridled, standardless official discretion. *Cox v. Louisiana [Cox I],* 379 U.S. 536 (1965).

c. *Nontraditional fora:* Not all public places are public fora open to all First Amendment activities. It is primarily the character of the property that determines what kind of forum it is or whether it is a forum at all and what standard to apply to limitations on speech rights on that property. The Court has determined the forum status of the following:

(1) Courthouses and jails: Courthouses and jails are not fora open to all First Amendment activities but are limited to certain kinds of public business. To protect the judicial process, state legislatures may prohibit picketing and parading near a courthouse. *Cox v. Louisiana [Cox II],* 379 U.S. 559 (1965). Similarly, to protect the security and functions of jails, states may prohibit demonstrations on jail grounds. *Adderley v. Florida,* 385 U.S. 39 (1966).

(2)   Public transportation: Display space on public transportation vehicles does not constitute a public forum, and consequently officials need not provide equal access to all messages. *Lehman v. Shaker Heights,* 418 U.S. 298 (1974) (plurality).

(3)   Public theaters: Publicly owned theaters are fora designed for and dedicated to expressive activities, and officials cannot, in effect, censor or restrain presentations by refusing them use of such facilities simply because they are controversial. *Southeastern Promotions, Ltd. v. Conrad,* 420 U.S. 546 (1975).

(4)   Military bases: Military bases are not traditional public fora, and even generally opening them to public access and activity does not make them public fora by designation. Consequently, military officials may properly ban political speeches and demonstrations and, given the necessity of maintaining and furthering military activities, may even require prior approval before permitting distribution of literature which might constitute a danger to military loyalty, discipline, or morale. *Greer v. Spock,* 424 U.S. 828 (1976).

(5)   Fairgrounds: Fairgrounds are temporarily open to the public for fairs and other exhibitions. Given the numbers of people attending fairs, crowd control is a significant state interest. In the interests of crowd control, officials may restrict distribution and sale of literature and solicitation of funds to fixed locations on the fairgrounds. At least, they may do so as long as those distributing or selling are not similarly restricted in communicating their views or − in other words − have adequate alternative fora on the fairgrounds to present their views. *Heffron v. International Society for Krishna Consciousness,* 452 U.S. 640 (1981).

(6)   Home letterboxes: By law, home letterboxes for U.S. mail become part of the Postal Service's mail system. Such boxes are not public fora and are subject to reasonable, content-neutral government regulation. Consequently, the government, in order to ensure mail revenues, may prohibit persons from using the boxes to deliver unstamped material. *U.S. Postal Service v. Greenburgh Civic Ass'ns,* 453 U.S. 114 (1981).

(7)   Public university facilities: When a university generally opens facilities to student groups, it creates a public forum by designation for students. It may not then exclude student groups from facilities' use on the basis of the content or subject of the group's meeting, even if the group wants to use them for religious purposes. *Widmar v. Vincent,* 454 U.S. 263 (1981).

(8)   Equal access in high schools: Under the Equal Access Act, 20 U.S.C. §§ 4071–4074, Congress adopted equal access rules for any public secondary school which received federal financial assistance and which opened its facilities to at least one "noncurricular related group." Under the Act, any such school must provide equal access to students who wish to conduct religious, political, philosophical, or similar meetings. This statute was upheld, predominantly on a *Widmar* theory, in *Board of Educ. of the Westside Community Schools v. Mergens,* 497 U.S. 226 (1990).

(9)   Public school facilities: Where a school district creates a nonpublic forum open to civic, social, or other meetings, it may not exclude speakers on the ground they would discuss permitted subject matters from a religious standpoint. The exclusion fails the viewpoint-neutrality test. *Lamb's Chapel v. Center Moriches Union Free School District,* 61 U.S.L.W. 549 (1993).

(10)   Internal mail systems: Some public organizations provide internal mail systems which organizational officials and employees use to communicate with one another. They also sometimes permit nonaffiliated groups or individuals to use the systems to communicate with those within it. As long as such systems are not open to indiscriminate use by the general public, they do not become public fora or limited public fora simply because nonaffiliated parties are allowed to use the system, but rather remain nonpublic fora. As such, officials may, as long as they do so on some reasonable basis related to the purpose of the forum, discriminate among those using the forum on the basis of subject matter or speaker identity. *Perry Ed. Ass'n v. Perry Local Educators' Ass'n,* 460 U.S. 37 (1983).

(11)   Utility poles: While public utility poles can certainly bear signs and thus serve a communicative purpose, there is no tradition of right of access to them for such a purpose. Unless the government so designates them, they do not constitute public fora. *City Council v. Taxpayers for Vincent,* 466 U.S. 789 (1984).

(12)   Government-facilitated workplace-charity drives: When the government permits use of its facilities to assist solicitation of charitable contributions from employees, it does not create a public forum. If the government has made reasonable, viewpoint-neutral distinctions in permitting charitable groups to use such facilities, or excluding groups, the government action will be upheld. In other words, simply because it permits some charities to solicit on government property, the government need not permit all charities to solicit. *Cornelius, supra.*

(13)   Airports: Although airport terminals in major metropolitian areas contain virtual shopping malls, having stores, restaurants, banks, cocktail lounges, private clubs, and other stores and businesses, they are not traditional public fora. Their principal purpose is the facilitation of passenger air travel, not expression, and they have no long-standing tradition of openness to all First Amendment activities. *International Society for Krishna Consciousness v. Lee, supra.* As airports are nonpublic fora, regulation of First Amendment activity in them need be only reasonable and viewpoint neutral.

   (a) Solicitation for funds in airports: Solicitation for funds in airports interferes with the efficient movement of travelers, who are often on tight schedules to meet interconnecting flights, and leads to pedestrian congestion. Consequently, a ban on funds solicitation, which is viewpoint neutral, is reasonable. *Id.*

   (b) Leafleting and distribution of literature in airports: Unlike fund so licitation, leafleting and literature distribution do not significantly interfere with airport traffic flow; banning them is therefore unreasonable. *International Society for Krishna Consciousness v. Lee, supra.*

J. Demonstrations and Protests at Abortion Clinics; Injunctions: Abortion remains a controversial choice, and substantial numbers of people, often for religious reasons, oppose it. To discourage – or interfere with – a woman's decision to have an abortion, some opposition groups have staged demonstrations at abortion clinics. The aim of some groups appears to be to intimidate women who seek clinic aid from doing so. Others may claim they intend only to use rational or emotional persuasion to dissuade women from obtaining abortions. Whatever the motivation, the antiabortion behavior has ranged from extreme intimidation – involving massing, blocking traffic, shouting, harassment, using loudspeakers, and the like – to efforts at quiet moral suasion. As access to most abortion clinics is via public streets, the tactics of antiabortionists pose problems. These are essentially those deriving from a conflict between rights to use the streets for expressive activities and rights to use them for other purposes, including the rights to decide whether or not to bear a child and visiting abortion clinics. Women have a right to seek pregnancy counseling, and the state has strong interests in public order, the free flow of traffic, and in protecting privacy rights and property. Against these must be set the free speech rights of abortion protesters.

Legislation usually fails at this juncture, for it is rarely specific enough to accommodate the actual confrontation problems of the street, when antiabortionists confront women, and their companions, apparently seeking abortions or abortion counseling and using the public streets to do so. Injunctions, however, serve a good purpose here, for courts can examine the details of particular street situations and craft solutions that accommodate the rights of all parties. Courts have issues, and the Supreme Court has reviewed, a number of these cases, and it is possible to articulate how free speech rules operate to manage these problems.

1. ***Buffer zones:*** Buffer zones are areas protesters cannot enter. They are intended to insure a free flow of sidewalk and street traffic and to protect relatively unfettered ingress and egress from abortion clinics. Courts may designate buffer zones, but if they involve property generally open to the public, such as streets and sidewalks, they should be no larger than necessary to effect their purposes. *Madsen v. Women's Health Center, Inc.,* 512 U.S. 753 (1994).

2. ***Noise levels:*** Demonstrators sometimes mass, engage in group singing or shouting, or use bullhorns and loudspeakers to amplify their message. If the noise levels are so great as to disturb the operation of an abortion clinic, they are enjoinable. *Id.*

3. ***Observable images:*** Anti-abortion demonstrators sometimes display signs that appear to convey threats, or that are offensive to some. But injunctions against the display of otherwise protected speech or images cannot issue on the basis of offensiveness to some. *Id.*

4. ***Physical approach:*** Injunctions against approaching persons in a public way, without a demonstration of intimidation or blocking of clinic ingress, or egress are unconstitutional. *Id.*

5. ***Picketing and demonstrating:*** Under *Frisby, supra,* targeted residential picketing is prohibitable. This means a court may prohibit pickets and

demonstrations that target a private abortion clinic. However, such a ban must be narrowly tailored, and a court cannot enjoin pickets and demonstrations in an entire neighborhood. *Id.*

Fixed and floating bubbles: Fixed buffer zones established to accommodate the interests of ingress and egress to and from abortion clinics and to permit the free flow of traffic are constitutional. *Id. Schenck v. Pro Choice Network of Western New York,* 519 U.S. 357 (1997). Floating buffer zones, however – those that move with the target persuasion – are unconstitutional because they burden more speech than is necessary. They prevent people from approaching others within conversational distance in a public forum, the public sidewalk. *Schenck, supra* (fifteen-foot floating buffer zone unconstitutional).

Example: A Colorado statute provides that, within 100 feet of the entrance to any health care facility, anyone knowingly approaching within 8 feet of another person, without consent, to leaflet, handbill, display a sign, or engage "in oral protest, education, or counseling with such other person" is guilty of a misdemeanor. Although clearly directed at abortion protesters, the statute is viewpoint neutral as it does not target particular content or positions. People have a privacy interest in avoiding unwanted communication. Although the speech in this instance occurs in a public forum, there is a degree of "captivity" for persons visiting health clinics.

The law is also a content-neutral time, place, and manner regulation. In its terms, the statute applies to all demonstrators and all speech content. The law is not content-neutral in the sense that, in order to determine whether there is a violation, someone must decide, by reference to speech content, whether an approacher was engaged in "oral protest, education, or counseling." However, looking at the content of speech to determine whether a law applies to a course of conduct (*e.g.,* threats, blackmail) is proper and does not violate the content-neutrality rule. *Hill v. Colorado,* 120 S.Ct. 2480 (2000).

The 8-foot separation zone allows speakers to communicate. While the separation zone may interfere with handbillers, people who want to accept handbills can easily do so. *Id.* Finally, free speech law recognizes special governmental intrests in particular places, such as courthouses and private homes, and health clinics are worthy of special concern. *Id.*

*RIGHTS OF
ACCESS IN
PUBLIC FORA*

II. RIGHTS OF ACCESS IN PRIVATE FORA

A. **Company Towns and Shopping Malls:** The public fora rules may apply to private property devoted to essentially public purposes and uses.

Examples: In *Marsh v. Alabama,* 326 U.S. 501 (1946), the Court overturned a trespass conviction of a Jehovah's Witness who had distributed literature in a town completely owned by a company. The *Marsh* decision, however, is rather unique, and the Court, after some vacillation, finally refused to extend *Marsh* to shopping malls. Private shopping malls, although in some senses the modern day functional equivalent of a public business district, are nonetheless private property. Unlike the situation involving company towns, those wishing to communicate with shoppers have available other means of communication. *Hudgens v. NLRB,* 424 U.S. 507 (1976); *cf. Lloyd Corp. v. Tanner,* 407 U.S. 551 (1972) (read in *Hudgens* as overruling *Amalgamated Food Employees v. Logan Valley Plaza,* 391 U.S. 308 (1968)).

B. State Law Opening Private Property to Free Speech Access: States may grant their residents broader free speech rights than those the federal Constitution grants.

Example: In *Pruneyard Shopping Center v. Robins,* 447 U.S. 74 (1980), the Court held constitutional California's action, through a state court ruling on state constitutional law, requiring that privately owned shopping centers open their premises to free speech unrelated to commercial or shopping center activities. In doing so, the Court rejected the Center's constitutional arguments that the rule violated its federal property and free speech rights.

C. Access to the Media and Other Institutions

1. ***Broadcast media:*** On the theory, once true, that there were a limited number of broadcast frequencies and that regulation was needed to prevent broadcasters from interfering with one another's signals, Congress adopted the Federal Communications Act and created the Federal Communications Commission to regulate the broadcast media. In effect, the public owns the airwaves and Congress can authorize the allocation of frequencies and permit broadcast operations under appropriate terms and conditions. Consequently, unlike the print media, which are not in any sense creatures at sufferance of the state, Congress can, if it chooses, regulate broadcast media speech and constrain the media's journalistic freedom in some ways.

   a. Perhaps most important, it can provide individuals or groups with a right of access to the broadcast media. Thus it can empower the FCC to adopt "fairness doctrine" requirements which impel stations to present discussions of public issues and assure fair, balanced coverage of differing sides and to permit responses to personal attacks and editorials; or to require broadcasters to give federal election candidates access to air time. *Red Lion Broadcasting Co. v. F.C.C.,* 395 U.S. 367 (1969); *CBS, Inc. v. Democratic Nat'l Committee,* 412 U.S. 94 (1973); *CBS, Inc. v. F.C.C.,* 453 U.S. 367 (1981).

   b. Although Congress can regulate the broadcast media to a certain degree and without showing a compelling need to do so, it may regulate the content of broadcasting only when its broadcast restrictions are narrowly tailored to further a substantial governmental interest. *F.C.C. v. League of Women Voters of California,* 468 U.S. 364 (1984).

2. ***Print media:*** By contrast, government has no authority to require that the press grant rights of access to its publications. The First Amendment prohibits laws abridging both the freedom of speech and the freedom of the press, and governments cannot interfere with journalistic freedom to decide what and whether to publish. Consequently, statutes such as "right of reply" statutes, which purport to require newspapers to grant to persons they criticize or attack equal space to respond, are unconstitutional. *Miami Herald Pub. Co. v. Tornillo,* 418 U.S. 241 (1974). Such statutes may force a newspaper to publish what it doesn't want to publish, cause a newspaper to refrain from some opinions for fear it will have to provide free space for replies, and may require government supervision.

3. ***Access to mailings:*** Requiring a private company, even one closely regulated such as a utility, to include in its mailings or billing the views of those disagreeing with its own views may deter such organizations from presenting their views and reduce

the free flow of information and ideas. The First Amendment therefore does not permit governments to require such access. *Pacific Gas and Electric Company v. Public Utilities Commission of California,* 475 U.S. 1 (1986) (plurality).

FREEDOM OF SPEECH, ASSOCIATION, AND THE PRESS

▶ **CHAPTER SUMMARY**

CHAPTER 13: FREEDOM OF SPEECH, ASSOCIATION, AND THE PRESS

Introduction. The constitutional jurisprudence of freedom of speech, and related concerns, forms a large, reasonably comprehensive, and detailed body of law having some similarities to a code. Like a code, the case law reviews and applies general principles in specific contexts, taking into account the distinctive features of the particular context. Part I of this chapter therefore treats the First Amendment doctrines and rules that arise in political campaigning; public schools and education; the administration of justice; and picketing and boycotting.

Part II discusses the important related First Amendment freedom of association, and reviews the right to join organizations; to associate for political, ideological, and social purposes; and the rights of public employees to speak out on matters of public concern and to political and ideological association. The chapter concludes, in Part III, with a discussion of freedom of the press, taking up matters not already touched upon in earlier discussions of the prior restraint and libel doctrines.

I. FREE SPEECH IN SPECIAL CONTEXTS

A. Money and Political Speech

FREE SPEECH IN SPECIAL CONTEXTS

1. ***Background:*** Modern election campaigns are highly organized and oriented toward mass and targeted audiences through the astute use of the media and polling. Name and issue identification is highly important, and politicians, and those promoting them, seek to find issues important, and positions attractive, to the largest number of voters. Campaigns for national and state level office rely heavily on political experts of various kinds – public relations specialists, pollsters, political consultants, advertising firms – to help create winning images and to promote them on television and in the other media. Such campaigns are very expensive, and raising money to fund a campaign is fundamental to political success.

   The need to seek money for a campaign creates risks for the integrity of a political system that assumes that its elected officials will represent their electorates and vote honestly on issues. In order to obtain campaign money, candidates may make promises, compromise their views, guarantee political access to important contributors, incline their votes toward their contributors' interests, or, in a worst case, in effect sell their votes on issues.

   Obviously, the system creates opportunities for and temptations to corruption. The wealthy, the well organized, and those who can otherwise command resources may obtain decisive influence or political power. The system may require candidates, including incumbents anticipating a reelection campaign, to spend great amounts of time cultivating money sources. Finally, the system favors incumbents, who have the resources of office and the leverage it provides in obtaining money from contributors, over nonincumbents – not because of their comparative merits, but because of the position they presently occupy.

   Issue elections involving voter initiatives or referenda raise a related set of problems. While there is no candidate to corrupt in such elections, no advantage of incumbency, and no question of influence on votes following election, special interest groups may be able to use their wealth to engage in issue demagoguery and defeat measures that otherwise would have wide popular support.

13

In an attempt to cleanse political campaigns of the undesired effects of money and the perhaps undue influences of wealth and existing arrangements of power, Congress and many states adopted political campaign financing laws. Such laws usually involve contribution and expenditure limitations and impose record keeping and detailed reporting and disclosure requirements.

As noted below, the Court treats regulation of campaign contributions quite differently than regulation of expenditures. In essence, "restrictions on contributions require less compelling justification than restrictions on independent spending." *Federal Election Comm'n v. Massachusetts Citizens for Life, Inc.,* 479 U.S. 238, 259–260 (1986); *Nixon v. Shrink,* 120 S.Ct. 897 (2000). As for personal or organizational expenditures, whether for candidates or issues, there are essentially no limits. This rule raises the famous "soft" money problem in campaign finance.

2. ***Free speech rules regarding campaign financing:*** Money talks and more money talks more.

   a. *Personal or campaign expenditures for political campaigns:* Free speech protects not only the right to speak, but also the right to speak with conviction and commitment. In the Supreme Court's view, using money to back one's speech – to reach a larger audience, to make views known more forcefully or artfully, to enhance one's ability to be heard, and the like – is integral to the right of political speech. Limiting expenditures which persons can make in election campaigns limits speech by reducing "the quantity of expression by restricting the number of issues discussed, depth of exploration, and size of the audience reached." *Buckley v. Valeo,* 424 U.S. 1 (1976). Furthermore, given the First Amendment's preference for a free market in ideas, government may not seek to enhance the speech of some by limiting others' speech resources. *Id.* Consequently, the government may not limit the amount individuals personally spend to advance a candidate or a cause, the amount candidates spend from personal or family resources, or the amount a candidate's campaign expends. *Id.* The same is true for political action committees truly independent of a candidate and her campaign. Such committees are independent if, even if they support a particular candidate, they do not attempt to coordinate their own expenditures with those of the candidate's campaign. Were they to do so, their expenditures would amount to campaign contributions, which, unlike expenditures, may be regulated. *Federal Election Comm'n v. National Right to Work Committee,* 459 U.S. 197 (1982).

   b. *"Voluntary" campaign expenditure limitations:* Presidential candidates can, on agreeing to limit campaign expenditures in their campaigns, receive federal campaign funds. As this particular expenditure limitation is voluntarily accepted, it is constitutional. *Buckley, supra.*

   Candidate election campaign contributions: Expenditures are those funds a person or a group devotes directly in some way to further its own speech to advance a cause or a person. Contributions, by contrast, are monies given by one to another for the latter's free use as an expenditure. While contributions, like expenditures, result in political expression, unlike expenditures, they result in expression by someone other than the contributor. Because the government has a compelling interest in preventing corruption or its appearance and because campaign contribution limitations do not limit a contributor's ability to speak on his own, such limitations are constitutional. *Buckley, supra; California Medical Ass'n v. FEC,* 453 U.S. 182 (1981).

As for state limitation of contribution amounts, there is no apparent minimum. The issue is not limitation on individual contributions, but rather whether the limits are so low that candidates cannot amass sufficient funds from all contributions to mount a campaign. *Nixon v. Shrink,* 120 S.Ct. 897 (2000).

c. *Political party expenditures:* Political parties exist in large measure to elect candidates to office, and one may assume that many of their activities are devoted to that end. The question arises, therefore, whether to treat political party expenditures as expenditures or as contributions to candidates. The Federal Election Commission went so far as to assume that all political party expenditures in support of a particular candidate's campaign for office were coordinated with the candidate and therefore were to be treated as contributions. In *Colo. Republican Federal Campaign Committee v. FEC,* 518 U.S. 727 (1996), however, the Court invalidated this rule. As long as the party spends its funds independently, and does not actually coordinate them with a candidate, the spending is to be treated as an expenditure for First Amendment purposes. *Id.* (Raising, but not deciding, question whether law limiting political party coordinated expenditures violates First Amendment).

d. *Corporate or union contributions or expenditures in candidate election campaigns:* The Federal Election Campaign Act, in order to prevent corruption, forbids corporations and unions from making contributions or expenditures in federal election campaigns. The Act, however, does permit such organizations to create, administer, and solicit funds for a special segregated fund to be used for political purposes. This exception is designed to prevent management from using organizational resources for its political purposes and to protect the interests of minority shareholders who might not wish to expend corporate funds for particular political purposes. These features of the Act or similar state statutes are constitutional, as applied to business corporations or unions, *F.E.C. v. National Right to Work Committee, supra; Austin and Kelley v. Michigan Chamber of Com.,* 459 U.S. 197 (1990). In such cases, the state has a compelling interest in ensuring that expenditures reflect actual public support for the political ideas the organization espouses rather than simple control of organizational treasuries.

(1) Exception: Political expenditure limitation laws may be unconstitutional as applied to some corporations that do not present the dangers that such laws are designed to foreclose. Thus, where a corporation is formed for political, rather than business, purposes, has no shareholders or other affiliated persons having a claim on assets or earnings, and is not an agent for corporate or union interests, imposing corporate expenditure limits on it would be unconstitutional. *Austin and Kelly, supra; F.E.C. v. Massachusetts Citizens for Life,* 479 U.S. 238 (1986).

e. *Corporate political speech on referenda:* Although creatures of the state and subject to extensive regulation, corporations may have something relevant to contribute to the public debate. The value of speech to the public debate does not depend on the source of the speech. Therefore, states may not, even in the interest of protecting the electorate from undue influence or dominance by corporate wealth, prohibit corporations from spending money to influence the outcome of referenda. *National Bank of Boston v. Bellotti,* 435 U.S. 765 (1978). On the other hand, states also have an interest in protecting corporate shareholder interests, possibly even by restricting corporate management's ability to use corporate resources as it pleases. States might therefore require that shareholders play a role in determining whether a corporation shall speak out on public matters and what it shall say, but such statutes must be narrowly tailored not to restrict corporate speech itself. *Id.*

Contributions in ballot measure elections: The compelling constitutional justification for limiting contributions is preventing corruption. Ballot measure elections, however, do not involve candidates, and only candidates – possible later public officials – can trade political favors for money. Consequently, there is no risk of corruption in ballot measure contributions. Since the constitutional justification fails, states may not limit contributions in ballot measure campaigns. *Citizens Against Rent Control v. Berkeley,* 454 U.S. 290 (1981).

Petition circulators: Sometimes, in order to obtain sufficient voter signatures to qualify a voter initiative for the ballot, campaigns hire and pay persons to circulate petitions and obtain signatures. Some states, in the interests of limiting the undue influence of wealth in voter initiative campaigns, have sought to prohibit paying petition circulators. However, as petition circulation is directed to politics, it involves core political speech that, under any theory of the Amendment, is most protected. In *Meyer v. Grant,* 486 U.S. 414 (1988), the Court held such laws unconstitutional as restricting the payer's right to communicate and to use the best communicative means to attempt to place an item on an election agenda.

(1) New developments. The Court recently struck down some Colorado efforts to regulate petition circulation in various ways. In an attempt to prevent fraud, Colorado required that petition circulators be registered voters, that they wear identification badges, and that the petition proponents make monthly reports regarding petition circulators and the amounts they were paid. The Court viewed the registered voter requirement as limiting the pool of potential circulators and thus reducing the chances that a measure would gain enough signatures to qualify for the ballot. It also noted that a decision not to register to vote implicates political thought and expression. The badge requirement also interfered with one to one communication in political expression, and was certainly inconsistent with case law recognizing the right of speakers to remain anonymous. As for the reporting requirements, as petition circulators had to submit affidavits, and proponents had to submit a final report containing the information Colorado sought monthly, these additional requirements were unwarranted. *Buckley v. American Constitutional Law Foundation, Inc.,* 525 U.S. 182 (1999).

f. *Other political campaign restrictions*

(1) States may not prohibit political parties from supporting or opposing candidates in primary elections. *Eu v. San Francisco County Democratic Cent. Committee,* 490 U.S. 214 (1989).

(2) Even in an attempt to ensure there will be no undue influence on elections, states may not prohibit press endorsements of candidates on election day. *Mills v. Alabama,* 384 U.S. 214 (1966).

(3) A candidate's campaign promise to confer some benefit on voters is protected speech, and state restrictions on such campaign promises are subject to strict scrutiny. *Brown v. Hartlage,* 456 U.S. 45 (1982).

(4) Statutes limiting the practice of exit polling whereby pollsters or news organizations seek to determine, by interviewing those who have just voted, the likely election result are probably unconstitutional as seeking to preclude communication, information gathering, and publication.

B. Free Speech in Public Schools

1. ***Student free speech rights:*** Students have free speech rights while on school grounds and may express themselves freely as long as they do not "materially and substantially interfere" with the work of the school or impinge on others' rights. *Tinker v. Des Moines School District,* 393 U.S. 503 (1969).

2. ***School officials' authority to limit students' speech:*** Student free speech rights in school, however, are not the same as those of adults in other settings, and school officials and teachers have the authority to inculcate values, including values relating to civil public discourse, as well as undertaking education. In other words, while schools cannot silence a student's personal expression not interfering with the school's educational mission, schools can impose standards – educational and civic – which have the effect of limiting certain kinds of student speech.

   a. *Imposing educational standards having the effect of limiting or channeling student speech:* Schools may limit student speech in ways compatible with the school activity in which students are engaged and may limit speech based on the maturity of the student audience. *Hazelwood School District v. Kuhlmeier,* 484 U.S. 260 (1988).

   b. *School as sponsor:* Schools sponsor many speech activities – plays, readings, newspapers – and educators, carrying out their educational mission, may exercise "editorial control over the style and content of student speech in school-sponsored educational activities so long as their actions are reasonably related to legitimate pedagogical concerns." *Hazelwood, supra.*

   c. *Improper student language:* Schools may ban and punish lewd, indecent, vulgar, or offensive student speech and conduct, even where not otherwise constitutionally proscribable. *Bethel School District No. 403 v. Fraser,* 478 U.S. 675 (1986).

3. ***School officials' authority to select educational materials:*** As a part of their authority to educate and transmit values, school authorities may make decisions regarding the suitability of books and other educational materials. In making suitability decisions, school officials may consider the sexual tenor, vulgarity, or bad taste of materials that might be used to educate. Nonetheless, the First Amendment does not permit school officials to censor material for noneducational reasons nor exercise their curricular discretion in partisan or political ways or in order to suppress ideas. *Board of Educ. v. Pico,* 457 U.S. 853 (1982).

C. Speech Interfering with the Administration of Justice

1. ***Contempt power:*** Courts have large powers to punish for contempt of court actions and conduct which hinder or prevent courts from carrying out their duties or which interfere with the administration of justice.

2. ***Clear and present danger test:*** A problem arises, however, when courts use the contempt power to punish the out-of-court expression of opinions, views, or information relating to the conduct of the courts or cases or business before them. To resolve such cases, the Supreme Court has applied a version of the clear and present danger test. In order to justify a contempt punishment of out-of-court speech, there must be a showing of some real, serious, and imminent danger to, or actual interference with, the administration of justice. *Wood v. Georgia,* 370 U.S. 375 (1962); *Craig v. Harney,* 331 U.S. 367 (1947); *Pennekamp v. Florida,* 328 U.S. 331 (1946); *Bridges v. California,* 314 U.S. 252 (1941). In general, public criticism of judges, courts, and other justice personnel and institutions does not constitute a clear and present danger, and injuries to official reputations are not a sufficient reason to punish critical speech. *Landmark Comm., Inc. v. Virginia,* 435 U.S. 829 (1978).

3. ***Litigating parties' public statements:*** States have substantial interests in protecting the integrity and fairness of the judicial system. In protecting those interests, states may restrict the extrajudicial statements of litigants and attorneys relating to pending litigation when such statements are substantially likely to materially prejudice an adjudication. *Gentile v. State Bar of Nevada,* 501 U.S. 1030 (1991). (Standard upheld, but state bar rule and reprimand of criminal trial attorney for press conference held following client's indictment overturned as unconstitutionally vague.)

D. Picketing and Boycotts as Free Speech

1. ***Picketing is protected, with limits:*** Picketing is generally protected First Amendment activity. There are features of picketing, such as massing, patrolling, and the occasional violence which sometimes accompanies a picket line, which fall on the conduct side of the speech-conduct distinction and permit special regulation, particularly in the labor context. Picketing is subject to reasonable time, place, and manner regulation. The state therefore can regulate conduct on the picket line to reduce the potential for violence or possible interference with other legitimate activities, for example, by limiting the number of pickets.

2. ***Boycott conduct may be regulated:*** Boycotts are concerted actions by which a group seeks to achieve an aim through economic pressure by persuading parties not to deal with the target of the pressure. Boycotts involve conversation, the communication of ideas, persuasion, and association and thus involve First Amendment activity. Boycotts involve conduct as well as speech, however, and the state may appropriately regulate the conduct associated with particular boycotts.

   a. *Labor speech:* The free speech rules relating to labor speech form something of a special regime, having been worked out through many years of industrial strife, labor unrest, and the adoption of major federal legislation regulating labor management relations. Such legislation allows ample opportunities for labor speech through certain channels and mechanisms. Labor speech is thus constrained within a framework not generally applicable to nonlabor speech.

(1) Labor picketing: Peaceful picketing for the purpose of disseminating information regarding a labor dispute is protected activity and the state may not ban it completely. *Thornhill v. Alabama,* 310 U.S. 88 (1940).

(2) Picketing with illegal goals: Picketing is sometimes aimed at achieving an aim that the state has defined as unlawful. Picketing directed at one employer could be part of a union effort to force other employers to hire union labor, as when a union pickets an employer to force it not to sell to nonunion employers. Many states define such secondary picketing as an unlawful form of economic coercion. Where picketing, by itself or as part of a larger course of conduct, is aimed at achieving a goal the state has defined as unlawful, the state may ban even peaceful picketing. In other words, the state may ban nonviolent picketing where it has an unlawful purpose. *Teamsters Union v. Vogt, Inc.,* 354 U.S. 284 (1957).

(3) Economic boycotts: In the heavily regulated labor context, the government has defined certain kinds of boycotts as illegal, and they are thus not protected First Amendment activity for labor. *Longshoremen v. Allied Int'l, Inc.,* 456 U.S. 212 (1982).

b. *Nonlabor boycotts for political ends:* As forms of economic coercion, the law often defines economic boycotts for economic aims as illegal. However, groups can undertake economic boycotts for political purposes, as, for example, would occur when a group organizes an economic boycott to bring pressure to bear on a business to force it to stop discriminating on the basis of race. For free speech purposes, economic boycotts for political purposes are treated differently from economically motivated boycotts. While the state can regulate economic activity and ban economically motivated boycotts, even though they involve the communication of ideas, persuasion, and association, the state cannot prohibit the free speech activities associated with a politically motivated boycott. *NAACP v. Claiborne Hardware Co.,* 458 U.S. 886 (1982). The state may, of course, regulate any unlawful conduct – violence, destruction of property, and the like – associated with any kind of boycott. *Id.*

FREEDOM OF ASSOCIATION

II. FREEDOM OF ASSOCIATION

A. **First Amendment Freedom of Association:** There is a First Amendment right to associate with others for the advancement of beliefs, ideas, and opinions, to communicate, and generally to engage in all protected First Amendment activities. *NAACP v. Alabama,* 357 U.S. 449 (1958). This right of association should be distinguished from another right of association, the right of intimate association, an aspect of liberty protected, at least in part, by the right of privacy.

B. **Compelled Disclosure of Associations and Other Information**

1. *Lawful associations:* Compelled disclosure of membership in lawful associations, without a compelling state interest, where disclosure may subject organizational members to sanctions, reprisals, vilification, or public embarrassment, violates the freedom of association. *NAACP v. Alabama, supra.* Such disclosures may affect organizational membership by inducing members to withdraw or by discouraging persons from joining for fear of exposure. *Id.*

2. ***Communist Party membership:*** The state's interest in discovering membership in the Communist Party, at least where the Party may be thought to be a genuine threat to the state, can justify a investigative demand for information regarding associational ties or activities. *Barenblatt v. United States,* 360 U.S. 109 (1959); *Uphaus v. Wyman,* 360 U.S. 72 (1959). (Given changes in First Amendment doctrine and the world during the last three decades, these cases are doubtful authority.)

3. ***Public employees and licensees***

    a. *Inquiries into fitness and competence:* Governments have a legitimate interest in inquiring into the fitness and competence of employment candidates or license applicants. But broad inquiries into ties may chill freedom of association. For that reason, while governments may make such inquiries, they must tailor them narrowly to their fitness and competence interests. *Shelton v. Tucker,* 364 U.S. 479 (1960). There is thus a strong relevancy requirement for governmental inquiries into fitness and competence, which the state has the heavy burden of meeting. *Baird v. State Bar of Arizona,* 401 U.S. 1 (1971).

        Example: The state can inquire into the fitness and competence of those who would be teachers, but a requirement that teacher candidates list all associational ties of all kinds over the previous five years is too broad and unrelated to the purpose of inquiry. *Shelton, supra.*

    b. *Inquiries as belief tests:* During the domestic communist scare period in the late 1950s and the 1960s, the state and federal governments sought in many ways to uncover whether public employees or candidates for public employment had ever been associated with the Communist Party. Governmental efforts to seek information of this kind led to many divided, agonized, and tortured Supreme Court decisions. What survives is essentially as follows: governments may not punish persons for their beliefs or because they are or have been members of particular organizations. The only exception to this is the rule that government may prohibit, and punish, knowing membership, with specific intent to further illegal aims, in organizations advocating violent overthrow of the government. As this is unprotected activity, government may inquire into it. *Law Students Research Council v. Wadmond,* 401 U.S. 154 (1971); *Baird, supra; In re Stolar,* 401 U.S. 23 (1971). *Cf.* Chapter 2, II.A., *supra.*

        (1) The scope of governmental inquiry, at least in cases where inquiry is into knowing membership in organizations advocating violent overthrow of the government, may be somewhat greater than the scope of disqualification. In other words, in such cases, the government may ask questions the answers to which will not of themselves disclose disqualifying information, but which may lead to other relevant inquiry. *Wadmond, supra; Konigsberg v. State Bar of California,* 366 U.S. 36 (1961).

    c. *Refusal to answer relevant inquiries:* Where a candidate or other person undergoing inquiry refuses to answer a relevant question, without a privilege to do so, the government may refuse to hire or otherwise sanction for failure to answer, but not for some assumed association. It may not, however, sanction persons who refuse to answer on grounds of the Fifth Amendment privilege against self-incrimination. *Lefkowitz v. Turley,* 414 U.S. 70 (1973); *Gardner v. Broderick,* 392 U.S. 273 (1968); *Garrity v. New Jersey,* 385 U.S. 493 (1967).

4. ***Compelled disclosure of political contributions:*** Contributing to a political campaign or a candidate reveals something about one's beliefs, views, and affiliations. In this respect, a government requirement that one disclose her financial contributions to political campaigns or causes is very much like a requirement that one disclose her associations and should be judged by the same strict standard. As seen before, however, there are governmental interests that can justify compelled disclosure of associational information, protection against internal security threats being one of them. Similarly, there are compelling interests in the proper functioning of democratic institutions, and these justify requiring political campaign contribution disclosures. These interests are: providing information to the public about where campaign money comes from and how it is spent; deterring of corruption, and avoiding its appearance, through publicity; and detecting violations of contribution limitations. *Buckley v. Valeo,* 424 U.S. 1 (1976).

   a. *Application to major parties and candidates:* While compelling campaign contribution disclosure may deter some from contributing or even expose contributors to harassment or retaliation, these risks are not great overall, at least with respect to the major or mainline parties, candidates, and causes. Regarding them, the protection of democratic institutions justifies burdening First Amendment associational rights in this way.

   b. *Application to minor parties and independents:* Minor parties, by definition, lack widespread political support, sometimes because their positions or platforms, although within First Amendment protections, are too controversial or too radical. Independent candidates, except in unusual situations, also often lack broad support. Requiring contributors to minor parties or independents to disclose their contributions poses greater exposure risks or burdens than the same requirement for major parties or candidates. Disclosure might so deter potential contributors that the minor party could not raise funds – as, for example, would likely be true of the Socialist Workers Party. For these reasons, if minor parties or independent candidates can show that there is a reasonable probability that compelled disclosure of contributors' names will result in threats, reprisals, or harassment, the First Amendment will require exemption from the requirement. *Buckley, supra.*

C. **Loyalty Oaths – Compelled Commitment to Association or Disavowal of Association:** Loyalty oaths are no longer the problem they once were, although many public institutions continue to require them of new employees. During the period of the domestic communist scare and purge, loyalty oaths – which required some kind of oath of allegiance to, or disavowal of desire to overthrow, the government – were required of new, or continuing, employees as a litmus test of allegiance. They were also a means to harass or embarrass individuals whose past affiliations or whose independence of mind precluded them from taking such oaths. As the oaths were often vague and broad, the Court often overturned oath requirements on vagueness and overbreadth grounds. The ultimate resolution of the general matter, however, was tied to the Supreme Court's development of the doctrine of unlawful advocacy. Once the Court drew a clear line between what kinds of advocacy the First Amendment protected and what it did not, it was clear that the only oath that government could require was an oath that one had not engaged in, or would not engage in, unprotected activity. In other words, government could require only that persons swear that they did not belong to an organization knowing that it advocated violent overthrow of the government with specific intent to aid in its unlawful activities when the time was ready – or that they did not believe in such ideas. *Cf.* Chapter 2, § II.A., *supra.* The net effect of the loyalty oath cases is that government cannot condition employment by requiring job applicants or employees to take oaths denying having engaged in, or forswearing future engagement in, protected First Amendment activity.

Example: New York disqualified from employment anyone who advocated the overthrow of government by force, violence, or unlawful means, published material so advocating, or organized or joined any group so advocating. Other state law required removal from employment of those that made "treasonable or seditious" utterances or engaged in such acts. In implementing these and related laws, the State Board of Regents adopted regulations which required University teachers to sign a statement that they had never been Communists. Failure to sign resulted in dismissal, as did disclosure of Communist Party or other listed subversive organization membership. The law regarding seditious utterances is vague. The law proscribing advocacy of overthrow punishes even abstract advocacy and therefore punishes constitutionally protected speech. The discharge law also punishes constitutionally protected activity, for it reaches inactive membership or membership without specific intent to further unlawful organizational goals. It is therefore overbroad and unconstitutional. *Keyishian v. Board of Regents,* 385 U.S. 589 (1967).

D. Litigation as Expression

1. *Litigation for political ends and association for the purpose of litigating constitutional rights are protected First Amendment activities: NAACP v. Button,* 371 U.S. 415 (1963). Consequently, states cannot, without a showing of some serious abuse, curb, as improper solicitation or unauthorized practice of law, political interest group informational activities designed to stimulate litigation. *Id.*

2. *Collective activity for the purpose of obtaining meaningful access to the courts is protected First Amendment associational activity:* States may not, therefore, use regulatory rules relating to the legal profession to bar or impede association for the purposes of recommending particular attorneys for group members or of employing attorneys to represent members regarding claims. *Brotherhood of Railroad Trainmen v. Virginia,* 377 U.S. 1 (1964); *United Mine Workers v. Illinois Bar Ass'n,* 389 U.S. 217 (1967).

E. Freedom Not to Associate: Just as freedom of speech entails the freedom not to speak, the freedom of association entails a freedom not to speak.

1. *Forced association:* Although a state, with good justification, may sometimes require individuals to associate involuntarily, as occurs with union shop or integrated bar rules, it cannot require them to provide support for political views, candidates, or ideological causes with which they disagree. *Abood v. Detroit Board of Educ.,* 431 U.S. 209 (1977). *Keller v. State Bar of California,* 496 U.S. 1 (1990). While individuals, in such circumstances, may be forced to pay dues to support the association's regulatory and beneficial activities, they cannot be required to contribute to the association's ideological or political activities with which they disagree.

Example: States may permit union shop agreements under which a single union represents the interests of all employees of a private employer. *Railway Employees' Dept. v. Hanson,* 351 U.S. 225 (1956). When there is a union shop, the union negotiates the collective bargaining agreement for all employees, even those employees not belonging to the union and those who may disagree with the union's bargaining position. Union shops eliminate the tensions and competitions existing when there are rival unions and avoid confusion and conflicting demands on the employer. These are important state objectives in the creation of an orderly and peaceful system of labor-management relations. To support unions and the benefits they confer, states authorizing union shops may require employees not members of a union or disagreeing with its position to contribute to finance the union's normal collective bargaining activities. Because of an individual's freedom not to associate, however, states may not require nonmembers to finance union political views, candidates, causes, or activities not related to bargaining collectively, administering contracts, or adjusting grievances. *Abood, supra; Communications Workers v. Beck,* 487 U.S. 735 (1988).

2. ***Mandatory student activity fee:*** Universities may charge students an activity fee used to fund viewpoint-neutral programs that facilitate extracurricular student speech and exchange of ideas. *Bd. of Regents, Univ. of Wisconsin v. Southworth,* 120 S.Ct. 1346 (2000). As most such university programs operate, a student organization controls some activity fee funds and uses them to fund various student organizations that apply for funding. Some of these organizations may use at least part of the funding to support ideological messages that offend some students who must pay the activity fee. As a university has an educational mission, rather than an associational one, as in *Abood* and *Keller,* and the speech germaneness test applied in those cases is unworkable in a university setting. One function of universities is to expose students to new and different ideas, even to challenge their beliefs. For this reason, the university can promote intellectual exchange even in extracurricular activities. In this context, a viewpoint neutral program for allocating funds to student organizations adequately protects objecting student's First Amendment interests. In effect, the aim of the university program is to create a space for extracurricular speech. As long as the university does not prefer some viewpoints over others, the program is constitutional.

   a. Student referenda to allocate activity funds. When a university allows activity funding decisions to be decided by referenda, the situation is different. Majority decision determines referendum results, and referenda do not respect minority wishes. Viewpoint neutrality appears unattainable through referenda. *Southworth, supra.*

3. ***Rule limited to political or ideological association:*** The *Abood-Keller* rule appears to be limited to cases in which individuals are forced to support political or ideological messages with which they disagree. *Glickman, Secretary of Agriculture v. Wileman Brothers & Elliott, Inc.,* 65 U.S.L.W. 3459 (1997). *Glickman* deals with commercial advertising and "marketing orders." As a part of New Deal legislation to help end the Depression, Congress passed the Agricultural Marketing Agreement Act in 1937. The aim of the Act was to establish and maintain orderly marketing conditions and fair prices for agricultural commodities. The Act authorized a supermajority of producers to issue marketing orders to set uniform product prices, quality and quantity standards, and other matters including product promotion and advertising in the interests of all producers. Expenses

involved in administering the marketing orders are paid from assessments imposed on producers.

Under this scheme, the issue arose whether the assessment for generic advertising violated the First Amendment because it compelled nonconsenting producers to support others' speech. The Court held that the First Amendment right not to contribute to speech with which one disagrees is limited to speech which conflicts with a party's beliefs. As the marketing orders in question only promoted tree fruit, there was no political or ideological issue involved in the advertising. There was also no message in the advertising with which the complaints disagreed, other than wishing to spend the assessed moneys on their own individual advertising. *Id.*

4. *Forced association and exclusive or expressive organizations:* Some organizations limit their membership to persons having certain qualifications or characteristics, such as membership in a particular religion, being of a certain gender, ethnic group, or race, having certain military service, having a certain community status, and the like. Other organizations may form, in part, in order to further, express, or promote certain ideologies or beliefs. Governmental attempts to open the membership of such exclusive or expressive organizations pose special associational problems.

    a. *Right of intimate association:* Some groups, most likely small groups, may form in order to enjoy the freedom of intimate association: For example, a book or gourmet club among good friends might compose such a group. State efforts to open such groups to broader membership would invade the right of intimate association.

    b. *Right of expressive association*: Still other groups may form for specific expressive purposes, purposes which themselves condition and define membership qualifications. For example, the group World War II Survivors of the Battleship Indianapolis' Sinking, if faithful to its name, cannot have nonsurvivors as active members. There is a close relationship between the group's selection criteria and the message the group wants to convey. Forcing such a group to accept members whose presence belies the group's message would violate the right of expressive association.

        (1) The Boy Scouts as an expressive association: The Boy Scouts of America is a private, nonprofit organization aimed at instilling certain values in young boys. As such, it engages in expressive activity promoting those values. In resisting a public accommodations law that would have forced the Boy Scouts to accept homosexuals as members, the Boy Scouts claimed that homosexual conduct was inconsistent with the values it was attempting to inculcate. Forcing the Boy Scouts to accept an admitted gay leader as an assistant scoutmaster would in effect force the organization to send a message about the acceptability of homosexuality. *Boy Scouts of America v. Dale*, 120 S.Ct. 2446 (2000).

        (2) Even large and amorphous groups, or collectivities of groups, may, depending on their purpose, have rights of expressive association which they may exercise to prevent the association of certain messages with them: For example, each year a group of private citizens organizes a St. Patrick's Day parade in Boston, Massachusetts. The group denied

13

permission for members of a gay and lesbian organization to march in the parade as an identified gay and lesbian group. The parade's sponsor, however, granted permission to many other different groups to join in the parade. Thus, the parade could be said to express many different messages, not a single, particularized message, and the parade's sponsor in some sense associated itself with those many messages. Nonetheless, the sponsor did not have to associate itself with a message it did not like or approve. Any speaker has the right to shape his or her expression by speaking out on some matters and not on others. Therefore, a Massachusetts law, interpreted to require the sponsor to allow the gay and lesbian group to march in the parade as an identified group, violated the sponsor's First Amendment rights of expressive association. *Hurley and South Boston Allied War Veterans Council v. Irish-American Gay, Lesbian and Bisexual Group of Boston*, 515 U.S. 557 (1995).

(3) There remain groups which, while private and discriminating regarding membership qualifications, are neither intimate associations nor expressive associations of the kind calling for a close relationship between the group's message and the group's membership selection criteria. These are organizations such as the Jaycees or Rotary, whose purposes are social or commercial. Requiring such organizations to open their membership violates neither the right of intimate association nor the right of expressive association. *Roberts v. United States Jaycees,* 468 U.S. 609 (1984); *Board of Directors of Rotary Int'l v. Rotary Club of Duarte,* 481 U.S. 537 (1987); *New York Club Ass'n, Inc. v. City of New York,* 487 U.S. 1 (1988). States may therefore require such private organizations not to discriminate in admission to membership on the basis of sex, race, religion, or such criteria.

c. *Political parties and freedom of association:* Political parties are free to associate for political purposes, and the right of association entails a right to exclude, or a right not to associate. In particular, political parties may limit participation in the process of selecting a party's nominees to party members. For these reasons, a California "blanket" primary law that permitted members of any party to vote for any candidate in a state primary, regardless of party affiliation, violated the right of freedom of association. *California Democratic Party v. Jones,* 120 S.Ct. 2402 (2000). The law forced political parties to allow their nominees to be selected, in least in part, by crossover voters not affiliated with the party. This could result in the selection of nominees the party did not want and in nominee induced shifts in party positions. *Id.*

F. **First Amendment Protection of the Speech and Associational Activities of Public Employees and Contractors:** Government may not condition public employment, contracting, or receipt of public benefits on relinquishing rights of free expression. It may, however, in the interests of efficient, fair, and effective government performance, restrict to a certain degree, the First Amendment rights of public employees and contractors.

1. *Proscribing public employee partisan political activity:* The government's interest in efficient and fair government, free of improper influences, justifies restrictions on the political activities of public employees. Consequently, government can, as long as it does so in content neutral ways, proscribe public employee involvement in political management and political campaigns. *United*

Public Workers v. Mitchell, 330 U.S. 75 (1947); *C.S.C. v. Letter Carriers,* 413 U.S. 548 (1973).

2. ***Public employee speech:*** The First Amendment protects public employee speech related to "matters of public concern," which is not knowingly or recklessly false, does not involve the disclosure of confidential information, and does not, by its nature, undermine or destroy employer-employee relationships requiring trust and confidence.

   a. *Particularized balancing:* Although public employees may speak on matters of public concern, they are not completely insulated from employment sanction for having done so. Instead, reviewing courts should balance the particular reasons for the employee's discharge against the nature of the employee's expression. *Connick v. Myers,* 461 U.S. 138 (1983); *Pickering v. Board of Educ.,* 391 U.S. 563 (1968).

   b. *Position:* The job or position the speaker holds makes a difference in the determination whether the speech can be said to affect working relationships or public confidence.

   c. *Matter of public concern:* The difficult cases in this area are those in which an employee makes some statement, usually critical of his agency or employer, in which the public could take some interest because it in some way bears on governmental functioning. At the same time, the statement may be nothing more than a personal grievance or personal grievance *plus* some expression on a matter of public concern. The problem here is to find some guide which protects citizenship-related speech but which also protects against disgruntled employees cloaking private grievance in public garb. The Court has said that this is in effect a judgment call, taking into account the content, context, and time, place, and manner of a public employee's speech, and balancing the nature of the expression against the reasons justifying discharge.

      (1) Speech critical of public employers is not automatically of public concern;

      (2) Even if a public employee speaks out on a matter of public concern, the public employer's interest in promoting the efficiency of the service it performs may, on balance, override the right of the public employee to speak as a citizen. Note that this rule authorizes content-based sanctions on speech depending on the effect the speech may have on working relationships or public confidence.

      Examples: In *Pickering v. Board of Educ., supra,* the Court overturned the dismissal of a teacher discharged for writing a newspaper a letter criticizing the school board for its handling of financial matters. This is obviously the kind of speech any citizen might engage in, and nothing in it could be thought to damage either the teacher's effectiveness as a teacher or the appropriate functioning of the employer-employee relationship.

      By contrast, in *Connick v. Myers, supra,* a deputy district attorney, unhappy with a decision to transfer her, prepared and distributed a survey questionnaire soliciting views of other staff. The survey asked questions regarding transfer policy, morale, the need for a grievance committee, confidence in supervisors, and pressure to work in political campaigns. She was discharged for her refusal to accept the transfer and insubordination in distributing the questionnaire. The content of most of the questionnaire did not relate to any matter of public concern. The item relating to pressuring employees to work on political campaigns did. The context of the questionnaire's preparation and distribution clearly suggested its motivation was a personal grievance. The time, place, and manner of its distribution – to other employees during office hours – demonstrated possible damage to office efficiency. Balancing the employee's expression on the single matter of public concern against the damage done to office efficiency and working relationships, the Court upheld the discharge.

In *Rankin v. McPherson,* 483 U.S. 378 (1987), a probationary clerical employee in a county constable's office was discharged for saying, following the attempted assassination of President Reagan, "If they go for him again, I hope they get him." The statement was made in a private conversation with her boyfriend, and, in context, it was clear that it was not a threat on the president's life but instead an expression of disapproval of his policies. The employee had no policy-making, law enforcement, or public relations duties. Under these circumstances, the Court held the employer could not discharge the employee for her speech.

d. *Restraining or sanctioning public employee disclosure of confidential information:* A majority of Supreme Court justices support the propositions that the government can prohibit employees from disclosing confidential information and that the government may require prepublication review of proposed employee publications. *Snepp v. United States,* 444 U.S. 507 (1980). There is thus no "whistleblower's privilege," that is, there is no First Amendment right to know which can insulate governmental employees disclosing confidential government information from government reprisal. Another way of looking at this is that the *Pickering-Connick* rules discussed *supra* do not call for balancing the value of the information disclosed to the public against the affront to confidentiality.

e. *Restraining employee speech unrelated to duties:* The government has strong interests in protecting the integrity and efficiency of public service and avoiding even the appearance of employee impropriety. These interests, however, do not justify a law forbidding rank-and-file government employees from receiving compensation for speech, outside of working hours, related to matters of public concern and unrelated to their public duties. *United States v. National Treasury Employees Union,* 63 U.S.L.W. 4133 (1995) (federal ethics law prohibiting government employees from accepting honoraria for speaking or writing on matters unconnected with employment unconstitutional as applied to employees grade GS-16 and lower).

3. **Public contractors:** The Pickering line of rules also applies to governmental contractors. The First Amendment protects even at-will governmental contractors from governmental termination or refusal to renew contracts in retaliation for an exercise of free speech rights. *O'Hare Truck Service, Inc. v. City of Northlake,* 518 U.S. 712 (1996).

4. **Patronage or political affiliation dismissals:** To avoid punishing public employees for their political affiliations or associations, public employers cannot fire, dismiss, transfer, or otherwise sanction employees whose effectiveness in their

positions does not depend on political affiliation. *Rutan v. Republican Party of Illinois*, 58 U.S.L.W. 4872 (1990); *Branti v. Finkel*, 445 U.S. 507 (1980); *Elrod v. Burns*, 427 U.S. 347 (1976).

Example: In *Branti, supra,* on taking office, a public defender office head, who was a member of the Democratic Party, fired assistant public defenders who were Republican Party members. Political affiliation had no relevance as a criterion of position effectiveness, and the firings were held unconstitutional.

5. ***Denial of benefits because of speech:*** Government may not deny persons governmental benefits because they have engaged in protected expression. *Speiser v. Randall*, 357 U.S. 513 (1958). On the other hand, government is not required to subsidize expression. Consequently, government does not violate free speech rights in refusing to grant tax-exempt status to organizations that devote a substantial part of their activities to lobbying. *Regan v. Taxation with Representation of Washington*, 461 U.S. 540 (1983).

G. **Legislative Investigations and Free Speech:** Congress and state legislatures have the implied power to conduct investigations to develop information to assist them in drafting or amending legislation or to gain an understanding of how legislation is operating. Legislative investigations, however, even when proper, may invade or abridge First Amendment freedoms, for legislative inquiry into beliefs or associations may discourage, or even punish, such activity. Consequently, need for a particular legislative investigation, when directed to beliefs, associations, or other protected First Amendment activities, must be balanced against the burden imposed on First Amendment rights. Legislative investigation into Communist Party activities is an important legislative purpose that overbalances an individual's First Amendment rights. *Barenblatt v. United States*, 360 U.S. 109 (1959). On the other hand, when investigating organizations not affiliated with the Communist Party, the legislature must demonstrate a compelling interest to infringe First Amendment rights. *Gibson v. Florida Legislative Committee*, 372 U.S. 539 (1963).

III. **FREEDOM OF THE PRESS**

A. **Background:** The prior restraint rules, *cf.* Chapter 12, I.B., *supra,* while applying broadly to restraints on any expression, constitute a principal protection for the press, as do the libel rules, *cf.* Chapter 11, II.F., *supra.* The Constitution, however, expressly protects the freedom of the press, and the Press Clause has given rise to arguments that the press has special rights beyond those conferred by the free speech guarantee. The basic argument for special protection is that the press plays important informational and checking functions – it uncovers, reveals, and publicizes social and political facts and conditions. In doing so, it informs the people, who then can decide what action to take, and it ensures the accountability of elected and appointed officials. The Court has not accepted such arguments, and at least one justice has suggested instead that the Press Clause confers no special status on the press. *First National Bank of Boston v. Bellotti*, 435 U.S. 765 (1978) (Burger, C.J., concurring). Nonetheless, there are problems specific to the press, and the Supreme Court has developed a small body of constitutional law, in addition to prior restraint and libel law, relating to the press. Some of this law does appear particularly sensitive and hostile to governmental actions that may "chill" the press or reduce its independence.

13

FREEDOM OF THE PRESS

B. No Special Press Immunity from Governmental Inquiries, Obligations, or Processes

1. ***Testimonial demands:*** When properly called or subpoenaed, all persons have an obligation to provide relevant, unprivileged testimony, to grand juries and trial courts. The governmental interest in investigating and prosecuting crimes is compelling, and news reporters have no special newsgathering privilege regarding confidential sources of information which protects them from compelled disclosure of sources if such disclosure is relevant to an investigation or criminal trial. *Branzburg v. Hayes,* 408 U.S. 665 (1972). Nonetheless, the First Amendment does pose some limits to investigative authority. Grand juries must have good reason to inquire into a reporter's relationship with news sources. They are subject to judicial control to ensure that their investigations do not constitute press harassment, and their subpoenas are subject to motions to quash to test their propriety. *Id.*

2. ***Search warrants:*** The press has no special privilege exempting it from the ordinary criminal processes to which every citizen is subject. Consequently, the government may execute a properly issued search warrant against the press rather than a subpoena duces tecum, notwithstanding that execution of a search warrant may cause business disruption and allow searching officers to see material the warrant doesn't cover. *Zurcher v. Stanford Daily,* 436 U.S. 547 (1978). However, when courts are asked to issue search warrants whose execution might endanger First Amendment interests, they should apply the warrant requirements "with particular exactitude." *Id.*

3. ***Laws of general applicability:*** The media are not exempt from laws of general applicability even where such laws have an incidental effect on the media's ability to gather and report news. *Cohen v. Cowles Media Co.,* 501 U.S. 663 (1991).

   a. *Contracts and promises of confidentiality:* Where the media explicitly promises a source confidentiality regarding the source of information, the source may sue the media for its voluntary disclosure of the source even though the disclosure provides truthful information. *Id.*

C. Public and Press Access to Information: The First Amendment requires that places and governmental institutions traditionally open to the public, such as trial courts, remain open unless the government has a compelling interest to close them. Generally speaking, the press has only the same right of access to public institutions, to acquire information, that the public itself has. In certain circumstances, however, because of the character of its work, governmental institutions may have to make reasonable accommodations to the press, to facilitate its work, not required for the general public.

1. ***Criminal trial courts:*** Although not explicitly stated in the First Amendment, the First Amendment rights of speech, press, and assembly imply a purpose of assuring free communication on matters relating to government functioning. Historically, criminal trials have been open to the public, and access to them has been important in ensuring the proper functioning of the judicial process and the government. Government therefore may not close criminal trials to the public or press unless closure is essential, and narrowly tailored, to serve an overriding governmental interest. *Press-Enterprise Co. v. Superior Court (I),* 464 U.S. 501

(1984); *Globe Newspaper Co. v. Superior Court,* 457 U.S. 596 (1982); *Richmond Newspapers, Inc. v. Virginia,* 448 U.S. 555 (1980).

Examples: State law cannot require the exclusion of the public and press from courtrooms during the testimony of minor sex offense victims. Protecting minor sex crime victims from further psychological trauma and from public embarrassment are compelling interests, but closure cannot be mandated in all cases. Instead, it is essential to determine the appropriateness of closure in such cases on a case-by-case basis. *Globe Newspaper, supra.*

The privacy interests of prospective jurors do not justify excluding the public or press from their *voir dire* examination even in high visibility or grisly cases. Public jury selection is an integral part of public trial and, historically, has been open to the public. It is possible that examination of some prospective jurors would "pose matter so sensitive, traumatic, or embarrassing" as to justify closing that particular examination, but that again should be decided on a case-by-case basis when triggered by juror request. *Press-Enterprise Co. v. Superior Court, supra.*

2. ***Disclosure of grand jury testimony:*** States may not permanently bar grand jury witnesses from disclosing testimony they gave before the grand jury. *Butterworth v. Smith,* 494 U.S. 624 (1990). Once a grand jury has been discharged, the reasons for barring disclosure of one's own grand jury testimony also end, and the state no longer has any overriding interest in prohibiting publication of truthful information. *Id.*

3. ***Fair trial as a compelling state interest:*** Ensuring that a defendant receives a fair trial is a compelling state interest, and there are possible cases where pretrial publicity is so great that a defendant could not obtain an unbiased and impartial jury. Nonetheless, criminal trial courts may not order the press not to publish material relating to a trial, including transcripts of preliminary hearings, unless there is no other way to ensure fairness. *Press-Enterprise Co. v. Superior Court (II),* 478 U.S. 1 (1986); *Nebraska Press Ass'n v. Stuart,* 427 U.S. 539 (1976). *Cf.* Chapter 12, I.B., *supra.*

4. ***Access to jails:*** The press has no greater right of access to jails than the general public does. As long as the government does not discriminate against press access to jails by according less access than the public, it has no duty to make available to journalists information not available to the public generally. Consequently, where jail or prison officials do not permit members of the public to interview specific inmates, the press has no constitutional right to such interviews. *Pell v. Procunier,* 417 U.S. 817 (1974); *Saxbe v. Washington Post Co.,* 417 U.S. 843 (1974). However, given the special role the press plays in our society, government may have to take steps to ensure that the press has effective access to all areas open to the public. *Houchins v. KQED, Inc.,* 438 U.S. 1 (1978) (plurality). For example, while members of the public do not normally bring video-recording equipment with them while touring jail facilities, to deny the press the right to do so would preclude their ability to report, and thus be unreasonable. *Id.*

D. **Laws Directed at the Press:** While the press is a business and is subject to laws generally applicable to businesses, government may not enact laws specially applicable to the press which create a risk of punishing or censoring the press or which discriminate between classes of publications.

13

1. ***Laws with punitive or censorial motives:*** States may not enact laws in an attempt to punish publications for their reporting or expression of opinion. *Grosjean v. American Press Co,* 297 U.S. 233 (1936) (Louisiana tax on newspapers keyed to circulation and calculated to limit circulation).

2. ***Taxes singling out the press:*** The government may tax publishing as a business and may properly subject newspapers and other publications to sales or other general taxes. However, the government may not direct a tax specifically at the press, even when the press is exempted from other taxes and pays a lower tax than if not exempted. Differential taxation of the press, even if initially favorable, creates the possibility of burdensome or punitive taxation. General taxes subject all to tax, and all can complain of the burden. Singling out a taxpayer for a special tax, however, separates it from the general taxpaying public and therefore disadvantages it before the legislature. *Minneapolis Star and Tribune Co. v. Minnesota Comm'r of Revenue,* 460 U.S. 575 (1983).

   Example: Minnesota exempted newspapers from its sales tax. Leaving the exemption in place, it adopted a use tax, directed at newspapers, on the cost of paper and ink newspapers used. The use tax was not a complementary tax, that is, it did not operate to tax products purchased out of state, but used in state. Consequently, it was not a sales tax under another name. The tax singled out newspapers, however, and this differential tax created the possibility, at some future date, of more burdensome tax treatment for newspapers than other businesses. *Minneapolis Star, supra.*

3. ***Discrimination between classes of publications:*** Laws that single out certain kinds or classes of publications, either on the basis of size or publication content, are unconstitutional. Such laws have a great potential for abuse, permitting the possibility of targeting particular publishers for vindictive or repressive treatment. *Minneapolis Star, supra; Arkansas Writers' Project, Inc. v. Ragland,* 481 U.S. 221 (1987).

   Example: Arkansas' sales tax taxed publications, but exempted newspapers and religious, professional, trade, and sports journals. The tax scheme discriminated between publications on the basis of content and was unconstitutional. *Arkansas Writers' Project, supra.*

FREEDOM OF RELIGION

▶ ## CHAPTER SUMMARY

14

CHAPTER 14: FREEDOM OF RELIGION

Introduction. There are two religion clauses in the First Amendment to the Constitution. They provide that Congress shall make no law respecting an establishment of religion, or prohibiting the free exercise thereof. The two clauses, the Establishment Clause and the Free Exercise Clause, reflect both the religious practice and tolerance in the United States at the time of the adoption of the Bill of Rights. Persons seeking to escape religious persecution in England formed some of the American colonies, which later became the founding states. Of these, some were theocratic and had established religions. In these, church and state were united, and people were not religiously free. In others, like those influenced by the Quakers, there was religious tolerance or a belief in voluntarism in religion. In yet other colonies, like Virginia, there were established religions, but yet some tolerance. Not everyone had to express belief in the state religion, but nonetheless all had to support it through paying taxes. In Virginia, Madison and Jefferson played leading roles in disestablishing the state church and laid the foundations for the separation of church and state in the later-formed United States. At the time of the drafting of the Bill of Rights, these various strands came together. Some states did not want Congress to have the power to interfere with state establishments. The voluntarists wanted neither a national religion nor interference with free exercise. Those who believed in a separation of church and state concurred.

Eventually, as seen in other contexts, the Supreme Court read the Fourteenth Amendment as applying the First Amendment to the states and therefore as forbidding state establishments of religion and state interferences with free exercise. There is, however, some tension between the two religion clauses. The Free Exercise Clause appears to require the state not to place barriers to or burdens on the exercise of religious belief, and one may read it even to require that the state facilitate the free exercise of religion. On the other hand, the Establishment Clause suggests that the state should not aid religion in any way, but instead that there should be a wall of separation between church and state. Does any aid or deference to religion constitute an establishment? If the state denies aid, at least in some circumstances, does it interfere with the free exercise of religion? The ideal, of course, is neither embrace nor hostility, but neutrality, yet this is quite difficult to accomplish, as the cases reveal.

THE ESTABLISHMENT CLAUSE

I. THE ESTABLISHMENT CLAUSE

A. Aid to Sectarian or Religious Schools

1. *The* Everson *no-aid formula and school transportation:* In the Supreme Court's initial foray into Establishment Clause jurisprudence, it propounded a so-called no-aid formula as setting the rule for state assistance of religion. Involved in *Everson v. Board of Educ.,* 330 U.S. 1 (1947), was a New Jersey statute which authorized public payment for transporting both public and secular school children to and from their schools. The majority, while acknowledging that the clause was intended to create a "wall of separation" between church and state nonetheless viewed the law as providing a general welfare service or benefit, much as the provision of police or fire services to all citizens. In addition, the Court concluded that while the Establishment Clause means that states should not provide aid to religion, the Free Exercise Clause prevents the state from punishing people because of their faith. To deny members of a religion the benefit of neutral laws providing general welfare benefits would in effect punish them. On this view, the New Jersey statute was held constitutional, as not providing aid to religion. In other words, some kinds of aid flowing to sectarian or religious schools do not constitute aid for Establishment Clause purposes.

a. *The* Everson *problem:* The provision of education of children is, of course, of ultimate benefit to the public at large. Secular schools, which are supported by parents and religions, provide a state-mandated education without cost to the public. Such education is expensive, and, over the years, many secular schools have found it difficult to remain open. If such schools close, however, children now attending them would attend public schools, increasing the costs of public education. In addition, there is something of an equity problem in the state's treatment of parents who send their children to religious schools. The state taxes everyone to support public schools, but these parents, although they pay their fair share for public education, do not use public schools. These facts, together with pressure from religious and parent groups for some form of public support, have led to many different kinds of state efforts to provide some form of aid to sectarian or religious schools. Because *Everson* permitted a certain kind of aid, by deeming it not aid, the Supreme Court was forced, in case after case, to distinguish between permissible and impermissible kinds of public aid to sectarian education. The effort ultimately required the Court to articulate exactly what was objectionable about aiding sectarian education.

b. *The religious character of sectarian education:* The Court has determined that the basic problem in the provision of state aid to sectarian or religious schools is that while such schools do provide all the elements of a general education, all the teaching is infused with religious values. This makes it exceptionally difficult, if not impossible, to separate out what is secular and what is religious in the education. Sectarian schools "(a) impose religious restrictions on admissions; (b) require attendance of pupils at religious activities; (c) require obedience by students to the doctrines and dogmas of a particular faith; (d) require pupils to attend instruction in the theology or doctrine of a particular faith; (e) are an integral part of the religious mission of the church sponsoring them; (f) have as a substantial purpose the inculcation of religious values; (g) impose religious restrictions on faculty appointments; and (h) impose religious restrictions on what or how faculty may teach." *Levitt v. Committee for Public Educ. and Religious Liberty,* 413 U.S. 472 (1973). In other words, in sectarian schools, religious values and atmosphere permeate all the education and teaching provided. This realization has played a major role in the Court's complicated and confusing resolution of sectarian school-aid issues.

2. *The* **Lemon** *formula:* The *Everson* no-aid formula was not a useful tool for analysis of potential establishment problems, and the Court later evolved a three-part formula known as the *Lemon* formula. It provides that in order for a state statute or program which arguably aids or endorses religion to pass constitutional muster under the Establishment Clause. It requires that the program (1) must have a secular, as opposed to a religious, purpose; (2) its principal or primary effect must be one that neither advances nor inhibits religions; and (3) must not foster excessive government entanglement with religion. *Lemon v. Kurtzman,* 403 U.S. 602 (1971).

a. *Secular purpose:* The Establishment Clause prohibits government sponsorship or endorsement of religion, partly because such government action excludes members of the "out-religions" or nonbelievers from the political community. Legislative purpose, however, is notoriously difficult to determine, and courts tend to give legislatures the benefit of the doubt and assume that statutes are properly motivated. In addition, statutes can have multiple purposes, both religious and secular. For these reasons, the purpose prong of the *Lemon* test is interpreted as follows: because the government cannot act from religious motivations, either to aid or harm religions, statutes whose motivations are either solely or predominately religious are constitutionally invalid. This means that some, but not all, statutes that have mixed religious and secular motives, may pass scrutiny.

b. *Primary effect:* In unclear or mixed-motive cases, the effect of a statute may suggest that it was religiously motivated or that it otherwise assists or harms religion or involves government in religion in some objectionable way. Even if a statute has a purely secular purpose, however, it could provide significant aid to religion or harm religion, and that alone would make it unconstitutional.

Note: There is some dispute on the Court about the importance of the primary effect prong of the test. Justice O'Connor, who takes strong view that government endorsement is the primary evil the Establishment Clause aims at, argues that the fact that a government statute or practice advances or inhibits religion should not by itself invalidate it. In her view, only those governmental actions that, as a part of their effect, communicate a message of government endorsement or disapproval are unconstitutional. *Lynch v. Donnelly,* 465 U.S. 668 (1984) (O'Connor, J., concurring); *Corporation of Presiding Bishop v. Amos,* 483 U.S. 327 (1987) (O'Connor, J., concurring). As her views have become increasingly influential in Establishment Clause cases, this position bears watching as a possible refinement of the *Lemon* test.

c. *Excessive entanglement:* The entanglement portion of the test reflects the idea that government involvement with religion, even through supervision of neutral programs, runs risks both of government influence on religion and religious influence on government. There is the related and further worry that church-state involvement would lead to the development of political constituencies along religious lines and create dangerous political divisiveness, a possibility that the history of religious conflicts and wars in England and Europe reveals to be both serious and real.

3. *Application:* In application, the *Lemon* test tends to collapse into its last two prongs. Given the reluctance of the Court to question the motivation of state legislatures, states can usually, although not always, satisfy the "secular purpose" prong of the test quite easily. Determining primary effect and "excessive" entanglement, however, is quite difficult, as is disclosed by the Court's treatment of the following issues.

a. *Textbook loans:* Indirect aid to sectarian schools involving the loan of secular textbooks to students attending them constitutes public welfare legislation primarily benefiting children and their parents, not the religions running the schools. *Board of Educ. v. Allen,* 392 U.S. 236 (1968).

b. *Teacher salary supplements:* Because of the nature of teaching in sectarian schools and the influence of teachers, it is difficult, if not impossible, to separate the secular teaching from their religious teaching. If government provides salary supplements for such teachers, it would have to watch over their teaching in order to ensure they did not teach religion. This, however, would create excessive government entanglement in religion. Provision of aid by way of busing or textbook loans, by contrast, requires no surveillance at all. Such aid goes directly to the children or the parent, and there is no need to examine any teaching. Salary supplements for sectarian teachers therefore violate the Establishment Clause. *Lemon v. Kurtzman, supra.*

c. *Recent developments:* Recent cases reveal that the Court is revisiting its Establishment Clause decisions and beginning to articulate new, or refined, tests that are less restrictive of state aid to sectarian schools. In *Agostini v. Felton,* 521 U.S. 203 (1997), it modified the *Lemon* test in school aid cases by examining only the first two factors, concluding that the excessive entanglement factor was really an aspect of determining a statute's effect. Now, in analyzing effect, the Court looks at whether the aid results in governmental indoctrination, defines its recipients by reference to religion, and creates excessive entanglement. *Agostini, supra.*

In *Mitchell v. Helms,* 120 S.Ct. 2530 (2000), operating under a federal government supplemental school aid program, Louisiana distributed educational materials and equipment – books, computers and software, projectors, televisions, and the like – to public and private schools, the latter mostly sectarian. The private schools received aid based on the number of children enrolled in them, and the aid itself was "secular, neutral, and nonideological." At issue in the case was only the possible impermissible effect of the aid. The plurality reasoned that under *Agostini,* that while there might be religious indoctrination in the sectarian schools, because the government was neutral in giving aid to all groups without regard to religion, no indoctrination was attributable to the government. Secondly, as the program was a per-capita program, the aid that went to the sectarian schools was a result of private choices of parents to send their children to such schools, and not because of a government choice. The program did not define its recipients by reference to religion since it was a neutral government program available to all schools.

The sum of the plurality position appears to be that government aid to religious schools does not violate the Establishment Clause if it is secular in content and is provided neutrally. Further, the plurality expressly rejected arguments that direct aid to sectarian schools was impermissible and that aid that was "divertible" that is, that lent itself to religious use was improper. On the latter point, the plurality opined that diversion of aid for religious indoctrination was not an act attributable to the government and therefore not of constitutional concern. Were the plurality view to become law, it would work a substantial shift in Establishment Clause doctrine.

The divertibility issue: Two Justices concurred in *Mitchell,* but disagreed on the divertibility question. For them, diversion was not permissible, but they concurred in result because in this case there were safeguards against diversion and such diversion as may have occurred was deemed minor. Given the position of the dissenters on this point, it is clear that a majority of Justices believe that diversion of aid for sectarian purposes is not permissible. Even the potential for diversion was an issue for the dissenters, but the concurring Justices were concerned primarily with actual diversions and were unwilling to assume that aid that could be diverted would be diverted.

The private choice issue: In *Witters* and *Zobrest, see infra,* neutral governmental aid programs directed aid to individuals. These individuals then used the aid in ways that may have supported religious indoctrination. In those cases, the Court reasoned that private, not public, choice directed the aid, so there was no Establishment Clause problem. In *Mitchell*, however, the aid was provided on a per-capita basis, and the plurality treated this as equivalent to private choice. The concurring and dissenting judges also disagreed on this point. As direct aid goes to the school based on the number of students, if the schools divert the aid for religious purposes, the government could be said to have supported the advancement of religion.

The direct aid question: Although the plurality in *Mitchell* opined that the direct-indirect aid distinction was invalid, one should not draw the conclusion that the directness of aid is of no concern. For example, it is clear that direct monetary subsidies to sectarian schools would violate the Establishment Clause, at least under prevailing law.

c. *Tuition and other financial assistance*

(1) Assistance provided directly: Direct aid solely to sectarian schools or to the parents of sectarian school children by way of reimbursements, tax relief, or direct grants, provided in order to aid such schools and actually supporting them, violates the Establishment Clause. *Levitt, supra; Sloan v. Lemon,* 413 U.S. 825 (1973).

(2) Assistance provided to all parents: State school aid programs which provide the parents of all children attending school, whether public or private, relief through a tax deduction for tuition expenses, are constitutional. As the aid goes to all parents, and to parents rather than the schools, there is no "imprimatur of State approval" of religion. *Mueller v. Allen,* 463 U.S. 388 (1983).

(3) General programs providing aid to individuals: States can offer general programs of financial assistance to individuals to help them attend schools of their choice. As long as such programs are neutral and offer assistance without regard to religion, they are not made unconstitutional simply because a beneficiary makes the private choice of using the assistance to attend a religious school. *Witters v. Washington Department of Services for the Blind,* 474 U.S. 481 (1986).

Examples: In *Witters,* the state, as a part of a general state program, provided financial assistance to a blind person studying at a Christian college. Although some financial aid may have gone to the religious institution, it resulted from the private, independent choice of the aid recipient.

In *Zobrest v. Catalina Foothills School District,* 61 U.S.L.W. 4641 (1993), parents of a deaf ninth-grader enrolled him in a Catholic high school. They asked the public school district to supply him with a sign-language interpreter to transmit to him everything that was said in his classes, a service allegedly required under the federal Individuals with Disabilities Education Act (IDEA). As the Catholic school was pervasively sectarian, the interpreter would undoubtedly convey religious as well as nonreligious messages. The district refused to provide the interpreter, asserting, among other things, that the Establishment Clause barred it from doing so. The IDEA, however, is a general government benefit program which distributes benefits to qualifying handicapped children. Under IDEA, parents may select their child's school, and, consequently, it is their private decision, not a governmental decision, that places the interpreter in a sectarian school. Furthermore, no aid flows to the sectarian school.

Note: When decided, *Zobrest* and *Witters, supra,* unless limited to their facts, seemed somewhat inconsistent with other, major Establishment Clause cases involving aid to sectarian schools. Relying on *Zobrest* and *Witters*, the Court has now overruled the earlier cases, *Grand Rapids School District v. Ball,* 473 U.S. 373 (1985) and *Aguilar v. Felton,* 473 U.S. 402 (1985), at least to the extent that those cases prohibited the use of secular teachers to teach secular courses in sectarian schools. *Agostini v. Felton, supra. See* subsection e, *infra.*

d. *Sectarian teachers offering secular courses on-site:* On occasion, some communities have attempted to make use of existing sectarian school facilities and resources to provide public education. One way to do this is to provide support for sectarian teachers to offer secular courses in sectarian schools, but at the end of the regular school day. Such programs are unconstitutional for they pose a substantial risk that the religious message the teachers convey during the school day will carry over and infuse their secular classes. *Grand Rapids School District v. Ball,* 473 U.S. 373 (1985).

e. Before *Agostini v. Felton, supra,* Establishment Clause jurisprudence drew a firm line between government-supported remedial instruction for eligible students offered at the site of a sectarian school and such instruction provided off-site. The latter was constitutional and the former was unconstitutional. *Grand Rapids School District v. Ball, supra; Aguilar v. Felton, supra.* The reasoning was that state-paid teachers holding secular classes in a sectarian atmosphere might convey religious messages. Further, providing secular instruction in religious schools would produce a symbolic union of church and state conveying a religious message. In addition, in providing the secular instruction, the state might relieve religions of the need to do so, and schools could use the savings to further religious teaching, in effect a government subsidy. Finally, were the state to attempt to remedy some of these problems by supervision, there was a risk of excessive entanglement of church and state. *Id.*

In an important recent case, *Agostini v. Felton, supra,* the Court overruled *Grand Rapids* and *Aguilar* on the issue of state-supported instruction in sectarian schools. Relying on *Zobrest* and *Witters,* the Court held that the assumptions on which the earlier cases had relied were in error. There was no good reason to assume that properly selected and instructed secular teachers teaching secular subjects in sectarian schools would convey religious messages. The "symbolic union" between church and state appeared to be no greater for on-site programs than for off-site programs as church-state cooperation was required in both programs. There was no evidence that state provision of supplemental remedial secular education to select students would displace sectarian remedial efforts, and therefore there was no government subsidy to religion. Finally, because there is no longer an assumption that secular teachers may inculcate religious beliefs if teaching on-site, there is no need for pervasive monitoring. There was therefore no excessive entanglement.

f. *Maintenance and repair*

(1) Elementary and high schools: A state, in providing direct money grants for equipment, upkeep, renovation, utilities, and janitorial services at sectarian schools may have a secular purpose of maintaining existing educational facilities. Nonetheless, where the state does not limit the use of such funds to secular purposes, the direct and immediate effect of such aid may be to aid religion; for example, the institution could use such funds to repair a chapel. *Levitt, supra.*

(2) Colleges: Government aid to colleges for facilities construction or maintenance and repair, where aid is restricted to nonsectarian use and the colleges are characterized by an atmosphere of academic freedom rather than religious indoctrination, is constitutional. *Tilton v. Richardson,* 403 U.S. 672 (1971); *Roemer v. Board of Pub. Works,* 426 U.S. 736 (1976).

g. *Teacher-prepared testing:* Testing is an integral part of teaching, and the state cannot divide sectarian teacher activities into discrete parts and subsidize some of them without in some way supporting their overall function. Consequently, a state program which reimbursed private schools principally for teacher services in conjunction with teacher-prepared tests, together with the costs of state-required tests, records, and reports, violated the Establishment Clause. *Levitt v. Committee for Public Educ., supra.*

h. *Standardized testing:* Unlike sectarian teacher-prepared testing, publicly prepared standardized testing cannot be used for religious instruction. States may therefore provide such testing for sectarian schools.

i. *Provision of instructional equipment, material, and auxiliary services*

Instructional equipment and materials: In *Meek v. Pittenger,* 421 U.S. 349 (1975); *Wolman v. Walter,* 433 U.S. 229 (1977), the Court took the view that teachers can readily use instructional equipment such as recorders, playback devices, projectors, maps, and instructional materials to convey a religious message. It therefore held that this form of aid was forbidden. In *Mitchell v. Helms, supra,* it overruled *Meek* and *Wolman* on this point.

(1) Auxiliary services

(a) On-site: *Meek* also held that the provision, on private school grounds and through public school personnel, of auxiliary services – counseling, testing, psychiatric services, speech and hearing therapy, teaching for exceptional children, students needing remedial aid, and the educationally handicapped – also poses problems. Even though those providing auxiliary services may be public school personnel, the religious atmosphere of sectarian schools is such that it is impossible to ensure, without constant government surveillance, that even such personnel would not inculcate religious values. *Meek's* view was that this would give rise to excessive entanglement problems. This holding is apparently inconsistent with *Mitchell* and should probably be deemed overruled as well.

(b) On-site diagnostic services: Where the relationship between the diagnostician and the student is quite limited and not likely to create a risk of fostering ideological views, the state may provide, on-site, simple diagnostic services, such as speech and hearing tests. *Wolman, supra.*

(c) Nonsectarian off-site therapeutic services: As there is no pervasive sectarian atmosphere off the premises of a sectarian school, states, using nonsectarian teachers, may provide sectarian school students with off-premises therapeutic services. *Wolman, supra.*

j. *Field trips:* Where the sectarian school controls field trips, selecting sites and sending accompanying teachers to make the trip meaningful, it is impossible to separate out possible religious messages that the teacher or trip may convey. Consequently, this is an unconstitutional form of state aid. *Wolman, supra.*

4. **Summary**

a. *Impermissible aid to sectarian elementary schools and high schools:* Because of the pervasive sectarian atmosphere and possibilities of church-state entanglement, the state may not provide:

(1) Tuition aid;

(2) Teacher salary supplements;

(3) Building funds.

b. *Permissible aid to sectarian elementary and high schools*

(1) Bus transportation;

(2) Secular book loans;

(3) Instructional materials and equipment;

(3) Simple on-site diagnostic services;

(4) Off-site therapeutic and auxiliary services provided by nonsectarian school personnel;

(5) Funds for teacher-designed testing or for field trips. (Once held unconstitutional, now, following Mitchell, probably constitutional.)

c. *Permissible aid to colleges:* For colleges not having a sectarian atmosphere, all of the above may be permissible.

B. **State Sponsorship of Prayer, Religious Practice, or Doctrinal Teaching in Public Schools:** The Court, for the most part, uses the *Lemon* test, *cf.* A, *supra,* first applied to resolve questions regarding public aid to secular education, as a general purpose test to analyze and resolve other issues regarding government involvement with religion. This includes the many ways in which governments have accommodated religion in public schools. The *Lemon* test, however, is one that developed over time, and the early cases in this area, hardly expressing a consistent body of law, do not use it.

1. ***Released-time programs:*** Historically in the United States, religions were in the forefront in providing education to children. Many sects created schools to provide a basic education and religious and practical training. When the states eventually created systems of public education, in many cases they simply took over existing systems – the buildings, the teachers, and the curriculum, which generally involved reading, writing, arithmetic, and religion. Continuing to offer religious instruction, however, was problematic as different denominations originally controlled different schools. When the state took over education, however, students from many denominations went to any given school. For the most part, all the denominations were Protestant, and they mostly had one thing in common, the Bible. In many schools, therefore, there was a compromise effected under which there was no teaching of the specific doctrines of any one particular religion, but instead nonsectarian teaching in the basic principle of mainstream religion and its foundational source, the Bible. There was also prayer, generally nonsectarian, albeit vaguely Protestant. This nonsectarian and limited religious praying was felt not to be enough, and in order to inculcate strong religious principles in children, it was thought necessary to reach them during school hours when they were readily available. The consequence was the creation of released-time programs that provided a period of time during the school day when children, with parental consent, were released to attend religious instruction, either inside or outside of the school. These programs eventually came under Supreme Court scrutiny under the Establishment Clause, with mixed results.

    a. *Sectarian teaching in public schools:* State programs under which sectarian teachers offer teaching in religious subjects in public schools during the school day violate the Establishment Clause. *McCollum v. Board of Educ.*, 333 U.S. 203 (1948). Such programs depend on compulsory school attendance, use public facilities and funds, and lend the authority of the state to religion, thus symbolically aligning the state with religion.

    b. *Sectarian teaching during school hours off-premises:* A different version of a released-time program involved releasing students, on written request of parents, during the school day so that they could leave school grounds to go to religious centers for instruction. The Court deemed this version of released time as an accommodation to the free exercise of religion. In effect, when there is no coercion of students, no use of state facilities or resources, and no symbolic alignment of the state behind religion, released-time programs that merely accommodate religious belief are constitutional. *Zorach v. Clauson,* 343 U.S. 306 (1952).

2. ***Prayer and Bible reading in public schools:*** The government may not compose nor require nor sponsor the recital of public school prayers, even prayers which are not sectarian but nondenominational. Doing so violates the Establishment Clause, for the government has no business composing prayers and may not constitutionally have the purpose of promoting religion over nonreligion, even if it promotes no particular religion. *Lee v. Weisman,* 112 S. Ct. 2649 (1992). The recital of the prayers, even when the state does not compel unwilling students to participate, also implicates the Free Exercise Clause. When the government lends its authority and support to religious belief and practice, it creates at least indirect

coercion on minorities to conform. *Engel v. Vitale,* 370 U.S. 421 (1962). The Establishment Clause forbids states from requiring the reading of the Bible or recital of the Lord's Prayer in public schools. The purpose and effect of such requirements is normally to promote or advance religion. *Abington School Dist. v. Schempp,* 374 U.S. 203 (1963). Similarly, a law having a religious purpose in requiring the posting of the Ten Commandments in public school classrooms is unconstitutional. *Stone v. Graham,* 449 U.S. 39 (1980). Objective, secular study of the Bible or religion, however, without a purpose to promote religion and not involving a religious exercise, is permissible. *Schempp, supra.*

3. ***Mandatory moments of silence for meditation or voluntary prayer:*** Under the first prong of the *Lemon* test, legislatures may not enact statutes having religious, but no secular, purposes. If a legislature's purpose in enactment is to endorse or disapprove of a religion, its statute is unconstitutional. Consequently, an Alabama statute providing for a period of silence in public schools "for meditation or voluntary prayer," which was intended to return prayer to the public schools and had no secular purpose, violated the Establishment Clause. *Wallace v. Jaffree,* 472 U.S. 38 (1985). "Moment-of-silence" statutes enacted with genuine secular purposes, unaccompanied in practice with any suggestion or pressure to use the silence for prayer, and having no effect of advancing or inhibiting religion, however, may be constitutional. *Id.*

   a. *"Permitted" prayer:* A public school district that authorized high school students to elect to have a student give a prayer or invocation before varsity football games violated the Establishment Clause. *Santa Fe Independent School District v. Doe,* 120 S.Ct. 2266 (2000). While students vote to have the prayer, the school district authorizes it, and the prayer occurs on school district property at a school district event. Because of the authorization and association, the prayer cannot be considered as merely private speech, in a public forum, but rather as governmental endorsement of religion. Under these circumstances the student election does not insulate the school district, nor does a majority vote protect the rights of minorities. Even though student attendance at games may be voluntary, some students who choose to attend are forced to participate in a religious exercise.

4. ***State prohibition or promotion of teaching certain theories in order to protect or promote religion:*** Some religions oppose the theory of evolution, believing instead in the biblical account of creation as a factually true account. Responding to such views, some state legislatures adopted laws either prohibiting the teaching of evolution or requiring that the "science" of creationism be taught along with evolution as a coequal theory. In the cases reaching the Supreme Court, the laws had an easily demonstrable religious purpose – either the proscribing of a scientific theory because of a conflict with religious doctrine or the requiring the teaching of a religious, essentially biblical, account of creation. In *Epperson v. Arkansas,* 393 U.S. 97 (1968), the Court held unconstitutional a Tennessee "antievolution" law which completely forbade the teaching of evolution. In *Edwards v. Aguillard,* 482 U.S. 578 (1987), the Court overturned a Louisiana requirement, adopted for clear religious reasons, that creationism be taught along with evolution.

C. **Grant of Government Powers to Religious Bodies:** Governments may not grant or cede the exercise of governmental powers to religions. In *Larkin v. Grendel's Den, Inc.,* 495 U.S. 116 (1982), a Massachusetts law permitted churches and schools to veto applications to open liquor stores located within 500 feet of them. Such a law both aids religions, by allowing them to control their environments, at least to a certain degree, and allows religions to exercise governmental powers.

D. State Conferral of Benefits or Exemptions

1. ***Benefits or exemptions generally available:*** Governments do not violate the Establishment Clause simply because some general benefit or exemption program, available to both secular and religious parties, happens to confer benefits on a religion. On the other hand, benefits or exemptions given solely to religions or religious groups and in effect sponsoring, or appearing to sponsor, religion are unconstitutional.

    Examples: State aid going to the parents of all school children, public and private, is permissible even if it aids parents of children attending sectarian schools and thus indirectly aids religion. *Mueller v. Allen, supra.*

    Public colleges do not violate the Establishment Clause when they open college facilities to religious groups for meetings or activities on the same terms as all other groups. *Widmar v. Vincent,* 454 U.S. 263 (1981). Similarly, where a school district permits after-hours use of its facilities for civil, social, or other meetings involving certain subject matters, it does not violate the Establishment Clause in allowing religious groups to use the facilities to make presentations to the public on the permitted subjects. The district's purpose in opening its facilities to public use is secular, its action does not have a principal effect of advancing or inhibiting religion, and there is no excessive entanglement. Given that the district does not sponsor the religious group's message, that the use is after-hours, and that the meeting is open to the public, there is no real danger that the community would conclude the district was endorsing religion. *Lamb's Chapel v. Center Moriches Union Free School District,* 61 U.S.L.W. 4549 (1993).

    Tax exemptions for property used for religious, educational, or charitable purposes, obviously intended to favor organizations, secular or sectarian, having benevolent public purposes, are constitutional. *Walz v. Tax Commissioner,* 397 U.S. 664 (1970).

    State laws providing sales tax exemptions for religious but not other types of publications violate the Establishment Clause. *Texas Monthly, Inc. v. Bullock,* 489 U.S. 1 (1989).

    Public universities making payments from student activities funds to outside contractors for printing services rendered for student group publications do not violate the Establishment Clause when making such payments for a student religious newspaper. The university action is neutral in treating all such groups evenhandedly, regardless of their message or viewpoint, and the university is pursuing a secular purpose of supporting student publications. *Rosenberger v. Rector and Visitors of the University of Virginia,* 63 U.S.L.W. 4703 (1995).

2. ***Benefits or exemptions conferred solely on religion:*** Singling out religious entities for benefits or exemptions is not invariably unconstitutional, for under some circumstances government may make an accommodation for the free exercise of religion, relieving a burden it might otherwise impose.

Example: The Civil Rights Act of 1964 prohibits religious discrimination in employment, but exempts religious organizations employing "individuals of a particular religion to perform work connected with [the organization's] carrying on . . . of its activities." In other words, the Act's exemption, which applies only to religious organizations, allows, but does not require, them to choose or discharge employees on the basis of their religion. Not permitting such organizations to select employees on the basis of religion might hamper their religious work, for employees of a different religion might not act with the same zeal, vision, sense of mission, or commitment – at least with respect to nonprofit activities. *Corporation of Presiding Bishop of Church of Jesus Christ of Latter-Day Saints v. Amos,* 483 U.S. 327 (1987).

14

Counterexample: A state law mandating that employers could not dismiss employees for refusing to work on any day of the week which their religion observed as a Sabbath was an unconstitutional establishment of religion. In effect, the state gave force of law to a particular religious practice of Sabbath observance and thus advanced religion. *Estate of Thornton v. Caldor, Inc.,* 472 U.S. 703 (1985).

E. **State Funding of Religious Groups:** Government may not, of course, directly fund religious groups to support them nor to advance their causes. Nonetheless, as seen above, when government has a secular purpose, such as promoting charitable activities or the public welfare, the fact that sectarian as well as secular organizations receive equal government assistance – via subsidies, exemptions, benefits, or grant funds – does not make out a violation of the Establishment Clause. This view presumes that religions or religiously affiliated groups receiving these forms of government assistance will, in fact, carry out the secular purpose. Depending on the program, however, there are risks that religious groups will use the government assistance not to realize the secular purpose, but instead to spread or advance a religious message. The government program would then have the primary effect of advancing religion and be unconstitutional *as applied. Bowen v. Kendrick,* 488 U.S. 589 (1988).

1. Where a public university uses mandatory student fees to support student activities, including speech activities in a limited public forum, payment of some of those funds to a printer for publication of a student journal having a Christian viewpoint is direct aid to religion in violation of the Establishment Clause. (For further discussion, *see* Chapter 12: Freedom of Speech, I.G.2.a., *infra.*)

F. **Government Association with Religion in Other Contexts**

1. *Sunday closing laws:* Sunday is a day particularly important to Christians, and laws requiring businesses to close on Sunday were originally religiously motivated. Nonetheless, their modern, and secular, purpose is to provide a uniform day of rest for all, and Sunday closing laws therefore do not constitute an establishment of religion. *McGowan v. Maryland,* 366 U.S. 420 (1961).

2. *Legislative prayer and chaplains:* Historically, legislatures in the United States have always had paid chaplains, and the chaplains have opened legislative sessions with a prayer, generally of Judeo-Christian derivation. Similarly, other official bodies, sometimes courts, have also opened their proceedings with a prayer. Given this long history and unbroken practice, these things more reflect an acknowledgment of belief than an establishment of religion. *Marsh v. Chambers,* 463 U.S. 783 (1983). (This is probably best viewed as an instance of "ceremonial deism". That is, one of a series of long-standing public rituals or acknowledgments – court oaths and the "In God We Trust" slogan on the dollar are other examples –

that actually carry little real religious meaning, but are simply familiar and part of accepted practice.)

3. ***Religious gerrymandering:*** Laws that on their face operate to create denominational preferences violate the Establishment Clause.

   Example: Minnesota provided that only religious organizations which received more than half their contributions from their members were exempt from the registration and reporting requirements of the state's charitable solicitation law. Such a law plainly favors religions soliciting most of their contributions from members, and disfavors religions, such as the Unification Church, the Hare Krishna religion, and the like, which obtain most of their contributions from nonmembers. Even if such a law is aimed at preventing fraud, the means it uses is not closely tailored to that end. Furthermore, as the law favors some religions while disfavoring others, it creates a risk of politicizing religion. *Larson v. Valente,* 456 U.S. 228 (1982).

   Counterexample: An Internal Revenue provision denying charitable contribution status, and therefore deductibility, of funds given to a church in exchange for services does not create an unconstitutional denominational preference. On its face, the provision does not differentiate between religions. There is an obvious secular purpose – to deny charitable contribution deductibility whenever there is an exchange of value, but not when there is a true gift. The provision, applicable to all charitable entities, has no effect of either advancing or inhibiting religion, and its administration does not risk excessive entanglement. *Hernandez v. Commissioner of Internal Revenue,* 490 U.S. 680 (1989).

4. ***Governmental use of, or association with, religious symbols:*** Government use of religious symbols, such as the cross or the star of David, to endorse religion or advance or hinder a religion or sect would clearly be unconstitutional. Governments, however, sometimes use or associate themselves with religious symbols in contexts where the message conveyed is equivocal on the question of support or endorsement of religion. Whether the government's use of religious symbols amounts to an endorsement depends very much on the context and setting in which the symbols are displayed.

   Examples: In *Lynch v. Donnelly,* 465 U.S. 668 (1984), Pawtucket, Rhode Island, in cooperation with a retail merchant's association, erected a Christmas display to observe that holiday season. The display included a creche, with Christ-child, shepherds, angels; a Santa Claus house, reindeer, a Christmas tree, a wishing well, cutout decorative figures, and other various implements of the Christmas holiday season. In erecting the display, the City asserted secular purposes of celebrating the holiday and depicting its origins. The context and setting of the display do not unequivocally suggest a message of government endorsement of Christianity; indeed, the cornucopia of symbols suggests, most generously, a celebration of everything Christmas has come to mean, and, most cynically, a celebration of a commercial holiday. In these circumstances, the Court concluded the primary effect of the display was not to advance religion.

   Contrast *Allegheny County v. Greater Pittsburgh ACLU,* 492 U.S. 573 (1989). There, the County displayed a creche, with flowers, a tree, and a sign revealing the creche had been donated by the Holy Name Society, a Catholic religious organization. There was nothing in the setting to dilute the clear religious message of the creche, and the Court held that government sponsorship of the display violated the Establishment Clause.

II. **FREE EXERCISE OF RELIGION: The First Amendment forbids the government from prohibiting the free exercise of religion. While the Establishment Clause ideal is governmental neutrality toward religion, there is some tension between this ideal and that of the Free Exercise Clause, which calls for government to allow people to believe and practice their religious beliefs without interference. Without doubt, there are governmental actions so clearly violative of free exercise that the government cannot undertake them. For example, the government may not require the affirmation of any religious belief nor punish its expression in speech, discriminate on the basis of religious views or status, nor take sides in religious controversies. On the other hand, many religiously neutral laws, adopted for quite legitimate secular governmental purposes, turn out to be "hostile" to religion – in the sense that they ignore the possibility that their requirements may interfere with the practices or beliefs a particular religion demands. For example, applying income tax law to exact taxes from a sincere religious pacifist who believes he cannot contribute in any way, even involuntarily, to war or enhancing the country's war-making capability will interfere with his practice of religion. In the United States, there is a great diversity of religious belief and practice, and sincere religious belief often dictates some practice or conduct that the government for legitimate secular reasons regulates or forbids. This kind of governmental regulation-religious practice conflict is therefore a significant problem, and the Supreme Court has been seriously divided over this issue. For a time, it appeared that the Court was verging on adopting a strict scrutiny-compelling state interest standard of review in all such cases. However, the Court recently retreated to adopt a rule holding that, in a large class of cases, the governmental interest in enforcing neutral laws of general applicability and effect overrides the individual interest in free exercise, without regard to the feasibility of granting exemptions. There remains a group of previously decided cases, mostly unemployment compensation cases, where the Court interpreted the Free Exercise Clause to require the government to exempt from the laws' operations those whom the laws would in some way religiously coerce or punish. This latter group of cases now comprises an exception to the more general rule.**

A. **Generally Applicable Laws:** With some exceptions, generally applicable laws, not specifically directed at religious practices, which happen to govern the performance of acts that a religious belief or practice requires or forbids are constitutional, and the government need not make exemptions in order to accommodate the religious practice. *Employment Division, Dept. of Human Resources of Oregon v. Smith,* 494 U.S. 872 (1990). However, laws that target religious practices thought to pose social problems, while not regulating other practices posing the same problems, are neither neutral nor of general applicability. Such laws are subject to strict scrutiny review and must be justified by a compelling state interest. *Church of Lukumi Babalu Aye, Inc. v. Hialeah, Fla.,* 61 U.S.L.W 4575 (1993) (ordinance proscribing religious, but not most secular, killings of animals unconstitutional).

1. *Sunday closing laws:* When states elect to make Sunday a uniform day of rest by proscribing labor on it, the Free Exercise Clause does not require them to make an exception for those whose religious convictions require them to observe a day of rest other than a Sunday. *Braunfeld v. Brown,* 366 U.S. 599 (1961).

2. ***State criminal laws:*** Without violating the Free Exercise Clause, states may adopt criminal laws which, while not aimed at particular religious practices, may have the effect of forbidding a particular religious practice.

Examples: Government could outlaw polygamy by making bigamy a crime, even though such action precluded Mormons from practicing polygamy as a religious duty. *Reynolds v. United States*, 98 U.S. 145 (1878).

Notwithstanding a religious motivation, the state could prosecute a parent for a violation of child labor laws for having her children dispense religious literature in the streets. *Prince v. Massachusetts*, 321 U.S. 158 (1944).

Oregon adopted a criminal law prohibiting the use of peyote, as a narcotic drug, under all circumstances. As Oregon could punish criminally all who used peyote, it could also take the lesser step of refusing to grant unemployment compensation to members of the Native American Church who used peyote sacramentally in conjunction with a religious rite. *Employment Division, Department of Human Resources of Oregon v. Smith, supra.*

3. ***Governmental regulatory and tax programs:*** With the exception of unemployment compensation schemes, and similar programs where individualized determinations are easy to make, the Free Exercise Clause does not require governments to exempt from regulatory and tax obligations those claiming interference with free exercise.

Example: Old Order Amish believe that they have a religious obligation to provide fellow church members with the kinds of assistance provided others by the Social Security system. Because of this religious belief, an Amish employer refused to withhold and pay Social Security taxes for his Amish employees. Permitting an exemption from tax payment in such circumstances might jeopardize a neutral governmental tax program of general applicability, and the Free Exercise Clause does not require an exemption. *United States v. Lee*, 455 U.S. 252 (1982).

a. *Licensing and taxation of religious publications or property*

(1) License tax: Governments may not require that those who solicit for religious purposes or who distribute or sell religious literature procure a license to do so by paying a flat fee. Such license taxes operate as a prior restraint on the exercise of religious liberty. *Murdock v. Pennsylvania*, 319 U.S. 105 (1943); *Follett v. McCormick*, 321 U.S. 573 (1944).

(2) Sales, use, or property taxes: States may impose generally applicable, nondiscriminatory sales and use taxes on the sale of religious literature or materials, or property taxes on religious property. Such taxes do not operate as a precondition for or prior restraint on religious activity and do not single out religious activity for special or burdensome treatment. *Jimmy Swaggart Ministries v. Board of Equalization of California*, 493 U.S. 378 (1990). Although imposing such taxes on religious literature or property reduces the amount of money available for the taxpayer to expend on religious activities, that burden, at least as long as the tax is not so high as to effectively choke off religious activity, is not constitutionally significant. *Hernandez v. Commissioner*, 490 U.S. 680 (1989); *Jimmy Swaggart Ministries, supra.*

4. ***Government regulation of its business and disposition of its property:*** The Free Exercise Clause protects an individual's own religiously dictated conduct but does not require government to conform its conduct to individuals' beliefs. Nondiscriminatory government practices or conduct regarding its own business do not violate the Free Exercise Clause even though they are offensive to someone's religious beliefs or they make it harder, perhaps even impossible, for someone to practice her religion.

Examples: Roy, a Native American, sincerely believed that control over one's life was essential to spirituality and that use of a Social Security number would "rob the spirit." He therefore objected to the government's use of a Social Security number for his two-year-old daughter, which was necessary to obtain food stamps and family aid. As Roy was objecting to government conduct and not to conduct the government required of him, he stated no free exercise claim. *Bowen v. Roy,* 476 U.S. 693 (1986).

The United States Forest Service proposed to build a road over National Forest public lands which, as it turned out, would substantially interfere with, perhaps even end, the religious value of the land to Indians whose religion was location based and for whom the land was a sacred spiritual place. While building the road might interfere with the Indians' ability to practice their religion, the government proposed neither to prohibit nor penalize their religious practices but was simply utilizing its own land. *Lyng v. Northwest Indian Cemetery Protective Ass'n,* 485 U.S. 439 (1988).

5. ***Exceptions***

   a. *Unemployment compensation cases:* In a series of cases, states denied employees unemployment compensation following discharge for refusing to work on their Sabbath or for resigning because of religious scruples concerning the nature of the work. In each of these cases, the state statute had some provision that, in effect, authorized the payment of unemployment compensation except where the unemployment was "without good cause." The states refused to consider the religious reason as good cause for unemployment. In these cases, the Court applied the strict scrutiny-compelling state interest test and held the denial of compensation to be an unconstitutional burden on the employees' free exercise of religion. *Sherbert v. Verner,* 374 U.S. 398 (1963); *Thomas v. Review Board, Indiana Employment Security Division,* 450 U.S. 707 (1981); *Hobbie v. Unemployment Appeals Comm'n of Florida,* 480 U.S. 136 (1987). Subsequently, in *Oregon Employment Division v. Smith, supra,* the Court interpreted these cases as holding that where a state has a system of individualized exemptions from a statute's operation, it cannot, without a compelling reason, refuse to consider religious hardship as a ground of exemption.

      (1) "Hybrid" cases and the double-trump theory: In an additional group of cases, which the Court now refers to as "hybrid" cases, the Court has held that the First Amendment bars application of neutral, generally applicable laws without a compelling state interest. *Oregon Employment Division v. Smith, supra.* These are cases in which the law burdens both free exercise and some other fundamental right, usually a First Amendment

communicative right or the parental right to educate children. Most representative, in the current context, is *Wisconsin v. Yoder,* 406 U.S. 205 (1972). There, the Court applied the strict scrutiny-compelling state interest standard to a Wisconsin statute which required parents, under threat of criminal sanction, to send their children to school to age sixteen. The state applied the statute to Amish parents who, for sincere religious reasons, refused to send their children, although they were under 16, to school beyond the eighth grade. The Court held that the state interests of preparing children as citizens to participate in the political system and to be self-reliant and self-sufficient participants in society did not justify the burden placed on the free exercise rights of the Amish parents. In so holding, the Court accepted the basic Amish claim that their children were sufficiently educated for the life they were brought up to lead as members of a separated agrarian community.

(2) Religious Freedom Restoration Act: Acting under its Fourteenth Amendment authority, Congress, in the Religious Freedom Restoration Act, attempted to restore the *Sherbert-Yoder* compelling state interest test for review of cases involving neutral government laws that burdened the free exercise of religion. As RFRA was neither remedial nor preventative – there having been no showing whatsoever that neutral laws were enacted or used to oppress free exercise – Congress exceeded its Fourteenth Amendment enforcement power, and RFRA was unconstitutional. *City of Boerne v. Flores, Archbishop of San Antonio,* 521 U.S. 507 (1997) (Historic Landmark Commission denial of a building permit to enlarge a landmark church upheld). *Cf.* Chapter 10, Section II. C., *supra.*

B. **Free Exercise in Special Contexts:** Although the strict scrutiny-compelling state interest standard of review is applied in a limited class of free exercise cases, the Court applies a much more deferential reasonableness standard of review to free exercise claims arising in special contexts such as the military or prisons.

Examples: An Air Force regulation mandating standardized dress for active duty officers prohibits the wearing of headgear indoors. Goldman, a Jewish rabbi and Air Force captain working as a clinical psychologist, refused to comply when ordered to stop wearing a yarmulke, a skullcap he wore as a religious observance. Although he had worn the yarmulke on duty without incident or objection from superiors, the Court, deferring to the professional judgment of the military regarding dress uniformity, upheld its action. *Goldman v. Weinberger,* 475 U.S. 503 (1986).

ADJUDICATION OR OTHER STATE SETTLEMENT OF RELIGIOUS MATTERS In *O'Lone v. Shabazz,* 482 U.S. 342 (1987), prisoners challenged work regulations which prevented them from attending the Friday religious service called for by their Islamic faith. The Court applied the reasonableness standard and deferred once again to the judgment of professionals.

III. **ADJUDICATION OR OTHER STATE SETTLEMENT OF RELIGIOUS MATTERS**

A. **Intrachurch Matters:** An interesting set of problems arises when there are intrachurch disputes and a court or other governmental body is called upon to settle the dispute. If adjudicating or settling the dispute turns on a determination of religious doctrine, state involvement would present major establishment and free exercise problems. The basic rule is that the state may not ally itself with any side in a controversy over religious authority or dogma. *Serbian Eastern Orthodox Diocese v.*

Milivojevich, 426 U.S. 696 (1976); *Presbyterian Church v. Hull Church*, 393 U.S. 440 (1969); *Kedroff v. St. Nicholas Cathedral*, 344 U.S. 94 (1952). Further, where courts can apply neutral criteria to resolve nondoctrinal matters, they may do so, although they may also choose to defer to church authorities or tribunals. *Milivojevich, supra; Jones v. Wolf*, 443 U.S. 595 (1979).

1. ***Church property disputes:*** Church property disputes sometimes arise when a particular church or parish wishes to split off from the main body of the church or when there are disputes over who has authority to appoint ministers and control church property. Without violating the First Amendment, states may provide neutral criteria for deciding such disputes, *e.g.*, require written constitutions to address such issues, apply secular corporation laws, and the like. *Presbyterian Church, supra.* In the absence of neutral criteria or an express trust, courts should defer to majority determination in a congregational church or to the highest church authority in a hierarchical church. *Watson v. Jones*, 80 U.S. 679 (1871).

   Examples: Until 1924, the Russian Orthodox Church in America, located in New York, was governed by the patriarchate in Moscow in the Soviet Union. That year, although some members of the congregation remained faithful to Moscow, the Russian Orthodox Church of America overthrew Moscow governance. In 1945, when Moscow sent a metropolitan to take over the church, New York passed a statute declaring that the Russian Church of America was the recognized church and entitled to possession of church property. New York's action violated both the Establishment and Free Exercise Clauses, as New York could not legislate which church represented the true faith. As the Orthodox Church was a hierarchical church and the highest authority was the Moscow Patriarchate, its determination of the issue was final. *Kedroff, supra.*

   Two congregations of the Presbyterian Church had grievances against the Church's General Assembly concerning the ordaining of women, taking public positions on moral and social issues, and the teaching of "alien" doctrines. The two congregations voted to withdraw from the Church. The Church responded by directing a takeover of the congregations' property. The congregations sued, and a jury decided that the General Assembly had been guilty of a substantial departure from doctrine and did not have a right to take the property. The Supreme Court reversed, holding that the jury, as an arm of the state, had violated the Establishment and Free Exercise Clauses by passing judgment on tenets of religious doctrine. *Presbyterian Church, supra.*

B. **Determining What Constitutes a Religion:** In order to qualify for a free exercise exemption, when the Constitution either requires it or when the state appropriately accommodates it, an individual must demonstrate that his claim has a religious basis. This suggests that the state must determine the bona fides of the religious claim, either that it is sincerely held or that it stems from a belief which is religious. To do the latter would be to inquire into and to decide what constitutes a religion and whether particular beliefs qualify as religious. This the state cannot do. *United States v. Ballard*, 322 U.S. 78 (1944).

C. **The Religion Clauses and the Conscientious Objection Exemption:** In the Universal Military Training and Selective Service Act of 1948, Congress provided for an exemption from combat service for those who, because of religious training or belief, were opposed to war in any form. The statute defined belief as "a belief in a relation to a Supreme Being involving duties superior to those arising from any human relation," but excluded political, sociological, or philosophical views or a personal moral code. As written, the statute posed serious Establishment Clause and Free Exercise Clause problems. It appeared to distinguish between theistic and nontheistic religions and prefer the former over the latter, in effect establishing theism and punishing, or at least treating discriminatorily, those believing in a nontheistic religion such as Buddhism. The statute also attempted to define what constitutes religious belief. The Court construed the statute in three separate cases, and, in effect, constitutionalized it by reading it in ways to avoid the establishment and free exercise problems.

1. *United States v. Seeger,* 380 U.S. 163 (1965): In *Seeger,* avoiding establishment and free exercise issues, the Court construed a statute to exempt those persons who had a sincere belief against war where the belief was equivalent to, and occupied the same role, as the conscientious objection beliefs of persons believing in God.

2. *Welsh v. United States,* 398 U.S. 333 (1970): In *Welsh,* the claimant refused to characterize his beliefs as religious. As the statute distinguished between religious and other views, it implicitly defined religion. The Court again avoided the problem by construing the statute to mean that a person was a conscientious objector if his objection to war stemmed from beliefs held with the strength of religious convictions.

3. *Gillette v. United States,* 401 U.S. 437 (1971): The issue in *Gillette* involved selective conscientious objection, that is, opposition to some wars, not all wars, as the statute required. As some religions do not oppose all wars, the statutory requirement appeared to favor only those religious beliefs opposed to all wars, as against those more discriminating. This problem the Court resolved directly by holding that the statute had a secular purpose of maintaining a fair system of conscription. There can be many reasons for objecting to particular wars, political and nonconscientious as well as religious and conscientious, and the difficulties in sorting these out administratively involve real dangers of unfair and discriminatory decision-making. The Court also rejected petitioner's free exercise claim, holding the government's interest outweighed the burden on free exercise.

EXAM PREPARATION

CONSTITUTIONAL LAW EXAMINATION ADVICE

Constitutional Law is a survey course, and it is a subject tested on the objective multi-state portion of many bar examinations. Many constitutional law instructors therefore write examinations having both objective and essay portions. Generally speaking, the objective portion tests substantive knowledge of rules and case law, while the essay portion essentially tests the student's skill and understanding in handling constitutional law material. This advice section focuses on answering essay questions.

Law professors vary considerably in their views of what comprises a good or excellent answer to an essay examination question. What constitutes a good answer may also vary with the subject matter tested and the way the particular instructor taught it. For example, some essay examinations are written primarily as "issue-spotting" examinations; some to test the student's ability to work with facts; others yet to test knowledge of the rules and ability to manipulate or use them creatively; others to test the student's ability to draw distinctions and to expand or restrict application of rules; and finally, some essay examinations attempt to test all of these things. The first advice to the law student preparing for an essay examination, therefore, is to talk to the instructor to discover what kind of essay examinations she typically drafts and what she is looking for generally as a well-formed answer.

In writing essay examination questions, professors usually try to draft fact patterns that present a range of issues from the obvious to the subtle. Roughly speaking, when they read students' answers to grade the examinations, they rank papers both by the issues discussed and the quality of the discussion. All other things being equal, an answer that discusses just the obvious issues will get a lower grade than the answer that discusses both obvious and non-obvious issues.

In reading student examination answers, professors are also interested in the quality of the discussion. Some issues in a question may have an answer under existing law; others will not. In either case, the grader's interest is to see whether the student properly identifies, and states, applicable existing law. This is often a baseline – in that the professor grades the answer downward if a student misidentifies or misstates the law.

Law professors also look for specificity in answers. When, for example, a question sets out a statute or regulation with several subsections, the grading professor will examine how discretely a student has worked through the various provisions. Holding quality of discussion constant, they are likely to rank higher the answer that examines the provisions closely and separately over the answer that just speaks generally about the statute or regulation as a whole. Indeed, connecting this grading standard to the one stated above, it is likely that specific statutory provisions or language will contain some of the more subtle issues the professor is looking for to help distinguish between answers.

Often, problem fact statements will be ambiguous or equivocal, or even lack some critical facts. What this means is that the problem is subject to interpretation. Where that is so, the professor looks to see whether the student understood this and dealt with it appropriately. The examiner knows the interpretive problems are there; in fact, she likely put them there deliberately to test a student's facility in handling alternate states of affairs or in demonstrating persuasive argument. Appropriate ways for dealing with the interpretation issue are either to assume alternative interpretations and analyze each or, depending on the problem, to argue that one particular interpretation is the best one, show why, and then apply the law to it. Many students fail to note interpretive problems in examination questions and often attempt to evade the issue by simply assuming or declaring, without any analysis or justifying argument, that the problem is one thing or the other. Most professors downgrade evasion and reward students who try to confront, and work through, the interpretive problems a question presents.

Constitutional law instructors often design constitutional law essay questions to test all the skills and knowledge described above – issue spotting, working with facts, knowledge of particular rules and cases, awareness and sensitive handling of interpretive problems, the ability to argue from facts and cases, to draw analogies, to draw intelligent distinctions, and to argue persuasively for extending or restricting the application of a given rule. They do this primarily by drafting fact patterns presenting debatable issues not yet clearly decided by the Supreme Court – legal problems which as yet have no definitive resolution, but which should have good arguments on both sides.

For example, in *New York Times v. Sullivan,* the Supreme Court held that the First Amendment required a libel plaintiff to prove that a publication was false and the publisher published it knowing its falsity or with reckless disregard of its falsity. The Court later clarified that the rule applied to plaintiffs who were public officials or public figures. But many questions remained about the scope and reach of the new rule, and shortly after the case was decided, one could have framed a nice constitutional law essay question around a fact pattern involving a completely private party suing for invasion of privacy where the information disclosed was true, but which a reasonable person would have found embarrassing to have disclosed. Neither *Sullivan* nor its immediate progeny answer that question or subsidiary questions that fact pattern raises. The libel cases and their rationales, as well as the constitutional status of the right of privacy (albeit of uncertain definition and scope), give rise to good arguments that the *Sullivan* rule should be extended to this situation and good arguments that it shouldn't. Of course, this problem could be complicated in various ways by adding facts suggesting that perhaps the material disclosed was not actually private or that, even though private, it was material of a kind that could possibly be important for the public to know. And so on.

Essentially, until the Supreme Court definitively decides the particular issues such a fact pattern presents, there is no "correct" answer to such a question. Instead, there are better or worse discussions of the problem, better and worse ways to use constitutional law materials to frame a decision resolving the issues the question presents, and perhaps better analyses and predictions of what the Court would likely do with such a case.

In reviewing answers to such questions, the instructor is generally not seeking a "correct" solution but, instead, a well-constructed essay which disposes of each issue by a carefully justified decision (or, as the case may be, depending on the call of the question, a well-defended prediction of how a court would rule or a carefully framed argument). The grade usually doesn't depend on what side the resolution favors on any given issue, but on the quality of the essay's justifications for the positions it takes on issues. Quality essays identify issues, state the best arguments for each side of an issue, decide between those arguments, and justify the decisions by reference to cases or rules, constitutional premises or values, and reasonable inferences from them. In stating "best arguments," the essay invokes stated facts, and reasonable inferences drawn from those facts, to claim and persuasively argue that certain constitutional law precedents or rules apply and are dispositive. Where other precedents or rules seem contrary or to lead in a different direction, the argument seeks to limit their effect or application by drawing distinctions between the situation involved in the essay question and those precedents.

More briefly stated, your aim in answering a constitutional law essay examination should not be to come up with the "correct" answer; it should be to articulate well-reasoned justifications for your decisions on how the issues presented should be resolved. Part of a well-reasoned justification involves noting arguments pro and con, disposing of those arguments you don't find persuasive by explaining why they aren't, and stating persuasive reasons for those arguments and conclusions you accept.

It should also be clear that, in drafting such essay examination questions, constitutional law professors typically seek to create fact patterns raising, as a major focus of the question, undecided points of constitutional law. They sometimes draft their questions after studying the advance sheets for new cases where lower courts have grappled with a puzzling new issue. These are often cases where the Supreme Court precedents, where applied, apparently lead to indeterminate or inconsistent results. Sometimes the question will be based on the facts of one or more cases in which the Supreme Court has granted certiorari but has not yet decided. In fact, one good way to find hypothetical questions to analyze to help you prepare for a constitutional law essay question is to look up in the advance sheets recent lower court decisions on matters of federal constitutional law. You may also find it valuable to look at those cases where petitions for writs of certiorari have been filed, and especially cases where the Court has granted certiorari. Citations to them are easy to find; just look in the current volume of *United States Law Week*.

While it is my view that issue-spotting is somewhat less important in constitutional law essay examinations than issue discussion, it is nonetheless important to be alert to certain issues that appear in many constitutional law cases but may not be immediately obvious, such as standing, state action, statutory construction to avoid constitutional questions, preemption, and the like. Preliminary questions of this kind often need to be resolved before turning to what seems to be the major constitutional issues a question presents.

For example, I once gave a constitutional law essay examination question involving a criminal defense attorney who exercised all her peremptory challenges to strike only women from a jury venire in a rape case – an improbable and somewhat artificial situation. Nevertheless, the major call of the question obviously was whether the holding and reasoning of *Batson v. Kentucky,* which made prosecutorial use of peremptories apparently based on race challengeable, could and should be extended to challenges based on female gender. The problem, however, also raises an important preliminary issue, that of state action: is the action of a private criminal defense attorney, in exercising peremptories authorized by statute, attributable to the state for Fourteenth Amendment state action purposes? Most students identified the *Batson* issue and discussed it at least reasonably well. Quite a few, however, missed the state action issue altogether. It was not that they did not know about the state action requirement, for they recognized it immediately when I pointed it out later. It was rather that the *Batson* issue shouted so loudly that these students didn't listen carefully for further calls in the question.

One further matter of note. Your essay answer to a constitutional law essay question should be responsive to the stated formal call of the question. It makes a considerable difference whether you are asked to answer the question as though you were a judge or court ruling on the issues presented or whether you are asked, in effect, to write a brief or memorandum of points and authorities for one side. In the former case, you are asked to assume a certain objectivity and to take a position reviewing the possible arguments that could be presented on either side of the question. In the latter case, you are asked to be an advocate for one side. That is not to say that you would not, as advocate, anticipate arguments for the other side. You should, of course, do that; it's simply that your emphasis would be different than if you were taking the role of a judge.

In sum, work the facts, work the issues, present arguments for both sides, decide the issues, and justify your decisions by persuasive reference to cases, constitutional principles, and reasoned distinctions between different fact situations.

REVIEW AND EXAMINATION PREPARATION QUESTIONS

I. MULTIPLE CHOICE QUESTIONS

Below you will find a set of fact statements. Each statement is followed by one or two multiple choice questions based on it. Answer all the questions by choosing the BEST answer from the set of four (4) answers. "Best answer," as used here, means the answer which is the best, or most correct, of the four. There may be other, better answers not stated; nonetheless, you should not concern yourself with the best of all possible answers but only with the best of those from which you are asked to choose.

1. Under the terms of an International Treaty known as the Beirut Agreement, to which the United States is a signatory, signatory nations agreed to exempt certain educational, scientific, and cultural materials from customs duties and licensing requirements. In order to qualify for such an exemption, an applicant must obtain certificates – from both the exporting country and the importing country – that the materials are of an educational, scientific, or cultural character. In the United States, the United States Information Agency (USIA) is the certifying agency. USIA has refused to give an exporting country certification to several films produced in the United States: *Save the Planet*, which deals with the debate over nuclear power; *The Secret Agent*, which examines the United States' use of Agent Orange during the Vietnam War; and *From the Ashes*, which is about the Nicaraguan National Liberation Movement, the revolution, and the history of U.S.–Nicaraguan relations. The USIA based its refusal on criteria set out in USIA regulations, concluding that the films "espoused a cause," were "inaccurate," and "were capable of being misinterpreted by foreign audiences lacking adequate American points of reference."

    Plaintiffs, the producers of these films, have filed suit in federal court alleging the foregoing facts and challenging the validity of the regulations the USIA used to deny certification. The Government has moved to dismiss on the ground that plaintiffs lack standing.

    The court should:

    (a) grant the motion because the plaintiffs have alleged no injury in fact;

    (b) grant the motion because even if the plaintiffs win there is no certainty importing countries will grant customs and licensing exemptions to the films;

    (c) deny the motion because the plaintiffs' films will be at a competitive disadvantage in foreign markets relative to other American films that receive customs and licensing exemption certificates;

    (d) deny the motion because plaintiffs have alleged injury to their ideological interests.

2. Assume that the Association of American Film Producers, of which the film-producer-plaintiffs are not members, is an additional party plaintiff in the suit in the foregoing question. The AAFP is a nonprofit corporation organized to promote the interests of American film producers. On a challenge to AAFP standing,

    The court should:

    (a) hold that AAFP has no standing because it is not seeking to represent the interests of any of its members before the court;

(b) hold that AAFP has no standing because there is no evident injury in fact to its interests;

(c) hold that AAFP has standing because it may lose membership if it fails to litigate the interests of American film producers whether or not they are Association members;

(d) hold that AAFP has standing because it has members who may produce films which the USIA might not certify under its current regulations.

3. The State of Georgia owns and partially funds a farmers' market known as the Columbus Farmers Market. Persons wishing to sell farm products at the market rent space in it. The market has two separate selling areas. One area, the "elevated-shed" area, is by far the better and more profitable selling area in the market. It is covered and provides protection from sun and rain, has better customer parking, and is more accessible to farmers for loading and unloading their products.

While Georgia originally made "elevated-shed" area space available on a first-come, first-served basis, last year it adopted a regulation giving "elevated-shed" preference to Georgia farmers.

Smith is an Alabama farmer who has been selling from an elevated shed at the Columbus market for five years. Under the new rule, however, Smith has been forced to move to the disadvantageous selling area. He has now sued the State of Georgia, alleging various constitutional violations.

Smith's best argument is:

(a) The Georgia rule is a protectionist measure facially discriminating against interstate commerce, and the state is unable to justify the discrimination;

(b) The Georgia rule infringes Smith's federal privileges and immunities;

(c) The Georgia rule denies equal protection by irrationally preferring Georgia over non-Georgia residents;

(d) The Georgia rule, while not barring out-of-state commerce, imposes a substantial and unjustifiable burden on it.

4. In the foregoing problem, Georgia's best argument is:

(a) Georgia has not prohibited or limited the flow of trade across its borders, for Smith can continue to sell his goods;

(b) Federal privileges and immunities are not involved in situations like this;

(c) By creating a tax-supported market, Georgia is acting as a market participant and can prefer its own residents;

(d) Georgia's preference for its own producers is a rational means of achieving the state goal of benefiting state taxpayers.

5. Illinois has a statute which provides that any contractor on "any public works project or improvement for the State of Illinois or any political subdivision, municipal corporation or other governmental unit thereof shall employ only Illinois laborers on such project or

improvement." The statute has an exemption in cases in which "the contractor certifies, and the contracting officer finds, that Illinois laborers either are not available, or are incapable of performing the particular type of work involved." Violation of the statute is a misdemeanor punishable by 30 days in jail or a fine of $500.

The public school board of Decatur, Illinois, using donated funds, hired the Window Company, an Illinois corporation, to replace some windows. Window, without the required certification and finding, subcontracted the work to Custom Contracting, an unincorporated Missouri association made up of ten Missouri residents who perform Custom's contracts. On hearing that the Director of the Illinois Department of Labor planned to file suit against them asking that they be enjoined from violating the law, Window and Custom immediately sued Illinois seeking a declaration that the statute was unconstitutional under the Commerce Clause, Article IV, § 2 Privileges and Immunities Clause, and the Equal Protection Clause of the Fourteenth Amendment.

On a standing challenge, the court should hold that:

    (a) Even though Window is an Illinois resident, it is derivatively injured and may assert the privileges and immunities claim;

    (b) Window has standing to assert the equal protection claim;

    (c) Custom has standing to invoke the Privileges and Immunities Clause for itself;

    (d) Custom can invoke the Privileges and Immunities Clause for its members.

6. In the foregoing problem, the court should also:

    (a) hold that under the market participant doctrine, Illinois may prefer its own residents in public employment and sustain the statute;

    (b) hold that given the scope of the statute, Illinois is a market regulator rather than a market participant, and overturn the statute;

    (c) hold that under the Equal Protection Clause, states cannot prefer their citizens in the award of any benefits and overturn the statute;

    (d) hold that it doesn't understand any of this stuff and ask the parties to please go away.

7. The Adolescent Family Life Act of 1981 provides for federal grants to public and private health care and other institutions to support programs aimed at preventing adolescent pregnancies and to promote adoption of children delivered by pregnant adolescents not wishing to care for them. The statute provides, however, that:

"Grants or payments may be made only to programs or projects which do not provide abortions or abortion counseling or referral, or which do not subcontract with or make any payment to any person who provides abortions or abortion counseling or referral, except that any such program or project may provide referral for abortion counseling to a pregnant adolescent if such adolescent and the parents or guardians of such adolescent request such referral; and grants may be made only to projects or programs which do not advocate, promote, or encourage abortion."

This provision of the statute is:

(a) unconstitutional because the First Amendment encompasses a right to receive information and ideas, and the statute, by skewing information through viewpoint subsidization and limiting the information pregnant teenagers receive, violates their right to receive information;

(b) constitutional because the government can be a speaker, has a right to speak and indoctrinate, and can promote certain ideas over others;

(c) unconstitutional because AFLA effectively constitutes a limited public forum for speech on a particular topic, and the government cannot exclude speakers from it on the basis of their message;

(d) constitutional because the statute is not a restriction on the free flow of information, but simply reflects a government refusal to subsidize speech with which it disagrees.

8. State *X* imposes a sales tax on all periodicals except "(1) periodicals that are published or distributed by a religious faith and that consist wholly of writings promulgating the teaching of the faith and books that consist wholly of writings sacred to a religious faith; and (2) periodicals sold by charitable organizations." *State X Monthly* magazine, which is a completely secular publication, is subject to this periodicals sales tax and has brought suit to invalidate it.

The tax exemption:

(a) violates the Establishment Clause;

(b) is compelled by the Free Exercise Clause;

(c) violates the Free Press Clause because it discriminates between publications on the basis of their content;

(d) is an accommodation of religion permissible under the Establishment Clause.

9. The Maryland Chapter of the Invisible Empire of the Knights of the Ku Klux Klan applied for a permit to parade on the streets of Thurmont, Maryland. After some delay, the Mayor, whose duty it was to issue such permits, agreed to grant the permit on the condition that the Ku Klux Klan open up the parade itself to participants of all races and religions. The KKK objected, stating that it had requested a parade for only "card-carrying" members of the KKK, which consists only of white Christians.

The imposed condition is:

(a) constitutional because Thurmont city streets are public fora, and the city may not discriminate against any speakers in their use of the fora;

(b) unconstitutional because the Mayor used standardless discretion in imposing the condition;

(c) constitutional because Thurmont has a compelling interest in ensuring that there is no racial, ethnic, or religious discrimination against its residents;

(d) unconstitutional because the condition violates the KKK members' rights of association.

10. The local county Grand Jury is conducting an investigation of the union corruption in the building trades. The investigation of union corruption has focused primarily on high ranking union officers, but, the prosecutor working with the Grand Jury told jury members she assumed that some rank-and-file union members might become targets of the investigation. Pursuant to her suggestion, the Grand Jury issued subpoenas for the membership lists of four union locals. The subpoenas request that each local provide a list of its members' names, addresses, and telephone and social security numbers. The subpoenas should be:

   (a) enforced because the information sought may be relevant and useful to the underlying investigation;

   (b) quashed because the subpoena requests are overbroad;

   (c) enforced because unlike *NAACP v. Alabama,* there is no showing of possible harassment and there is a compelling need for the information;

   (d) quashed because the subpoena requests violate the union members' associational rights.

11. Assume that the Student Conduct Legislative Council on a public university campus is proposing to adopt an amendment to the Student Conduct Code which would ban "harassment by vilification." The draft amendment reads:

   "Any student who, intending to hurt or harass, makes a personal attack by directly addressing to another words, pictures or symbols that are commonly understood to convey, in a direct and visceral way, hatred or contempt for human beings on the basis of the sex, race, color, handicap, religion, sexual orientation, or national and ethnic origin commits the student conduct offense of harassment by vilification and is subject to disciplinary action as otherwise provided in this code."

   The proposed amendment is:

   (a) constitutional because the University has a compelling interest in diversity, protecting students from discriminatory harassment and maintaining standards of decorum in speech;

   (b) unconstitutional because it is vague;

   (c) constitutional because the proposed amendment simply embodies and updates the "fighting words" doctrine;

   (d) unconstitutional because the state may not proscribe or punish speech merely because it is offensive.

12. Randy and Alice Blackwelder are the parents of two grade-school-age children, Carmon and Kathy. New York, where they live, permits "homeschooling." In other words, New York permits parents to educate their children at home provided that certain standards regarding teaching, subject matters, and testing are met. Specifically, New York requires that children schooled at home receive instruction in basic subjects such as arithmetic, reading, spelling, writing, English, geography, history, science, civics, conservation, health and sex education, music, visual arts, and physical education. New York also requires that a team of local school district representatives conduct a preapproval scheduled visit at the home where homeschooling is to take place and that the team conduct one or two scheduled on-site inspections during the school year.

The Blackwelders wish to give their children a "Christian education" at home. They contend that allowing their children to attend public schools, where religion is not integrated into studies, would violate their religious beliefs. They further assert that the New York state homeschooling requirements, including the subjects of instruction, testing, and the necessary state supervision violate their religious beliefs. In their sincere view, fulfilling the state requirements would violate their religious beliefs by requiring them to teach their children matters their religion forbids them to teach and by allowing the state to review "God's work."

New York:

(a) must, on the reasoning of *Wisconsin v. Yoder,* grant the Blackwelders an exemption from statutory homeschooling requirements;

(b) must, before denying the Blackwelders an exemption, exhaust other, less restrictive alternatives;

(c) may, for accommodation reasons, grant the Blackwelders an exemption;

(d) must, for Establishment Clause reasons, deny the Blackwelders an exemption.

13. The Washoe County, Nevada School District has a written policy which permits community groups to use school facilities. The policy provides that "the district's facilities shall be open to organizations for public, literary, scientific, recreational or educational meetings, or for discussions of matters of general or public interest, and community groups shall be permitted and encouraged to use school facilities for worthwhile purposes."

Northgate Community Church is an unincorporated association organized as a church. It is a relatively new church and has no facilities of its own but has been meeting for Sunday services and Sunday school at the Washoe County Oddfellows Hall. Northgate asked the School District to permit it to use a District high school auditorium for regular and permanent Sunday Church services and Sunday school, but the School District has refused.

The School District's action is:

(a) constitutional as applied;

(b) unconstitutional because it is a content-based exclusion;

(c) constitutional because the District policy did not create a public forum by designation;

(d) unconstitutional because it was taken pursuant to a regulation which conferred standardless discretion.

14. (The following fact pattern is the basis of multiple choice questions 14 and 15. Answer both.)

Escort services are companies which provide their clientele with companions or "escorts" for a fee – in effect, escorts are paid dates. Clark County, Nevada was concerned about the large number of "escort services" operating there, fearing that many of them were little more than prostitution agencies. Consequently, it adopted a regulation to license and control escort services. The regulation distinguishes between "service-oriented" and "sexually-oriented" escorts and escort bureaus. The former are permitted and the latter proscribed.

Under the regulation, a "service-oriented escort" is an escort which "does not advertise that sexual conduct will be provided to the patron and does not offer to provide sexual conduct." A "sexually-oriented escort" is an escort which "advertises that sexual conduct will be provided; or solicits offers to provide or does provide acts of sexual conduct to an escort patron."

The regulation defines "an offer to provide acts of sexual conduct" so as to include "all conversations, advertisements, and acts which would lead a reasonably prudent person to conclude such acts were to be provided." Finally, the regulation defines sexual conduct as "the engaging in or commission of an act of sexual intercourse, oral-genital contact or the touching of the sexual organs, pubic region, buttock or female breast of a person for the purpose of arousing or gratifying the sexual desire of another person."

The regulation is:

(a) unconstitutional because it seeks to regulate the freedoms of intimate and expressive association;

(b) constitutional because it regulates what is essentially a commercial transaction;

(c) unconstitutional because it regulates truthful advertising;

(d) constitutional because the regulation is aimed primarily at conduct the county can outlaw and the speech proscription is a means of achieving that end.

15. The regulation is:

(a) facially overbroad and vague and therefore unconstitutional;

(b) not substantially overbroad or vague on its face and therefore not constitutionally challengeable by one whose conduct the statute properly reaches;

(c) basically an obscenity regulation and therefore constitutional;

(d) simply a regulation of commercial speech and therefore not susceptible to an overbreadth challenge.

16. An Indiana statute provides that in order to receive county poor relief, an indigent had to reside in the state for three continuous years and in the county for one continuous year. The statute's three-year residency requirement is:

(a) constitutional because the Court does not require a state to support poor persons from out of state;

(b) unconstitutional on its face as a denial of equal protection through imposition of a penalty on the exercise of the right to travel;

(c) constitutional because rationally related to state interests of saving money and deterring fraud;

(d) unconstitutional as a denial of due process.

17. As applied to an Indiana resident who has lived in the state for five years, but in the county of application for only six months, the foregoing statute is:

(a) constitutional because rationally related to state interests of saving money and deterring fraud;

(b) unconstitutional because it denies a fundamental right to travel;

(c) constitutional because the statute deals with social and economic legislation;

(d) unconstitutional because it could not be applied to indigents migrating interstate and therefore irrationally discriminates against intrastate migrants.

18. A federal statute regulates federally provided life insurance benefits for deceased service personnel where no beneficiary is designated. The state treats illegitimate posthumous children of insured servicemen differently than similarly situated legitimate children. In order for a posthumous illegitimate child to receive benefits, the alleged father must either have acknowledged the child in writing; have been named, with his knowledge, as father on a birth certificate or other public record; or have been judicially declared the father. As applied to a servicemen's illegitimate child who lacks the statutorily required proof of fatherhood, the statute is:

(a) unconstitutional because not substantially related to an important governmental objective;

(b) constitutional because the statute does not discriminate against illegitimates;

(c) unconstitutional because the statute denies an illegitimate child the opportunity to prove paternity at a hearing;

(d) constitutional because reasonably well-tailored to the governmental objectives of deterring fraudulent claims and administrative efficiency.

19. City authorities closed two "adult" movie theaters in Denver, Colorado after a hearing in which the City Attorneys proved that many public sex acts had taken place regularly in the dimly lit theater areas. As part of its proof, the City showed over 200 citations of theater patrons for acts of masturbation, fellatio, and sexual intercourse in the theaters. The theater owners argue that the closings are unconstitutional because their theaters are devoted to showing films which are protected First Amendment expression. The theater closings are:

(a) constitutional, as actions directed to conduct and having only an indirect effect on speech;

(b) unconstitutional because the closures impact heavily on free speech activities;

(c) constitutional because there was a prior hearing;

(d) unconstitutional because obviously motivated by a desire to prevent the showing of sexually explicit films.

20. Ten federal statutes presently authorize *qui tam* actions. *Qui tam* actions, a part of the American colonial tradition, and initially adopted by the First Congress, authorize private citizens to prosecute other private citizens, for a bounty, for violations of certain federal statutes. *Qui tam* actions are:

(a) unconstitutional because prosecution is an executive power, and it would violate separations of powers principles for Congress to attempt to confer executive power on private citizens;

(b) constitutional because the enforcement of *qui tam* actions does not trench on critical executive functions;

(c) constitutional because Congress has the authority to regulate civil and criminal prosecutions;

(d) unconstitutional because it interferes with judicial power to oversee enforcement of statutes.

21. The Child Protection and Obscenity Enforcement Act makes criminal the production and distribution of sexually explicit images of nude children, where the model is under 18 years old. Among other things, the statute authorizes civil forfeiture of any "property, real, or personal, used or intended to be used to commit or to promote the commission" of the offense. The statute allows preliminary seizure of such property through a warrant issued on an *ex parte* showing of probable cause. The civil seizure and forfeiture provision is:

(a) constitutional because sexually explicit depictions of children are not constitutionally protected First Amendment expression;

(b) unconstitutional because they allow the government to seize materials protected by the First Amendment;

(c) constitutional because Fourth Amendment search and seizure requirements are satisfied;

(d) unconstitutional because it authorizes a wholesale seizure of possibly protected materials without a prior judicial authorization of obscenity following an adversary hearing.

22. A Utah statute provides that a divorced person having an outstanding, unpaid support obligation to a prior spouse cannot enter a lawful marriage. Cooper, a divorced Utah resident owing support to his former spouse, remarried. Having discovered that his marriage was not lawful in Utah, he filed suit in federal district court seeking a declaration that the Utah statute was unconstitutional and that his marriage was lawful. Cooper should:

(a) lose, because the state statute regulates social matters and is therefore subject only to rational basis scrutiny;

(b) win, because the state statute denies him a liberty interest without a prior hearing;

(c) win, because the statute denies equal protection and due process;

(d) lose, because states have substantial interests in their marriage laws and protecting former spouses and children of lawful marriages.

23. Rose Erhard was director of the Western Office of the Massachusetts Secretary of State. Erhard's position, which was not a civil service position, among other things involved her in public affairs activities of the office, providing information to, and doing some

casework service for, voters and also providing referral services by directing citizens' problems and inquiries to the proper agency. Erhard did not have any formal policy-making authority but was a participant in some policy discussions. For example, she attended monthly Directors' meetings at which the Secretary's future political strategy was discussed. The Secretary dismissed Erhard after, and because, she expressed opposition to the Governor at a local political meeting. Erhard's dismissal is:

(a)   unconstitutional because it violates her First Amendment rights of expression;

(b)   constitutional because she was in a noncivil service position;

(c)   unconstitutional because she had a property interest in her position which precluded firing her without cause and without a prior hearing;

(d)   constitutional because her position was one which legitimately required political affiliation or loyalty.

24.   Wisconsin provides that prospective adoptive parents may, after a child placed in their home has been there six months or more, petition to adopt the child. If, during the six months after placement, the agency placing the child wishes to remove it from the home, it may do so without a preremoval hearing. The prospective parents are, however, entitled to a hearing after removal. Catholic Social Services placed a child in the Thelens' home but removed the child four months later following an investigation into a report that the prospective mother, Laura Thelen, had an adulterous relationship with a man who later committed suicide in her presence. The Thelens, who wish to adopt the child, have filed suit, alleging a violation of constitutional rights. The Thelens should:

(a) win, because they have been deprived of their liberty interest in the preadoptive family unit without due process of law;

(b) lose, because the state has a compelling interest in seeing that the best interests of the child are served, and a post-removal hearing is adequate to protect the Thelens' interests under the circumstances;

(c) win, because in this case the state procedure authorizes what amounts to an establishment of religion;

(d) lose, because the Thelens have no vested interest of any kind in the child.

25.   Daley Plaza in Chicago is a large, open public space. The Chicago Building Commission has opened the Plaza to cultural, political, ethnic, musical, commercial, military, and educational uses. It has also permitted many demonstrations, rallies, celebrations, exhibits, displays, and other types of events on the Plaza. A Jewish group wishes to erect a succah, a Jewish religious symbol, on the Plaza for a period of eight days, in observance of the eight-day Feast of Tabernacles (Succot) to which the succah relates. During this holiday, observant Jews eat outdoors in the succah, a temporary hut, symbolizing the manner in which the ancient Hebrews lived during the forty years spent wandering in the desert. The exhibit would be approximately 20-feet square and have an eight-foot-high hut and a temporary house. The house would have posted on it a sign saying "Lunch with the Rabbis." Chicago should:

(a) permit the group to erect its display because the Daley Plaza is a completely open public forum;

(b) deny the group permission to erect the display because doing so would raise Establishment Clause problems;

(c) permit the display because of its overwhelmingly secular character;

(d) deny permission because the display is incompatible with other uses of the Plaza.

26. Minneapolis has adopted an ordinance providing that adults-only bookstores may locate only within the B4 Central Business District, a district 375 acres in size and comprising 150 blocks. Further, adults-only bookstore restrictions, preventing such businesses from locating within 500 feet of other specified uses, also limit adults-only bookstore locations within the Central Business District. The ordinance defines a regulated bookstore as "an establishment having as a substantial or significant portion of its stock in trade, books, magazines [or other material] characterized by their principal emphasis on matters depicting, describing, or relating to nudity, sexual conduct, sexual excitement or sadomasochistic abuse." The ordinance further provides for administrative enforcement. The ordinance is:

(a) constitutional because it regulates the secondary effects of sexually explicit expression;

(b) unconstitutionally vague;

(c) constitutional because it leaves adequate opportunities to publish, sell, and distribute sexually explicit expression;

(d) unconstitutional because it reaches protected First Amendment expression.

27. Purdy School District, a rural district located in Southwestern Missouri, has always had a rule prohibiting dancing on school property. While the original motivation behind the rule is unknown, religion is an important force in the Purdy area. Over the years, various groups have unsuccessfully sought to change the no-dance rule. Most recently, a community group that wanted to assist a student organization to sponsor a dance at the high school proposed that the Board of Education change the rule. At a Board meeting on the question, several ministers who had organized community members to attend the meeting, appeared to voice opposition to the proposed change. Following the meeting, the Board voted unanimously, without discussion, to leave the rule as it was. The no-dancing rule is:

(a) an unconstitutional establishment of religion;

(b) constitutional because school officials have considerable discretion regarding education and the use of school facilities;

(c) constitutional because the rule has evident secular purposes and does not have the effect of establishing religion or entangling government in it;

(d) constitutional because the Board's motivation in refusing to change the rule is constitutionally irrelevant.

28. In one of the immigration statutes, Congress provided that children, born outside the United States, of male, but not female, American citizens were also American citizens. While the law was amended in 1934 to provide that female, as well as male, citizens could transmit American citizenship to foreign-born children, the amendment was not

retroactive. Ms. Elias was born in Canada in 1921 of an American mother and a Canadian father. She applied for an American passport but was denied on the ground she was not a United States citizen. She has filed suit in federal district court seeking a declaration that she is an American citizen notwithstanding the statute's applicability to her. She should:

(a) win, because the Court will, under the circumstances, apply more than minimal scrutiny in reviewing the statutory denial of citizenship;

(b) lose, because Congress' control over immigration is plenary;

(c) lose, because the original rule was designed to discourage American women from having children abroad and is therefore rational;

(d) win, because the classification is irrational.

29. Jones applied to the City of Fort Smith for permission to build a convenience store to be associated with a gasoline station he was already operating on Phoenix Avenue. City officials responded that, under City ordinances, they could not give him permission unless he granted the City an expanded right-of-way along his property fronting the street, for purposes of street expansion. He refused and brought suit to enjoin the application of the ordinances to him. The City's proposed action is:

(a) a constitutional police power zoning regulation;

(b) a permissible conditional exaction;

(c) an unconstitutional taking of private property for a public use without just compensation;

(d) constitutional because plaintiff's property will receive a reciprocal advantage.

30. Operation Rescue is an anti-abortion organization. Among other things, it organizes picketing of, and demonstrations at, abortion clinics. Operation Rescue picketed and demonstrated at abortion clinics in New York City. On a number of occasions, Rescue members tried to block clinic entrances, filled clinic offices, screamed epithets at women seeking to enter the clinics, and engaged in other activities designed to deter women from entering the clinics. In these actions, Operation Rescue members asserted they were expressing their beliefs that abortion was morally wrong. The National Organization for Women sued and obtained a permanent injunction against Operation Rescue. The injunction enjoined defendants from "(a) trespassing on, blocking, or obstructing egress from any facility at which abortions are performed; (b) physically abusing or tortiously harassing persons entering or leaving such facilities. The injunction specifically permitted "sidewalk counseling, consisting of reasonably quiet conversation of a nonthreatening nature by not more than two people." The injunction is:

(a) an unconstitutional overbroad restriction, reaching protected First Amendment activities;

(b) an unconstitutional content-based regulation of speech;

(c) a constitutional regulation of conduct alone;

(d) a constitutional time, place, and manner regulation of expressive conduct and other First Amendment activities.

ANSWERS TO MULTIPLE CHOICE QUESTIONS

1.	c.	16.	b.
2.	d.	17.	d.
3.	a.	18.	d.
4.	c.	19.	a.
5.	d.	20.	b.
6.	b.	21.	d.
7.	d.	22.	c.
8.	a.	23.	d.
9.	d.	24.	b.
10.	c.	25.	a.
11.	d.	26.	b.
12.	d.	27.	c.
13.	a.	28.	d.
14.	d.	29.	c.
15.	d.	30.	d.

EP

II. ESSAY QUESTIONS

Below you will find three sets of essay questions to test your constitutional law knowledge and your ability to use constitutional law materials. The first set of essay questions, ten in all, was complied from decided cases. The cases themselves provide generally good discussions of the issues and arguments and appropriate reference to relevant case law and controlling principles. Once you have sketched out your response, you can turn to the case to compare your understanding with that of a federal court. You will find the citations for these cases at the end of Section **A**.

In Section **B**, you will find a second set of essay questions, four in all. These were compiled from constitutional law examinations and bar examinations. Following this set of questions you will find essay answers discussing them.

In Section **C**, you will find a third and final set of essay questions, five in all. I provide no answers for these, and you may find it useful to work through them and discuss them with your classmates or study partners.

A. Essay Questions from Decided Cases

1. Delaware passed a law, called the Coastal Zone Act, "to control the location, extent, and type of industrial development in Delaware's coastal areas" in order to "better protect the natural environment of its bay and coastal areas and safeguard their use primarily for recreation and tourism." Among other provisions, the Act totally bans new offshore gas, liquid, or solid bulk product transfers.

    Norfolk Southern Corp., a coal shipping company, applied for a Delaware permit to establish a coal "topping-off" facility at Big Stone Anchorage in Delaware. Because of the shallow depth of most East Coast ports, Norfolk Southern was unable to load its coal ships fully and, instead, shipped coal to foreign countries in partially loaded ships. Big Stone Anchorage, however, has a depth of 55 feet, deep enough for fully loaded coal ships; indeed, Norfolk Southern believed it was the only East Coast location capable of handling its fully loaded ships. It thus proposed to establish a facility there to receive its coal ships, partially loaded with coal in other East coast ports; and then add coal, or "top-off," to make a full load.

In its permit application, Norfolk Southern noted that coal topping-off was the most efficient means of exporting coal and that it would reduce the per-unit transportation cost of United States coal, making it more competitive on the world market. It also claimed that the facility would enable it to export an additional three million tons of coal a year. Finally, it asserted that increased exports of coal would improve the United States' balance of payments by $150 million a year and lead to increased employment at coal mines, on railroad lines transporting coal, and at East Coast ports.

As a part of its consideration of the permit request, Delaware commissioned an environmental study of the effects of the proposed facility. The study concluded that the operation would discharge 252 tons of coal dust into Delaware Bay annually, that it would routinely spill coal into the Bay, and that it would measurably degrade air quality in the area. Norfolk Southern submitted affidavits from its experts which asserted that only one and one-half tons of coal dust would be discharged into Delaware Bay, and that the operation would not be a significant source of toxic pollutants.

The Delaware State Coastal Zone Industrial Control Board determined that the coal top-off service was a "bulk product transfer facility" within the meaning of the Coastal Act and denied Northern Suffolk a permit.

Is Delaware's Coastal Zone Act constitutional as applied to Norfolk Southern?

2. In 1985, Virginia amended its Highway Code to provide that any motor vehicle engaged in "either escorting, or towing overdimensional materials, equipment, [or] boats" must carry high intensity amber flashing lights, visible for at least 500 feet. As used in the statute, the term "overdimensional" refers to freight having a width greater than 102 inches.

Virtually all the states have highway statutes regulating overdimensional loads. These statutes vary greatly from state to state. Maryland bans flashing lights on such loads. California, Texas, and Tennessee require lights different than those called for by Virginia.

In addition, Congress has established a scheme of highway safety regulation. In the Motor Carrier Safety Act, Congress statutorily imposed some safety regulations and authorized the Secretary of Transportation to promulgate others. One part of the statute reads: "Notwithstanding the provisions of this section or any other provision of law, a State may grant special use permits to motor vehicles that exceed 102 inches in width."

Before promulgating regulations, the statute directed the Secretary to "consider state laws and regulations pertaining to commercial motor vehicle safety in order to minimize unnecessary preemption. As finally issued, the regulation covering lighting equipment requires that "[all] exterior lighting devices shall be of a steady-burning type." The regulations also have a section dealing with projecting loads and call for equipping them with "dimension or marker lights, red or orange fluorescent flags, and a warning sign."

Acme Trucking Association is a nonprofit association composed of haulers of heavy and oversized machinery, equipment, building materials, and supplies. On behalf of its members, it filed suit in federal district court challenging the constitutionality of the Virginia statute. Acme alleged that the lights the statute requires, when installed, cost approximately $220, and that the lack of uniformity as between states regarding regulation of overdimensional loads meant that interstate traffic would be subjected to multiple, costly, inconsistent requirements. It contended that the Virginia statute violated the Supremacy Clause, Congress having preempted the field, and that the statute imposed an unreasonable burden on interstate commerce in violation of the Commerce Clause.

What result and why?

3. In the Submerged Lands Act, Congress conveyed to the states title to the land underlying the nation's harbors and seas from the high-tide mark to the three-mile limit. In California, the State Lands Commission administers the tidelands and submerged lands. California law authorizes the Commission to lease such lands on terms it deems to be in the best interests of the state.

   California leases some of these lands, which the state has not improved in any way, to oil companies which own and operate refineries on the California coast. The leases hold the oil companies responsible for any environmental damages caused by their use of the lands and require that the companies post a surety bond and public liability insurance.

   The oil companies have constructed oil pipeline facilities on the lands in order to offload crude oil transported by tanker to the refineries for processing. Approximately 95% of the oil entering the pipeline facilities is of foreign origin, and depending on the vagaries of demand, between 46–98% of the refined products leaving the refineries move into interstate or foreign commerce.

   When it initially leased the lands, California charged a flat annual rate of six percent of the appraised value of the land. Recently, however, the state enacted a statute which raised the basic annual rate to eight percent and added an additional charge, known as the "volumetric" rate, which was based on the volume of oil passing through the pipelines. These changes were designed to bring leasing policies and charges in line with those commonly used by California ports.

   Some oil companies negotiated leases under the new schedule, and an analysis of the leases and projected throughput volumes discloses that new charges California imposes will equal annual rates of return on the appraised values of the respective leased lands ranging from 12.5% to 29%.

   An association of oil companies representing the refineries which lease the submerged lands from California have now sued the state, asserting that California's volumetric rate violates the Commerce Clause.

   Does it?

4. Blackstone Valley Disposal, a Massachusetts company, is a commercial hauler of refuse, trash, and other solid waste and does business both in Massachusetts and Rhode Island. In 1974, Rhode Island created a public agency, the Rhode Island Solid Waste Management Corporation (R.I. Solid Waste), to plan, construct, operate, and maintain a state-wide system of solid waste management facilities and services. In 1980, this public agency, using funds raised through issuance of tax-exempt bonds, purchased the Central Landfill, the largest sanitary landfill in New England, and the only such landfill in Rhode Island which accepts all kinds of nonhazardous solid waste. In 1985, when the last privately owned sanitary landfills in Rhode Island reached capacity and closed, the Central Landfill remained as the only nonhazardous, solid-waste sanitary landfill in Rhode Island. There are now, however, at least four pending applications for new private sanitary landfills.

   In 1987, Blackstone and R.I. Solid Waste agreed to allow Blackstone to dispose of its collections, regardless of state of origin, at the Central Landfill. That same year, Blackstone used the Central Landfill to dispose of approximately 400 tons of solid waste it collected in Massachusetts and Rhode Island. In 1988, however, Rhode Island enacted a statute prohibiting the disposal of out-of-state waste at the Central Landfill. R.I. Solid Waste then notified Blackstone that it would refuse to accept any more Massachusetts waste.

Blackstone has now sued in federal district court alleging that the statute is unconstitutional. Is it?

5. Montana has 25% of the United States' coal reserves. Much of Montana's coal is low-sulfur coal which, when burned, produces less sulfur pollutant than other coal. Low-sulfur coal is therefore much in demand for use in coal-burning electricity-generating plants, which can use the coal without the installation of expensive anti-pollution devices.

    Ninety percent of Montana's coal is shipped out-of-state while 10% is used in state. Montana imposes a tax on the severance of coal, whether mined on state or private lands. The tax equals 30% of the contract sales price of the coal, substantially higher than similar coal severance taxes imposed by other states. Montana uses the proceeds to help fund state government, and the tax produces almost 20% of the state's revenue.

    The test the United States Supreme Court uses to determine the constitutionality of state taxation of interstate commerce is as follows: to be constitutional, a state tax on interstate commerce must "be applied to an activity with a substantial nexus with the taxing State, [must be] fairly apportioned, [must] not discriminate against interstate commerce, and [must be] fairly related to services provided by the state."

    Assume that purchasers of Montana coal sue in federal district court to overturn the coal severance tax. Restricting yourself to the issue of discrimination, does Montana's coal severance tax discriminate against interstate commerce?

6. Woodward was an aviator in the United States Naval Reserve. At the time of his original enlistment, he noted in his fitness questionnaire that he "was sexually attracted to, or desired, sexual activity with" members of his own sex, but that he had never engaged in homosexual conduct. Notwithstanding this statement, he was accepted into the Reserve, completed flight school, and was assigned to a squadron in the Philippines.

    While stationed in the Philippines, Woodward visited the Officer's Club with an enlisted man awaiting discharge on grounds of homosexuality. Woodward's commanding officer questioned him about the incident, and Woodward admitted homosexual tendencies but denied having had homosexual sexual relations. He also stated that he would continue to associate with other homosexuals.

    The Commanding Officer wrote to the Chief of Naval Personnel recommending Woodward's discharge. Normally, the Naval Personnel Office would not conduct a transfer deactivation review except on regularly scheduled occasions. When the Office reviewed Woodward's field performance records, it discovered that he had received poor fitness reports prior to the incident at the Officer's club. His ratings were so low that he fell below the cut-off point for retention as a reservist.

    The Navy decided not to discharge Woodward but instead to release him from active duty. He then served without pay in an inactive reserve status. By the time his six-year service term ended, he had been twice passed over for promotion, and the Navy then discharged him.

    Woodward has brought an action in United States District Court seeking back pay and reinstatement to active status. He alleges that his release from active status had violated his constitutional rights of freedom of association, due process, and equal protection.

Write a memorandum resolving the constitutional issues which Woodward's case presents.

7. Several plaintiffs, as detailed below, have filed suit seeking a declaratory judgment that the Anti-Terrorist Act (see précis of the Act, below) violates their rights of free speech and association.

Ibrahim Abu-Lughod, a United States citizen, is Chairman of the Political Science Department at Northwestern University in Evanston, Illinois. He asserts that he has been asked to attend various meetings throughout the United States to explain the position and views of the Palestine Liberation Organization (PLO) on the current situation in the Middle East but is unable to do so unless his travel expenses are reimbursed by the PLO. Victor A. Ajlouny, also a United States citizen, similarly declares that the Palestine Red Crescent Society, a constituent group of the PLO, has requested that he undertake a series of speaking engagements in the United States with its funds. He, too, declares he is unable to do so unless his travel expenses are paid. Lughod and Ajlouny therefore claim that the ATA impermissibly forecloses their right to solicit and receive funds from the PLO in order to facilitate the exchange of views and information.

Nubar Hovsepian, also a United States citizen, asserts that the PLO has requested that he establish and maintain an office in the United States to gather, write, and disseminate materials on the subject of Palestinian people. He also declares that the PLO has requested him to arrange, through that office, for speakers and forums in which these subjects will be discussed. He has sworn that he is prepared to open the office immediately, has laid out his initial plans for the office's undertakings, and has received a commitment from individuals for the necessary funding, contingent only on the determination that it would be lawful under the ATA to open the office. According to Hovsepian, "this office will not be authorized to present official views and positions of the PLO, to speak on behalf of the PLO or to represent the PLO."

Is the Anti-Terrorist Act constitutional as applied to these plaintiffs?

---

*The Anti-Terrorist Act

(a) The Congress finds that –

    (1) Middle East terrorism accounted for 60 percent of total international terrorism in 1985;

    (2) The Palestine Liberation Organization (hereafter in this title referred to as the "PLO") was directly responsible for the murder of an American citizen on the Achille Llauro cruise liner in 1985, and a member of the PLO's Executive Committee is under indictment in the United States for the murder of that American citizen;

    (3) the head of the PLO has been implicated in the murder of a United States ambassador overseas;

    (4) the PLO and its constituent groups have taken credit for, and been implicated in, the murders of dozens of American citizens abroad;

    (5) the PLO covenant specifically states that "armed struggle is the only way to liberate Palestine, thus it is an overall strategy, not merely a tactical phase";

    (6) the PLO rededicated itself to the "continuing struggle in all its armed forms" at the Palestine National Council meeting in April 1987; and

(7) the Attorney General has stated that "various elements of the Palestine Liberation Organization and its allies and affiliates are in the thick of international terror."

(b) Therefore, the Congress determines that the PLO and its affiliates are a terrorist organization and a threat to the interests of the United States, its allies, and to international law and should not benefit from operating in the United States.

It shall be unlawful, if the purpose be to further the interests of the Palestine Liberation Organization or any of its constituent groups, any successor to any of those, or any agents thereof, on or after [March 21, 1988] –

(1) to receive anything of value except informational material from the PLO or any of its constituent groups, any successor thereto, or any agents thereof; or

(2) to expend funds from the PLO or any of its constituent groups, any successor thereto, or any agents thereof; or

(3) notwithstanding any provision of law to the contrary, to establish or maintain an office, headquarters, premises or other facilities or establishments within the jurisdiction of the United States at the behest or direction of, or with funds provided by the Palestine Liberation Organization or any of its constituent groups, any successor to any of those, or any agents thereof.

---

8. Are the following statute and regulation vague or overbroad? Who may challenge them? If vague or overbroad, can they be narrowly construed so as to make them constitutional? How?

(a) Failure-to-Move-On Statute

Whoever, with intent to provoke a breach of the peace, or under circumstances such that a breach of the peace may be occasioned thereby –

*****

(2) congregates with others on a public street and refuses to move on when ordered by the police;

*****

shall be fined not more than $250 or imprisoned not more than ninety days, or both.

(b) Police Line Regulation

When fires, accidents, wrecks, explosions, parades, or other occasions cause or may cause persons to collect on the public streets, alleys, highways, or parking areas, the Chief of Police, inspector, captain of police, or officer acting for him, may establish such area or zone as he considers necessary for the purpose of affording a clearing for: (1) the operation of firemen or policemen; (2) the passage of a parade; (3) the movement of traffic; (4) the exclusion of the public from the vicinity of a riot, disorderly gathering, accident, wreck, explosion, or other emergency; and (5) the protection of persons and property. Every person present at the scene of such an occasion shall comply with the necessary order or instruction of any police officer. No person shall enter such area or zone, unless duly authorized by the person in command on such an occasion; provided that bona fide representatives of the press and bona fide insurance adjusters or underwriters and such other persons as the Chief of Police may authorize to be within such space, and who shall have plainly exposed to view the press pass or fire pass described in this section, shall be permitted within the lines established by the Police Department under the conditions named in the following paragraph.

9. The City of Los Angeles proposes to enact the following ordinance. Assume that you are an attorney working in the Office of the Chief Legislative Analyst (CLA) of the City of Los Angeles. CLA asks you to assess the constitutionality of the ordinances. Write a memorandum addressing any constitutional issues raised by the proposed ordinances. If you find the ordinance constitutionally defective in any respect, state the ways in which it should be changed to make it constitutional.

Use of City Ways

Except when otherwise authorized by law or rules of the City Streets and Transportation Department, it is unlawful to make any commercial use of the right of way of any city-maintained road, street, sidewalk, alley, highway, or other ways open to the travel by the public. Such prohibited uses include, but are not limited to, the sale, or the display for sale, of any merchandise; the solicitation for the sale of goods, property, or services or for charitable purposes; and the display of advertising of any sort, except that any portion of such city ways may be used for an art festival, parade, fair or other special event if permitted by the Streets and Transportation Department. The violation of any provision of this section or of any Departmental rule promulgated pursuant to this section shall constitute a misdemeanor.

10. Write a memorandum addressing the constitutional issues raised by the statute quoted below. If you find the statute constitutionally defective or suspect, state how it should be changed to make it constitutional.

Child Pornography and Obscenity

Whoever in the State of Arcadia produces any book, magazine, periodical, developed or undeveloped film or videotape, or other matter which contains one or more visual depictions made after February 6, 1978 of actual sexually explicit conduct shall create and maintain individually identifiable records pertaining to every performer portrayed in such a visual depiction. Such records shall include the performer's correct name and date of birth as well as any other name ever used by the performer including maiden name, alias, nickname, stage or professional name. Failure to keep the records provided by this section constitutes a misdemeanor.

As used in this ordinance,

(1) the term "actual sexually explicit conduct" means actual

  (a) sexual intercourse, including genital-genital, oral-genital, anal-genital, or oral-anal, whether between persons of the same or opposite sex;

  (b) bestiality;

  (c) masturbation;

  (d) sadistic or masochistic abuse (for the purpose of sexual stimulation); or

  (e) lascivious exhibition of the genitals or pubic area of any person.

(2) the term "produces" means to produce, manufacture, or publish and includes the duplication, reproduction, or reissuing of any material; and

(3) the term "performer" includes any person portrayed in visual depiction engaging in, or assisting another person to engage in, actual sexually explicit conduct.

Any person to whom this section applies shall affix to every copy of any matter described in this section a statement describing where the records required by this section may be located. In any prosecution for child pornography, failure to provide this statement regarding any performer shall raise a rebuttable presumption that such performer was a minor.

Citations.

1. *Norfolk Southern Corp. v. Oberly*, 822 F.2d 388 (1987); 632 F. Supp. 1225 (1986).

2. *Specialized Carriers v. Virginia*, 795 F.2d 1152 (1986); 619 F. Supp. 1199 (1985).

3. *Western Oil and Gas Ass'n v. Cory*, 726 F.2d 1340 (1984).

4. *Blackstone Valley Disposal v. Rhode Island*, 669 F. Supp. 1204 (1987).

5. *Commonwealth Edison Co. v. Montana*, 453 U.S. 609 (1981).

6. *Woodward v. United States*, 871 F.2d 1068 (1989); *Watkins v. United States*, 875 F.2d 699 (1989), 837 F.2d 1428 (1988).

7. *Mendelsohn et al. v. Meese*, 690 F. Supp. 1226 (1988).

8. *Leonardson v. City of East Lansing*, 896 F.2d 190 (1990); *Washington Mobilization Comm. v. Cullinane*, 566 F.2d 107 (1977).

9. *News and Sun-Sentinal Co. v. Cox*, 702 F. Supp. 891 (1988).

10. *American Library Association et al. v. Thornburgh*, 713 F. Supp. 469 (1989).

B. Essay Questions with Sample Answers

1. Arcadia Government Code Sections 19790 et seq. authorize the State's affirmative action program. Code Sections 19790 and 19791(a) call for affirmative action goals and timetables designed to overcome *"any identified underutilization of minorities and women...."* Section 19791(c) defines *"underutilization"* as *"having fewer persons of a particular group in an occupation or at a level in a department than would reasonably be expected by their availability."*

The Arcadia State Affirmative Action Manual, Section 2200 states that Arcadia's overall affirmative action policy goals are to:

(1) *assure all persons equal access to and consideration for employment; and*

(2) *achieve a civil service work force that is fully representative of and has each ethnic group, females, and the disabled represented (by occupational group,*

responsibility level, and salary level) in proportion to their representation in the State's labor force.

Following a recent review of relevant law, the Arcadia State Personnel Board has proposed to set affirmative action goals and timetables for Arcadia State Agencies. Once approved, State Agencies will use the Personnel Board's guidelines in creating their own affirmative action policies. The Board has made the following findings and recommendations, *inter alia*:

(1) It is not clear whether the courts consider goal-setting, which is designed to monitor an employer's progress in achieving work force representation and not to set hiring quotas, as a race/gender conscious affirmative action.

(2) Because of the lack of legal guidance from the courts, the SPB (State Personnel Board) does not believe that it is necessary to establish a "firm basis" for setting goals by establishing a prima facie case of employment discrimination.

(3) The SPB believes that goals are justified to facilitate the recruitment and hiring of women and minorities based only on an identified underutilization.

(4) Statistics used to measure underutilization must compare the ethnic and gender composition of the State's combined full-time and other than full-time work force with the composition of those qualified in the relevant area labor force.

(5) "Relevant area labor force" is defined as either (1) the pool of potential job applicants possessing requisite minimum qualifications in the geographic area in which the States expects to recruit for the job, or (2) the pool of applicants meeting the minimum qualifications for the job who have been accepted to compete in civil service examinations for the job.

(6) General labor force representation may be used as a base against which to measure the State's overall progress in achieving a fully diverse work force.

(7) To foster accountability for the achievement of affirmative action hiring goals, the SPB annually will publish the hiring goals of departments and the extent to which they were achieved in its *Annual Census of State Employees and Affirmative Action Report.*

Assume that you are a Deputy State Attorney General. In that capacity, you have been asked to review the SPB's proposed recommendations for conformity with federal constitutional law. Write a memorandum analyzing the federal constitutionality of the recommendations. You should note and discuss any constitutional problems; if appropriate, you should also suggest such changes in the recommendations as will likely insure their federal constitutionality.

The following three essay questions have been taken from recent bar examinations.

2. There has been a recent substantial rise in residential mortgage loan interest rates in State *X*. This has resulted in numerous complaints to the state legislature by home buyers about mortgage lenders who raise rates after the initial loan commitment but before execution of loan documents. In response, the legislature enacted the State *X* Residential Mortgage Banking Act (RMBA), requiring a ninety-day period during which a residential loan rate commitment cannot be increased by the lender. If the loan closes during this ninety-day period at a higher interest rate than

EP

that initially committed to by the lender, the lender is subject to a penalty. For example, the penalty for breaching an interest rate commitment on a $100,000 loan would be $15,000.

Under RMBA, lenders whose principal places of business are in State X can obtain a reduction of the penalty to 10% of what the penalty would otherwise be by demonstrating a reasonable business justification to the State X Commissioner of Banks. This reduced penalty provision does not apply to lenders doing business in State X whose principal places of business are in other states.

When RMBA was enacted, out-of-state banks making residential loans had 75 branches in State X. Of these, forty were branches of Lendco, a large out-of-state lender. RMBA limits to ten the number of branches that any out-of-state lender may have in State X. There is no similar limitation for lenders whose principal places of business are in State X. The sponsors of RMBA justified the ten-branch limitation by citing the need to supervise lending operations closely, given the limited enforcement budget for the Commissioner of Banks, who was responsible for enforcement of RMBA. When the State X governor signed RMBA into law, he stated, "this will bring those eastern banking conglomerates down to size."

Lendco has filed an action against the State X Commissioner of Banks in United States District Court in State X seeking a declaration that RMBA violates the U.S. Constitution. Lendco can present proof that market economics require it to have at least twenty branches in State X to compete effectively and that it will cost Lendco in excess of $ 10 million to close down at least thirty of its existing branches in State X.

What arguments under the U.S. Constitution should be made for and against Lendco's challenge to the validity of the provisions of RMBA governing: (1) the interest rates and penalties, and (2) the limitation on the number of branches for out-of-state lenders? How should the court decide these arguments? Discuss.

3. The number of recipients of funds from State Assistance to Families with Dependant Children (SAFDC) in State X, a totally state-funded welfare program, has been dramatically increasing. In an effort to stem the rising costs of this program, three bills have been introduced in the State X Senate and referred to its Welfare Committee.

One bill, S.B. 1, would require that any mother who receives SAFDC benefits for a single eligible child be sterilized after the birth of a second child who would be eligible for such benefits.

Another bill, S.B. 2, would require sterilization of any woman with two or more eligible children, as a condition to continued receipt of SAFDC benefits.

A third bill, S.B. 3, would deny SAFDC benefits for more than two children in any family. It would also deny SAFDC funds to pay for medical services in the delivery of any child of a mother who already has two children for whom SAFDC benefits are being paid. However, free abortions would be provided by State X for women receiving SAFDC benefits.

As counsel for the Senate Welfare Committee, you are asked to advise it if each bill, if enacted as law, would violate the United States Constitution; and if so, on what bases. Discuss.

4. A new State *X*-owned office building has an interior ground floor mall area with spaces for leasing to privately owned retail businesses on the perimeter of the mall. Each lease with State *X* as lessor incorporates Office Building Rules, provided by State *X*. One rule permits each lessee to display floor advertising at designated spaces throughout the mall, limited to only commercial advertising. Another rule provides that another designated space in the mall, next to the main entrance to the building, is the only place available in the mall for public demonstrations. This space is to be assigned to the first group of demonstrators to arrive each day. The office building has two side entrances as well.

The Olde Tobacco Shoppe (OTS), a mall lessee, has set up large signs in all designated commercial advertising areas of the mall, advertising its sales of cigarettes at discount prices.

Citizens for Clear Air (CCA), a citizens' group protesting air pollution, began picketing at the mall with placards protesting both the leasing of State *X* property to OTS, and OTS' advertising in the mall. The first day the CCA picketers, including Dan, appeared, they were not allowed to use the one designated space for public demonstrations because a small anti-nuclear power protest group had arrived earlier and had been assigned use of the space. CCA members therefore began picketing at the two side entrances. The building manager called State *X* police who, after some resistance from the protesters, succeeded in escorting them from the premises.

Later that same day, the State *X* Attorney General obtained an *ex parte* order from a State court prohibiting members of CCA from picketing at any place in the mall, other than in the one designated area. The following day, CCA picketers were first to arrive at the mall and were assigned use of the designated area. The picketers, including Dan, were each given copies of the *ex parte* order. However, Dan left the designated area and stood in front of one of the OTS' mall advertisements near one of the side entrances. He held a poster with a graphic depiction of a fully nude, terminally ill cancer patent with tubes projecting from the patient's body and a caption which read, "The Governor Sticks It To You By Supporting Smoking."

Dan was arrested by State police and charged in State *X* court with criminal contempt of the *ex parte* order, with criminal trespass, and with violation of a State criminal statute proscribing the "public display" of an "obscene picture."

In the prosecution of Dan, what defenses should Dan assert under the United States Constitution to charges of (1) contempt of the *ex parte* order, (2) trespass and (3) violation of the statute, and how should they be decided? Discuss.

Essay Questions: Sample Answers

1. This particular question predominately poses an exercise in interpretation, but also includes a test of the student's ability to get into, and analyze, detail.

The discussion which follows explains what I think is really at issue in the problem. I write this as a commentary on the problem and what is involved in it rather than as a model answer. A model student answer would include statements of the relevant law, arguments on both sides of the issues, application of legal standards to the facts and inferences of the facts, and the like. A student answer might also appropriately raise issues I do not discuss below. For example, the state seems concerned with ethnic minorities, women, and the disabled, but the Personnel Board's recommendations address only minorities and women. Similarly, a student answer would likely, and properly, note

EP ▶

that there are different standards of review applicable to racial and gender classifications. Applying the differing standards to the Board's recommendations might give rise to different constitutional results, etc.

The first question is just what is it that the Personnel Board is up to? The Board is apparently attempting to reconcile state law, as found in the cited provisions, and the federal constitutional rules regarding affirmative action. But there is a real tension between the two. State law is concerned primarily with "underutilization," defined as "having fewer persons of a particular group in an occupation or at a level in a department than would reasonably be expected by their availability." "Availability," as used in the statute, is a vague term. One could construe it strictly – as referring only to persons appropriately qualified for positions. And one could construe it broadly – as referring to relevant group population percentages. In fact, Arcadia's Affirmative Action Manual states as a policy goal the achievement of "a civil service work force that is fully representative of each ethnic group [etc.] ... represented ... in proportion to their representation in the State's labor force." While also not free of ambiguity (and thus needing interpretation), this policy statement arguably states an aim of proportional representation in the state work force. Without some further qualification, this, of course, would clearly be unconstitutional.

In its proposed recommendations, the Personnel Board attempts to reconcile state and federal law by proposing a formula that it hopes will evade constitutional requirements. It treats the state "underutilization" requirement as a "goal" rather than as a quota, tracking federal law that says as long as goals are not rigid (and therefore quotas) a party can use them as guidelines to see how well it's doing. Using a flexible "goal" may not only evade the quota issue; the Board clearly also wants to use "goals" as a way of helping state agencies avoid having to make any findings regarding employment discrimination. (Board's proposed recommendation 2.) Such findings , at least where there is a "firm basis" for them, would support affirmative action remedies. But the Board apparently wants to avoid the necessity of making them.

While the Board's strategy would work if the goals it describes are merely "guidelines," there is a real question whether they are something more. Regardless of what the Board says it is doing, one has to examine the actual impact of the recommendations as they would play out were they to be adopted and followed. Recommendation 3 says, in effect, that the "goals" will be used to facilitate the hiring of women and minorities "based only on an identified underutilization." This sounds more like a quota than a guideline because it smacks of proportional representation. The Board, however, then qualifies that statement in Recommendations 4, 5, and 6. According to recommendation 4, "underutilization" is to be determined by comparing ethnic and gender composition of the State's work force (assumedly for a given region) with the ethnic and gender composition of qualified persons in the relevant area labor force.

Now, depending on how the Board defines "relevant area labor force," what the Board has done with recommendation 4 – without actually saying so – is to lay a predicate for establishing a "firm basis" for a prima facie statistical case of employment discrimination. For example, if there is a manifest statistical imbalance in the racial composition of the relevant State agency work force and the relevant population of qualified applicants, that would make out a prima facie case. In that situation, even if the Board's "goals" were quotas, there is some justification for them.

Recommendation 5, however, defines "relevant labor force" in a way that invalidates a statistical demonstration of employment discrimination. "Relevant labor force" is: 1.) the pool of potential applicants having minimum qualifications, or 2.) the same pool, but with the added qualification of having been "accepted to compete in civil service examinations." Neither of these groups comprise an appropriate reference group for establishing a statistical case of employment discrimination. The appropriate reference pool is *qualified applicants who have passed the civil service examinations for particular jobs.* This is so because it is from this group that persons are hired rather than from either of the two prior groups. Consequently, to the degree that the Board's "goals" are actually quotas, they are not appropriately supported by a prima facie case of discrimination. (Indeed, cannot be, for the Board has chosen the wrong reference pools. Note, the analysis would be different if there was some reason to believe the state's civil service testing was itself discriminatory or had a significant disparate impact. Nothing in the problem suggests this, however, nor that the Personnel Board was concerned with civil service testing.)

In Recommendation 6, the Board says "[g]eneral labor force representation may be used as a base against which to measure the State's overall progress in achieving a fully diverse work force." By itself, this statement is unexceptionable as it is but guideline language. Taken together with the other recommendations, however, the Board seems to be sending conflicting messages. In effect, it is waffling on the meaning of "goals." But this is a poor way to bridge the gap between the state's "underutilization" standard and federal constitutional requirements. To the degree that it imposes *any* affirmative action *requirements,* the 'underutilization" standard must be construed compatibly with federal constitutional requirements — that is, essentially meet *Croson* "firm basis" standards. To the degree that the state standard is merely hortatory, or an expression of good intentions, but lacking any effect on actual hiring decisions, they are fine. But the Board must choose one interpretation or the other; it cannot have both simultaneously.

As a final matter, there is a subsidiary question whether the Personnel Board's adoption of affirmative action "policy goals and timetables" have any binding legal effect on state agencies. If they do, there's clearly a constitutional problem, as stated above. Even if the Board's adoption of goals is in some way merely advisory to state agencies, however, there may remain a constitutional problem. In Recommendation 7, the Board states that it will annually publish "the hiring goals of departments and the extent to which they were achieved...." It is a factual question, but this publication is a form of pressure. If, in practice, state agencies feel obliged to follow Board personnel polices, it may be possible to view the adopted goals and timetables as virtual mandates and so treat them.

2. **(a) Interest Rates and Penalties**

Lendco would separately challenge (1) the restriction on raising interest rates; (2) the penalty imposed on raising interest rates during the 90-day period following initial loan commitment and preceding execution of the loan documents; and (3) the penalty reduction.

(1) The interest rate restriction

Although Lendco and other lenders obviously dislike the legislative restriction on their ability to raise interest rates following an initial loan commitment, Lendco will have some difficulty arguing it has some constitutional right which this particular legislation infringes. At one time, Lendco could have asserted a "liberty of contract" theory and claimed that the state could not regulate this kind of arms-length transaction between mature parties. But the Court no longer recognizes any liberty of contract in any strong sense, and states may undertake any social and economic regulation which is rational even though it arguably interferes with the parties' shaping of a contract. States have long regulated credit transactions and, for a long time, many even have had strict usury

EP

laws limiting the amount of interest which could be charged on a loan – all without constitutional difficulty or infirmity.

Alternatively, Lendco might seek to argue that the restriction amounts to a law impairing the "Obligation of Contracts," but this argument is weak as well. There is here both a factual and a legal problem. Whether there is even any Contract Clause argument at all turns on whether there is any arguable kind of impairment of Lendco's contracts. The facts are not clear, but it would appear that in any ordinary mortgage contract, Lendco, as a part of its initial loan *commitment,* would guarantee some interest rate. If so, this legislation only makes Lendco stand by its word, and there is not even an arguable impairment. On the other hand, it is possible that Lendco, in its loan commitment contracts, reserves the right to raise rates. A home buyer's agreement to such a provision would create a corresponding buyer obligation to pay the increased rates. Under this reading, the legislation arguably impairs the obligations of a contract between private parties. Unfortunately for Lendco, Contract Clause jurisprudence permits the state, when it has a justifying public purpose, to reasonably adjust the rights and responsibilities of contracting parties. There is certainly a significant public interest in the general housing market and the protection of the public from possibly fraudulent, or at least devious or misleading, credit advertising or offers. Lendco could argue that the 90-day period is too long and therefore an unreasonable condition, but given the length of time it takes for loans to close ordinarily, this argument appears to have no force at all. Indeed, given that persons buying new houses may need to sell old ones in order to obtain a down payment, or for other quite understandable reasons need some decent period of time to get their affairs in order to finally take out a loan, the 90-day period appears quite reasonable. In any case, unless the interest rate increases are fairly large, it would be difficult to characterize this particular state interference with contracts as "substantial," a basic requirement for triggering Contract Clause scrutiny of state legislation affecting contracts.

All the foregoing assumes that the initial loan commitment constitutes some kind of contract. But, of course, there may be no contract at all, for the commitment may simply amount to a unilateral offer to make a loan. In such a case, the state is merely involved in economic regulation or regulation of credit transactions, rationally justifiable as regulating a potential abusive sort of "bait and switch" advertising, if not on other grounds. Under these circumstances, there also doesn't appear to be any sort of commercial speech right argument of any avail that Lendco could raise.

(2) The penalty

Lendco's argument concerning the penalty is somewhat stronger. Under the facts, it is impossible to say exactly what the penalty structure of the statute is – whether flat rate or percentage or some other formula. It is therefore difficult to determine whether the penalty has a rational relationship to any lender violation of the legislative restriction on raising interest rates. Of course, under a rational basis test, the legislature has great freedom to choose appropriate remedies. Nonetheless, the most appropriate remedy for the identified problem would appear to be simply to require the lender to honor its initial interest rate commitment. Indeed, depending on how the statute is actually elaborated, the penalty imposed may not really deter violators. For example, if the lender who breaches must pay the penalty, but nevertheless can impose the higher interest rate, the legislation may actually encourage lenders to raise rates even higher – to cover both the cost of the penalty and to ensure higher profit on the loan. On the other hand, if the statute actually has no such effect, even though the penalty structure is not the most rational response to the problem, it isn't possible to say it's irrational or that it would have no tendency to solve the problem the statute is meant to reach. As long as the penalty appears to be a rational, albeit not necessarily optimal, response to the problem, a court should uphold it.

Lendco might attempt to argue that the penalty amounts to a taking of property without due process of law, but the argument is exceptionally weak. A violation of the law triggers the penalty, and, in this respect, the penalty does not appear different than any other kind of civil penalty. The penalty may be high, but nothing in the problem suggests that it is so excessive as to trigger due process concerns.

(3) The penalty reduction

The penalty reduction provision presents another question altogether. Lendco would argue that the provision permitting in-state business to obtain a 90% penalty reduction by demonstrating a reasonable business justification violates both the Commerce Clause and Equal Protection. The provision plainly discriminates against out-of-state lenders. The provision may or may not have a discriminatory purpose. The statement of the governor suggests that he had that purpose and there may be some evidence, albeit not conclusive, that there was an intent to discriminate against out-of-staters. Aside from any direct legislative expression of discriminatory purpose, however, the provision itself seems to speak loudly enough, for it is difficult to imagine a non-discriminatory purpose which could justify its particular shape. Out-of-staters may, of course, present certain regulatory problems not presented by in-staters, but whatever those might be, none could conceivably justify a penalty reduction only for in-staters. Indeed, the structure of the provision, considered together with the provision limiting the number of branches an out-of-stater can hold, impels a conclusion that it is intended to disadvantage out-of-staters in their competition with in-staters and amounts to unconstitutional state economic protectionism. While a state can condition the right of a foreign corporation to do business in the state, it cannot impose more onerous burdens on foreign corporations than on domestic corporations unless the discrimination between them bears some rational relationship to a legitimate state purpose. The provision therefore similarly violates equal protection, for there does not appear to be any rational reason – other than the improper one of discriminating against out-of-staters – for giving relief to in-staters, but not out-of-staters. The court consequently should hold this in-state preference unconstitutional as a violation of both the dominant Commerce Clause and the Equal Protection Clause.

(b) Out-of-state branch limitation

Lendco's arguments against the branch limitation essentially tracks its arguments against the penalty reduction. The only difference here is that the state proffers a regulatory justification. But the regulatory justification, which is essentially one of economy, is inadequate to justify the discrimination against branch-banking by out-of-state corporations. There is no demonstration that the regulatory problem regarding out-of-state branch banking is any different than the regulatory problem regarding in-state branch-banking. Consequently, while the limitation certainly would save money, it does so by preferring, or advantaging, in-state lending interests. The state could equally well save money through a branch-banking limitation applicable equally to in-staters and out-of-staters. Whether or not a discriminatory purpose lies behind the limitation, it does not treat in-staters and out-of-staters evenhandedly. It certainly has a discriminatory effect and certainly imposes, as Lendco's figures demonstrate, a significant burden on interstate commerce. Under the balancing approach to interstate commerce questions, the burden clearly outweighs the justification, and the limitation should be held unconstitutional. For reasons given above, the limitation also violates the Equal Protection Clause, although it really isn't necessary to reach that question.

3. **(a) S.B. 1:** S.B. 1 should not be passed, as it violates the United States Constitution. Although the United States Supreme Court, in *Buck v. Bell,* once sustained a state law

calling for the sterilization of institutionalized persons having severe mental deficiencies, the Court subsequently, in *Skinner v. Oklahoma,* recognized that marriage and procreation were fundamental human rights. In *Skinner,* the Court determined that strict scrutiny review was appropriate to review state classifications adversely affecting the right to procreate and overturn a state statute calling for sterilization of felons convicted a third time of felonies of "moral turpitude," but not other felonies, such as embezzlement. Although *Skinner* was decided on equal protection rather than substantive due process grounds, subsequent cases have affirmed the right to procreate as a fundamental human right and that state actions affecting it trigger strict scrutiny review. The Court's treatment of laws attempting to regulate the sale of contraceptives and its recognition of a woman's right to choose whether to bear a child in *Roe v. Wade* also evidence, and strongly support, the conclusion that the right to procreate is an established fundamental right.

The proposed legislation both punishes a woman who has, in effect, exercised her right to procreate, and, more importantly, by requiring sterilization, takes away her ability to procreate. These are among the worst imaginable infringements of the right to procreate.

The avowed purpose behind S.B. 1 is a desire to save money. The Court has made clear, however, that the saving of money is an insufficient justification for a state to infringe a fundamental right. *Shapiro v. Thompson.* Indeed, even if money savings were a compelling state interest, as called for by strict scrutiny review, the state could not show that the means it has chosen for that end, the sterilization of women receiving SAFDC benefits who have a second child eligible for such benefits, is the least restrictive means available to achieve that end. The provision of contraception, counseling, even reducing welfare benefits would likely save greater amounts than forced sterilization after a second child.

For these reasons, the bill is clearly unconstitutional and should be killed.

(b) S.B. 2: S.B. 2 is similar to S.B. 1 in many respects and subject to many of the same arguments of unconstitutionality. It differs, however, in conditioning continued receipt of benefits on the agreement of the woman, who has two or more SAFDC eligible children, to sterilization. This introduces an ersatz patina of voluntariness into the situation, giving the appearance of leaving the choice of sterilization up to the woman. Although a person can voluntarily waive constitutional rights, it is almost unimaginable that any reasonable person would conclude that a woman's choice to be sterilized under such circumstances was in fact voluntary. Furthermore, the state cannot require, as a condition of its distribution of benefits, that persons give up their fundamental rights; else the state could disregard fundamental rights by in effect buying them up.

The legislation classifies mothers of recipient children into two groups: those having only one child and those having more than one child. This classification obviously affects those women who have exercised their right to procreate more than once *on the basis of their having procreated.* As discussed above, it is therefore subject to strict scrutiny review. The state has no compelling interest in the saving of money which would justify this kind of discrimination between these classes of women, and S.B. 2 is also unconstitutional.

(c) S.B. 3: S.B. 3 is a rather different bill and calls for a different constitutional analysis.

First, the bill would deny benefits for more than two children in any family. While this is undoubtedly harsh, it is not unconstitutional. The Court considers the state provision of welfare benefits to be a matter of social and economic regulation. Where the state enacts such legislation, in ways not clearly impinging on a fundamental right, it is subject only to rational basis review. Under rational basis review, the saving of money is a legitimate state goal, and limiting the amount of benefits going to a welfare family is certainly one rational way to help reach that goal. The Supreme Court has explicitly held, in *Dandridge v. Williams,* that persons or indigents have no constitutional right to the basic necessities of life and that it is permissible for states to refuse to increase welfare benefits on a basis proportional to the number of eligible children in a recipient family. For these reasons, this portion of the bill, while ungenerous and perhaps punitive, and probably not good social policy, is constitutional.

The remainder of S.B. 3 is rather more complicated. Of itself, the denial of SAFDC funds for medical services for delivery of additional children for an SAFDC mother already receiving benefits for two children appears to be merely another instance of *Dandridge*-type social and economic regulation and subject to the same analysis. The statute, however, goes on to provide for free abortions for women receiving SAFDC benefits. Again, of itself, this provision is not problematic.

The combination of the two provisions, however, does raise different considerations. In effect, the state is funding abortions and refusing to fund childbirth. Under present constitutional law doctrine, the state can certainly do the reverse, that is, fund childbirth and refuse to fund abortions. *Harris v. McCrae.* In general, while the state itself cannot deprive anyone of their fundamental rights nor infringe on their exercise, the state is not required to fund the exercise of fundamental rights. Furthermore, it is not unconstitutional for a state to have a policy favoring childbirth over abortion. Id. There appears to be no reason in constitutional law to limit this doctrine to a pro-childbirth social policy. Consequently, there is no constitutional barrier to a pro-abortion, anti-childbirth policy.

The argument that in refusing to pay for medical services for childbirth the state is infringing upon the woman's fundamental right to procreate collides with the *Harris* holding. While *Harris* deals with the somewhat different right of a woman to decide whether to bear a child, the right is a closely related one and equally fundamental. Consequently, the *Harris* situation and this situation appear to be on all fours, and *Harris* should control.

There is, however, one further argument in opposition to the bill which is of some importance. The Supreme Court's abortion rulings since *Roe v. Wade* have almost all dealt with attempted state regulation of the abortion decision. While the individual holdings in those cases deal with specific state regulations regarding abortion procedure, consent, and various other requirements, the Court has perceived that many state efforts to regulate abortion were aimed at influencing a woman not to have an abortion. Until recently, the Court has made it clear that it would not tolerate state efforts, whatever their guise, to unduly influence a woman not to have abortions. The proposed legislation presents the reverse: the state is here attempting to encourage women *to have* abortions and *not* to have children by funding abortions and not paying for childbirth medical services. There is certainly a reasonable argument that this is undue state interference in the woman's right to decide whether or not to bear a child. This argument, however, appears to be irreconcilably in conflict with the *Harris* holding, for it is clear that a state policy of funding childbirth and not funding abortion must have some influential effect on at least some women's decisions regarding the bearing of children.

There is consequently a significant constitutional question here and the bill faces an uncertain litigation future. If anything, however, the current Supreme Court appears minded to retreat somewhat from its prior abortion law decisions. This suggests there is little likelihood that the Court would overrule *Harris* or otherwise hold that state funding or refusal to fund childbirth or abortion amounts to undue interference in the deci-

EP

sion whether or not to bear a child. As harsh and punitive as the bill is, it would appear to pass federal constitutional scrutiny.

There are, however, perhaps some subsidiary problems which the bill should address. The provision for free abortions makes no reference to when such abortions would take place. As the Court would undoubtedly acknowledge that a viable fetus capable of life outside the womb is a person for Fourteenth Amendment purposes, the proposed statute raises the possibility of the strange spectacle of state-authorized killing of third-trimester fetuses. This would raise issues of the taking of life without due process of law, and it would be well to draft the statute so that the abortions it funds comply with the constitutional law of abortion as laid down by the Supreme Court.

4. **(a) Contempt of the *ex parte* order:** Picketing is expressive activity protected by the First Amendment. While some of the conduct involved in some kinds of picketing, e.g., massing or intimidating patrolling, are regulable, nothing in these facts suggests the state is concerned about the conduct associated with picketing, as opposed to the message or *place* of the picketing involved here. For that reason, the *ex parte* order is a prior restraint on First Amendment activity. Normally, in order to obtain a valid restraint on, or injunction against, First Amendment activity, the state must first provide an adversary hearing and provide the *Freedman v. Maryland* procedural safeguards. It is possible that some dire emergency might justify issuance of an *ex parte* order restraining speech for a brief period pending a proper adversary hearing, but nothing in the facts suggests any dire emergency.

On the other hand, the collateral bar rule requires that court orders be obeyed and permits punishment of one who refuses to abide by a court order, even if it later turns out that the court order was itself unconstitutional or otherwise improper. Thus, in this case, the fact that the *ex parte* order may not be valid does not really help Dan, for his proper course should have been to challenge the underlying constitutionality or legality of the order. Again, nothing in the facts suggests that any of the exceptions of the collateral bar rule would operate in this case to excuse Dan – the court order was not a sham, time was not of the essence, and it is not possible to say that Dan could not have obtained judicial review of the *ex parte* order if he had tried.

Nonetheless, criminal contempt as punishment is normally visited only on those who were a party to a proceeding which resulted in the order which is the predicate for the criminal contempt. This is not the case here. Dan, however, did have actual notice of the *ex parte* order, and it was therefore binding on him, assuming it was certain and specific regarding the enjoined conduct and it actually covered what Dan in fact did.

On the other hand, as the original proceeding was *ex parte,* it lacked the adversariness required when the state imposes a restraint on free speech activities. An adversary proceeding, at which a party can contest the propriety of a restraint on free speech, is essential to validate the restraint. It would therefore appear that in any hearing on the issue of criminal contempt, which will be an adversary proceeding, Dan should be able to raise and contest the issue of the unconstitutionality of the original *ex parte* order. Under these circumstances, therefore, the collateral bar rule should not operate to preclude Dan from raising the question of the constitutionality of the state rule regarding public demonstrations at its building and the *ex parte* order based on it.

(b) Trespass: The state rule permits public demonstrations at only one designated space in the mall, and the trespass charge is evidently based on violation of this rule. In the context of the fact pattern, this trespass charge raises several First Amendment problems.

Public places such as streets, sidewalks, and parks are traditional public fora open to all First Amendment expressive activities. A state can, of course, open other areas to expressive activities. It can create public fora by designation, open to all expressive activities, and it can also create more limited public fora and restrict speech activities in them to those consistent with the character of the fora. The state may also create fora which are nonpublic and need not open them to any but those having business there. The question in this case is just what kind of fora the state has created, if it has created any. If Dan was in a place where he had a right to be, because it was a forum open to what he was doing there, he cannot be charged with trespass. Whether the place where he was was a public forum and what kind of forum it was is actually a factual question which the facts as stated in the problem do not clearly resolve.

The first problem therefore is simply a factual one. The state is leasing at least portions of a public building, and its ground floor mall area, to private parties for private business purposes. The problem describes the office building as having three entrances, a main entrance – where public demonstrations are permitted – and two side entrances, where such demonstrations are not permitted. The problem, however, does not state the character of the property at the entrances and outside the building. If a public sidewalk or street abuts the building at the entrances, those areas of entry would be traditional public fora open to all forms of First Amendment expressive activity and subject only to reasonable time, place, and manner regulation. A rule forbidding all use of a traditional public forum for expression would not be a reasonable time, place, and manner regulation. Consequently, if it is determined that the entries to the building were located on public streets or sidewalks, the statute limiting expression to only the main entrance is invalid, and Dan had a right to be where he was when he was arrested.

If the building is surrounded by a public plaza rather than streets or sidewalks, the case is somewhat complicated and a factual hearing may be necessary to determine to what uses the plaza is generally put. Indeed, it may also be necessary to consider the public and private uses to which the building is put, for these will reveal the relative openness, or forum character, of the building and its environs, as well as expectations of the public regarding it.

As the building is a public office building, it could be a building limited to certain public functions and not one which should be thought generally open to all expressive activities, but only to those relevant to the public business in the building. On the other hand, the fact that the state has leased the ground floor to private businesses complicates the matter, for it has opened at least that portion of the building to all the activities associated with shopping malls – which, generally speaking, would include a large range of expressive activities of the kind the First Amendment protects in public places. The opening to private business suggests that whatever public business goes on in the building will not in any way suffer from the commercial activity. It is therefore not comparable to a public courthouse or a jail where demonstrations outside, at least in some circumstances, could threaten or otherwise jeopardize functions inside.

As the state also permits commercial advertising throughout the mall, it is favoring commercial speech over noncommercial speech. Cases such as *Metromedia* suggest that the state cannot regulate so as to prefer commercial to noncommercial speech. On the other hand, cases such as *Lehman,* which upheld a ban on political advertising on advertising space in public transportation vehicles, indicate there are some circumstances under which the state can make content-based speech distinctions which appear to favor commercial over noncommercial advertising. This question need not be decided in this case, for there is no issue concerning the interior use of the mall, but the fact that the state is favoring commercial speech inside the mall does have a bearing on what the state is apparently attempting to do outside the mall. Although the problem does not state what justification the state has for allowing demonstrations at the main entrance, but not the other entrances, the limitation does not appear to serve any purpose but limiting noncommercial expression or ingress and egress problems that might be created by certain kinds of expression at the side entrances.

Depending on the physical character of the latter, the state might well be able to solve congestion and traffic flow problems with reasonable place and manner regulations. If so, its total ban on demonstrations at the side entrances is not the least restrictive alternative. If, on the other hand, such problems are otherwise insurmountable, the situation is more like that found in *Heffron*, where the Court upheld a literature distribution and fund solicitation limitation on Hare Krishnas at a public fairgrounds. Nonetheless, even in *Heffron*, the Krishnas were not limited in their ability to communicate their views where they wished on fairground property. In this case, the limitation on places where demonstrators may demonstrate *does* limit their ability to communicate. On the facts as stated in the problem, it would not appear that the state could bear its burden of showing its need to ban demonstrations at the side entrances, for nothing in the facts suggests that the state is seeking to solve significant access problems.

Generally speaking, the state may not limit noncommercial expression in order to aid commercial expression – although there might be some circumstances where the state itself was effectively acting only as a business proprietor and not as a state, in which case it should be treated simply as a business proprietor. That does not appear to be the case here, as the state is clearly seeking to act both in the regulatory role of the state and in a proprietary role. It may be that the commercial enterprises in the building may attract demonstrations which are so large as to interfere with the public functions of the building, but this is a problem of the state's own making in having combined public and private functions in a single facility. Viewed from this vantage, the question appears to be whether the state can, by privatizing through lease, strip the public area surrounding a public building of its status as a public forum open to First Amendment activities. On the facts as presented in the problem, I would conclude not.

(c) Violation of the statute: Dan is charged with violation of a state criminal statute proscribing the public display of an obscene picture for having held up a poster depicting a fully nude, terminally ill cancer patient. The poster also had a caption which read, "The Governor Sticks It To You By Supporting Smoking."

It is clear that under the circumstances, Dan cannot be successfully prosecuted for publicly displaying an obscene picture as the picture is not obscene. Expression is obscene if (1) to the average person, applying contemporary community standards, the dominant theme of the material taken as a whole appeals to the prurient interest, and (2) the work depicts or describes, in a patently offensive way, sexual conduct specifically defined by statute as unlawful to portray, and (3) the work taken as a whole lacks serious literary, artistic, political, or scientific value.

Mere photographic display of a person nude, of itself, cannot establish obscenity. Depending on the context in which the display occurred, and the whole of the message with which it is associated, the display might or might not be obscene. The context of the display in this case, however, and the message associated with it, makes it clear that it does not constitute obscene expression. The picture obviously does not appeal to the prurient (or morbid sexual) interest, nor, under the circumstances, could it be considered to be sexually stimulating. The clear message of the poster is political, social, and perhaps medical, and the nude display of a dying cancer patient may in fact contribute to the poster's effectiveness, for it attempts to show the condition to which smokers may ultimately be reduced.

C.   Essay Questions to Play With

1. In order to control welfare costs and decrease dependency on welfare payments, Governor Hooloomooloo has sponsored an initiative to amend the state constitution to include provisions regarding welfare and welfare payments. In relevant part, the proposed amendments provide:

Welfare Aid Payments: After aid has been received for any six months, aid for the seventh month shall be reduced by 15% of the amounts which would otherwise be paid. This reduction shall not be applied to families in which all parents or other caretaker relatives living in the home are age 60 or over, or are disabled.

Although welfare payments are based on family size, and each additional child in a family normally increases the aid payment by a statutorily set amount, welfare payments shall not be increased for families having a child who was conceived while either of the parents of the child was receiving welfare aid.

Notwithstanding the maximum aid payments specified in any statutory schedule, families who have resided in this state for less than twelve (12) months shall receive, as a maximum aid payment, only the level of assistance they could have received from their state of prior residence. Length of residence in this state while not on welfare shall be credited toward the twelve months.

Neglected and Abused Children; Foster Homes: Whenever a court declares a child a ward of the court, the court may place the child in the legal custody of Child Protective Services (CPS). CPS may place the child in foster care with relatives or non-relatives. [For the purposes of this statute, relatives are defined as a "grandparent, sister, brother, aunt or uncle who is related by blood, adoption, or marriage."] Whenever possible, CPS shall give preferential consideration to a request by a child's relative for placement with that relative.

When CPS places the child in foster-care with non-relatives, the state shall pay the care-provider a stipend reasonably calculated to support the child and compensate the provider for the care. The state shall not provide a stipend when CPS places the child with relatives.

The state estimates that these provisions may annually save as much as $100 million in welfare costs. Child welfare advocates have criticized the proposals severely.

State, discuss, and resolve the arguments for and against the federal constitutionality of these provisions. Please give your reasons for your conclusions.

2. Oo-oh Shipyards, Inc., is an Arcadia company shipbuilder that maintains small vessels for the United States Navy under defense contracts. Under the contracts, Oo-oh occupies premises and utilizes facilities and equipment at the former U.S. Navy small boat repair base at Mare Island.

After a series of very unpleasant and disturbing incidents, some of Oo-oh's employees complained to the federal Equal Employment Opportunity Commission about bias and harassment by other employees at Oo-oh . EEOC officials consulted with Oo-oh's management, informed it of its obligations, under Title VII of the Equal Employment Opportunity Act, to prevent sexual harassment in its workplace, and advised it on how to comply with the law.

Oo-oh's management immediately adopted a new harassment policy. Pursuant to this policy, which was reviewed, without comment, by the EEOC, Oo-oh issued a statement of prohibited conduct. In relevant part, that statement provided:

The following conduct is forbidden. Oo-oh employees found to have engaged in such conduct shall be subject to discipline or discharge as the case may warrant.

A. *Unwanted sexual advances, propositions or other sexual comments, such as:*

   (1) sexually-oriented gestures, noises, remarks, jokes, or comments about a person's sexuality or sexual experience directed at or made in the presence of any employee who indicates or has indicated in any way that such conduct in his or her presence is unwelcome;

   (2) subjecting, or threats of subjecting, an employee to unwelcome sexual attention or conduct or intentionally making performance of the employee's job more difficult because of that employee's sex.

B. *Sexual or discriminatory displays or publications anywhere in Oo-oh's workplace by Oo-oh employees, such as:*

   (1) displaying pictures, posters, calendars, graffiti, objects, promotional materials, reading materials, or other materials that are sexually suggestive or pornographic, or sexually, racially, ethnically, or religiously demeaning, or bringing into the OSI work environment or possessing any such material to read, display or view at work.

   (2) reading or otherwise publicizing in the work environment materials that are in any way sexually revealing, sexually suggestive or pornographic, sexually, ethnically, racially, or religiously demeaning.

C. *Intimidation:* Any employee who, because of his perception of another employee's race, color, religion, national origin, or sexual orientation, intentionally, knowingly, or recklessly causes physical injury to another employee shall be discharged.

Oo-oh fired Caliban, a computer programmer, for violations of these policies. Each week for several months, Caliban brought small reproductions of famous artworks and displayed them on his desk and on the walls of his work cubicle. These included several statues of female nudes, including the Venus de Milo and Rodin's Eve, and several paintings of nudes, including Botticelli's Birth of Venus, and Boucher's Nude on a Sofa. He also repeatedly brought Playboy, Hustler, the Ku Klux Klan Klaxon, American Nazi Party literature, and other magazines to Oo-oh's facilities and read them openly in the cafeteria during the lunch hour. Caliban admitted that some of the magazines he brought were sexually explicit and graphic, that one or two of them were definitely pornographic, and that some of the material he had been reading preached racial hatred.

In addition, other employees had reported that they had heard Caliban arguing heatedly with a new employee, a Mexican immigrant, in a tavern off-site after work one night. He was overheard to shout "Talk in English, bastard," "Damn Mexican wetback," and

"I'm for white power – America for white Americans." After that, the two engaged in a brief fist fight.

Proceeding under 42 U.S.C.§1983, Caliban has filed suit against Oo-oh in federal district court alleging a violation of his civil rights. He seeks reinstatement, back pay, damages, and an injunction against further unconstitutional application of the policy.

Assume you are a law clerk working for the federal district judge assigned this case. She has asked you to write a memorandum on the constitutional issues it raises. She has also directed that you sketch out arguments on both sides of all issues and that you indicate how you think she should rule on them, giving your reasons. Write the memorandum.

3. Disturbed by numerous citizen complaints about aggressive panhandling, the behavior of homeless persons, and instances of hate speech, the city council adopted a set of ordinances designed to relieve the problems. Police and other public officials and employees have begun to enforce these new ordinances systematically. The ordinances read as follows:

City Streets and Public Places:

1. A person is guilty of loitering when he loiters, remains, or wanders about in a public place for the purpose of begging.

2. A person is guilty of aggressive begging when

    (a) he positions himself in the immediate vicinity of any automatic teller machine and solicits funds for himself from patrons using any such machine;

    (b) he positions himself in or in the immediate vicinity of a subway or bus terminus during the morning or evening rush hour and solicits funds for himself;

    (c) he solicits funds for himself from another in an aggressive, intimidating, or harassing manner.

Libraries:

1. Patrons shall be engaged in activities associated with the use of a public library while in the building. Patrons not engaged in reading, studying, or using library materials shall be asked to leave the building.

2. Patrons shall respect the rights of other patrons and shall not harass or annoy others through noisy or boisterous activities, by staring at another with the intent to annoy that person, by following another person about the building with the intent to annoy that person, by playing walkmans so that others can hear, by singing or talking to oneself, or by any other behavior which may reasonably result in the disturbance of others.

3. Patrons shall not improperly interfere with the use of the library by other patrons, or improperly interfere with library employees' performance of their duties.

4. Patrons shall not be permitted to enter the building without a shirt or other covering of their upper bodies or without shoes or other footwear. Patrons whose bodily hygiene is so offensive as to constitute a nuisance to other persons shall be required to leave the building.

EP

5. Any patron not abiding by these or other rules and regulations of the library shall be asked to leave the library premises and shall in the future be denied the privilege of access to the library.

To enforce the anti-begging ordinances in a humane fashion, the police department adopted a "move-on" policy. Under that policy, police warned beggars seen begging on the street that their conduct was illegal and that they would be arrested unless they moved on. Police would then issue summons to, or arrest as necessary, only those who failed to comply with the move-on order or who were begging in an aggressive or intimidating fashion. This policy clearly had the effect of reducing the number of people begging.

Solitaire is a homeless person who has been charged both with loitering and with aggressive begging. Sundance is a homeless person who the police have, on a number of occasions, ordered to stop begging and to "move on." Lonesome is a homeless woman ejected from the public library, after library patrons complained about her staring, talking to herself, and her smell. When she was removed from the library, she had been in it for four hours. During the time she was in the library, she had been seen sleeping with her head down on a reading table in the reference section, and bathing in the restroom, but had not been seen to use any books or other library materials.

With the help of the Legal Aid Society, Solitaire, Sundance, and Lonesome have sued, on behalf of themselves and others, to enjoin enforcement of these ordinances.

State, discuss, and resolve the arguments for and against the federal constitutionality of these provisions. Please give your reasons for your conclusions.

Each of the two following questions presents a factual statement posing one or more constitutional issues. For each factual statement, assume that you are a law clerk for a United States Supreme Court Justice. She has assigned you the task of writing a memorandum on the constitutional issues raised by each problem statement. As is customary, she has asked that you detail the arguments on both sides of all issues raised in the problem statements and that you conclude each separate memorandum by stating how you think the Court should rule on the constitutional issues raised and giving your reasons for your conclusions.

4. Concerned with massive budgetary shortfalls, and desperate to economize, the Arcadia State Legislature has passed the following provisions relating to undocumented aliens. Lower courts have ruled the provisions constitutional.

No state funds appropriated in the annual Budget Act or available from any other state source shall be expended for

(1) the education of undocumented aliens at the Arcadia Community Colleges, the Arcadia State University, or the University of Arcadia;

(2) the provision of housing or welfare benefits, or medical and health care services to undocumented aliens;

(3) the provision of job training benefits or unemployment and workers' compensation to undocumented aliens whose employment is unlawful under the laws of the United States regulating the employment of aliens.

(4) On or before September 15, 1998, each public school district shall require the parent and guardian of each pupil enrolled in its schools to submit proof of legal citizenship of, or residence in, the United States. Thereafter, the district shall report the names of any pupils failing to provide proof of citizenship or legal residence to the federal Immigration and Naturalization Service. Where the Service begins deportation proceedings against the pupil, the district shall no longer provide a free education for the pupil.

5. Green is a federal Environmental Protection Agency employee. Since the early 1980s, he has traveled across the country, in his spare time, giving unofficial speeches explaining and criticizing EPA policies. He has routinely accepted travel expense reimbursement from organizations sponsoring his speeches. EPA regulations permitted this.

Recently, the EPA has adopted a regulation prohibiting its employees from receiving travel expense reimbursement for unofficial speeches. The new regulation reads as follows:

The standards of conduct prohibit an employee from receiving compensation, including travel expenses, for speaking or writing on subject matter that focuses specifically on his official duties or on the responsibilities, policies and programs of the Agency.

The EPA has construed this regulation to apply only to "non-official" travel expenses. The effect of this construction is that EPA employees can receive travel reimbursements from other parties for official travel. For the EPA, speech or writing is official " if it results from a request to EPA to furnish a speaker, author or editor. If an invitation is addressed to an employee, the invitation is official if it is tendered because of the employee's EPA position rather that his or her individual knowledge or accomplishments."

Because Green acknowledged his speeches were "unofficial" under this definition, the regulation barred him from accepting travel reimbursements when he gave a speech. Consequently, since the regulation has been in effect, he has declined speaking invitations from organizations located outside the Washington, D.C. metropolitan area. Green wanted to continue speaking, however, and he filed suit in Federal District Court, asserting that the new regulation deprives him of his constitutional rights. WARN (Waste Awareness and Reduction Network), a North Carolina group that has invited Green to speak, joined his suit as a co-plaintiff. The District Court ruled in their favor, but the Court of Appeals ruled against them.

6. Out of concern for prostitution, Whodoo County regulates "escort" services within the county. It has a licensing board which may deny, suspend, and revoke escort services licenses. The board may deny an application if the applicant is not a person "of good character, honesty, and integrity"; if the applicant's prior activities, reputation, habits, or associations pose a threat to the public interest of the county; if the escort service's source of financing is not suitable; and if the applicant is not "in all other respects qualified to be licensed." The board can also suspend or revoke a license if the licensee or any of its partners, managers, or employees has "conducted or

maintained the business in a manner contrary to the peace, safety, general welfare, or morals of the community."

Is Whodoo County's escort service regulation constitutional? Why or why not?

7. The City of Torpedo passed an ordinance authorizing its Housing Authority to devise plans for low and middle income housing and to obtain federal funding for projects. The Authority proposed and obtained federal funding for a new housing development project for low and middle income families. Known as The Woods, the project was to consist of sixteen single family, detached homes. The Authority planned to build the project in an outlying area adjacent to a well-established upper middle class residential area.

The proposed project created considerable controversy, and the City Council considered rescinding its Housing Authority ordinance. Instead, it voted 5-4 not to extend city sewer services to the project, services without which the project could not be built. The federal Housing Assistance Administration, however, pressured Torpedo by threatening to withhold all federal housing monies unless Torpedo built the new project. The Council then reversed itself and voted 5-4 to extend the sewer lines.

Following this last vote, project opponents forced a referendum vote on the sewer extension and won, thereby insuring that the City would not extend sewer service to the project. Minority and low income persons eligible for public housing then filed suit alleging that the referendum was racially based and had a substantial discriminatory impact, in violation of Fourteenth Amendment equal protection. Torpedo moved to dismiss the suit.

Should the court dismiss the suit? Why or why not?

8. Suppose that a future Congress and President enact legislation which reads in part:

Section 1.

(a) The Congress finds that the life of each human being begins at conception.

(b) The Congress further finds that the Fourteenth Amendment to the Constitution of the United States protects all human beings.

Section 2. Upon the basis of these findings . . . the Congress hereby recognizes that for the purpose of enforcing the obligations of the States under the Fourteenth Amendment not to deprive persons of life without due process of law and not to deny them the equal protection of the laws, each human life exists from conception . . . ., and for this purpose "person" includes all human beings.
Is this legislation constitutional? Why or why not?

9. After a report to its legislature, the state of Threestrikes Department of Corrections adopted a policy that required that only female personnel work in contact positions at female correctional institutions. The report stated that many women in such institutions had a history of being abused by men and (a) would benefit by seeing women exercise authority and (b) would react adversely to male exercises of authority, such as

male officer pat-down searches for drugs or weapons. Women correctional officers, however, work in contact positions in male correctional institutions.

Male correctional officers have sued Threestrikes and its Department of Corrections claiming a denial of equal protection.

Is the Threestrikes Department of Corrections' new policy constitutional? Why or why not?

10. The state of Ohno allows independent school districts to consolidate. When they do so, they are called a "unified" district. Ohno further provides that unified school districts must provide free school bus services for their students. Nonunified districts, however, may charge students' parents for transportation to school. Pauvre is an indigent parent who lives sixteen miles from the closest school and who has two children attending a nonunified district school. She has no other means of transporting her children to school than using a school bus, but she cannot afford to pay the school bus fee, and the school district has threatened to withdraw bus service to her children. She has brought suit in federal district court challenging the withdrawal of bus service as unconstitutional.

Will Pauvre win or lose her suit? Why?

11. Four police officers wrote a letter to their Chief. In the letter, they notified him they were resigning from Noplace City's SWAT team, but not from the police force. They also distributed the letter to the Mayor and City Council Members. In relevant part, the letter stated:

We are fed up with internal strife within our department, the talk of current grievances against the SWAT team program, the inability of your office to take a firm stance against anti-SWAT complainers, and your consistent reminders about how much money we cost and the headaches you endure because of the program. Another reason for our disgruntled attitude is your recent decision not to activate the SWAT units for the dedication of the new Mega plant. Your decision to send only one SWAT officer, because of fear of police union retaliation, was certainly not a take-charge type of decision.

After accepting the resignation, the Chief brought charges against the officers for violating City Code provisions that prohibit officers from "publicly criticizing orders given by a superior officer" and "giving information to any person concerning the business of the police department, which is detrimental to the police department." He proposes to discipline the officers by suspending them, without pay, for three months.

Is the Chief's proposed action constitutional? Why or why not?

12. The Board of Education of Whoville established an equal opportunity employment program policy. The policy states that the program's purpose "is to provide equal educational opportunity for students and equal employment opportunity in every aspect of employment, to attract minority personnel, and to prohibit discrimination in employment. In all cases, the most qualified candiate will be recommended for appointment. When candidates appear to have equal qualifications, candidates identified as minorities will be recommended."
The Board's affirmative action policy did not have a remedial purpose, and at all relevant times, black teachers employed by the Board exceeded the percentage of blacks available in the work force. Recently, the Board acted to reduce the teaching

staff in the business department at Whoville High by one person. Two of the teachers in the department, who were the last hired, had equal seniority, having both been hired on the same day. They were also equally qualified. One of the teachers was white, while the other, the only minority teacher in the business department faculty, was black.

Prior to adoption of the affirmative action policy, in layoff decisions as between employees of equal seniority, the Board broke the tie by drawing lots. In this case, however, the Superintendent recommended that the Board lay off the white teacher because the black teacher was the only minority teacher in the business department. The Board agreed and laid off the white teacher.
Was the Board's action constitutional? Why or why not?

The following fact statement provides the basis for the next two questions:

Appalled by the skyrocketing number of murders, assaults, and robberies, the state of Valhalla recently passed a "controlled access" law. The law authorized Valhalla municipalities to grant permits to neighborhoods having single entrances or exits to surround their communities with physical barriers to keep out outsiders. Neighborhoods which house a government-owned building or facility "maintained for the use and enjoyment of the general public" — excluding schools, recreational parks, and community centers — cannot obtain such permits. Furthermore, a neighborhood may not keep out public employees nor people who wish to attend private schools, churches, hospitals, civic clubs, and similar institutions located within its boundaries.

To obtain a permit a neighborhood must elect a board to represent the community, three-fourths of the homes in the community must approve of the plan to close the community, and the community must bear the costs of financing the installation, operation, and maintenance of the system.

The closed neighborhood system usually operates as follows. The neighborhood erects an iron gate or gates to block street access into the community. The gates can be opened using an electronic "beeper," and only residents who have such a device can open the gate. An iron gate also blocks pedestrian walkways leading into the community, and only residents who have a key can open the walkway gate. In addition, there is an intercom system so that visitors who wish to contact a neighborhood resident can use an intercom located at gate entrances. Neighborhood residents who voted for the system pay a monthly charge for the installation and maintenance of the gates, for the beeper, the key, and intercom, and for any security guards the neighborhood hires. Residents who voted against the system receive the beeper and key, but not the intercom, for free.

The residents of Keep Away, a neighborhood in the Valhalla city of No More, obtained a permit from Mayor Wodin to close their neighborhood. They set up the closure system described above, and they adopted a rule making it each resident's responsibility to impede the entrance of strangers to the community. As the neighborhood interprets the rule, residents must refuse to open gates to all interlopers, newcomers, transients, and unknown visitors.

13. May Keep Away residents who object to the closure or nonresidents sue the Keep Away Closure Board, Mayor Wodin, and Valhalla for a violation of their civil rights? Why or why not?

14. Is the controlled access law constitutional on its face and as applied? Why or why not?

GLOSSARY

GLOSSARY

Most of the terms used in this outline are either generally understood, self-explanatory, defined where they first appear, or are understandable from context. The following list is limited to terms most likely to cause some difficulty for a beginning student.

A

Abstention: The action of a federal court in refraining from exercising its jurisdiction to hear a state case involving application of a state statute not yet authoritatively construed by a state court.

Ad valorem: A Latin phrase meaning "in proportion to the value."

Article I courts: Courts created by Congress under its Article I powers and not having the authority to exercise with finality the federal judicial power the Constitution confers on the judicial branch.

Article III courts: The United States Supreme Court, federal courts of appeal, and federal district courts, which constitute the judicial branch of the federal government and derive their authority from Article III of the Constitution.

B

Bicamerality: The feature of having two legislative chambers, *e.g.,* the United States House of Representatives and Senate, as separate organized bodies within one legislature.

C

Case or controversy: A real dispute between opposing parties, appropriate for judicial remedy, which is a precondition for federal court jurisdiction.

Certiorari: A Latin phrase meaning "to be certified" and now used to refer to a discretionary writ issued by a superior court to an inferior court in order to review the lower court's decisions; the Supreme Court's writ ordering such review.

Court martial: A military court for the trial of military or martial law offenses, or a particular prosecutorial proceeding in such a court.

D

Denaturalization: The taking away of citizenship rights and status.

Discriminatory effect: A statistically significant selecting out, for relatively adverse or detrimental treatment — as compared with the population as a whole or other groups or classes, of a definable group or class.

Disproportionate impact: A discriminatory effect or the way some criterion operates to selectively disadvantage or burden some particular group as opposed to others.

E

Enabling Clause: Provision in a constitutional amendment authorizing Congress to adopt legislation to further the purposes of the amendment.

Enclave: A portion of territory belonging to one sovereign state completely surrounded by territories belonging to one or more other sovereign states.

Erotica: Visual or written material concerned with sexual love.

Executive agreements sole: Executive agreements which the President can enter into on the sole basis of presidential authority and thus not needing congressional authorization or approval.

Expatriation: The banishment of a citizen from his country.

Extradition: The process or action of surrendering up a person, especially a fugitive from justice, to a foreign state.

F

Federalism: A system of government in which two or more states form a political unity, usually with an overarching government common to all in some matters, while remaining more or less independent of each other with regard to their distinctly internal affairs.

Full faith and credit: A constitutional phrase referring to the legal obligation of the states of the United States to give effect to the valid legal actions of other states.

G

Gerrymander: The process of drawing electoral district lines so as to confer an electoral advantage on the party drawing them.

Group libel: Defamation of a specific group or class, usually a race, ethnic group, nationality, or religious sect.

I

Immunities: A protection from legal proceedings of various kinds.

Informed consent: Consent given by an affected party to some action or procedure, but only after receiving a full informational statement concerning the nature and consequences of the action or procedure.

J

Judicial review: As it relates to constitutional law, the practice of American courts in reviewing legislative or executive action for consonance with constitutional requirements.

Jurisdiction-stripping: A phrase referring to legislation withdrawing jurisdiction formerly exercised by a court.

Justiciability: The quality of being capable of court trial or adjudication.

M

Market participant: The state, or its agents, when it enters the market as an ordinary actor rather than in its governmental capacity.

Moot: A case or issue no longer in need of, or capable of, decision.

N

Neutral criteria: Criteria having the appearance of not discriminating on an invidious or improper basis.

O

Occupying the field: A phrase referring to comprehensive federal regulation of some matter which otherwise might be subject to individual state regulation.

Overbreadth: That quality or characteristic of a statute, regulation, or order which reaches beyond the problem it was meant to solve causing it to sweep within it activity it cannot legitimately reach.

P

Preemption: The action of Congress legitimately exercising its powers to preclude state legislation or regulation in areas where states might otherwise act.

Presentment: The constitutional requirement that legislation which has passed both houses of Congress be presented to the President for his signature before becoming law.

Procedural bar: The barrier to judicial review created when a litigant fails to follow a procedural rule which is a precondition to such review.

Proportional representation: A system of legislative representation in which political parties obtain a number of legislative seats proportional to their voting strength in an election.

Prudential considerations: A phrase referring to the nonconstitutional, nonstatutory reasons a federal court has or might have to refuse to hear a case otherwise justiciable.

Prurient: Having a morbid or unwholesome, lascivious craving.

R

Reciprocity: Mutual action between parties.

Restrictive covenants: Agreements in a property deed, passing with the land, which in some way restrain its use or disposition.

Retroactivity: The condition or fact of the application of a law or rule to actions or proceedings completed prior to adoption of the law or rule.

S

Secondary effects: A phrase used to refer some of the externalities or effects of particular kinds of speech or expressive activity; for example, the "massage" parlors, viewing arcades, topless bars, and the like that sometimes operate in the vicinity of bookstores or theaters offering sexually explicit materials, together with other associated effects, such as an increase in the number of transients in the area, solicitation for prostitution, drug sales, or other kinds of crime or antisocial activity.

Sectarian: Of, or adhering to, a particular religion, religious sect, or doctrine.

Seizure: The action of government, in taking as evidence, contraband, or forfeiture, of physical items belonging to private parties.

Self-executing treaties: Treaties not needing enabling legislation in order to become operative.

Severability: That feature or characteristic of legislation or legislative provisions which permits valid portions to remain in effect when an invalid portion is stricken as unconstitutional or otherwise unlawful.

Stacking: A form of gerrymandering by creating a few districts with an overwhelming majority of one party and many districts with a thin majority for the other.

Standing: A word used to describe the position of a party with respect to meeting the substantive jurisdictional requirements to sue.

State action: The action of the state, its subdivisions, or agents, or the action attributable to them; the limitation on the application of Fourteenth and Fifteenth Amendment rights.

Supermajority: A majority significantly larger than one-half of an electoral body plus one, *e.g.,* a two-thirds majority vote is a supermajority vote.

V

Vagueness: The quality or condition of being indefinite, imprecise, indistinct, or indeterminate.

TABLES OF AUTHORITIES

TABLE OF CASES

TA

TA

TA

TA

TA

TA

TA

TA

TA

TA

TA

Matthews v. Lucas,
427 U.S. 495 (1976) 8-28

Mazurek v. Armstrong,
117 S. Ct. 1865 (1997) 7-12

McCardle, Ex parte,
74 U.S. (7 Wall.) 506 (1868) 1-6

McCollum Illinois ex rel. v. Board of Education,
333 U.S. 203 (1948) 14-10

McCray v. United States,
195 U.S. 27 (1904) 3-6

McCulloch v. Maryland,
17 U.S. 316 (1819) 2-3, 2-5

McDonald v. Board of Election Comm'rs,
394 U.S. 802 (1969) 8-9

McGowan v. Maryland,
366 U.S. 420 (1961) 8-9, 14-13

McGrain v. Daugherty,
273 U.S. 135 (1927) 3-9

McKleskey v. Kemp,
481 U.S. 279 (1987) 8-21

McLaurin v. Oklahoma State Regents,
339 U.S. 637 (1950) 8-12

Meachum v. Fano,
427 U.S. 215 (1976) 7-17

Meek v. Pittenger,
421 U.S. 349 (1975) 14-8

Memorial Hospital v. Maricopa County,
415 U.S. 250 (1974) 9-22

Mesquite, City of, v. Aladdin's Castle, Inc.,
455 U.S. 283 (1982) 1-8

Metro Broadcasting, Inc. v. FCC,
497 U.S. 547 (1990) 9-4, 9-5, 9-9

Metromedia, Inc. v. City of San Diego,
453 U.S. 490 (1981) 12-9

*Metropolitan Washington Airports Authority v.
Citizens for Abatement of Aircraft Noise,*
501 U.S. 252 (1991) 5-4

Meyer v. Grant,
486 U.S. 414 (1988) 13-5

Meyer v. Nebraska,
262 U.S. 390 (1923) 7-5, 7-6

Miami Herald Pub. Co. v. Tornillo,
418 U.S. 241 (1974) 12-24

Michael H. v. Gerald D.,
491 U.S. 110 (1989) 7-7

Michael M. v. Superior Court,
450 U.S. 464 (1981) 8-23

Michelin Tire Corp. v. Wages,
423 U.S. 276 (1976) 6-16

Michigan v. Long,
463 U.S. 1032 (1983) 1-3

Milk Control Board v. Eisenberg Farm Products,
306 U.S. 346 (1939) 6-5

Milkovich v. Lorain Journal Co.,
497 U.S. 1 (1990) 11-9

Miller v. California,
413 U.S. 15 (1973) 11-12, 11-15, 11-18

Miller v. Johnson,
515 U.S. 900 (1995) 9-15

Miller v. Schoene,
276 U.S. 272 (1928) 6-19

Milligan, Ex parte,
71 U.S. 2 (4 Wall.) (1866) 3-7

Milliken v. Bradley,
418 U.S. 717 (1974) 8-17

Mills v. Alabama,
384 U.S. 214 (1966) 13-6

Mills v. Habluetzel,
456 U.S. 91 (1982) 8-28

*Minneapolis Star and Tribune Co. v. Minnesota
Comm'r of Revenue,* 460 U.S. 575 (1983) .. 13-20

Mississippi University for Women v. Hogan,
458 U.S. 718 (1982) 8-21, 8-24, 10-11

TA

TA

TA

TA

TA

TA

TA

TABLE OF CONSTITUTIONAL PROVISIONS AND STATUTES

TA

CASEBOOK CROSS-REFERENCE CHART

Please visit www.casenotes.com for the latest version of the cross-reference chart.

CR ▶

CONSTITUTIONAL LAW Casenote Law Outline Cross-Reference Chart	Brest 4th Ed. 2000	Stone 3rd Ed. 1996	Rotunda 6th Ed. 2000	Lockhart 8th Ed. 1996	Gunther 13th Ed. 1997	Farber 2nd Ed. 1998	Cohen 10th Ed. 1997
CHAPTER 1: Judicial Power, Functions, and Jurisdiction							
I. Federal Courts	730-735	145-147		43-51	1-2		44-79
II. The Doctrine of Judicial Review and Its Consequences	75-100	20-57	1-28	1-25	2-27	57-69	25-38
III. Constitutional Limits on Federal Judicial Review	469-470	88-120	28-69	55-57	27-45	1080-1088	80-123
IV. Judicially Imposed Limits on Federal Constitutional Review	401-410	121-145	28-69	25-43	45-60	1005-1029	125-147
CHAPTER 2: Federal Structure of American Government							
I. Federal-State Relations in General	551-614	266-288			87-141	749-819	361-371
II. Intergovernmental Immunities	608-609	331-342	78-81	139-158	328-337	819-855	339-361
III. Relations Between States		289-297		273-280	351-353	866-903	272-338
IV. State Relations to Citizens of Other States	164-169			274-281	328-336		
CHAPTER 3: Powers of the Federal Government							
I. The Principal Congressional Legislative Powers	499-503	182-289, 425-474, 482-495	70-81, 271-277	58-137	141-258	766-819	184-240
II. Powers of the President	621-730	387-424, 474-482	271-368	172-181	404-415	916-956	408-421
CHAPTER 4: Presidential Powers, Privileges, and Immunities							
I. Presidential Powers	621-730	392-423	271-368	181-212	365-374	916-956	408-421

CONSTITUTIONAL LAW Casenote Law Outline Cross-Reference Chart	Brest 4th Ed. 2000	Stone 3rd Ed. 1996	Rotunda 6th Ed. 2000	Lockhart 8th Ed. 1996	Gunther 13th Ed. 1997	Farber 2nd Ed. 1998	Cohen 10th Ed. 1997
II. Presidential Immunities and Privileges	634-640, 644-645	423-424	337-367	212-220	404-415	945-956	448-456
CHAPTER 5: Separation of Powers							
I. The Doctrine of Separation of Powers	80	385-391	337-428		354-355	905-1025	407-456
II. Major Issues Under the Doctrine of Separation of Powers	464-546	385-492	337-428	172-219	355-404	905-1025	407-456
CHAPTER 6: State Regulation/Commerce, Contracts, and Private Property							
I. The Dormant, or "Negative," Commerce Clause	614-619	289-328	82-147	220-233	259-328	866-903	251-272
II. State Taxation of Interstate Commerce	355-374	343-369	162-163	233-272	350-351	866-903	272-281
III. State Taxation of Foreign Commerce			163-164	313			
IV. The Contract Clause	442-445	1627-1645	463-470	362-370	505-516		525-541
V. Takings and Just Compensation Clause	446-453	1645-1693	524-541	338-362	486-505	429-448	567-570
CHAPTER 7: Fourteenth Amendment Liberty and Due Process							
I. The Bill of Rights and the Fourteenth Amendment	241-255	785-841	470-474, 883-899	370-549	418-448	381-404	480-503
II. The Meaning of Fourteenth Amendment "Liberty" and "Due Process"	241-255	785-841	470-474, 883-899	314-328	448-472	381-578	1069-1100
CHAPTER 8: Equal Protection (I)							

Please visit **www.casenotes.com** for the latest version of the cross-reference chart.

CR

Please visit **www.casenotes.com** for the latest version of the cross-reference chart.

CR

CONSTITUTIONAL LAW *Casenote Law Outline* Cross-Reference Chart	Brest 4th Ed. 2000	Stone 3rd Ed. 1996	Rotunda 6th Ed. 2000	Lockhart 8th Ed. 1996	Gunther 13th Ed. 1997	Farber 2nd Ed. 1998	Cohen 10th Ed. 1997
I. Overview	241-255	495-550	612-619	1148-1163	231-289	33-132	670-677
II. Rational Basis Review	985-1007	554-581	561-595	612-619	292-304	287-298	677-692
III. Strict Scrutiny Review: Suspect Classifications	801-830	595-697	619-741	1163-1226	133-163	133-171	962-743
IV. Heightened Scrutiny for Certain Other Classifications	985-1007	697-785	619-741	1270-1323	305-350	298-342	743-786, 896-926
CHAPTER 9: Equal Protection (II)							
I. "Benign" Suspect or Quasi-Suspect Classifications	1053-1129	648-697	619-741	1226-1270	366-394	238-286	810-887
II. Fundamental Rights and Equal Protection	1131-1155	785-1073	741-882	1323-1411	397-559	381-407, 441-479	926-1068
CHAPTER 10: State Action and Congressional Authority to Reach Private Action to Protect Civil Rights							
I. State Action	285-296	1694-1717	542-611	1411-1425	174-200	172-234	1101-1107
II. Congressional Authority to Reach Private Action Infringing Civil Rights	867-894	1725-1767	562-570	1425-1468	926-984	202-231	1116-1146
CHAPTER 11: Freedom of Speech (I)							
I. Theories of the First Amendment	60-70	1073-1087	931-1294	621-626	1022-1034	561-577	1180-1198
II. The First Amendment and "Dangerous" Speech Having Social or Political Aims	60-70, 382-387	1087-1132	931-944	614-661	1034-1076	577-591	1198-1232
III. Erotic, Obscene, and Pornographic Expression	60-70, 382-387	1249-1272, 1298-1322	1245-1294	696-723	1125-1175	604-619	1274-1290

CONSTITUTIONAL LAW Casenote Law Outline Cross-Reference Chart	Brest 4th Ed. 2000	Stone 3rd Ed. 1996	Rotunda 6th Ed. 2000	Lockhart 8th Ed. 1996	Gunther 13th Ed. 1997	Farber 2nd Ed. 1998	Cohen 10th Ed. 1997
IV. Indecent and Offensive Speech	382-387	1132-1154	1034-1057	723-734	1076-1091	620-635	1290-1339
V. Commercial Speech		1226-1249	1103-1135	808-832	1175-1202	635-644	1334-1360
VI. Noncommercial Speech			1206-1225	832-837		644-652	
CHAPTER 12 Freedom of Speech (II)							
I. First Amendment Variables	1434-1449	1172-1195	1058-1078	850-874	1203-1230, 1325-1357	672-705	1232-1248
II. Rights of Access in Private Fora	1533-1536		961-1033	898-909	1092	655-671	1378-1439
CHAPTER 13: Freedom of Speech, Association, and the Press							
I. Free Speech in Special Contexts		1434-1485	1079-1102, 1136-1170	910-937	1361-1374, 1400-1420	672-705	1439-1449
II. Freedom of Association	1415-1419	1426-1434	1171-1206	963-1011	1374-1400	705-710	1457-1482
III. Freedom of the Press	60-70	14868-1512	1079-1103	957-963	1420-1460	591-604	1553-1602
CHAPTER 14: Freedom of Religion							
I. The Establishment Clause	1571-1593	1547-1590	1295-1332	1039-1105	1500-1551	725-745	1602-1687
II. Free Exercise of Religion	1481-1490	1590-1610	1332-1380	1105-1147	1471-1500	710-725	1687-1790
III. Adjudication or Other Settlement of Religious Matters	1481-1490	1610-1627	1381-1411	1132-1146		746-747	

Please visit **www.casenotes.com** for the latest version of the cross-reference chart.

CR

INDEX

ID

ID

ID

ID

NOTES

NOTES

NOTES

NOTES

the Ultimate Outline

➤ **RENOWNED AUTHORS:** Every **Casenote Law Outline** is written by highly respected, nationally recognized professors.

➤ **KEYED TO CASENOTE LEGAL BRIEF BOOKS:** In most cases, **Casenote Law Outlines** work in conjunction with the **Casenote Legal Briefs** so that you can see how each case in your textbook relates to the entire subject area. In addition, **Casenote Law Outlines** are cross-referenced to most major casebooks.

➤ **FREE SUPPLEMENT SERVICE:** As part of being the most up-to-date legal outline on the market, whenever a new supplement is published, the corresponding outline can be updated for free using the supplement request form found in this book.

ADMINISTRATIVE LAW (1999) **$21.95**
 Charles H. Koch, Jr., Dudley W. Woodbridge Professor of Law, College of William and Mary
 Sidney A. Shapiro, John M. Rounds Professor of Law, University of Kansas

CIVIL PROCEDURE (1999) **$22.95**
 John B. Oakley, Professor of Law, University of California, Davis School of Law
 Rex R. Perschbacher, Professor and Dean of University of California, Davis School of Law

COMMERCIAL LAW (see SALES ● SECURED TRANSACTIONS ● NEGOTIABLE INSTRUMENTS & PAYMENT SYSTEMS)

CONFLICT OF LAWS (1996) **$21.95**
 Luther L. McDougal, III, W.R. Irby Professor of Law, Tulane University
 Robert L. Felix, James P. Mozingo, III, Professor of Law, University of South Carolina

CONSTITUTIONAL LAW (1997) **$24.95**
 Gary Goodpaster, Professor of Law, University of California, Davis School of Law

CONTRACTS (1999) **$21.95**
 Daniel Wm. Fessler, Professor of Law, University of California, Davis School of Law

CORPORATIONS (2000) **$24.95**
 Lewis D. Solomon, Arthur Selwin Miller Research Professor of Law, George Washington University
 Daniel Wm. Fessler, Professor of Law, University of California, Davis School of Law
 Arthur E. Wilmarth, Jr., Associate Professor of Law, George Washington University

CRIMINAL LAW (1999) **$21.95**
 Joshua Dressler, Professor of Law, McGeorge School of Law

CRIMINAL PROCEDURE (1999) **$20.95**
 Joshua Dressler, Professor of Law, McGeorge School of Law

ESTATE & GIFT TAX (2000) **$22.95**
 Joseph M. Dodge, W.H. Francis Professor of Law, University of Texas at Austin

EVIDENCE (1996) **$23.95**
 Kenneth Graham, Jr., Professor of Law, University of California, Los Angeles School of Law

FEDERAL COURTS (1997) **$22.95**
 Howard P. Fink, Isadore and Ida Topper Professor of Law, Ohio State University
 Linda S. Mullenix, Bernard J. Ward Centennial Professor of Law, University of Texas

FEDERAL INCOME TAXATION (1998) **$22.95**
 Joseph M. Dodge, W.H. Francis Professor of Law, University of Texas at Austin

LEGAL RESEARCH (1996) **$21.95**
 Nancy L. Schultz, Professor of Law, Chapman University
 Louis J. Sirico, Jr., Professor of Law, Villanova University

NEGOTIABLE INSTRUMENTS & PAYMENT SYSTEMS (1995) **$22.95**
 Donald B. King, Professor of Law, Saint Louis University
 Peter Winship, James Cleo Thompson, Sr. Trustee Professor, SMU

PROPERTY (1999) **$22.95**
 Sheldon F. Kurtz, Percy Bordwell Professor of Law, University of Iowa
 Patricia Cain, Professor of Law, University of Iowa

SALES (2000) **$22.95**
 Robert E. Scott, Dean and Lewis F. Powell, Jr. Professor of Law, University of Virginia
 Donald B. King, Professor of Law, Saint Louis University

SECURED TRANSACTIONS (1995 w/ '96 supp.) **$20.95**
 Donald B. King, Professor of Law, Saint Louis University

TORTS (1999) **$22.95**
 George C. Christie, James B. Duke Professor of Law, Duke University
 Jerry J. Phillips, W.P. Toms Professor of Law, University of Tennessee

WILLS, TRUSTS, & ESTATES (1996) **$22.95**
 William M. McGovern, Professor of Law, University of California, Los Angeles School of Law